"Given the socio-ecological crises facing the world today, we need to look not just at conserving the planet, but healing it, not just modifications to existing systems and institutions, but radical transformations. In this textbook, the authors provide students with critical information to help us move in this direction."

Kent Walker, *University of Windsor, Canada*

"The authors succinctly present the story timeline of how many businesses have become unsustainable globally and how we can systematically address the need to turn this around. They have effectively tied together philosophy, business, economics, culture, and politics to set the stage for today's students' study of sustainable enterprises. Furthermore, they provide potential solutions for moving forward with a holistic approach to sustainable business systems. I have been waiting for a book like this and will look forward to using it in my teachings."

Claudia G. Green, *Pace University, USA*

"By directly challenging the profit maximization orthodoxy of the existing system of 'Destructive Advanced Capitalism' and by proposing a new system for socially sustainable business, this book will force business students and faculty to engage in a conversation that envisions business as part of a new social movement for justice."

Thomas Abraham, *Kean University, USA*

SOCIAL SUSTAINABILITY FOR BUSINESS

Social Sustainability for Business demonstrates the need for a transformational change to the way businesses across the globe operate. What has become the standard, accepted "business model," with a focus on corporate profit, shareholder wealth maximization, and GDP growth, is no longer a sustainable business model for workers, consumers, communities, society, the planet, or any of its inhabitants and ecosystems.

The authors argue that the current commercial system depletes natural resources, denigrates human rights, and inhibits positive social and technological innovation. To address these issues, they focus on societal goals—such as a sustainable planet, meeting human rights of workers, and safe products for consumers—and outline steps that organizations and individuals must take to achieve them. Readers will gain insight into the psychological barriers to and influences on sustainable behavior. They will also learn how reconsidering corporate social responsibility and business ethics can stop and reverse the destruction of a profit-based approach. Cases on modern examples of sustainability or lack thereof explain how establishing and maintaining a socially sustainable business system can protect the environment, meet the rights of its people, and ensure that their needs are met tomorrow.

End-of-chapter and end-of-case discussion questions will help students in sustainability classes to think critically about the practical impact of the topics discussed.

Jerry A. Carbo is Professor of Management at the John L. Grove College of Business at Shippensburg University, USA.

Viet T. Dao is Professor of Management Information Systems at the John L. Grove College of Business at Shippensburg University, USA.

Steven J. Haase is a Professor in the Psychology Department at Shippensburg University, USA.

M. Blake Hargrove is Professor of Organizational Behavior at the John L. Grove College of Business at Shippensburg University, USA.

Ian M. Langella is Professor of Supply Chain Management at the John L. Grove College of Business at Shippensburg University, USA.

SOCIAL SUSTAINABILITY FOR BUSINESS

Jerry A. Carbo, Viet T. Dao, Steven J. Haase,
M. Blake Hargrove, and Ian M. Langella

NEW YORK AND LONDON

First published 2018
by Routledge
711 Third Avenue, New York, NY 10017

and by Routledge
2 Park Square, Milton Park, Abingdon, Oxon, OX14 4RN

Routledge is an imprint of the Taylor & Francis Group, an informa business

© 2018 Taylor & Francis

The right of Jerry A. Carbo, Viet T. Dao, Steven J. Haase, M. Blake
Hargrove, and Ian M. Langella to be identified as authors of this work
has been asserted by them in accordance with sections 77 and 78 of the
Copyright, Designs and Patents Act 1988.

Library of Congress Cataloging-in-Publication Data
A catalog record for this book has been requested

ISBN: 978-1-138-18888-4 (hbk)
ISBN: 978-1-138-18892-1 (pbk)
ISBN: 978-1-315-64198-0 (ebk)

Typeset in Bembo
by Apex CoVantage, LLC

I want to first thank my family for their patience and support during the process of completing this book: my wife, Betty, daughters, Suzanne and Adrienne, and sons, Anthony and Giovanni. Thanks for sticking with me and understanding why we do not buy certain unsustainable products or shop at certain places that your friends might. I also want to thank those who helped to set me in the direction of being passionate about human rights in the workplace and socially sustainable systems—Lance Compa, who first turned me on to the concerns with corporate codes of conduct and the problems with globalization and the race to the bottom; David Lipsky, who pushed me to think about systems of justice and fairness; James Gross, who inspired me to view the workplace from the perspective of human rights; and Risa Lieberwitz, a never-ceasing advocate for workers' rights who inspired me to pursue my passions and to be an advocate and to try to make my academic work meaningful to real lives each and every day. Most importantly to my father, Jerry Carbo, who was the most ethical and caring business leader I ever met. I miss him every day and know that there is so much of him in this book.

Jerry A. Carbo

To mom and dad for bringing me up and supporting me through all my endeavors. To Quynh and Michelle, the best wife and daughter I could ever wish for.

Viet T. Dao

I wish to dedicate this book to family and friends, who have always been so supportive of my academic endeavors over the years, and to my late Ph.D. mentor in cognitive psychology, John Theios, who provided me the space to think outside the box—I would not be the scholar today were it not for him. Lastly, I dedicate this book to all future inhabitants of our tiny planet in the cosmos that we call Earth. May your lives be better than if we were to maintain our current unsustainable trajectories.

Steven J. Haase

For my mother and father, who taught me to strive for a better world,
for my wife, who makes our world better,
and for Katherine and Alice, who will live in the world we make.

M. Blake Hargrove

To my children, Jonah, Colin, Ida, and Luke, the fulfillment of dreams from my younger years, and the embodiment of my hopes for the future. *Ad majorem Dei gloriam.*

Ian M. Langella

CONTENTS

FIGURES

TABLES

1

INTRODUCTION TO SOCIALLY SUSTAINABLE BUSINESS SYSTEMS (SSBS)

> We demand that big business give the people a square deal; in return we must insist that when anyone engaged in big business honestly endeavors to do right, he shall himself be given a square deal.
>
> *Teddy Roosevelt, Letter to Sir Edward Gray,*
> *November 15, 1913 (Theodore Roosevelt Association)*

> I hope we shall crush in its birth the aristocracy of our monied corporations which dare already to challenge our government to a trial by strength, and bid defiance to the laws of our country.
>
> *Thomas Jefferson to George Logan,*
> *November 12, 1816 (National Archives)*

> We do not inherit the land from our ancestors; we borrow it from our children.
>
> *Native American Proverb (indigenouspeople.net)*

Introduction

Socially sustainable business systems (SSBS) entail a new way of looking at business practices, business policies, and business regulation in such a way as to assure the sustainability of the planet and all of its inhabitants. From a planetary standpoint it no longer merely means not destroying the planet, but also means healing much of the damage that has been done to the planet. From the people side of the equation this means more than mere survival. As McGhee and Grant (2016) suggest, sustainability is about flourishing, or thriving. It means assuring all human rights for all humans at all levels and assuring socially just procedures and outcomes. In short, SSBS means that every human being is entitled to a life with dignity on the planet on which he or she was born. SSBS is not only about meeting these goals, but also about establishing the system and the path to the system that will assure we work towards these goals.

SSBS has a content component (substantive outcomes and goals) and procedural component (systems and processes). Perhaps for business students, the best analogy would be to the content and process theories of motivation. The content theories explain the *what*, and the process theories explain the *how*. SSBS is a combination of both content and process—the *what* we are looking to achieve as well as the *how* to achieve it.

When we review the various concepts and theories around social responsibility of businesses in Chapter 3, we will see that one of the strongest critiques of these concepts is that they have failed to work because they have *failed to question the system*. "Critiques" are often attempts to make minor changes within the current system or to change some of the inputs or influences from the outside to the current system of business practices. SSBS is predicated on the idea that the current system itself is flawed and that to overcome and to halt the destruction we see within the current system, we must fundamentally change the system itself. The system itself drives the behaviors and the destructive practices and is too strong to be overcome by minor internal changes or external influences. As Meadows explained, "The system, to a large extent causes its own behavior! An outside event may unleash that behavior, but the same outside event applied to a different behavior is likely to produce a different result" (Meadows, 2008, p. 2). We are currently stuck producing the same destructive results because we have not fundamentally changed the system. The application of different events or influences to such a strong system is not likely to change behaviors or outcomes.

The largely voluntarist concepts of corporate social responsibility, corporate citizenship, and business ethics discussed in Chapter 3 rely on voluntary behavior. It is our contention that voluntarism has not been and will not be sufficient to transform the current commercial system. As will be presented in detail in this chapter and in Chapter 2, the destructive processes in the present commercial system are accelerating. The system is too powerful and entrenched to be changed by incremental volunteer measures. SSBS offers a transformative path to stop and reverse the destruction from within the current system. SSBS is a broad-based global system that includes the systems of commerce, politics, and ecology around the globe. SSBS includes establishing new parameters, new rules, new institutions, new structures, and new goals to provide the planet and its people with a positive future in which every life can be lived with dignity. This text offers a broader notion of SSBS that seeks to preserve and protect our planet and meet the needs and rights of the people, and assure those needs will be met tomorrow.

SSBS seems on its face to propose a radical transformation of the current system of commerce. However, step back and consider the stated goals of the dominant conceptualizations of commerce, markets, and economic systems and see that SSBS is a return to these fundamental goals. Both Adam Smith's free market system and Karl Marx's proletarian utopia were intended to create the greatest benefits for all. Economists of every stripe have sought to promote systems that generate needed goods and services to provide for the commonwealth of all. The current system has failed to meet these laudable goals because it is no longer assessed based on broad utility or commonwealth but on erroneous economic measures such as profit and shareholder wealth. Because the measurements are wrong, the current system has failed to achieve the intended outcomes. The current measures have produced a system that destroys the very outcomes it was intended to produce by endangering our planet and its people. Simply stated, the measures must be changed if the system is to be transformed. This is the radicalism of SSBS; it offers a basic alteration in the measures of economic success. In the following sections, we examine the evolution of thought that led to the current system of capitalism, which we call destructive advanced capitalism (DAC).

The Foundations of Capitalism

Adam Smith

How did the current system that claims to maximize economic utility become the single most destructive force on the planet? Well, nothing happens all at once. The current commercial system, like all significant phenomena (positive and negative), emerged over time within a complex system due to a web of causal factors. However, there can be no doubt that the major underlying cause of the current system was the widespread acceptance of market capitalism in the United States and Western Europe during the 19th century. So, the underlying question is, How did capitalism come to be adopted?

Though features of market capitalism go back thousands of years and were present in all historical societies, the rationale for this economic system is relatively young. Adam Smith (1723–1790) is often held to be the parent of modern free market economics. He certainly did not see himself as that. He saw himself as a moral philosopher and was a central figure in the late 18th century Scottish Enlightenment. During the Enlightenment, intellectuals turned away from religion as a source of authority. Smith and others looked to reason rather than faith as the proper structure for organizing society. Predicating much of the work of Smith were the concepts of the *rational man* and of *rational choices*. In his view, human motivation is driven by reason and rational choice. Here is the important part: the argument that humans are motivated by rational choice is just that—an argument. Furthermore, it is a metaphysical argument rather than an evidence-based theory. Smith and other 18th and 19th century intellectuals built their philosophies before even the rudiments of scientific exploration into human behavior began. Smith and his contemporaries relied on a pre-scientific worldview in which human behavior was a function of souls, spirits, hearts, and minds rather than an outcome resulting from electro-chemical reactions among millions of neurons in the brain. Smith's rational choice argument is a metaphysical argument made more than two centuries before psychologists and neuroscientists began to have even a basic understanding of human brain function and the behaviors that are determined by that function. Arguments made without evidentiary support are a risky way to organize society, and that risk has come home with DAC.

During the last sixty years, psychology and neuroscience revolutionized thinking about human behavior. Overwhelming evidence supports that people act for a wide variety of reasons. Experiment after experiment has demonstrated that, taken as a whole, Smith's rational choices (maximizing economic utility) explain only a small fraction of behaviors. In fact, evidence indicates that most people are far more behaviorally responsive to social and emotional motivators than to purely cognitive decisions.

The Chicago School of Economic Thought

In the late 20th century Milton Friedman (1912–2006) championed many of Smith's arguments as a part of the Chicago School of Economics. This academic school, along with all neoclassical economists, bases its theories, calculations, and economic models on a set of assumptions. One central assumption is rational choice—the same 18th century metaphysical notion of behavior proposed by Smith. In 1962, Friedman wrote "there is one and only one social responsibility of business—to use its resources and engage in activities designed to increase its profits." The Friedman doctrine, also known as Stockholder Theory, strongly argues that the goal of every firm is to maximize shareholder value. Stockholder Theory posits that it is the rational choice for all businesses to seek only profit. This argument since has come to dominate American and Western business schools, multinational boardrooms, and both the conservative and libertarian political movements. The problem with this is that Stockholder Theory is firmly based upon a metaphysical assumption that has almost no support in the behavioral sciences. In other words, a huge edifice has been built on a defective foundation. The current commercial system rests on this shaky footing. The discredited notion that people behave by making rational economic choices has brought our society and our planet to a perilous state.

Defenses for the Current Commercial System

One of the principal defenses of the current commercial system is that it meets the utilitarian test. As previously mentioned, Smith, Marx, and subsequent economists have sought to conceptualize economic systems that create the greatest good for all concerned. Proponents of the current system have proffered the argument that profit-driven market capitalism, for all its many flaws, provides the best for the most. This apology for the current system chiefly rests on the belief that a rising tide will lift all boats (Mintzberg, Simons, & Basu, Fall 2002). However, the evidence for the rising tide has been questioned by many, and the premise has been called erroneous by others (Mintzberg, Simons, & Basu, Fall 2002). Utilitarian apologists point to increased Gross Domestic Product (GDP) and increased per capita incomes as "proof" that the current system is the best alternative for

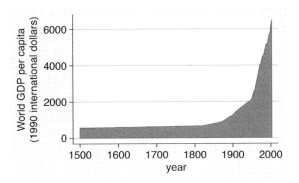

FIGURE 1.1 World GDP per Capita 1500–2003 (in 1990 International Dollars)

Source: https://en.wikipedia.org/wiki/World_economy

organizing economic efforts. Figure 1.1 appears to offer compelling evidence to support the utilitarian position.

Notice the y-axis in the graph—dollars. The utilitarian defense of capitalism relies almost entirely on these "dollars and cents" measures, and when dollars are the metric, the current financial system seems fully defensible. In the current system's assessment model, financial success equals economic success. Jeremy Bentham, John Stuart Mill, and other utilitarian philosophers would be confused by this equivalency. These thinkers never conceptualized pleasure, happiness, or utility with money alone. In fact, there is a great deal of evidence that many countries with high levels of GDP have relatively low levels of happiness (O'Brien, 2008). Those with high GDP and high inequality have high levels of mental illness, incarceration, crime, and obesity and low levels of educational attainment, social mobility, and physical health (Wilkinson & Pickett, 2010).

INFORMATION BOX 1.1   PLEASURE, PAIN, AND HAPPINESS—BENTHAM AND MILL

Jeremy Bentham (1748–1832) and John Stuart Mill (1806–1873), like Adam Smith, believed that societies are best ordered based on reason. Bentham and Mill were moral philosophers who held that it is the consequences of an action that make it moral or immoral as opposed to its conformity with some principle or law. The rightness of action is, therefore, a function of the consequence of that action; the action with the best consequences has the most utility. For Bentham, right action maximizes "pleasure" and minimizes "pain," while for Mill right action maximizes "happiness." For both of these consequentialists, pleasure and happiness should not be understood in the way we usually speak about them. For Bentham, *pleasure* depended on the real interests of each person, which ought to include sympathy and charity. For Mill, *happiness* meant to participate in distinctively human activities. For both philosophers, utility was not about maximizing efficiency; utility maximizes human potential.

Another defense of the current commercial systems revolves around notions of individual liberty. Libertarians argue that market capitalism bestows the maximum schema of liberty upon all constituents of society. This argument goes like this:

People should be free to do what they want to do.

People have a right to personal property.

People should be free to do what they want with their property.

Markets provide opportunities for consenting constituents to come together to exchange goods and services.

Unregulated free market capitalism is the best system to allow maximum economic liberty.

Libertarians, in theory, oppose any regulation that limits individual freedoms. For example, according to libertarians, owners of real property should in no way be constrained as to how they extract resources from their property. The property is theirs. The resources are theirs. The owners should be freely allowed to do what they want with them.

For libertarians, the role of government is principally to enforce contracts rather than to restrict action. The current commercial system often benefits from this libertarian defense. In fact, multinational corporations (MNCs) often seek out locations in which regulation is absent or minimalized so that their actions will be unconstrained by anything other than consensual contractual obligations. MNCs and libertarian-influenced politicians who support them regularly oppose legislative and administrative regulation as unacceptable constraints on their "rights." The current commercial system emphasizes the "free" in free market capitalism. Of course, it is only the beneficiaries of the system whose freedom and rights are protected. As Michelle Alexander points out, it would be difficult to argue that the seven million people (one in every thirty-one adults) imprisoned in the United States are enjoying high levels of liberty or freedom (2012).

INFORMATION BOX 1.2   JOHN RAWLS—THE THEORY OF JUSTICE AND AN ALTERNATIVE VIEW OF LIBERTY

John Rawls (1921–2002) arguably produced the most significant original moral theory of the 20th century. The Theory of Justice shared some common ground with libertarians. With his Liberty Principal, Rawls (1971) argued that all individuals are entitled the same basic schema of liberties including the right to private property. However, here Rawls departed from other libertarians. Rawls argued that the basic schema of liberties granted to any individual person must not infringe on the basic liberties of any others. In other words, one person's scheme of freedoms must never come at the expense of another. For Rawls, just societies are societies in which all members can share the same scheme of liberty rather than societies in which all persons are free to act in any way.

The Current DAC System

For many business students, a great deal of time is spent in their courses discussing the benefits of globalization. While the fast growing globalized economy has been a boon for many people around the globe, it has been a disaster for others. While globalization has created a tremendous amount of wealth for many and even lifted millions of people out of the worst forms of poverty, the current system has also produced tremendous and increasing levels of inequality between and within nation states; massive levels of unemployment, poverty, homelessness, and food insecurity in third and first world countries alike; unsafe working conditions; the exploitation of child labor; unsafe products; and devastation of the natural environment on which the entire globe depends. Just as business practices are credited for many of the benefits and gains, business practices and economic decisions are directly and indirectly responsible for a great deal of this destruction. The Schumpeterian shocks resulting from globalization pose an existential risk to the people and the planet.

The reality is that business practices do not occur in a vacuum. The astute business student quickly learns that what they do in individual business departments (e.g., accounting, marketing, human resources) impacts the rest of the organization. However, what is sometimes lost is that what happens within the organization impacts entities both within and outside the walls of any business.

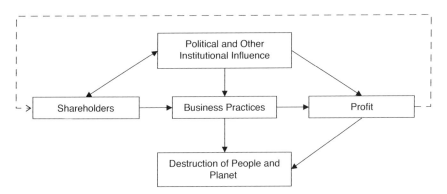

FIGURE 1.2 The Model of DAC

Business practices impact employees, their families, buyers, suppliers, consumers, communities, society as a whole, the environment, and the many millions of species inhabiting the planet. Today, business practices may even have an impact beyond the boundaries of the planet Earth. Unfortunately, the business practices that may benefit the internal operations of a business, or that may benefit a select class of business executives or owners, oftentimes create problems and destruction for these other stakeholders (all of which are referred to as negative externalities).

INFORMATION BOX 1.3   PROFESSOR SCHUMPETER AND HIS FAMOUS SHOCKS

Joseph Schumpeter (1883–1950) was an Austrian-born economist and founding member of the "Austrian School" of economics. A fierce proponent of market capitalism, he coined the term *creative destruction* for the "process of industrial mutation that incessantly revolutionizes the economic structure from within, incessantly destroying the old one, incessantly creating a new one" (Schumpeter, 1942). Schumpeterian shocks are the economic and social disruptions related to this process of creative destruction. Despite Schumpeter's argument that this destruction is on balance positive, the magnitude of the consequences is always difficult to measure. Today, a mismeasurement of the potential costs of creative destruction could result in irreversible damage to the inhabitability of the planet and destruction of human rights so painfully gained.

Many of these problems for both the planet and its inhabitants have received recent attention. Researchers, activists, and academics have cast an ever brighter light on these concerns. Political movements from the left and right have developed across the industrialized world as a result. The Occupy Movement, the Fight for $15, general strikes in France, and widespread protests over Greek austerity are all examples of the left's response to the economic disruption to workers. The right too has been active. Workers' anger with the elite's deafness to their pain has provided energy to far-right xenophobic movements in Europe and the United States and such outcomes as the Brexit vote and Trump election in 2016.

Occasionally, these environmental concerns and social concerns are addressed together. Authors such as Naomi Klein (*This Changes Everything*), Van Jones (*The Green Collar Economy*), and Annie Leonard (*The Story of Stuff*) have written about both environmental and social concerns and problems with the current global economy. In this book, we will follow the lead of Klein, Jones, and Leonard by looking at both social and environmental concerns and the relationships between them. We will begin by exploring the problems or destruction we see to the environment, workers, communities, families, and society as a whole. As stated previously, we define the current system that creates these problems as destructive advanced capitalism (DAC). We will also explore how business practices are related to these destructive practices and outcomes. We will then explore a part of the history of proposals to address this destruction in this system of commerce. In Chapter 3, we will review many of the past responses to DAC in the business ethics and social responsibility literature. In Chapter 4, we develop our proposed system as a solution to these problems—a socially sustainable business system (SSBS). Beginning in Chapter 5, we will explore the various business functions and how they relate to both the current destructive system of advanced capitalism and SSBS. This will include an exploration of human resource management, operations management, supply chain management, information technology, leadership, and strategy. We will also explore how psychology plays a role in both SSBS and DAC. We will explore why we continue to be tied to the current destructive system and, finally, present potential paths forward for a more sustainable and just system of commerce.

Problematic Outcomes of the Current DAC System

The current system of commerce destroys and depletes natural resources; denigrates the human rights to which workers, consumers, and communities are entitled; inhibits positive social and technological innovation; and even imperils democracy. This system is far removed from Adam Smith's original ideas and assumptions about capitalism. Instead, our current economic system creates a vicious cycle, focusing on the creation of profit and shareholder wealth at the expense of all else. The focus on profit has shifted from a fair profit to profit maximization, in no small part due to the Chicago School theories about the role of business and the functioning of the marketplace (Marens, 2008). This ideology of profit maximization has led to a proliferation of the idea that everything else is subservient to this goal. Today, that includes the very livelihood of the people who produce the profit and even the planet upon which those who produce the profit and those who benefit from the profit both depend to survive. So, what we have seen is that the system has advanced not in a productive way, but in a way of advancing towards more and more destructive behaviors and outcomes. These are the reasons we refer to this current system of commerce as DAC.

Destruction of the Planet

As human beings each of us depends on the Earth for the air we breathe, the food we eat, and the water we drink. The unbridled forces associated with DAC have the potential to deny any reasonable level of human thriving. From an ecological standpoint, the current business methods of marketing, extraction, production, and disposal push us away from a sustainable planet and towards a catastrophic level of destruction. Business practices are currently leading to an environment that is not conducive to human life in the long run and ecological problems that are leading to sicknesses and deaths in the short run.

INFORMATION BOX 1.4   THE SOUTHEAST ASIAN HAZE

The drive to meet the increasing corporate demand for palm oil has greatly increased slash-and-burn agriculture across Southeast Asia. This disastrous practice, in combination with seasonal monsoons, climate change, and other sources of air pollution, generates what has come to be known as the Southeast Asian Haze. Beginning in 2006 and regularly recurring since then, this condition has compromised the air quality of Southeast and East Asia. While slash-and-burn has destroyed the rain forests and the enormous bio-diversity dependent on these habitats, the resulting air pollution has caused more than 100,000 premature deaths (www.wsj.com/articles/u-s-study-calculates-death-toll-of-southeast-asia-haze-1474273547). Companies such as Johnson & Johnson, Sodexo, Nestlé, Mars, and many others continue to make huge profits selling questionably beneficial goods dependent upon an ever-increasing flow of palm oil. Corporations can make other choices. Colgate Palmolive, Frito-Lay, and Avon make profits and adhere to sustainable palm oil sourcing (http://greenpalm.org/the-market/green-palm-members).

Our planet has seen major destructive changes over the past several decades, changes that have been occurring since and accelerated with the industrialization of the global economy. Human practices have been tied to these changes. This current period of human impact on the global atmosphere and climate is referred to as the Anthropocene. According to the United Nations, throughout this century we will see the overall temperatures warm by 3°C. This increased temperature is expected to lead to heat waves, droughts, and other disastrous weather patterns as well as the melting of Arctic and Antarctic ice and resulting rising sea levels (Klein, 2014). These rising temperatures are increasing at rates unprecedented in the past 1000 years (Milman, 2016). Despite a recent international agreement to keep temperatures from rising more than 2°C, implementing the agreement will remain very challenging, given the difficulties of converting from carbon-based to non-carbon-based energy sources. Warming temperatures and the coinciding increased melting of the ice caps have led to the loss of land, hundreds of billions of dollars, and most importantly hundreds of thousands of lives (Schmidt, 2012).

Even in the industrialized world, the increase in sea water levels has already had a dramatic impact. For instance, the city of Miami has had to institute measures such as pumps and raised roads to keep the rising sea water out of city homes and buildings (Flechas & Staletovich, 2015). These pumps have already cost the city $500 million and really present only a band-aid or short-term solution to the rising sea waters engulfing the city. Carlisle, England is another city in the developed world that has been devastated by climate change. The town of Carlisle suffered three 200-year floods in a 5-year time frame. At one point, one of the rivers surrounding the town swelled to thirty times its normal volume. These floods are estimated to have been made 40% more likely as a result of climate change and have led to more than $33 million being allocated to Carlisle for flood defense (Schlossberg, 2016).

In addition to the climate change we have also seen the destruction through over-use and abuse of all of the resources of the planet. Our oceans are littered with garbage patches the size of Texas (Lovett, 2010), while similar patches of plastic waste collect in the Great Lakes of the northeastern and midwestern United States (Koe-bler, 2013). Water supplies have been polluted by industrial waste in West Virginia and government cuts to benefit corporate interests in Flint, Michigan. In 2008 in Bangladesh, seventy million people were drinking water that did not meet World Health Organization standards (Leonard, 2010, p. 13). According to a study by Environmental Working Group (EWG) in 2016, the water supply for more than 200 million Americans in all fifty states is contaminated with the carcinogen chromium-6 (Andrews & Walker, 2016). The air has also been polluted as a result of this system of DAC. The transportation of goods to and across the United States has led to massive decreases in air quality across the country. In emerging economies such as Brazil and China, the air quality is so bad that many days citizens are unable to go outside.

Destruction of the People

DAC and Poverty and Inequality

As a result of their relentless drive for profit with little regard for the environment and societal welfare, American corporations are earning the highest profits as a percentage of GDP that they have ever earned while paying their employees the lowest wages as a percentage of GDP that they have ever paid (Blodget, 2012). Meanwhile, with a particular focus on the United States, wealth disparity has been increasing at an alarming rate over the last few decades. For example, while productivity increased nearly 75% from 1977 to 2005, median family income increased by only 10%, with 40% of the total growth from 1979 to 2001 going to a mere 1% of Americans (Mishel, Bivens, Gould, & Shierholz, 2012). Since that time median family income has continued to decrease with 2014 being the first year in more than two decades with a real dollar increase in the median family income (Real median family income, 1947–2013, 2014). While the annual household income of the top 1% increased by more than 240% from 1979 to 2007, the bottom fifth of Americans saw an increase of only 10% (Mishel, Bivens, Gould, & Shierholz, 2012). The share of income going to the top 1% in the United States ballooned from around 10% in the 1960s to more than 20% of the total national income by 2008 (Mishel, Bivens, Gould, & Shierholz, 2012). The share of the United States wealth held by the top 1% increased from 23% in 1978 to 42% by 2012 (Leopold, 2015). As a result, the United States has become the most unequal society of any of the industrialized countries and has a current level of inequality not seen since the Great Depression (Krugman, 2013). Poverty, foreclosures, bankruptcy, and homelessness have impacted millions of American families.

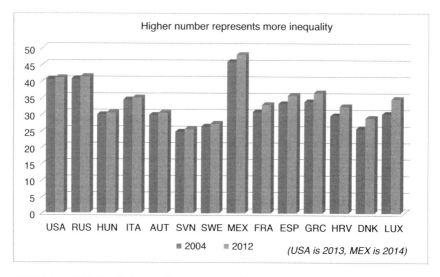

FIGURE 1.3 Gini Coefficients of Income Inequality 2004 and 2012 (World Bank)

The United States is not alone in this growing inequality. The United Kingdom closely mirrors the United States in terms of the increased share of income going to the top 1%. Other countries have also seen increases in their Gini coefficients of inequality (see Figure 1.3 and Table 1.1). The Gini index (Gini coefficient) indicates income distribution of residents in a country. The number ranges from 0 to 1, with 0 representing perfect equality and 1 representing perfect inequality. The Gini index is typically expressed as a percentage.

However, many other countries actually grew more equal during this time, as can been seen in Table 1.1.

While there can be arguments for inequality (i.e., competition drives innovation), high levels of inequality have been shown to have disastrous effects for all. According to studies by Wilkinson and Pickett, inequality leads to mental health problems, drug use, decreased life expectancy, obesity, increased teen birth, increased violence, increased incarceration rates, and decreased upward mobility (Wilkinson & Pickett, 2010). Nobel Laureate economist Joseph Stiglitz has found that unequal societies are less efficient and tend to be unstable (Stiglitz, 2012, p. 83). A 2016 International Monetary Fund (IMF) study found that the growing inequality has a dramatic downward effect on consumption and spending (Drum, 2016). Stiglitz explains that higher income individuals spend less of their income. Therefore, as a higher percentage of income goes to these upper level earners, less of the overall income is spent into the economy, decreasing demand. This decreased demand leads to increased unemployment and even more reduced incomes for those at the lower socio-economic levels. The inequality in the United States has led to a drastic reduction in upward class mobility with one's future earnings having a greater link to heredity than height or weight (Noah,

TABLE 1.1 Gini Coefficients of Income Inequality 2004 and 2012 (World Bank)

Country	2004	2012
NOR	31.72	25.9[+++]
PER	51.2	44.14[+++]
HND	58.41	50.64[+++]
URY	47.13	41.6
GTM	54.84[*]	48.66
GBR	36.22	32.57
BEL	30.63	27.59
SVK	28.94	26.12
POL	35.43	32.08[+++]
CHL	55.59[*]	50.45[++]
NLD	30.74	27.99
ROU	30.04	27.45[++]
DEU	32.78[**]	30.13[+]
PRT	38.9	36.04
CZE	27.53	26.13
ISL	28.11	26.94
LVA	36.77	35.48
FIN	27.92	27.12
TUR	41.29	40.18[++]
EST	33.96	33.15

Lower number represents less inequality.
Notes: [*] 2000
[**] 2006
[+] 2011
[++] 2013
[+++] 2014

2012). In the United States, "the greater likelihood is that your relative [economic] position will be merely as good as, or possibly worse than your parents" (Noah, 2012, p. 31).

In addition to inequality, poverty is another economic issue that has a destructive effect on individuals, families, communities, and society as a whole. In 2010 the overall US poverty rate was 15.1% with 1.5 million Americans living on less than $2 per day (Stiglitz, 2012). When the United States poverty rate is measured in the same way as the rest of the world, the poverty looks even worse. The United States relative poverty rate is more than double that of Denmark, Iceland, Slovakia, the Netherlands, France, Norway, Austria, Slovenia, Finland, Sweden, and Luxembourg, and nearly twice that of Germany, Switzerland, and Belgium. The United States rate of relative poverty is 1.8 times the rate of Organisation for Economic Co-Operation and Development (OECD) peer countries (Mishel, Bivens, Gould, & Shierholz, 2012). The children in the United States fare even worse. While business executives and capital owners continue to reap huge rewards, nearly one in four

American children lives in poverty (Mishel, Bivens, Gould, & Shierholz, 2012). These US children living in poverty live further from the median income than the children in any other peer OECD country, and to further exacerbate this problem, the United States does less through transfers to alleviate this poverty than any of these peer countries (Mishel, Bivens, Gould, & Shierholz, 2012). According to the Census Bureau 31.7% of American citizens live at or below twice the poverty level as of 2015 and 6% of the population lives at half or less of the poverty level (an income of $24,300 for a family of four in 2016). Even when accounting for tax adjustments and social safety nets, the United States poverty level does not change significantly, with the Earned Income Tax Credit (EITC) reducing it by just two percentage points and other social safety net measures having even less of an impact. The United States, despite being one of the richest countries, has a large percentage of its population who struggle to make ends meet each day (Census Bureau).

However, this is not to say that other developed countries around the world do not have concerns with poverty and inequality. Increasing inequality is a theme across the globe. Other countries including Germany and the United Kingdom have also seen increases in inequality (Report: Income Inequality Rising in Most Developed Countries, 2013). Poverty, including childhood poverty, is also prevalent in other developed countries. Two million children in Germany live in poverty. The United Kingdom, Italy, Greece, Japan, as well as other OECD peer countries with the United States also have child poverty rates exceeding 10% (Leopold, 2015).

For people in the developing world, the conditions are even worse. Globally we still find billions of people living on less than $2 of purchasing power equivalent (PPE) per day while millions of others toil in sweat shop conditions working for Apple, Dell, and other MNCs in China, Bangladesh, India, and Africa. As of 2001, more than one billion people are living in severe poverty defined as less than $1.08 of PPE in 1993 dollars (Ghose, Majid, & Ernst, 2008, p. 127). Even in countries that have shared in global growth "the money that is being made is not being distributed among the population" (Hertz, 2003, p. 47). For instance, one-fifth of China's population lives on less than one dollar a day, and half of the population in India lives on less than $1.50 per day (Hertz, 2003, p. 48). In Bolivia, following trade liberalization, the average wage for all workers fell from $845 per year to $789 (Klein, 2007, p. 149).

The inequality and poverty we see across the globe have devastating impacts on those living in poverty as well as all individuals in unequal societies. Inequality has been shown to have the strongest link to health indicators, murder rates, crime rates, prison rates (Hertz, 2003, p. 58), weaker communities, poor mental and physical health, teen pregnancies, and obesity (Wilkinson & Pickett, 2010).

The corporate focus on profit and growth does nothing to alleviate inequality. In fact, growth may actually lead to greater inequality (Ghose, Majid, & Ernst, 2008, p. 124). Corporate greed and profit have come before even the most basic necessity of life, and this corporate greed has been supported by international organizations and policies under the current free market system. The combination of the forces of decreasing wages, longer hours, and increasingly smaller shares of the wealth has led to an unsustainable living environment for the working class.

Destruction to Consumers

Individuals are also exploited and harmed in their role as consumers under our current system. DAC has led to a proliferation of unsafe and destructive products for consumers. From defective brakes to unsafe and even deadly air bags, auto products have been rushed to the market or produced in dangerous ways to cut down on costs. In the pharmaceutical industry, unsafe drugs are fast tracked into the marketplace, drugs meant for adults are pushed onto children causing deaths and major illnesses, and needed medicines are oftentimes priced out of access for consumers. Cost-cutting measures and profit-increasing measures in the food industry have led to unsafe products being sold in our supermarkets. In the financial sector consumers are often tricked into exorbitant levels of debt and financing fees, and even in one case placed into phony accounts and charged fees. In the United States, total debt increased from around 20% of disposable income in 1946 to more than 118% of disposable income by 2011, with consumer debt increasing from just more than 5% to nearly 22% in that same time period (Mishel, Bivens, Gould, & Shierholz, 2012). Student debt in the United States alone now exceeds $1.4 trillion (Berman, 2016), and 43% of the debt holders are behind on payments (Close, 2016). This debt has been a drain on graduates' ability to engage in the economic system through normal acts such as purchasing homes and vehicles.

Destruction of Communities

The current system of DAC is not only destructive at the individual level, but is also destructive at every conceivable collective level—families, communities, and the macrosocial level. For families it is hard to imagine anything more destructive than becoming homeless, yet we see that homeless families are the fastest growing segment of homelessness in the United States (Laham, 2016). While millions of American families have lost their homes and continue to suffer as a result of the financial recklessness of Wall Street and mortgage companies, the entities that caused these problems have been bailed out. We are left with a situation of children and their families living in shelters and on the streets while hundreds of thousands of homes remain unoccupied. We see that business practices of longer hours and greater responsibilities and pressures at work have led to negative family outcomes for an increasing percentage of workers (Cavanaugh, 2010). As workers share less and less of their own productivity, their families suffer.

Corporate practices of outsourcing, offshoring, and moving work to non-union facilities leave communities devastated. The remnants of the exodus of the Big Three manufacturers and their supplies turned Detroit from a thriving metropolis to a town full of abandoned and boarded up buildings. Exits from small towns such as Carrier's exit from McMinnville, Tennessee have devastating impacts on the local business community and families that depend on these employers. The corporate push for deregulation has even been linked to the actual physical destruction of communities. In West, Texas in 2013, an unregulated fertilizer plant exploded, destroying 150 buildings, injuring 160 people, and killing 15 others.

Just as the current system has proven to be destructive to our environment, likewise it is destructive to the people of this planet. We see that workers around the globe suffer at the hands of those who run the system. Consumers and communities are left in the path of destructive practices that lead to injuries, illnesses, and deaths from unsafe products, unsafe processes, and unsafe disposal practices. Around the globe billions of people are left unable to meet their most basic needs, much less to live fully as human beings with the dignity that each of us deserves. Even in the United States, millions of Americans are unable to adequately meet their needs for nutrition, health care, and shelter. Nearly one in four US children lives in conditions of poverty, and more and more families find themselves without a home. Food scarcity and insecurity are no longer just a third world problem, but are a problem for millions of Americans and others living in the first world, industrialized, and wealthy countries. For the American worker, wages have stagnated or decreased for thirty years, benefits such as pensions and health care have begun to vanish, and a middle class life of security and dignity is becoming a thing of the past.

INFORMATION BOX 1.5   ECOCIDE IN THE NIGER DELTA

The Niger delta located in the West African nation of Nigeria is home to millions of residents and enormous biodiversity. During the past decades, Royal Dutch Shell subsidiaries and other energy MNCs have been engaged in intensive extraction and refining activities in this region. Hand in hand with the economic "benefits" to the region have come social dislocation and environmental destruction that amount to ecocide. Studies estimate that more than 1.89 million barrels of oil out of a total of 2.4 million barrels extracted were spilled into the delta between 1976 and 1996 (Vidal, 2010). Within DAC, this astounding 78% loss is accounted for as shrinkage, cost of production, or loss of profits rather than wanton destruction. The loss of livelihood and basic property rights of tens of thousands of Nigerians was, of course, left out of this calculation. The millions of plants and animals killed by the release of these toxic chemicals also never appeared on corporate earnings reports. Despite this long and troubled history, oil companies are still actively damaging this region. During 2016, Shell was sued again by local communities seeking remuneration for their devastated fishing rights, farmland, and undrinkable water (Ellyatt, 2016).

Destruction of Creativity

Capitalism is often credited as a system that spurs innovation and creativity and that improves the lives of all. As can be seen from the previous discussion, the latter accomplishment is no longer present in this DAC. Certain innovations that change the technology of process or product in radical ways that could reduce the value of existing technologies and competences (and in extreme cases render many of them obsolete) are defined as creative destruction and are the vehicle at the heart of Schumpeter's theory of innovation and economic development (Schumpeter, 1934). However, even the two former accomplishments seem to be lacking. Creative destruction by itself is not destructive. The process of this innovation is often referred to as *creative destruction*. However, unfettered creative destruction could be destructive to society.

Over the course of history, creative destructions such as the steam engine and electricity have improved human productivity and bettered people's lives (Brynjolfsson and McAfee, 2012). However, such creative destruction can also result in the dismantling of many jobs. This trend has been reflected in both academic and commercial publications (Brynjolfsson and McAfee, 2012) as robots increasingly replace many manufacturing jobs. While this could help increase productivity, the impacts of such technological developments reach far beyond efficiency and must be evaluated from the social perspective. Left to their own devices with the DAC, the laid off workers will remain unemployed, while much of the profit will be concentrated in the small number of capital owners. This trend is one of the many factors that have contributed to the stagnant middle class income and increase of inequality in the United States of the last thirty years.

Without appropriate social structure to retrain these workers, they will end up long-term unemployed and even get trapped in poverty. There are several implications of this that will actually slow, or negatively influence, the development of society and lead to subsequent creative destructions. First, such phenomena occurring on a large scale will result in people with lost income who will not be able to afford the products that were produced by machines that replaced them. Second, without social mechanisms to educate replaced workers or provide education to children of impoverished workers, the potential contributions of these workers and their children will be lost to society.

While the current DAC's focus has been on profit maximization, deregulation, and competition (Meyer & Kirby, 2012), such a focus can be stifling to "fair" competition and the development of the market via innovations. Without a regulating body or arbiter of rules, technological development with a profit maximization mentality drives companies to grow and industries become concentrated into oligopolistic "competitors." Such large companies could become sufficiently powerful in certain industries that they not only control markets but also use their power to set policy (Meyer & Kirby, 2012), creating unfair competitive markets.

Additionally, such oligopolies often stifle freedom of experimentation and technological innovation since many innovations of a disruptive nature would reduce their power and influences. An example of such oligopolies is the consolidated mobile phone industry, dominated by AT&T and Verizon. As such, pseudo-competition created by an unregulated competitive market would be detrimental to innovation and creative destruction.

The focus on profit maximization and meeting quarterly profitability targets actually inhibits innovation and creative destruction since radical innovations require a long-term view of investment. This has been reflected by reduction in basic research investments by companies (Slywotzky, 2009). Xerox's Palo Alto Research Center (PARC) and Bell Labs these days are the ghosts of their former mighty research organizations.

Destruction of Democracy

Marin Wolf (2016), an esteemed economist and a firm believer that capitalism and democracy are compatible, argued that this compatibility between democracy and capitalism has been strained to a breaking point. Wolf called for steps to be taken to assure that capitalism be "reoriented towards promoting the interests of the man." Wolin (2008) suggests that the incompatibility of culture needed for democracy with the culture needed for capitalism is one of the great challenges of our time. For Richard Wolff (2012), an American economist, capitalism is the antithesis of democracy, and Wolff suggests the need for the democratization of the economy. Klein points to the political spending by corporations and corporate leaders as having a huge impact on democratic processes around the world, suggesting that the political spending by corporations leads to business-friendly political decisions.

Matten and Crane (2005) recognize the power of the corporation over nation state politics. They call for corporations to step in as the power brokers (formerly nation states) in the citizenship relationship, assuring and protecting the rights of the citizenry. Of course, as we have seen from the other disasters, corporations have clearly failed to do so. In fact, corporations use their powers to carve out exceptions to laws allowing them to exploit labor and the environment with impunity. This power has led to third world countries developing special economic zones, or what Kennard and Provost (2016) refer to as Corporate Utopias. In these zones, investors are promised tax breaks, cheap resources including land and water, and a guaranteed labor supply that can be exploited with no right to organize for the workers. A 2016 study by Gilens and Page (2014) found that in the United States, where capitalism has of course run rampant, the political system is no longer a real democracy.

This corporate takeover of democracy is seen and felt around the globe. In the United Kingdom the realization that the European Union was more concerned with serving corporate interests than the people of Europe played a role in the United Kingdom voting to exit the European Union. In Germany, this same frustration has led to the growth of the right-wing populist Alternative for Germany

(AfD) party. While reformers such as Jeremy Corbyn in the United Kingdom and Bernie Sanders in the United States have seen some political success, corporate control has pushed back against these reformers, with many corporate Labour MPs opposing Corben and even leaving the party, and the Democratic Party taking a tack back to the corporate side with both the 2016 Presidential and Vice Presidential candidates receiving high marks from business organizations.

Conclusion

Our current system of commerce has led to disastrous results to the people and the planet that we all inhabit. This destruction is not an unavoidable consequence of the advancement of the human race. Instead, this destruction is the consequence of a flawed system of commerce that benefits a select few at the expense of the many. It is hard to argue today that big business as a whole is indeed providing a square deal to the people of not only the United States, but also the planet. Instead, it would appear that many of Thomas Jefferson's fears about the "monied corporations" have become a stark reality.

In this textbook we will lead students down a path to understanding and ending this destruction. We will help students to identify some of the specific business practices that have led to this system of DAC. We will also help students to explore the solutions from the past that have failed to adequately address these problems. In Chapter 4, we present students with one proposed path to solve these problems that we define as SSBS. Of course, we do not suggest that we are the first to argue for social sustainability or suggest that this solution is the singular, or perfect, solution to the world's problems. Rather we recognize and hope that the students reading this book recognize that the problems of global commerce and global society are too complex for any one basic solution. Up front, we believe students should be aware of some of the potential problems with even the solution of SSBS. Boström (2012) discusses several problems in defining the concepts of social sustainability:

> The first is theoretical and concerns how we should define and understand this fluid concept of social sustainability. The other involves the practice: how are the social sustainability aspects to be operationalized and incorporated into various sustainability projects and planning? Partly due to its contested character, a number of scholars argue that the social dimension garners less attention or is dismissed altogether.
>
> *(Boström, 2012, p. 1)*

As Boström recognizes, the limitations of social sustainability are both a strength and a weakness. We hope that this text will allow us and each of you as future business leaders to utilize the strengths of SSBS and to overcome its weaknesses.

Chapters 5 through 10 are dedicated to helping business students to understand how to engage in specific business practices in a socially sustainable way and to actually use these business practices to help to achieve SSBS. In Chapter 11, we discuss the psychology of sustainability, including the psychological barriers and paths to social sustainability. Finally, in the two concluding chapters, we present students with an explanation as to why we are so tied to the current system of destructive commerce and how we can break free from these ties that bind us to DAC.

Discussion Questions

1. How would you define SSBS?
2. How would you define DAC? Do you see evidence of DAC in our society?
3. Are business practices responsible for the social outcomes discussed in Chapter 1? What specific practices are leading or might lead to destruction of the planet and the people of the planet?
4. What are the goals of your ideal society? What would the system of commerce look like in such a society? What rules would you set for businesses within that society? Why?

References

Alexander, M. (2012). *The New Jim Crow: Mass Incarceration in the Age of Colorblindness.* New York: The New Press.

Andrews, D., & Walker, B. (2016, September 20). *'Erin Brockovich' Carcinogen in Tap Water of More Than 200 Million Americans.* Retrieved January 15, 2017, from www.ewg.org: www.ewg.org/research/chromium-six-found-in-us-tap-water

Berman, J. (2016, January 19). *America's Growing Student-Loan-Debt Crisis.* Retrieved January 16, 2017, from marketwatch: www.marketwatch.com/story/americas-growing-student-loan-debt-crisis-2016-01-15

Blodget, H. (2012, June 22). *Corporate Profits Just Hit an All-Time High, Wages Just Hit an All-Time Low.* Retrieved January 15, 2017, from Business Insider: www.business insider.com/corporate-profits-just-hit-an-all-time-high-wages-just-hit-an-all-time-low-2012-6

Boström, M. (2012). A missing pillar? Challenges in theorizing and practicing social sustainability: Introduction to the special issue. *Sustainability: Science, Practice, & Policy, 8*(1), 1–15.

Brynjolfsson, E., & McAfee, A. (2011). *Race Against the Machine.* Lexington, MA: Digital Frontier.

Cavanaugh, G. F. (2010). *American Business Values* (6th ed.). Upper Saddle River, NJ: Prentice Hall.

Close, K. (2016, April 7). *The Number of People Behind on Student Loan Payments Is Staggering.* Retrieved January 16, 2017, from Time.com: http://time.com/money/4284940/student-loan-payments-debt-college/

Drum, K. (2016, September 29). *New Study Says Rising Inequality Is Killing the Economy.* Retrieved January 15, 2017, from Mother Jones: www.motherjones.com/kevin-drum/2016/09/new-study-says-rising-inequality-killing-economy

Ellyatt, H. (2016, March 2). *Shell Faces Further Suit Over Nigeria Oil Spills.* Retrieved June 6, 2017, from CNBC: http://www.cnbc.com/2016/03/02/shell-faces-further-suit-over-nigeria-oil-spills.html

Flechas, J., & Staletovich, J. (2015, October 23). *Miami Beaches' Battle to Stem Rising Tides*. Retrieved January 15, 2017, from Miami Herald: www.miamiherald.com/news/local/community/miami-dade/miami-beach/article41141856.html

Ghose, A. K., Majid, N., & Ernst, C. (2008). *The Global Employment Challenge*. Geneva: International Labor Organization Publications.

Gilens, M., & Page, B. I. (2014, September). Testing theories of American politics: Elites, interest groups, and average citizens. *Perspectives on Politics, 12*(3), 564–581.

Hertz, N. (2003). *The Silent Takeover*. New York: HarperBusiness.

Kennard, M., & Provost, C. (2016, August). Corporate utopias: To entice capital, many countries are carving out union-free zones. *In These Times*, pp. 24–31.

Klein, N. (2007). *The Shock Doctrine: The Rise of Disaster Capitalism*. New York: Metropolitan Books.

Klein, N. (2014). *This Changes Everything: Capitalism vs. the Climate*. New York: Simon & Schuster.

Koebler, J. (2013, April 9). *Now There's Also a Great Garbage Patch in the Great Lakes*. Retrieved January 15, 2017, from U.S. News: www.usnews.com/news/articles/2013/04/09/now-theres-also-a-great-garbage-patch-in-the-great-lakes

Krugman, P. (2013). *End This Depression Now!* New York: W.W. Norton & Company, Inc.

Laham, M. T. (2016, June 7). *Fastest-Growing Segment of the Homeless Population May Surprise You*. Retrieved January 16, 2017, from The Huffington Post: www.huffingtonpost.com/martha-ts-laham-/fastest-growing-segment-of-homeless-population_b_10201782.html

Leonard, A. (2010). *The Story of Stuff: How Our Obsession with Stuff Is Trashing the Planet, Our Communities, and Our Health—and a Vision for Change*. New York: Free Press.

Leopold, L. (2015). *Runaway Inequality: An Activist's Guide to Economic Justice*. New York: Labor Insitute Press.

Lovett, R. A. (2010, March 2). *Huge Garbage Patch Found in Atlantic Too*. Retrieved January 15, 2017, from National Geographic: http://news.nationalgeographic.com/news/2010/03/100302-new-ocean-trash-garbage-patch/

Marens, R. (2008). Recovering the past: Reviving the legacy of the early scholars of corporate social responsibility. *Journal of Management History, 14*(1), 55–72.

Matten, D., & Crane, A. (2005). Corporate citizenship: Toward an extended theoretical conceptualization. *Academy of Management Review, 30*(1), 166–179.

McGhee, P., & Grant, P. (2016). Teaching the virtues of sustainability as flourishing to undergraduate business students. *Global Virtue Ethics Review, 7*(2), 73–116.

Meadows, D. H. (2008). *Thinking in Systems: A Primer*. Junction, VT: Chelsea Green Publishing Company.

Meyer, C., & Kirby, J. (2012). *Standing on the Sun: How the Explosion of Capitalism Abroad Will Change Business Everywhere*. Cambridge, MA: Harvard Business Press.

Milman, O. (2016, August 30). *Nasa: Earth Is Warming at a Pace 'Unprecedented in 1,000 Years.'* Retrieved January 15, 2017, from The Guardian: www.theguardian.com/environment/2016/aug/30/nasa-climate-change-warning-earth-temperature-warming

Mintzberg, H., Simons, R., & Basu, K. (Fall 2002). Beyond selfishness. *MIT Sloan Management Review, 44*(1), 67–74.

Mishel, L., Bivens, J., Gould, E., & Shierholz, H. (2012). *The State of Working America* (12th ed.). Ithaca, NY: Cornell University Press.

Noah, T. (2012). *The Great Divergence: America's Growing Inequality Crisis and What We Can Do about It*. New York: Bloomsbury Press.

O'Brien, C. (2008). Sustainable happiness: How happiness studies can contribute to a more sustainable future. *Canadian Psychology, 49*(4), 289–295.

Rawls, J. (1971). *A Theory of Justice.* Cambridge, MA: Belknap.

Real Median Family Income, 1947–2013 (2013 Dollars). (2014, September 23). Retrieved January 15, 2017, from State of Working America: www.stateofworkingamerica.org/chart/swa-income-figure-2a-real-median-family/

Report: Income Inequality Rising in Most Developed Countries. (2013, May 16). Retrieved January 16, 2017, from The Washington Post: www.washingtonpost.com/news/worldviews/wp/2013/05/16/report-income-inequality-rising-in-most-developed-countries/?utm_term=.fd3abcfff9b7

Schlossberg, T. (2016, September 12). *In an English Village, a Lesson in Climate Change.* Retrieved December 1, 2016, from New York Times: http://nyti.ms/2cGnXb2

Schmidt, J. (2012, September 26). *Global Warming Is Already Causing Loss of Life and Damage to the Economy around the World: New Report.* Retrieved January 15, 2017, from nrdc. org: www.nrdc.org/experts/jake-schmidt/global-warming-already-causing-loss-life-and-damage-economy-around-world-new

Schumpeter, J. A. (1934). *The Theory of Economic Development: An Inquiry into Profits, Capital, Credit, Interest, and the Business Cycle* (Vol. 55). Transaction publishers.

Schumpeter, J. A. (1942). *Capitalism, Socialism and Democracy.* New York: Hamper Brother.

Slywotzky, Adrian. (2009, August 27). *Where Have You Gone, Bell Labs?* Retrieved from Bloomberg Business week: https://www.bloomberg.com/news/articles/2009-08-27/where-have-you-gone-bell-labs

Stiglitz, J. E. (2012). *The Price of Inequality: How Today's Divided Society Endangers Our Future.* New York: W.W. Norton & Company, Inc.

Vidal, J. (2010, May 29). *Nigeria's Agony Dwarfs the Gulf Oil Spill. The US and Europe Ignore It.* Retrieved June 6, 2017, from The Guardian: https://www.theguardian.com/world/2010/may/30/oil-spills-nigeria-niger-delta-shell

Wilkinson, R., & Pickett, K. (2010). *The Spirit Level: Why Greater Equality Makes Societies Stronger.* New York: Bloomsbury Press.

Wolf, M. (2016, August 30). *Capitalism and Democracy: The Strain Is Showing.* Retrieved January 16, 2017, from Financial Times: www.ft.com/content/e46e8c00-6b72-11e6-ae5b-a7cc5dd5a28c

Wolff, R. (2012). *Democracy at Work: A Cure for Capitalism.* Chicago: Haymarket Books.

Wolin, S. S. (2008). *Democracy, Inc: Managed Democracy and the Specter of Inverted Totalitarianism.* Princeton, NJ: Princeton University Press.

CASE 1   BIG ENERGY AND BIG DISASTERS

On January 2, 2006 at 6:26 in the morning an explosion rocked the Sago coal mine in Upshur County, West Virginia. One coal miner was killed instantly by the blast, sixteen escaped, and twelve were trapped. Forty-one hours later, the twelve miners were found by rescue efforts that began more than two hours after the blast. By the time they were found eleven of the twelve had died of carbon monoxide poisoning. While the explosion at Sago might not have been avoidable, as the report from investigator Davitt McAteer concludes, the trag-edy could have been avoided. First, the explosion at Sago should have been contained. Unfortunately the seals to contain such an explosion failed (McAteer et al., 2006). The seals may or may not have met the required standards in the United States at the time, but they fell well short of internationally applied stan-dards (Pittsburgh Post-Gazette Editorial, 2006). Even after this failure the eleven miners who died from carbon monoxide poisoning could have survived had they been equipped with working self-contained, self-rescue devices (SCSRs). Perhaps most troubling is the following from McAteer's report:

> There would have been no disaster if it had been possible for rescuers to communicate with the miners on Two Left. They could have been told that there was respirable air at the mouth of the section, not far from where they were. But the mine's phone system—an outmoded, vulnerable system typical of underground mines—was knocked out by the explosion.
>
> *(McAteer et al., 2006)*

By the time McAteer's report on the Sago disaster came out in July 2006 a total of nineteen miners had been killed on the job in West Virginia in 2006 (McAteer et al., 2006).

Prior to the explosion, the Sago mine had a nonfatal injury rate that was three times the rate for similar mines (Ward, Jr., 2006). The mine had been cited more than 200 times in 2005 by the Mine Safety and Health Administra-tion (MSHA) and had more than a dozen roof collapses. The last MSHA visit to the Sago mine before the disaster led to forty-six citations for safety violations.

Just more than four years after the explosion at Sago, on April 5, 2010 an explosion rocked the Upper Big Branch (UBB) mine in West Virginia. Twenty-nine miners perished in the coal dust explosion. According to the MSHA investigation of the disaster, this tragedy like the Sago tragedy was completely avoidable. Basic safety violation and "unlawful policies and practices" implemented by Massey Energy led to the tragedy. Investigators found that Massey Energy under the leadership of its CEO Don Blankenship had engaged in systemic, intentional, and aggressive efforts to avoid compliance with safety and health standards. UBB management threatened miners to prevent them from reporting violations, relayed advance notice of safety inspections to conceal violations, and "kept two sets of books" on safety records and hazards. Massey Energy could have prevented the explosion by following basic and required safety standards; instead they allowed the conditions to exist that led to the explosion and the deaths of twenty-nine miners, all in the pursuit of profit (Brown et al., 2010). Prior to the UBB disaster, MSHA had ordered evacuation of the mine due to safety concerns on sixty-four occasions since 2009. The UBB's safety violation was more than eleven times the national average (Mufson, Kindy, & O'Keefe, 2010). The mine had received 129 violation citations in the three plus months of 2010, twenty-nine related to coal dust (Ahrens, 2010).

Fifteen days after the UBB disaster, yet another disaster occurred in the energy industry. This time an explosion rocked the Deepwater Horizon drilling station in the Gulf of Mexico. The rig was owned by Transocean, which had been contracted by BP to drill the oil. Eleven workers were killed in the explosion or the ensuing fires, and twenty-two million gallons of oil spilled into the Gulf of Mexico. Hours before the explosion pressure tests indicated potential problems with the newly cemented well, yet an hour before the explosion the decision was made to continue extracting mud (Washburn, 2010). Further, BP decided to skip a cement test earlier in the day saving $128,000, a test that could have prevented the disaster (Tilcsik & Clearfield, 2015). A report from the United States Coast Guard and the Bureau of Ocean Energy Management concluded that BP, Halliburton, and Transocean all had culpability for the disaster. Specifically the report faulted BP for a failure to supervise activities, a failure to fully assess the risks associated with operations, and making cost and time savings decisions without concern for safety (Mason, 2011). Transocean was faulted for serious safety violations and "poor safety culture." Halliburton was faulted for using a cement mixture they knew to be unstable (Krause, 2013). There is ample evidence that numerous Transocean employees warned their employers of safety concerns well before and on the day of the disaster (Caeser, 2010). As Ed Caeser wrote, "between the companies who owned and drilled the oil, the people who thirsted for oil, and the governments who suckled on the oil, the acquisition of profit became more important than the protection of human life."

Discussion Questions

1. Are these disasters in the energy industry a problem with DAC or are they simply an unavoidable risk?

2. Is the energy industry socially sustainable? Is coal a socially sustainable industry? Is oil a socially sustainable industry?
3. How can the energy industry become more socially sustainable? What steps will need to be taken?
4. What role could you play, if any, in preventing disasters like Sago, UBB, and Deepwater from happening in the future?

References

Ahrens, F. (2010, April 10). Mine's 'gassy' coal was in high demand. *Washington Post*, p. A12.

Brown, A. L., Page, N. G., Caudill, S. D., Godsey, J. F., Moore, A. D., Phillipson, S. E., . . . Vance, J. W. (2010). *Report of Investigation, Fatal Underground Mine Explosion—Upper Big Branch Mine-South, Performance Coal Company, Montcoal, Raleigh County, West Virginia, ID No. 46–08436.* Arlington, VA: Department of Labor Mine Safety and Health Admininstration.

Caeser, E. (2010, September 12). Deepwater Horizon: The big picture. *The Sunday Times*, pp. 22–29, 31, 33, 35, 37.

Krause, C. (2013, July 26). Halliburton will admit destroying data on spill. *The New York Times*, p. 1.

Mason, R. (2011, September 15). BP decision to cut costs 'aided Gulf oil disaster'. *The Daily Telegraph*, Business, p. 3.

McAteer, J. D., Bethell, T. N., Monforton, C., Pavlovich, J. W., Roberts, D., & Spence, B. (2006). *The Sago Mine Disaster: A Preliminary Report to Governor Joe Manchin III.* Buckhannon, WV: J. Davitt McAteer and Associates.

Mufson, S., Kindy, K., & O'Keefe, E. (2010, April 9). Mine avoided harsh penalties despite violations. *Washington Post*, p. A01.

Pittsburgh Post-Gazette Editorial. (2006, July 23). The Sago report: U.S. mines are behing the times and other countries. *Pittsburgh Post-Gazette*, p. H-2.

Tilcsik, A., & Clearfield, C. (2015, April 28). Five years after Deepwater Horizon oil spill, we are closer than ever to catastrophe: Important changes have been made since 2010, but the oil and gas industry has not learned from the historic oil spill in the Gulf of Mexico. Retrived June 5, 2017, from The Guardian: www.theguardian.com/sustainable-business/2015/apr/17/deepwater-horizon-oil-spill-catastrophe-five-years

Ward, Jr., K. (2006, January 9). '05 Sago safety record worse than most. *Charleston Gazette*, p. 1A.

Washburn, M. (2010, May 16). Deepwater Horizon lucky streak rant out productive oil rig's final day was one of frustration, cascading problems and ultimately, calimity. *St. Louis Post-Dispatch*, p. A11.

2

BUSINESS PRACTICES OF DAC

Exemplary persons help out the needy, they do not make the rich richer.

Confucius (Ames & Rosemont, 1998)

The Great Companies did not know that the line between hunger and anger is a thin line.

John Steinbeck, The Grapes of Wrath *(Steinbeck, 1982)*

Introduction

What do the quotes from Confucius and Steinbeck mean? How do they apply to business practices? Do the business practices you have been taught meet the definition of being an exemplary person? Do current companies recognize the line that Steinbeck suggests is a thin line? What happens when hunger crosses over into anger? What does this suggest about current business practices?

The destructive outcomes discussed in Chapter 1 are in large part due to the culmination of specific business practices. A key learning outcome of this book is to help students to understand these connections. The first step is understanding how specific business practices can lead to negative outcomes for people and the planet at the micro level. The second step is to consider how these micro-destructive practices contribute to the macro, global-level destruction we see for the planet, its resources, and its inhabitants. This chapter examines a range of business practices across multiple fields that are destructive to the planet and the people.

Business Practices and the Destruction of the Planet

Manufacturing and Planned Obsolescence

The warming planet, melting ice caps, and corresponding rising sea levels discussed in Chapter 1 are not naturally occurring. Planned obsolescence of business practices with regards to mineral and raw material extraction, production, and disposal of products is linked to climbing temperatures, resource depletion, and environmental destruction (Leonard, 2010). *Planned obsolescence* (PO) is the strategy of making products that have a short useful lifespan. For instance, companies may manufacture home appliances that do not last as long as appliances manufactured decades ago.

INFORMATION BOX 2.1   PLANNED OBSOLESCENCE

PO is a practice of producing goods with uneconomically shortened useful lifespans that will induce customers to make repeat purchases, maximizing producers' profit. Started in the 1920s by automobile companies to make consumers purchase new cars more frequently, PO is practiced widely these days. An example is the gadgetry industry, with smartphone producers adopting PO through practices including:

- *Prevention of repairs*: For example, it is almost impossible for individual users or independent repair shops to even make simple repairs of smartphones, including replacing batteries.
- *Style obsolescence*: For example, new smartphone models are introduced frequently with design changes that reduce the desirability of current phones as unfashionable items.
- *System obsolescence*: For example, many smartphones are not forward compatible so that new upgrades (e.g., software) are not compatible with older phones, requiring replacement.

PO has negative financial (on consumers) and environmental impacts. Globally only 12% of smartphone upgrades involve old devices being sold or traded in. Thus, many functioning smartphones will end up in landfills.

Sources:
Guiltinan, J. (2009). Creative destruction and destructive creations: environmental ethics and planned obsolescence. *Journal of Business Ethics, 89*(1), 19–28.
https://en.wikipedia.org/wiki/Planned_obsolescence
www.theguardian.com/sustainable-business/2015/mar/23/
were-are-all-losers-to-gadget-industry-built-on-planned-obsolescence

---

A similar but distinct marketing strategy, perceived obsolescence, is employed to convince consumers that they should replace their goods, even if they are still functioning. For example, mobile phone companies compete in an ever shorter time frame to get the next model of their phone to market; the "updated" models frequently have few meaningful improvements, and consumers typically discard their gently used devices. Both the planned and perceived obsolescence have produced shorter product lifespans that generate more and more profit (Leonard, 2010, pp. 161–163).

Kleindorfer, Singhal, and Van Wassenhove (2005) report that less than 1% of the material sold in the United States remains in use after a mere six months. Shrinking product life cycles have led to depletion of natural resources for inputs and landfill space for waste outputs. The increased level of disposal pollutes our land, water systems, air, and water supplies. These business practices are not necessary; they are the predictable outcomes associated with maximizing profit and shareholder wealth.

The Energy Industry

The push to consumption, production, and extraction plays a large role in pushing an ever-growing need for energy to power this cycle of consumption. The use of and exploration for more and more fossil fuels to meet this growing energy need have led to massive levels of destruction to the planet and one of the main causes of climate change. The fossil fuel industry plays the largest role in environmental destruction and is viewed as the dirtiest industry on the planet (Fast Fashion Is the Second Dirtiest Industry in the World, Next to Big Oil, 2015). In North Carolina, waterways and water supplies were polluted by the coal byproduct of ash from Duke Energy (Zucchino, 2015). The coal mining technique of strip mining (or mountain top removal) has tremendous environmental impacts on the surrounding communities, burying water tributaries, contaminating water supplies, destroying forests, and pushing species of wildlife out of the area or to the brink of extinction (Ecological Impacts of Mountaintop Removal, 2017). This mountain top removal has also been linked to the increased flooding in West Virginia, including a flood in 2016 that destroyed more than one thousand homes and took twenty-three lives (Heyman, 2009; Visser & Savidge, 2016).

As discussed in the previous chapter, BP's Deepwater Horizon oil rig explosion caused the most catastrophic environmental disaster in American history. The effects of this spill may be felt for decades if not longer (Elliott, 2015; Deepwater Horizon Oil Spill, 2017). Statistically, oil spills occur so often in the United States that even the large, ecologically devastating spills, such as the Mayflower spill in Arkansas, are so common as to garner little media attention (Rivers of Oil in Arkansas Town: Many 'Didn't Even Know' Exxon Pipeline Ran under Their Homes, 2013; List of Oil Spills, 2017). Despite these spills and the stark reality that eventually every pipeline will leak and cause some level of environmental damage, there is a continued push for more and more pipelines and more extraction of oil and other fossil fuels.

Natural gas is often held up as a clean and abundant source of energy. Fracking has been touted as a safe, environmentally friendly alternative. However, a 2016 report on the total impact of fracking stated that since 2005 the 137,000 fracking wells that have been permitted and drilled in the United States have produced more than 239 billion gallons of toxic wastewater. Additionally, a growing body of evidence suggests that fracking has led to not only the contamination of drinking water through contamination of water wells, streams, rivers, and lakes, but also a destruction of ecological systems, air pollution (Ridlington, Norman, &

Richardson, 2016), and even the proliferation of earthquakes in Oklahoma, Texas, and Ohio (Conca, 2016). Despite this, many politicians on both sides of the aisle keep supporting fracking in one way or another. If the fossil fuel companies extract the reserves that they have claims over, that they have promised in their disclosures to shareholders, they will burn five times the amount of carbon fuels the planet can absorb between now and 2050 (Klein, 2014, p. 148).

Nuclear energy, which is often looked at as an alternative to the fossil fuels, has also been destructive to our environment. Disasters such as the meltdowns at Three Mile Island, Chernobyl, and most recently Fukushima have had a devastating impact on the planet and the people inhabiting the planet in both the short term and long term. We still have no viable solution for how to deal with the waste from the production of nuclear energy. Despite these dangers, countries such as Germany have replaced the "dirty" fossil fuels not entirely with renewables but also by increasing nuclear production (though they have been phasing out nuclear power and pledge to shut down all plants by 2022). Germany's nuclear power decision illustrates some of the problems we will still face with upscaling to clean energy technologies such as wind and solar (McCathie, 2015; Kucera, 2016). Similarly, in the United States, nuclear power generation is transparently unsustainable, because there are simply no plans to store nuclear waste safely; instead, waste is stored on site at each facility, hoisting a radioactive sword of Damocles above the surrounding communities.

Renewable energy sources such as wind, solar, and hydroelectric present viable options. With current technology, these sources are not likely to completely replace fossil fuels, but they may drastically reduce their usage. However, the transition to such energy options would require that corporations leave many of the fossil fuels to which they have rights in the ground where they lie. These companies would need to abandon assets on their balance sheets and forego profits associated with extraction. These potential decreases in shareholder wealth are simply not an acceptable practice in our current system of commerce. Therefore, the revenues, profits, and shareholder wealth in the fossil fuel industries continue to grow while the planet and its populace suffer.

Factory Farming

Farming under the current DAC system also creates a great deal of destruction to the planet. The factory farming practices in our advanced system of commerce produce a trifecta of disaster—destruction of the environment, consumers, and workers. According to a WorldWatch report, factory farming is estimated to contribute 18% of the planetary greenhouse gas (GHG) emissions. In fact, when accounting for all factors, factory farming may actually contribute more than one-half of all GHG emissions (Goodland & Anhang, 2009).

Factory farms also divert much needed water supplies away from citizens into their profitmaking practices. For example, the Resnick Farms in California, producers of Pom Wonderful, mandarin oranges, almonds, and pistachios, use more California water than the residents of the entire city of Los Angeles at a time when California has been suffering a drought for more than four years (Harkinson, 2016). Like many other corporate practices within DAC, these agricultural practices are not necessary. The same products can be grown sustainably if corporations were willing to forego short-term profits for longer-term priorities.

Fast Fashion

Despite the enormous environmental damage caused by corporate agribusiness, EcoWatch rates "fast fashion" as the second dirtiest industry (Fast Fashion Is the Second Dirtiest Industry in the World, Next to Big Oil, 2015). While arguments are often made that fossil fuels are needed to power our lives and factory farms make the food we need to survive more affordable, fast fashion represents a more discretionary industry. Cotton production soaks up water supplies and leads to the pervasive use of insecticides, while the dyes pollute water supplies, harming millions of inhabitants of communities downstream from the production. The cotton supply chain produces tremendous GHG emissions as the cotton travels from farm to dying to cutting to sewing to the stores in which it is sold (Jane, 2014). Of course, clothing retailers are full participants in obsolescence strategies. Cheap clothing has a short economic life, and retail marketing strategies help to ensure that higher quality durable clothing must also be replaced because of the rapid rate at which clothes fall out of fashion (with the ample pushing of corporate merchandisers).

Nearly Every Industry Contributes to the Destruction

Though there are a number of particularly destructive industries, environmental damage is the rule not the exception within DAC. Worldwide air quality has been degraded by pollutants from a wide variety of business operations. Similarly, water supply has been compromised not only by the petroleum and agribusiness industries, but also by mining and manufacturing. Toxic tort cases concerning corporate contamination of community water supplies have been well-publicized and even made into popular movies such as *Erin Brokovich*. Moreover, chromium-6, the chemical found in the water supply in the case depicted in *Erin Brokovich*, has been found in the water supply of two-thirds of the United States population according to a report from EWG (Andrews & Walker, 2016). Likewise, when *Consumer Reports* tested grape and apple juices, they found 25% exceeded legal limits for lead and 10% exceeded the legal limits for arsenic (Arsenic in Your Juice, 2012). The pollution of our natural resources, including those we depend on to survive, has become so common it has morphed into an accepted business practice that is rarely discussed.

Even if the fossil fuel, factory farming, and fast fashion industries were to disappear, the remaining industries would still engage in destructive practices to the

Earth and to its inhabitants. Information Box 2.2 provides an example of how widespread the problem is.

INFORMATION BOX 2.2   THE TOLL THAT INDUSTRIES HAVE ON HUMAN LIFE (DALYS)

Even if the fossil fuel, factory farming, and fast fashion industries were to disappear, the remaining industries would still engage in destructive practices to the Earth and to its inhabitants. In fact, according to the Blacksmith Institute, the ten worst polluting and destructive industries are, in terms of disability adjusted life years (DALYs):

1. Lead-Acid Battery Recycling—4,800,000
2. Lead Smelting—2,600,000
3. Mining and Ore Processing—2,521,600
4. Tannery Operations—1,930,000
5. Industrial/Municipal Dump Sites—1,234,000
6. Industrial Estates—1,060,000
7. Artisanal Gold Mining—1,021,000
8. Product Manufacturing—786,000
9. Chemical Manufacturing—765,000
10. Dye Industry—430,000

(New Pollution Report Measures Global Health Impact Across 49 Countries, 2012)

Many if not most destructive industries exist to serve other destructive industries, forming a disastrous spiral of environmental damage. For example, the mining industry extracts the precious metals and rare earth elements used in the manufacturing of the planned obsolescence products produced by high tech industries. The problem is not specific to any one industry but is attributable to the whole system of DAC with its focus on increasing profits and shareholder wealth. Environmental costs simply do not matter as much as profit margins in DAC. A dangerous and false dichotomy of jobs versus the environment is often posed by those that profit from DAC. Corporations (often with little substantiation) posit that they cannot make profits and, therefore, afford to create jobs without some capability to compromise the environment. Unfortunately, societies immersed within DAC consistently choose jobs (corporate profits) over the planet (Jones, 2008). Fracking, a case in point, is permitted and expanded despite the evidence of environmental damage it causes. Shortly after the Deepwater Horizon spill wreaked havoc on the ecosystem of the United States Gulf Coast, there were calls for more offshore drilling to further line the pockets of the energy companies and their executives (Obama Granted Over 1,500 Underwater Fracking Permits in Gulf of Mexico After Deepwater Horizon, 2016).

We reached 387.81 parts per million (ppm) of CO_2 in the atmosphere in July 2009 (Leonard, 2010, p. xiv). The levels have now surpassed 400 ppm and are not likely to decline any time soon.[1] Leading scientists have identified 350 ppm as the maximum level that the atmosphere can contain for the planet to remain as we know it (Rockström et al., 2009). Further, toxic industrial and agricultural chemicals now show up in everybody tested anywhere in the world, including newborn babies (Leonard, 2010). The current damage to the environment as a result of current business practices is so severe that a 2009 article in *Nature* suggests we have already surpassed six out of ten boundaries for a sustainable planet. (Rockström et al., 2009). Weber (2015, p. 561) refers to this climate challenge as "perhaps the most daunting challenge of the twenty-first century." Halting climate change requires dramatic change to the current global economic system typified by DAC.

Business Practices and Destruction of People

Not only have business practices created a great amount of harm to the environment, but they have also harmed the people who inhabit the planet. People in their roles as consumers, workers, and members of their families, communities, and society are harmed by the destructive practices of the current economic system. People are harmed financially, psychologically, and physically. Too often destructive business practices violate the human rights of the people across the globe.

The Financial Sector

In the financial sector, "creative" financial managers have invented products that have led to bankruptcies and broad financial disasters. In 2010, the Justice Department filed suit against Goldman Sachs for defrauding its customers through the sale of mortgage backed securities and then betting against these securities. Investors in these mortgage backed securities lost billions of dollars in wealth, while banks such as Goldman Sachs were bailed out for their losses. Such irresponsible actions of Goldman Sachs as well as other financial institutions caused the worst economic recession since the economic depression of the 1930s, having devastating effects on the finances of families both in the United States and worldwide. Direct consumers of mortgage services were also left in the path of destruction of these behemoth banks and their pursuit of profit. In 2008, more than two million foreclosure processes were begun and more than one million American families lost their homes not as a result of poor personal planning, but as a result of mortgage company deception and hard sales techniques.

In fact, the industry has a history of financiers taking advantage of the public and the consumers in their pursuit of ever greater profit—perhaps indicative of sociopathy. Examples of such abuses include the Savings and Loan scandal in the early 1990s, Milken's sale of junk bonds in the 1980s, and Enron's creative accounting and financing that led to what was then the largest US bankruptcy. Even since

2008 there are strong indicators that the industry is back to its old tricks with new tactics—from producing and bundling subprime auto loans, to taking advantage of students and their needs to finance their education. In 2016, Wells Fargo, a major player in the 2008 crisis, was exposed for pressuring employees to create or "sell" fake accounts to current customers the same way they had been during the subprime bubble. Wells Fargo management created an environment of either "make the sale or lose your job" in pursuit of maximizing profit and shareholder wealth.

The Auto Industry

The auto industry has harmed consumers through both fraudulent practices and the use and production of unsafe products. In 2015 Toyota was caught covering up a problem with its braking system. Eventually it paid out more than $1 billion in damages, but not before drivers and passengers were injured or killed. Takata Corporation, an auto parts manufacturer, currently faces huge fines and potential criminal charges for selling defective air bag inflators to Honda, Chrysler, Nissan, and other manufacturers. Takata sold these inflators for more than a decade after knowing they were defective and could cause major injuries or death (Sokolove Law, 2016). Much like the financial industry, the auto industry is not new to these abusing behaviors: the Ford Pinto and the Chevrolet Corvair were both mass produced and sold to consumers despite industry knowledge that these cars were unsafe for drivers and passengers.

Big Pharma

The pharmaceutical industry is yet another industry that causes a path of destruction for consumers. GlaxoSmithKline sold Avandia to treat diabetes for at least three years after having knowledge the drug led to heart problems (Wolfe, 2010). Avandia led to as many as 100,000 heart attacks, strokes, and deaths that would not have occurred had patients used the older, more common diabetes treatments (Freeman, 2010). Avandia is not the only drug recently on the open market that was known to harm consumers well before being taken off the market—the work of Public Citizen has led to twenty-three such drugs being pulled off the market, but dozens of others are still readily available while making its "worst pills" list.[2]

When medications do work as intended, the industry has a way of making the pills inaccessible to consumers, especially in the United States, where the health insurance and health care industries are in the private sector. For instance, in 2014, Martin Shkreli, CEO of Turing Pharmaceuticals, purchased the rights to Daraprim, a drug produced in the 1950s. Daraprim costs very little to produce, and Turing had no research costs involved in the decades old drug, but Shkreli decided to jack the price up from about $14 per dose to $750 per dose (Ramsey, 2015). Mylan Pharmaceuticals under the leadership of CEO Heather Bresch, daughter of US Senator Joe Manchin, jacked up the price of the EpiPen from $50 to $600. The EpiPen is a lifesaving device relied upon by millions of children and adults with life-threatening allergies such as peanut allergies (Cha, 2016). The drugs in the EpiPen cost approximately $30 to produce (White, 2016). These increases in drug prices are not a necessary part of the industry. They are not needed for R&D as Shkreli and Bresch both have suggested, nor are they due to regulatory burdens. Instead, according to a Harvard study, they are due to monopolistic practices in the industry—in other words companies raise the prices because they can (Flavio, 2016).

Food and Water

If taking medication is not unsafe enough or expensive enough for consumers, eating and drinking present many unnecessary dangers thanks to today's business practices. Consumers have been exposed to mercury in high fructose corn syrup (Wenner, 2009); salmonella in pot pies (Moss, 2009); and salmonella contaminated peanut butter, alfalfa sprouts, and cereal (Services, 2009). Factory farming again plays a role here, feeding consumers massive amounts of antibiotics through the chicken they eat. The overuse of antibiotics to produce edible chicken faster and cheaper has led to the ingestion of antibiotics through the meat, and this has led to antibiotic resistance. These antibiotics are also found in beef and pork and even in the milk consumed across the globe (Philpott, 2016).

These same factory farms have pushed the federal government to ease back US Department of Agriculture (USDA) inspections and even to allow for self-inspection. In the pilot program of this self-inspection of hog farms, the companies were found to have failed to remove fecal matter from the meat before packing it for consumption. Similar programs in Australia and Canada led to massive recalls over E. coli concerns. In New Zealand where consumers must rely on meat producers' self-inspection, government inspectors warn of a significant contamination problem (Edwards, 2013). *Caveat emptor!*

In West Virginia, Freedom Industries allowed 10,000 gallons of MCHM—a toxic chemical mixture used in the coal production process—to leak into the Elk River, a tributary flowing into the water supply of more than 300,000 people in southern West Virginia (Kroh, 2014). This spill led to 400 people visiting the emergency rooms with burns from the chemicals and left more than 300,000 people without access to potable water or even water that was safe for bathing (Reuters, 2014). The CEO of Freedom Industries was eventually found to be criminally negligent and was fined $20,000 and sentenced to one month in jail (in other words, about 7 cents per citizen impacted and about 9 seconds of jail time per individual actually involved in the perpetration). Flint, Michigan is another example of corporate greed contaminating the water supply. While corporate taxes were slashed by Governor Snyder in 2011, the state looked to cut costs by finding a cheaper water supply for the city of Flint. This led to the transition of Flint's water to the Flint River. Further, costs were saved by avoiding the $100 per day chemical needed to assure the new water supply would be safe for the people of Flint. These cost-cutting measures in the name of corporate tax relief led to every citizen of Flint being poisoned with lead. For the children of Flint, this assured learning and developmental disabilities (Kelley, 2016).

Water issues and corporate greed go hand in hand across the globe. In addition to the actions by Freedom Industries and the Resnicks and the corporate led political decisions, Coca-Cola and Nestlé are two more examples of corporations with a history of pilfering water supplies for profit across the globe. The CEO of Nestlé has made it clear that he sees this as acceptable because he does not believe water is a human right (McGraw, 2013). Nestlé has purchased the rights to many local water supplies, often leaving citizens with questionable access to their water in their own communities (Nestlé SA, 2005; Michigan's Water Wars, 2016). In another example, Coca-Cola has a history of depleting water supplies in parts of India that are often most desperate for clean water. In both 2004 and 2014, Coca-Cola was fined by the Indian government for its excessive depletion (Hansia, 2014).

Even when we are just looking at what are considered "normal" business practices, the destruction to water is a common theme. According to Annie Leonard, it takes 300 to 4400 tons of water to produce 1 ton of paper, 256 gallons of water to produce one T-shirt, and 36 gallons of water to produce your morning cup of coffee, all while one-third of the world lives in countries experiencing water shortages or insecurity (Leonard, 2010).

It has become a common corporate practice for businesses to harm the very consumers they claim to serve. Businesses could make their products less harmful, they could assure drugs are safer before they are put into the marketplace, they could use more sustainable water practices, and they could eliminate toxic chemicals from their products and prevent toxic chemicals from seeping into water supplies. However, the current system sends the message that corporate executives and leaders are not only not obligated to take such measures, but such measures might lead to less than the maximization of shareholder wealth or profit, so they should avoid these types of sustainable decisions.

Destruction of Worker Health and Safety

The global employment system is destructive not only economically but also emotionally, psychologically, and physically to workers. According to Hornstein (1996) more than 90% of American workers will suffer from abusive supervision at work. Millions of American workers are unnecessarily injured on the job each year, and approximately 65,000 American workers die as a result of work-related illnesses and injuries (Spieler, 2003). Often overlooked in the Deepwater Horizon gulf oil spill disaster is the fact that 12 workers died in this explosion or the fact that, in 2005, another disaster at a BP oil refinery cost 15 workers their lives and injured 180 other workers.

INFORMATION BOX 2.3 WORKER SAFETY: WHY DOESN'T THE GOVERNMENT DO A BETTER JOB PROTECTING US?

"The Occupational Safety and Health Administration was born with a heavy load to bear—the obligation of ensuring that every worker in America has a safe and healthful workplace for his or her entire working life."

(McGarity, Steinzor, Shapiro, & Shudtz, 2010)

In the 1970s, the Occupational Safety and Health Administration (OSHA) was established during the Nixon administration. OSHA ushered in regulations such as protecting workers' hearing in noisy environments, protecting workers from falls, and other on-the-job hazards.

While government organizations such as OSHA have led to improved worker safety, by dramatically reducing deaths on the job by more than 50%, it and other organizations (such as the Mine Safety and Health Administration) do not currently have the resources to monitor sites to the extent that they *should be* and do not have sufficient fine-levying and other types of punitive powers (Environmental Law Institute, 2016). The problems and safety issues are even worse in other countries, as indicated by the annual estimates of miner deaths in India and China numbering in the thousands. Of course, there are many other safety issues involved in the energy sector such as petroleum distillation and the effects of air pollution (regulated in the United States by the EPA)—worldwide estimates of deaths due to air pollution number in the millions.

Sources:
Is OSHA a Failed Agency—Or an Unheralded Success? (2016). The Environmental Forum, Environmental Law Institute, Washington, D.C. www.eli.org/sites/default/files/forum/eli_forum_article-2016-08-the_debate_2016_sept.pdf
McGarity, T., Steinzor, R., & Shapiro, S. (2010). *Workers at Risk: Regulatory Dysfunction at OSHA.* www.progressivereform.org/articles/osha_1003.pdf
www.resourcesandenergy.nsw.gov.au/__data/assets/pdf_file/0009/182484/International-Mining-Fatality-Database-project-report.pdf
https://en.wikipedia.org/wiki/Energy_accidents

At the Upper Big Branch mine in West Virginia, twenty-nine workers lost their lives due to the mine owner's negligence. The United States MSHA had ordered evacuation of the mine on sixty-four occasions in a one year time frame before the disaster, but was unable to take steps to shut the mine down due to a lack of enforcement regulations (Mufson, Kindy, & O'Keefe, 2010). In fact, the mine had stepped up production due to a high demand for the gassy coal it produced (Ahrens, 2010). The CEO, Don Blankenship, was eventually found guilty of conspiracy to violate mine safety regulations. His actions cost twenty-nine men their lives; he was fined $250,000 (1.4% of his $17.8 million 2009 salary) and sentenced to one year in prison—12.5 days for each man his pursuit of profit killed (Blinder, 2016). The United States is not alone in these disasters—in 2007, 100 miners were trapped and killed in a disaster in Ukraine; in Chile an average of 34 miners die in accidents each year; and 3000 miners die in China each year—all of these deaths are preventable and are in the pursuit of greater profit (Lang, 2010).

For immigrant workers in the United States the reality of the workplace is even worse. For instance, in Compa's comprehensive report on the meat packing industry, an industry heavily staffed by immigrant workers, the workers suffer cumulative and catastrophic debilitating injuries. Nearly every worker Compa interviewed during his two-year study "bore physical signs of a serious injury suffered from working in a meat or poultry plant (Compa, 2004, p. 24). In 2001, the reported injury rate was 20%, or twenty out of every one hundred workers suffering an OSHA reportable injury (that employers actually reported) (Compa, 2004, p. 30). Other injuries, both physical and to the other rights of these workers, go unreported. The workers are denied their rights, and their employers use the fear of deportation of the workers or their family to prevent them from complaining or asserting their rights. Employers in the United States have even been caught holding immigrant workers as indentured servants after luring them to the United States with the promise of professional work (*Chellen v. John Pickle Co.*, 2004).

US and European MNCs also spread the destruction to third world countries via manufacturing facilities such as the Foxconn facility in Shenzhen, China where eighteen workers attempted to leap to their deaths from the roof of the building, leading to fourteen deaths (Bilton, 2014). The workers in the facilities are reported to suffer from extremely harsh working conditions that result in uncontrollable ticks and twitching. The workers are exposed to hard labor with long hours, and are exposed to harsh chemicals, including the use of a known neurotoxin used to clean iPhone screens as a last step of production. The accumulation of aluminum dust has even led to explosions in the facility. However, this is not the only example of large MNCs exploiting workers overseas. In April 2013, fast fashion and the push for ever cheaper stuff led to the largest industrial disaster in the world, as more than 1100 factory workers were crushed to death as their building crumbled around them (Bangladesh Factory Death Toll Soars Past 1,100, 2013). This incident took place in the Rana Plaza of Bangladesh. Despite concerns from workers about the building where they were producing cheap clothes for Walmart, the Gap, F&M, and other MNCs from the industrialized North, they were ordered back into work or to give up their jobs. Shortly after returning to work, the workers' worst fears were indeed realized and the building crumbled to the ground.

The workers suffering this harm are often the most vulnerable. According to the International Labor Organization (ILO), as of 2012 more than 160 million children are engaged in child labor and more than 80 million of these children work in hazardous conditions (Making Progress Against Child Labour—Global Estimates and

Trends, 2000–2012, 2013). According to ILO estimates, 115 million children ages 5–17 work in hazardous conditions across the globe and 22,000 children die at work each year (Hazardous Child Labour, 2017). Child labor supports US and European MNCs in the chocolate industry, textile industry, fashion industry, and technology industries as well as many others. According to a 2000 Department of Labor report, even in the United States, around eighty children die at work each year.

While Namie and Namie (2009) suggest that work should not hurt, the harsh reality is that for American workers and workers abroad, work does hurt—physically, psychologically, and emotionally. This current system of advanced capitalism is, simply stated, destructive to all but a few that would benefit from the exploitation of the planet and the majority of people around the globe. However, this current system is not the only alternative—there are other options and paths that we can and must take, from the micro-level options presented by employers such as the SAS Institute, Costco, and Patagonia, to the macro-level solutions to poverty and inequality that have been instituted in many countries that are poorer than the United States (Stiglitz, 2012). This destruction of the global workers is no less of a business decision than the decisions during the American industrialization period to use child labor or the decision by the plantation owners of early US history to engage in slave labor. Likewise, these current practices are no less destructive than the earlier practices that we readily recognize as blights on our history.

Destruction of Education

The advanced system of capitalism has also led to the destruction of education in the United States. At the higher education level, both Marens (2008) and Lieberwitz (2002) point to a takeover of the university system (and especially business schools) by corporations. Lieberwitz (2002) explains that as universities became more and more dependent on corporate financing (generally due to a lack of state support), corporate leaders were able to exert more and more influence and to limit the academic freedom faculty once enjoyed in teaching and research. Marens (2008) points to a 1979 *Harvard Business Review* article in which Mallot, a CEO of a defense contracting company, demanded that business schools teach more Friedman along with Galbraith if they wanted financial support. Of course, as Marens points out, this demand was to teach a centrist neoliberal economist—Galbraith—along with a free market, extreme right-leaning economist—Friedman. This article as well as the corporatization of the university described by Lieberwitz severely limited the discourse in business schools and universities (it limited the ability of researchers to address problems for social benefit if such benefits would potentially harm business interests). This corporatization continues to push to end the discourse and discussion that has long been the heart of higher education.

However, DAC has not only impacted colleges and universities. K–12 education in the United States has also faced its own form of corporatization. For more than thirty years, American K–12 education has been systematically compromised by the mania of high-stakes testing. Many trace the origins of such business-model "accountability" testing to a 1983 education task force in Texas (Blakeslee, 2013). For this committee, comprising mainly business professionals and led by billionaire Ross Perot, the answer to American educational woes was to hold schools and teachers more accountable. To reform schools, businesses held that school performance should be measured by student testing so that schools and communities would be forced to compete with one another in a marketplace in which parents could be informed by "objective" measures. Thirty years later, the business model and its standardized testing help-mate have consumed public K–12 education. Many teachers spend 30% or more of their class time preparing students for testing; test-prep comes at the expense of content, skills, and other critical pedagogical goals (Long, 2014). How has it worked? Terribly for students, parents (Brown, 2015), teachers, and communities (Amrein & Berliner, 2002; Blazer, 2011). Wonderfully for the testing industry (Ujifusa, 2012; Cavanagh, 2015), for profit corporate consultants (Friedman, 2013), resegregation (Renzulli & Evans, 2005), and private K–12 schools that enroll the privileged children of parents seeking to escape public education (GreatSchools Staff, 2017) and justifiably shield their kids from questionably valid standardized tests (Brown, 2016).

In 2001, in his appropriately sub-titled article, "Only Some Children Matter," James Gross lamented the fact that in the United States and really across the globe we fail to view education as a human right (Gross, 2001). As a result, there are stark differences between the educational opportunities between affluent and impoverished children. Further, this view of education allows us to accept the use of child labor to produce our stuff, as we do not see this as violating the human rights of these children.

According to Barry, the poorer children in the industrialized world face a host of disadvantages to their education, many before they even enter school. Because their parents are less likely to have been able to afford pre-natal health care, the disadvantages for these children often start before they are born. They are then born to parents who have more stress, must work longer hours to survive, and are less able to supply educational learning toys, tutors, or the nannies that the most well-off children receive. Then these children, who are lagging behind by the time they enter school, enter schools that have much lower funding levels and fewer resources than those of their wealthier peers (Barry, 2008). Rather than address these inequities due to socio-economic status, education reformers in the United States looked to take advantage of the situation to convince taxpayers to funnel public dollars into privately run charter schools. Despite the claims by these private actors, these charter schools have failed to produce any better results than the traditional public schools. In fact, according to a 2013 Stanford study, less than one in three charter schools outperforms public schools (Noguera, 2014) even while refusing to admit many of the more challenging students (Ravitch, 2014). However, these private charter schools have done a great job of funneling taxpayer money into the hands of these for-profit corporations and their executives. In 2013, the Philadelphia school district budgeted $729 million for charter networks (Noguera, 2014), and D.C. spends more than $600 million per year to fund charters (Brown & Chandler, 2015). Executives at these charter schools are often pulling in salaries of $500,000 or more, including the CEO of one charter program, Community Academy, pulling in a salary of $1.3 million (Brown & Chandler, 2015). In addition to treating children as a source of revenue, private organizations also pull money out of school districts through tax subsidies and Local Economic Revitalization Tax Assistance (LERTA) programs.

Conclusion

In this chapter, we have examined multiple industries and how the business practices of businesses within such industries that follow the DAC model cause severe harmful effects on the environment and the people across the globe. At the macro level of analysis, we see severe negative outcomes for communities, workers, consumers, society at large, and the environment. All of these outcomes have connections to our current system of commerce. These outcomes can also be linked to specific business practices at the micro or organizational level. We will explore these connections further in Chapter 3.

Discussion Questions

1. Consider the various industries in which we have described destructive business practices. How could these industries operate in a different manner to avoid these destructive practices?
2. Consider all of the products you purchased six months, twelve months, and up to twenty-four months ago. How many of these do you still use? Why? Why not? How many of the products are no longer "in style" and thus are not used? How many are broken or have been discarded because they became difficult to use?
3. Consider the tactics and strategies you have learned throughout your business courses—accounting, finance, economics, management, marketing, and so on. How many of these practices could lead to the types of destruction described in this chapter?
4. How are the specific business practices and outcomes discussed in this chapter linked to the macro-level outcomes from Chapter 1? Does this mean that these business practices should be a focus of public policy? Why or why not?
5. Review several major newspapers or periodicals from the past week. Can you find other examples of destructive business practices? What are the negative outcomes, and what specific practices led to these outcomes? How could the destruction be avoided?

Notes

1 See https://scripps.ucsd.edu/programs/keelingcurve/.
2 See Public Citizen Drug Projects at www.citizen.org/Page.aspx?pid=4374.

References

Ahrens, F. (2010, April 10). Mine's 'gassy' coal was in high demand. *Washington Post*, p. A12.

Ames, R. T., & Rosemont, H. (1998). *The Analects of Confucius: A Philosophical Translation*. New York: Ballantine Books.

Amrein, A. L., & Berliner, D. C. (2002). *An Analysis of Some Unintended and Negative Consequences of High Stakes Testing*. Tempe, AZ: Education Policy Studies Laboratory.

Andrews, D., & Walker, B. (2016, September 20). *'Erin Brockovich' Carcinogen in Tap Water of More Than 200 Million Americans*. Retrieved January 15, 2017, from www.ewg.org: www.ewg.org/research/chromium-six-found-in-us-tap-water

Arsenic in Your Juice. (2012, January). Retrieved January 16, 2017, from Consumer Reports: www.consumerreports.org/cro/magazine/2012/01/arsenic-in-your-juice/index.htm

Bangladesh Factory Death Toll Soars Past 1,100. (2013, May 11). Retrieved from CBC News: www.cbc.ca/news/world/bangladesh-factory-death-toll-soars-past-1-100-1.1370852

Barry, B. (2008). *Why Social Justice Matters*. Cambridge, UK: Polity Press.

Bilton, R. (2014, December 18). *Apple 'Failing to Protect Chinese Factory Workers'*. Retrieved from BBC News: www.bbc.com/news/business-30532463

Blakeslee, N. (2013, May). *Crash Test*. Retrieved from Texas Monthly: www.texasmonthly.com/politics/crash-test/

Blazer, C. (2011). *Unintended Consequences of High Stakes Testing*. Miami, FL: Miami-Dade Public Schools Information Capsule Research Services.

Blinder, A. (2016, April 6). *The Blankenship Sentencing: A Judge Finds an Abuse of Trust*. Retrieved from The New York Times: www.nytimes.com/2016/04/07/us/the-blankenship-sentencing-a-judge-finds-an-abuse-of-trust.html?_r=0

Brown, E. (2015, March 7). *Some Parents Across the Country Are Revolting against Standardized Testing*. Retrieved from The Washington Post: www.washingtonpost.com/local/education/some-parents-across-the-country-are-revolting-against-standardized-testing/2015/03/05/e2abd062-c1e1-11e4-9ec2-b418f57a4a99_story.html

Brown, E. (2016, April 5). *Alaska Cancels All K–12 Standardized Tests for the Year, Citing Technical Problems*. Retrieved from The Washington Post: www.washingtonpost.com/news/education/wp/2016/04/05/alaska-cancels-all-k-12-standardized-tests-for-the-year-citing-technical-problems/

Brown, E., & Chandler, M. A. (2015, February 23). *D.C. Charter School Executive Salaries Vary Widely, Post Analysis Shows*. Retrieved from The Washington Post: www.washingtonpost.com/local/education/dc-charter-school-executive-salaries-vary-widely-post-analysis-shows/2015/02/23/5191b3fc-b38c-11e4-886b-c22184f27c35_story.html

Cavanagh, S. (2015, August 10). *Assessing the State of the K-12 Testing Market, as Dynamics Shift*. Retrieved from Ed Week Market Brief: https://marketbrief.edweek.org/marketplace-k-12/assessing_the_state_of_the_k_12_testing_market_as_dynamics_shift

Cha, A. E. (2016, August 24). Lawmakers call for probe of Epipen price hike. *The Washington Post*, p. A13.

Chellen, Babu Thanu et al., Plaintiffs v. John Pickle Co., Inc. and John Pickle, Jr., 344 F. Supp. 2d 1278 (N.D. Okla 2004).

Compa, L. (2004). *Blood, Sweat, and Fear*. New York: Human Rights Watch.

Conca, J. (2016, September 7). *Thanks to Fracking, Earthquake Hazards in Parts of Oklahoma Now Comparable to California*. Retrieved January 16, 2017, from Forbes.com: www.forbes.com/sites/jamesconca/2016/09/07/the-connection-between-earthquakes-and-fracking/#32b24c307f65

Deepwater Horizon Oil Spill. (2017, January 16). Retrieved from NOAA: http://response.resto ration.noaa.gov/oil-and-chemical-spills/significant-incidents/deepwater-horizon-oil-spill

Ecological Impacts of Mountaintop Removal. (2017, January 16). Retrieved from Appalachian Voices: http://appvoices.org/end-mountaintop-removal/ecology/

Edwards, D. (2013, September 9). *USDA Privatizing Meat Inspections with Program That Allowed 'Chunks' of Feces.* Retrieved from Rawstory.com: http://rawstory.com/rs/2013/09/09/usda-privatizing-meat-inspections-with-program-that-allowed-chunks-of-feces/

Elliott, D. (2015, April 20). *5 Years after BP Oil Spill, Effects Linger and Recovery Is Slow.* Retrieved January 16, 2017, from NPR: www.npr.org/2015/04/20/400374744/5-years-after-bp-oil-spill-effects-linger-and-recovery-is-slow

Fast Fashion Is the Second Dirtiest Industry in the World, Next to Big Oil. (2015, August 17). Retrieved January 16, 2017, from EcoWatch: www.ecowatch.com/fast-fashion-is-the-second-dirtiest-industry-in-the-world-next-to-big—1882083445.html

Flavio, A. (2016, September 13). *Harvard Study: Spike in US Drug Prices Stem from Gov. Granted Monopoly Rights.* Retrieved from Mint Press News: www.mintpressnews.com/harvard-study-spike-us-drug-prices-stem-gov-granted-monopoly-rights/220328/

Freeman, D. W. (2010, June 29). *Diabetes Drug and Risk: Avandia Linked to Stroke, Heart Trouble, Deaths.* Retrieved January 16, 2017, from CBS News: www.cbsnews.com/news/diabetes-drug-and-risk-avandia-linked-to-stroke-heart-trouble-deaths/

Friedman, S. (2013, April 4). *$90 Million Tab for STAAR Testing Includes Pricey Meetings, Travel, Consultants.* Retrieved from NBCDFW Investigates: www.nbcdfw.com/investigations/90-Million-Tab-for-STAAR-Testing-Includes-Pricey-Meetings-Travel-Consultants-201520411.html

Goodland, R., & Anhang, J. (2009). *Livestock and Climate Change: What If the Key Actors in Climate Change Are Cows, Pigs and Chickens.* World Watch. Retrieved from www.world-watch.org/files/pdf/Livestock%20and%20Climate%20Change.pdf

GreatSchools Staff (2017). Private versus public. Retrieved from: https://www.greatschools.org/gk/articles/private-vs-public-schools/

Gross, J. A. (2001). A human rights perspective on U.S. education: Only some children matter. *Catholic University Law Review, 50,* 919–956.

Hansia, F. (2014, July 10). *Coca-Cola Forced to Shut Bottling Plant in India.* Retrieved from CorpWatch: www.corpwatch.org/article.php?id=15963

Harkinson, J. (2016, May/June). Some kind of wonderful. *Mother Jones,* pp. 32–38, 66–67.

Hazardous Child Labour. (2017, January 17). Retrieved from International Labour Organization: www.ilo.org/ipec/facts/WorstFormsofChildLabour/Hazardouschildlabour/lang—en/index.htm

Heyman, D. (2009, June 8). *Expert Says Mountaintop Removal Causes Flooding.* Retrieved January 16, 2017, from Public News Service: www.publicnewsservice.org/index.php?/content/article/9231-1

Hornstein, H. A. (1996). *Brutal Bosses and Their Prey.* New York: Riverhead Books.

International Labor Organization. (2013). *Making Progress Against Child Labour—Global Estimates and Trends 2000–2012.* Geneva: International Program on the Elimination of Child Labour, ILO.

Jane. (2014, April 7). *Top 10 Most Polluting Industries in the World.* Retrieved from What a Green Life: www.whatagreenlife.com/top-10-polluting-industries-world/

Jones, V. (2008). *The Green Collar Economy: How One Solution Can Fix Our Two Biggest Problems.* New York: HarperOne.

Kelley, A. R. (2016, January 16). *Budget Cuts and Negligence Poisoned the Drinking Water in Flint, Mich.* Retrieved January 16, 2017, from Truthdig: www.truthdig.com/eartotheground/item/budget_cuts_and_government_negligence_poisoned_flints_drinking_20160116

Klein, N. (2014). *This Changes Everything: Capitalism vs. the Climate.* New York: Simon & Schuster.

Kleindorfer, P. R., Singhal, K., & Wassenhove, L. N. (2005). Sustainable Operations Management. Production and operations management, 14(4), 482–492.

Kroh, K. (2014, February 9). *The Complete Guide to Everything That's Happened Since the Massive Chemical Spill in West Virginia.* Retrieved January 16, 2017, from Think Progress: https://thinkprogress.org/the-complete-guide-to-everything-thats-happened-since-the-massive-chemical-spill-in-west-virginia-1a7d09185b7d#.1n5m4qgbj

Kucera, J. (2016, March 24). *The German Conundrum: Renewables Break Records, Coal Refuses to Go Away.* Retrieved January 16, 2017, from Energy Post: http://energypost.eu/german-conundrum-renewables-break-records-coal-refuses-go-away/

Lang, O. (2010, October 14). *The Dangers of Mining around the World.* Retrieved from BBC News: www.bbc.com/news/world-latin-america-11533349

Leonard, A. (2010). *The Story of Stuff: How Our Obsession with Stuff Is Trashing the Planet, Our Communities, and Our Health—and a Vision for Change.* New York: Free Press.

Lieberwitz, R. (2002). The corporatization of the university: Distance learning at the cost of academic freedom? *The Boston University Public Interest Law Journal, 12*(1), 73–135.

List of Oil Spills. (2017, January 16). Retrieved from Wikipedia: https://en.wikipedia.org/wiki/List_of_oil_spills

Long, C. (2014, June 17). *The High-Stakes Testing Culture: How We Got Here, How We Get Out.* Retrieved from NEA Today: http://neatoday.org/2014/06/17/the-high-stakes-testing-culture-how-we-got-here-how-we-get-out/

Marens, R. (2008). Recovering the past: Reviving the legacy of the early scholars of corporate social responsibility. *Journal of Management History, 14*(1), 55–72.

McCathie, A. (2015, October 29). *Germany Pays the Price for Switching Off Nuclear Power.* Retrieved January 16, 2017, from ABC.net.au: http://mobile.abc.net.au/news/2015-10-29/germany-pays-the-price-for-switching-off-nuclear-power/6895192

McGarity, Thomas., Steinsor, Rena., Shapiro, Sydney, & Shudtz, M. (2010). *Workers at Risk: Regulatory Dysfunction at OSHA.* Washington, DC: Center for Progressive Reform.

McGraw, G. (2013, April 25). *Nestlé Chairman Peter Brabeck Says We Don't Have a Right to Water, Believes We Do Have a Right to Water and Everyone's Confused.* Retrieved January 17, 2017, from Huffington Post: www.huffingtonpost.com/george-mcgraw/nestle-chairman-peter-brabeck-water_b_3150150.html

Michigan's Water Wars: Nestlé Pumps Millions of Gallons for Free While Flint Pays for Poisoned Water. (2016, February 17). Retrieved January 17, 2017, from Democracy Now: www.democracynow.org/2016/2/17/michigans_water_wars_nestle_pumps_millions

Moss, M. (2009, May 15). Food companies are placing the onus on safety on consumers. Retrieved June 5, 2017, from New York Times: http://www.nytimes.com/2009/05/15/business/15ingredients.html

Mufson, S., Kindy, K., & O'Keefe, E. (2010, April 9). Mine avoided harsh penalties despite violations. *Washington Post*, p. A01.

Namie, G., & Namie, R. (2009). *The Bully at Work: What You Can Do to Stop the Hurt and Reclaim Your Dignity on the Job.* Naperville, IL: Sourcebooks, Inc.

Nestlé SA: Corporate Crimes. (2005, October 6). Retrieved January 17, 2017, from Corporate Watch: https://corporatewatch.org/company-profiles/nestl%C3%A9-sa-corporate-crimes

New Pollution Report Measures Global Health Impact across 49 Countries. (2012, October 23). Retrieved January 16, 2017, from Blacksmith Institute: www.blacksmithinstitute.org/press-release-2012-world-s-worst-pollution-problems-report.html

Noguera, P. (2014, October 13). Charter schools as black boxes. *The Nation, 299*(15), pp. 27–28.

Obama Granted over 1,500 Underwater Fracking Permits in Gulf of Mexico after Deepwater Horizon. (2016, June 29). Retrieved January 16, 2017, from Mint Press News: www.

mintpressnews.com/obama-granted-1500-underwater-fracking-permits-gulf-mexico-deepwater-horizon/217944/

Philpott, T. (2016, May–June). Playing chicken. *Mother Jones*, pp. 40–47, 74.

Ramsey, L. (2015, September 22). *A Pharma CEO Tried to Defend His Decision to Jack Up the Price of a Critical Drug by 5,000%—and It Backfired*. Retrieved January 16, 2017, from Business Insider: www.businessinsider.com/martin-shkreli-defends-daraprim-price-2015-9

Ravitch, D. (2014, October 13). The secrets of "success". *The Nation, 299*(15), p. 29.

Renzulli, L. A., & Evans, L. (2005). School choice, charter schools, and white flight. *Social Problems, 52*(3), 398–418.

Reuters. (2014, January 10). *Chemical Spill in West Virginia Leads to Tap Water Ban for 300,000 People*. Retrieved January 16, 2017, from The Telegraph: www.telegraph.co.uk/news/worldnews/northamerica/usa/10562583/Chemical-spill-in-West-Virginia-leads-to-tap-water-ban-for-300000-people.html

Ridlington, E., Norman, K., & Richardson, R. (2016). *Fracking by the Numbers: The Damage to Our Water, Land and Climate*. Retrieved from Environment America Research and Policy Center, Frontier Group: www.environmentamerica.org/sites/environment/files/reports/Fracking%20by%20the%20Numbers%20vUS.pdf

Rivers of Oil in Arkansas Town: Many 'Didn't Even Know' Exxon Pipeline Ran under Their Homes. (2013, December 25). Retrieved January 16, 2017, from RussiaToday: www.rt.com/usa/exxon-oil-spill-arkansas-168/

Rockström, J., Steffen, W., Noone, K., Persson, Å., Chapin, F. S., Lambin, E. F., . . . & Nykvist, B. (2009, September). A safe operating space for humanity. *Nature, 461*(24), 472–475.

Services, D. O. (2009, July 28). *Center for Disease Control and Prevention*. Retrieved from CDC Investigation of Outbreak of Infections Caused by Salmonella Agona: www.cdc.gov/salmonella/agona

Sokolove Law. (2016, September 30). *Takata Racks up $400M in Losses While Prosecutors Consider Criminal Charges for Air Bag Explosions*. Retrieved from Sokolove Law: www.sokolovelawfirm.com/blog/takata-criminal-charges-air-bag-explosions/

Spieler, E. A. (2003). Risks and rights: The case for occupational safety and health as a core worker right. In J. A. Gross (Ed.), *Workers' Rights as Human Rights* (pp. 78–117). Ithaca, NY: Cornell University Press.

Stiglitz, J. E. (2012). *The Price of Inequality: How Today's Divided Society Endangers Our Future*. New York: WW Norton & Company.

Ujifusa, A. (2012, November 29). *Standardized Testing Costs States $1.7 Billion a Year, Study Says*. Retrieved from Education Week: www.edweek.org/ew/articles/2012/11/29/13testcosts.h32.html

Visser, S., & Savidge, M. (2016, July 1). *West Virginia Floods Devastate 1,200 Homes, Many Lives*. Retrieved January 16, 2017, from CNN.com: www.cnn.com/2016/06/28/us/west-virginia-flooding-weather/

Weber, E. U. (2015). Climate change demands behavioral change: What are the challenges? *Social Research, 82*(3), 561–580.

Wenner, M. (2009, September). Children of the corn. *Mother Jones*, pp. 16–17.

White, M. C. (2016, September 7). *It's Jaw-Dropping How Little It Costs to Make an EpiPen*. Retrieved from Money: http://time.com/money/4481786/how-much-epipen-costs-to-make/

Wolfe, S. (2010, July 3). *FDA: Cautious on Food Safety—Reckless on Prescription Drug Safety*. Retrieved January 16, 2017, from Huff Post Social News: www.huffingtonpost.com/sidney-m-wolfe/fda-cautious-on-foid-safe_b_499344.html

Zucchino, D. (2015, May 4). *Coal Ash Contamination Upsets Residents Near North Carolina Plants*. Retrieved January 16, 2017, from LA Times: www.latimes.com/nation/la-na-coal-ash-pollution-20150504-story.html

CASE 2 BIG PHARMA AND THE EXPLOITATION OF LIFE

Between 2015 and 2016 there were numerous news stories and even Congressional hearings concerning business practices in the pharmaceutical industry in the United States. According to an article from the Daily Beast reporter Samantha Allen (Allen, 2015), Martin Shkreli was "Big Pharma's Biggest A**hole" in 2015. Shkreli, a hedge fund manager, then just 32, had recently purchased the rights to the little known drug Daraprim for his company, Turing Pharmaceuticals. Daraprim is a sixty-three-year-old drug, and it is also a necessary lifesaving drug for some patients (Johnson, 2016). Overnight, Turing increased the price of Daraprim from $13.50 per pill to $750 per pill.

Daraprim treats toxoplasmosis, a common condition in the United States population that can be deadly for those with weakened immune systems such as AIDS patients and cancer patients (Allen, 2015). These patients are in essence a captive consumer for Turing and Shkreli. The drug is the only treatment available, and Shkreli raised the price more than 5000% overnight. Shkreli is on record admitting that the vast majority of the revenue from the drug would be profit and that he expected to make a billion dollars off Daraprim (Johnson, 2016). In December 2016, a group of high school students in Australia came up with a process to produce the same drug for $2 per pill. At press time for this book, the price of Daraprim is still $750 per pill (Johnson, 2016).

Another lifesaving drug and device, the EpiPen, produced by Mylan Pharmaceuticals, received attention in 2016. In the first half of 2016 Mylan increased the price of a two pack of EpiPens to $600, an increase of 600% since 2007, and an increase of $100 since the beginning of the year (Cha, 2016). The EpiPen delivers a dose of epinephrine to individuals who are in anaphylactic shock due to allergic reactions. The device is a staple for parents whose children suffer from peanut allergies or are allergic to bee stings.

The CEO of Mylan, and daughter of Senator Joe Manchin, Heather Bresch, defended Mylan's price increase and argued that its price increase was not nearly as bad as the actions by Shkreli, while at the same time admitting the price increase was driven by the company's profit motive (Thomas, 2016). The medication in the EpiPen costs approximately $1, and a competing device can be found for under $150 (Cha, 2016). However, doctors are often hesitant to recommend the cheaper device because nurses and teachers are commonly trained on the use of the EpiPen (Cha, 2016). Mylan conducted no R&D into the EpiPen, as the product was fully developed when Mylan purchased it in 2007 (Spencer, 2016). Bresch's total compensation as CEO of Mylan in 2015 was nearly $19 million (Thomas, 2016). During her time as the President of the National Association of State Boards of Education,

Bresch's mother, Gayle Manchin, pushed for the EpiPen to be available in all schools (O'Donnell, 2016). According to Representative Mulvaney of South Carolina, Bresch has also lobbied Congress to require schools to purchase the EpiPen (Sabatini, 2016).

Shkreli's actions and similar actions by other pharmaceutical companies led to a Congressional hearing in early 2016 (Johnson, 2016). During the hearing Shkreli refused to answer questions about why he increased the price of Daraprim 5000%, instead pleading the Fifth Amendment (Brait, 2016). Bresch's actions also received Congressional attention and scrutiny. Senator Grassley of Iowa noted that many first responders have considered making their own epinephrine devices in response to the price increase. Senator Klubachar asked the Federal Trade Commission to investigate Mylan's practice, and Senator Bernie Sanders argued that there was no reason for Mylan to charge $600 for a device that costs them a few dollars to produce. Bresch was also called into a Congressional hearing, where representatives sought an explanation for Bresch's EpiPen price increase and questioned her over her $19 million compensation package and her mother's actions in pushing the EpiPen (Sabatini, 2016).

In late 2016, Representative Elijah Cummings and Senator Sanders called for yet another Congressional investigation, this time into the increase in Insulin medications from $231 to more than $736 per year per patient since 2002. In late 2016, it was also reported that Valeant had acquired the treatment for lead poisoning and immediately increased the price from $950 to more than $7000, only to further increase the price to more than $26,000 over the following months (Keown, 2016). These increases occurred at the same time that the lead poisoning in Flint, Michigan was in the national news.

The price increases have also been noticed by the American public. According to a Harris Poll in 2016, 90% of Americans blame the pharmaceutical industry at least in part for the rising costs of health care. More than eight out of ten of those polled supported some form of price controls over the pharmaceutical industry. Ninety percent of respondents believe that these price increases are an example of the industry exploiting consumers (Solutions, 2016). According to a Harvard study, the steep price increases on pharmaceuticals in the United States has nothing to do with research and development, but instead is a result of monopolistic practices of drug companies and the laws that allow for such practices (Flavio, 2016).

Discussion Questions

1. Is Big Pharma a DAC or SSBS industry in its current state?
2. Are the current profit margins fair? Why? Why not?

3. How can we address the issues with dangerous drugs being put into the marketplace?
4. What steps can be taken to make the pharmaceutical industry more socially sustainable?

References

Allen, S. (2015, September 21). *Martin Shkreli Is Big Pharma's Biggest A**hole.* Retrieved January 18, 2017, from The Daily Beast: www.thedailybeast.com/articles/2015/09/21/martin-shkreli-is-big-pharma-s-biggest-asshole.html

Brait, E. (2016, February 4). *Pleading the Fifth: Five Notorious Times People Refuse to Give Answers.* Retrieved from The Guardian: https://www.theguardian.com/law/2016/feb/04/fifth-amendment-martin-shkreli-michaele-tareq-salahi

Cha, A. E. (2016, August 24). Lawmakers call for probe of Epipen price hike. *The Washington Post*, p. A13.

Flavio, A. (2016, September 13). *Harvard Study: Spike in US Drug Prices Stem from Gov. Granted Monopoly Rights.* Retrieved from Mint Press News: www.mintpress news.com/harvard-study-spike-us-drug-prices-stem-gov-granted-monopoly-rights/220328/

Johnson, C. Y. (2016, February 3). Martin Shkreli boasted of drug price hikes, memos show. *The Washington Post*, p. A17.

Keown, A. (2016, October 12). *Controversy Over Lead Poisoning Drug Pricing.* Retrieved January 18, 2017, from Pharma Live: www.pharmalive.com/anger-behind-the-scenes-when-valeant-jacked-up-price-by-2700-for-lead-poisoning-drug/

Kleindorfer, P. R., Singhal, K., & Van Wassenhove, L. N. (2005). Sustainable operations management. *Production and Operations Management, 14*(4), 482–492.

McGarity, T. O., Steinzor, R. I., Shapiro, S. A., & Shudtz, M. (2010). Workers at risk: regulatory dysfunction at OSHA. Center for Progressive Reform White Paper No. 1003; U of Maryland Legal Studies Research Paper No. 2010-14; Energy Center Research Paper No. 09-10.

O'Donnell, J. (2016, September 21). CEO's mother used post to push EpiPen into schools: Mylan, subject of antitrust inquiry and consumer ire over price hikes, took over allergy market. *USA Today*, p. 1A.

Sabatini, P. (2016, September 22). Mylan CEO Gets Grilling Over Epipen: Lawmakers Sought Explanation of Price Hike. *Pittsburgh Post-Gazette*, p. A-1.

Solutions, P. M. (2016). *Washington: Americans Fed Up with Soaring Drug Prices: Health Day/Harris Poll.* New York: Plus Media Solutions.

Spencer, J. (2016, August 24). Investigation sought of Epipen price jump allergic reaction product cost $100 in 2008, $500–$600 today. *Spokesman Review*, p. A10.

Stiglitz, J. E. (2012). *The Price of Inequality: How Today's Divided Society Endangers Our Future.* W.W. Norton & Company.

Thomas, K. (2016, August 30). Drug maker's chief says she's no villain; Executive defends fourfold increase in price for allergy medication. *International New York Times*, Finance, p. 13.

3

THE ADVENT OF SOCIALLY SUSTAINABLE BUSINESS SYSTEMS

Let us not be afraid to say it: we want change, real change, structural change, from a system that has imposed the mentality of profit at any price, with no concern for social exclusion or the destruction of nature. This system is by now intolerable: farm workers find it intolerable, labourers find it intolerable, communities find it intolerable, people find it intolerable. The earth itself—our sister, Mother Earth—also finds it intolerable.

Pope Francis (Francis, 2015)

But the alliance between working people and public minded intellectuals is also crucial—it is all about standing up to entrenched economic power and the complacency of the affluent. It's an alliance that depends on intellectuals being critics, and not the servants, of economic privilege.

I am here tonight at the Kennedy School of Government to say that if you care about defending our country against the apostles of hate, you need to be part of the fight to rebuild a sustainable, high wage economy built on good jobs—the kind of economy that can only exist when working men and women have a real voice on the job.

Richard Trumka at the Kennedy School of Government,
April 12, 2010 (Trumka, 2010)

Our shared belief is that management of the modern firm (and often other types of organizations too) is guided by a narrow goal—profits—rather than by the interests of society as a whole, and that other goals—justice, community, human development, ecological balance—should be brought to bear on the governance of economic activity.

Critical Management Studies (CMS) Mission Statement (Adler, 2002)

The world runs on individuals pursuing their self-interests. The great achievements of civilization have not come from government bureaus. Einstein didn't construct his theory under order from a bureaucrat. Henry Ford didn't revolutionize the automobile industry that way.

Milton Friedman (Friedman, 2017)

Capitalism is based on self-interest and self-esteem; it holds integrity and trust-worthiness as cardinal virtues and makes them pay off in the marketplace, thus demanding that men survive by means of virtue, not vices. It is this superla-tively moral system that the welfare statists propose to improve upon by means of preventative law, snooping bureaucrats, and the chronic goad of fear.

Alan Greenspan (Greenspan, 1963)

Introduction

What are your thoughts on the opening quotes? What are the different views of the roles and functions of business? How do the quotes indicate differing views about the goals of business? Many academics and business leaders take the quotes from Friedman and Greenspan as representing the current and historical role of business or the traditional view of business. However, the reality is there is nothing historical or traditional about this role of business. This view of the firm as a profit maximizer and tool for shareholders is clearly a Westernized view of the firm, and it is also clearly a man-made adaptation of the firm that has occurred in recent history. In fact, a more historical (and traditional) view of the firm is a skepticism of the cor-poration, with a strong expectation and legal obligation to serve the public interest or to have the very existence of the firm revoked (Mintzberg, Simons, & Basu, Fall 2002). However, through misinterpretation of the legal status of the corporation, and through well-placed and timed articles by the Chicago School academics and practitioners such as Greenspan and Friedman, the modern view of the firm became widely accepted in business circles including business schools, business organiza-tions (the Chamber of Commerce and the National Association of Manufacturers as examples), and business leaders. This view of business is narrow and focuses on a narrow set of goals—profit, GDP, and shareholder wealth. This view of the firm is also responsible for a great deal of the destruction we see in the current system.

Mintzberg, Simons, and Basu (Fall 2002) make a strong case that this view of the firm is built on a series of myths or half-truths. The fabrications presented by Mintzberg, Simons, and Basu are as follows: we are all economic man, corporations exist and have always existed to maximize shareholder wealth, businesses need heroic leaders, effective organizations are lean and mean, and a rising tide of prosperity lifts all boats. Each one of these fabrications supports the narrow profit maximization focus we see causing the destruction discussed in Chapters 1 and 2. For instance, if we believe everyone is economic man, then why should we also not engage as economic man? If we buy into the myth that businesses require heroic leaders, then we can justify CEO pay that is 200, 300, even 400 times that of the average worker. If we believe the fallacy that corporations exist (and have always existed) only to maximize shareholder wealth, then we accept the terrible business practices that increase stock prices while harming workers, consumers, communities, and the environment as normal business practices. When we see workers being laid off or even when we ourselves are caught up in the ever more common mass lay-offs, if we believe that the best way to run any business is lean and mean, then we accept these lay-offs. Finally, if we buy into the myth that a rising tide of prosperity (through the maximization of shareholder wealth) will bring us all up, then of course we will not only support, but will cheer the ever greater wealth accumulation in the hands of the top 1% or even top 0.1% of the country and world.

The quotes from Richard Trumka, Pope Francis, and the CMS Mission Statement suggest that there should be a broader or even different view about the goals of business. Their quotes suggest that current business practices both in the United States and across the globe erroneously focus on narrow goals of profit, GDP, and shareholder wealth. They suggest that this narrow focus can no longer be accepted by the broader community/society. These quotes suggest that there are more important goals to business functioning than these purely economic outcomes. The United Nations (UN) has recognized the broader role of businesses and corporations. In 1983 via the Brundtland Commission and again in 2015 the UN has developed broader goals for businesses, including the goal of operating in a sustainable manner for the planet and its inhabitants. The goals of these works coming from the UN are enumerated in Table 3.1.

How do these goals compare to those of Friedman and Greenspan? How might societies differ depending on the set of goals adopted? Over the years a number of different concepts and theories have emerged addressing the role for the corporation. From the narrow focus on profit to the expansive ideas of broad social responsibilities to a broad group of shareholders, theorists, academics, and business leaders have debated the question of the exact role of business in the global economy.

The Views of the Firm

Over the course of history, there have been many views about business practices and how businesses should engage within the larger realm of society. These views date back to the Ancient Greeks and their view of work and the relationship between citizens and slaves, through the early periods of Christianity and through the Enlightenment. All of these early views have an impact on how business is viewed and how business operates around the globe. In Chapter 1, we discussed the laissez faire views of the Chicago School and the somewhat more regulated (at least morally) view of capitalism of Adam Smith. In this chapter we will review many of the theories and concepts that argue that businesses do indeed have a broader social role and lay out the path to achieve these roles. These theories range from a complete rebuke of the system of capitalism to a call for minor variations to business and managerial practices.

TABLE 3.1 Brundtland Commission and UN Sustainable Development Goals

Brundtland Commission UNWCED 1987 Policy Directions (www.un-documents.net/ our-common-future.pdf)	*UN Transforming Our World: The 2030 Agenda for Sustainable Development— Sustainable Development Goals (https://sustainabledevelopment.un.org/sdgs)*
1. Population and Human Resources: Addressing unsustainable population increases in parts of the world, assuring access to resources for all of the world's population	1. No Poverty
	2. Zero Hunger
	3. Good Health and Well-Being
	4. Quality Education
	5. Gender Equality
2. Food Security: Policies to support small farmers, incentives for food production in the developing world, and global food security	6. Clean Water and Sanitation
	7. Affordable and Clean Energy
	8. Decent Work and Economic Growth
	9. Industry, Innovation, and Infrastructure
3. Species and Ecosystems: Protection of Earth's species, assurance of maintaining diverse species	10. Reduced Inequalities
	11. Sustainable Cities and Communities
	12. Responsible Consumption and Production
4. Energy: Safe and sustainable energy to the developing world to improve living standards	13. Climate Action
	14. Life Below Water
	15. Life on Land
5. Industry: Producing more with less resources, avoiding toxic production practices, and avoiding exportation of toxic manufacturing	16. Peace, Justice, and Strong Institutions
	17. Partnerships for the Goals
6. The Urban Challenge: Assuring resources for the growing percentage of the population living in cities	

The Marxist Critique of the Burgeoning System of Capitalism

Karl Marx and Friedrich Engels's critique of capitalism is perhaps the most complete and most well-known rebuke of the system of capitalism. Marx and Engels lived during the earliest days of the expansion of capitalism and industrialization. From the earliest days of capitalism Marx and Engels saw the problems of growing inequality, exploitation of the worker, dangerous working conditions, and declining wages. Marx and Engels argued that the system of capitalism itself was the cause of this exploitation and alienation of the working class. They argued that this exploitation by the owners of capital would create an imbalance of power leading to big businesses dominating the political process and even exploiting other countries. While Marx and Engels's work *Das Capital* is the perhaps the most complete critique of the expanding capitalism of their time, *The Communist Manifesto*, a much more succinct work, also demonstrates the primary Marxist critiques of the system. In Marx and Engels's *Communist Manifesto*, they claimed that under the system of capitalism, the "power of the modern state is merely a device for administering the common affairs of the bourgeois class (the class of owners)" (Marx & Engels, 1996, p. 3). They argued that the bourgeoisie would exploit the workers, stealing the surplus value of the workers' (proletariat's) labor, and would alienate workers from their work by treating them as appendages of their machines capable of doing only the most mundane task. The Marxist argument is that a system that divides the ownership of capital from those who work the capital will always lead to the owners looking to steal the surplus value of the laborers—that this is not a flaw in the system of capitalism, but instead *is* the system of capitalism. For Marx and Engels, the only hope for the proletariat (the working class) was to "fling into the air the whole superstructure of social strata from the establishment" (Marx & Engels, 1996, p. 11). Marx famously called for the overthrow of the system through a workers' revolution: "Let the ruling class tremble at a communist revolution. Proletarians have nothing to lose in it but their chains. They have a world to win. Proletarians of all countries unite!" (Marx & Engels, 1996, p. 30).

INFORMATION BOX 3.1   EXPLOITATION OF THE VALUE OF LABOR

Moody points out some interesting evidence of the exploitation of the surplus value of labor by the owners of capital. While the ILO reported that the share of the global population engaged in wage labor increased to nearly 50% of the population by 2006, the share of the GDP going to capital of the seventeen richest OECD countries increased from 25% in 1975 to 33% by 2005, with the share in the United States increasing from 18.8% to 26.2% (Moody, 2014).

The proletarian revolution never occurred. Instead, there were some instances of stated communist revolutions—the most well-known being the Leninist Bolshevik Revolution. However, these revolutions did not lead to an empowering system of communism and worker control as envisioned by Marx. Instead, they were much closer to what Wolff (2012) refers to as *state capitalism*. They still had all four of the problems that Marx and Engels pointed to under the system of capitalism—worker exploitation, worker alienation, the dominance of national goals by a ruling elite, and the exploitation of other nation states. However, rather than these problems being in the name of private sector industries, they were to support the state-owned industries and the ruling elites or oligarchy. The results were nothing better than the results we have seen under DAC.

The Great Depression and the Early Scholars of Social Responsibility

Rather than calling for an all-out revolt against the system, other theories have focused on working within the system to reform the system. Shortly after and at least partially in response to the Great Depression, a group of business scholars emerged who argued for broader social roles for businesses. These scholars came from industry and governmental service and brought with them a great deal of practical experience from the pre-Depression era through the New Deal era. These scholars argued that the role of business must include (if not be primarily focused on) the business impact on society.

According to Marens (2008), the main focus of these early scholars was on three issues: the need for independent oversight and regulation of business, the role of employee representation, and the distribution of wealth and income. These scholars saw the need for wealth and income redistribution to those at the bottom of the economic ladder. They found that employee representation and collective bargaining led to higher wages, safer and more secure working conditions, and stronger benefits, all of which they saw as important societal goals. Finally, already being skeptical of any possible success of voluntary social responsibility efforts, they found the clear need for independently developed legislation around the business environment. They did not believe that industrial leaders would ever take measures that might go against their own self-interests and would never widely adopt socially responsible business practices.

These scholars played a large role in the development of the New Deal era. At least in part as a result of these scholars, this era saw the types of macroeconomic outcomes for which these scholars had argued. There was indeed a redistribution of wealth during this time frame (1940s–1970s), with a decrease in the levels of inequality and strong growth across all income quintiles, with the strongest growth in the bottom four quintiles (see Table 3.2). There was an expansion of labor union density, and there were numerous regulations passed concerning the operations of businesses. However, in the 1970s, business interests (perhaps business traditionalists, at least as we would refer to them today) lashed out against these ideas of the early scholars. Marens (2008) points to a specific article by a defense contractor CEO, Robert H. Malott, published in the *Harvard Business Review* in 1978 as leading to a push back against these early scholars. This article suggested that business schools would receive corporate support but only if they would support limited government and put more focus on Milton Friedman and

TABLE 3.2 Income Growth During the New Deal and After

Income Group	1947–1979	1979–2007
Bottom fifth	2.5	0
Second fifth	2.2	0.4
Third fifth	2.4	0.6
Fourth fifth	2.4	0.9
Top fifth	2.2	1.5
Top 5%	1.9	2.0

Source: State of Working America

the Chicago School system of economics (focusing on profit maximization as the only goal of a corporation). This article and the backlash led to the Chicago School view of the firm discussed earlier becoming the primary view not just of business, but also in the field of business ethics.

Carroll's Pyramid of Corporate Social Responsibility

As the early scholars of business and society disappeared from business schools and business journals, a new field emerged of business ethics, and the concept of voluntary social responsibility became a big part of this field. One of the earliest concepts within this field is known as corporate social responsibility (CSR). Archie Carroll has been one of the major researchers and developers in this field. It builds on Stakeholder Theory recognizing owners, customers, employees, communities, competitors, suppliers, social activist groups, and the public at large as stakeholders. In 1991, Carroll developed what he termed the *pyramid of corporate social responsibility*. This pyramid set out four levels of responsibility for corporations—economic, legal, ethical, and philanthropic.

These responsibilities were defined as:

1. Economic Responsibility: to be profitable, to make an acceptable profit while producing needed and desired goods and services. Carroll suggests this is the foundation upon which all others rest. Businesses cannot or would not exist without meeting this primary obligation.
2. Legal Responsibility: to comply with the law and regulations—part of the social contract.
3. Ethical Responsibility: to meet societal expectations and norms as well as higher level ethical principles such as "justice, rights and utilitarianism."
4. Philanthropic Responsibility: "actively engaging in acts or programs to promote human welfare or goodwill." This is not expected; rather, this responsibility is discretionary.

(Carroll, 1991)

A hallmark of CSR, including Carroll's model, is the reliance on corporations and their leaders to voluntarily engage in socially responsible behavior. Rather than looking to abolish capitalism, or even looking to regulate capitalism, Carroll along with many other CSR researchers called for a form of voluntary moral management.

Corporate Codes of Conduct

Corporate codes of conduct are often viewed as a method of corporations implementing CSR. The corporate codes of today are another form of voluntary social responsibility emerging through the development and expansion of corporate codes of conduct. These codes tend to be developed internally, they are largely voluntary, and many of them have no monitoring (Baker, 2007). These codes grew in popularity and prevalence throughout the late 1980s and through the 1990s, and still exist today. The codes present a sort of implied contract between businesses and society, with businesses agreeing to carry out their operations in specific ways. These codes have been internal—Levi, Reebok, and Nike, as three examples—and external—the Sullivan Principles. Baker points out a number of problems with these codes:

1. They are not developed without external pressure and often result from a scandal or violation.
2. They are often not taken seriously by managers and employees.
3. They seldom contain any adequate monitoring or enforcement.
4. When they are enforced against suppliers, it is often the workers of these suppliers who are harmed.
5. The areas of business impacted have been limited.

Jenkins, Pearson, and Seyfang (2002) suggest that internal voluntary corporate codes have largely been ineffective and that the only codes that have had any success are those that have been written and enforced (or at least monitored) by outside non-governmental organizations (NGOs) and labor organizations. Despite these problems with corporate codes of conduct, Compa (2008) suggests that they can indeed play a role in addressing the social issues in business, but they cannot do so alone. Rather, Compa argues that these codes should be one leg of a three-legged stool consisting of strong laws, strongly enforced; strong labor unions; and the corporate codes or voluntary CSR.

Corporate Citizenship

Corporate citizenship (CC) is yet another conception of a means to convince corporations to focus on broader social issues. The idea of corporate citizenship is that the responsibility of a business shifts from being socially responsible to being a "good corporate citizen." In 1998, Carroll (1998) shifted towards using the term *corporate citizenship*. He presented four "faces" of corporate citizenship that matched his prior responsibilities of the corporation—economic, legal, ethical, and philanthropic. Interestingly, in 1998, Carroll's shift also led to a shift in his definition of the economic responsibility from "a fair profit" to "a strong return for investors." It could be that Carroll himself was caught up in a half-truth that corporations exist to maximize shareholder wealth—a myth that Mintzberg, Simons, and Basu (Fall 2002) point out we are all susceptible to believing.

Matten and Crane (2005) suggested that a shift to corporate citizenship made sense, but that such a shift had to have some meaningful difference from the concept of CSR. The corporations could not be treated in the same way as they had been in the CSR literature as just another member of society, or in this case citizen, with the same rights and responsibilities as any other citizen. Instead, Matten and

Crane explained that citizenship is not about a state of being; it is about a relationship. The relationship is based on power. At least in theory, citizenship is about power given to a smaller group (traditionally government) by the large mass of citizens, in exchange for the smaller group assuring and protecting certain rights for the masses. Matten and Crane explain that while governments were traditionally the holders of this power, today in large part due to globalization corporations now hold such power. As a result, they should have the responsibility to assure and protect the civil, social, and political rights of the masses—or the larger groups of stakeholders.

The Catholic Social Tradition (CST)

Pope Francis's quote at the beginning of this chapter was not the first time the Catholic Church or the church's doctrine called for a broader social focus for businesses. Pope John Paul II focused on man's right to dignity at work in *Laborem Exercens*. Both Pope John Paul II and Pope Francis were describing at least in part what is known as the Catholic Social Tradition (CST) in relation to work and business. Naughton (2006) argues that the CST requires that managers view the corporation or business as a community of persons and that it must thus be concerned with the growth and development of those associated with the business. Naughton suggests that one's work is one of the primary institutions in one's life and that the right to dignity is an inherent part of such an institution. Naughton also addresses profit as being necessary for survival, but not the purpose of the corporation. Kennedy (2006) places the focus of the CST on the right to dignity in the workplace. He argues that under the CST:

1.   Every person is possessed of irreducible value.
2.   People are never merely instruments of their work.
3.   People have capacities to reason and choose freely.
4.   People are social by nature.

INFORMATION BOX 3.2   CATHOLIC SOCIAL TEACHING AND SOCIAL JUSTICE

The Catholic Church has a rich tradition dating back hundreds of years of advocating for the environment, workers, and families. This work, regardless of one's personal, private religious beliefs, contains messages that speak of responsibility and a clear call to try to make the world a better place for both those living now as well as those who will come after us. Starting as early as 1891 with the Pope Leo XIII encyclical *Rerum Novarum*, most heads of the church have written on social justice issues, including Pope Francis with his apostolic exhortation *Evangelii Gaudium*. The seven main themes of Catholic social teaching fit very well with this book and include:

1. Sanctity of life and dignity of the person. Every human being has the right not only to live, but live a dignified life.
2. Call to family, community, and participation. We exist as social beings, not mere individuals, and have responsibilities to our family, communities, and society at large.
3. Rights and responsibilities of social justice. Every human being is endowed with human rights; among these are food, water, shelter, medical care, and work. We have both a right to these as well as a clear responsibility to protect the rights of others.
4. Option of the poor and vulnerable. More powerful voices must make policy decisions as well as personal, private decisions that always consider those least powerful voices first.
5. Dignity of work and rights of workers. Workers have an absolute and indelible right to unionize and freely associate.
6. Solidarity. No ethnic or political divisions can diminish our responsibility to protect the rights of others.
7. Care for creation. We have a responsibility to be good stewards of the planet, and to pass it on to future generations in as good a condition as or better than we received it.

In reading this book, you will see numerous examples in which every one of these major themes is broken by the status quo of destructive capitalism. Regardless of our individual beliefs, we believe that we all have an obligation to create a more just world, and this book is part of our (the authors') efforts to make good on this responsibility.

Sources:
https://en.wikipedia.org/wiki/Catholic_social_teaching
www.loyolapress.com/our-catholic-faith/scripture-and-tradition/
catholic-social-teaching
www.osjspm.org/catholic-social-teaching/

All of these premises of human being should be respected and afforded in the workplace, and work should allow for the meeting of social needs. Much like the ideas of CSR, corporate codes, and corporate citizenship, the Catholic Social Tradition is a call to managers and business leaders to make decisions from a moral viewpoint.

Business Ethics

Marens points to business ethics as the field of study that took over for the early scholars of business and society. He critiques this group as being focused on acceptable behaviors within the system—a form of descriptive ethics. The very name of this field can cause such objections—a way of qualifying what ethics means. As Shaw and Barry (2007, p. 4) explain, *business ethics* is the study of what constitutes right and wrong, good and bad—human conduct in a business context. Ferrell, Thorne, and Ferrell (2016, p. 155) go a bit further, explaining that business ethics "comprises the principles and standards that guide the behavior of individuals and groups in the world of business." Both of these definitions suggest that what is ethical is determined from within the field of business. If the practices discussed in Chapter 1 are the accepted norms of the business world, then the question becomes, Are these practices, unethical in any other environment, ethical in the business environment context? The field of business ethics is perhaps the clearest acceptance of the current system of capitalism of any of these theories. Not only does this field accept the current system, but it suggests that only the insider within the system, within the businesses, should play a role in defining the moral responsibilities of the organizations and their leaders.

Critical Management Studies

Critical Management Studies (CMS) is yet another field that has recognized the problem with the narrow, profit-driven view of the firm. CMS is a field of study that has emerged out of business researchers, practitioners, and academics. The original mission statement of CMS was quoted at the beginning of this chapter. Unlike the field of business ethics, the field of CMS suggests that there are indeed broader social goals that businesses must meet.

According to Alvesson and Deetz (2000), CMS research comprises three components: insight, critique, and transformative redefinition. The idea is to understand what social goals are not being met, to understand the role that business practices and actions play in this failure, and then to come up with the solutions to these failures. Adler (2002), a CMS researcher, suggests a bit more practical detail in suggesting that CMS as a whole and CMS researchers in particular should identify for whom and of what they are being critical. The CMS literature often does look at the broader system within which business practices occur and is thus a building block for the SSBS discussed in Chapter 4. The transformative redefinition called for under CMS can lead down the path of broad systemic changes. In fact, Adler (2002) suggests a common purpose of CMS is exploring deep-rooted problems in our current economic system and capitalism in general.

Sustainability

Since the 1980s, the impacts of business activities on the environment have become more profound and recognized as resulting in climatic change, a term proposed by the World Meteorological Organization (WMO) in 1996. As a result, the concepts of the social responsibility of businesses have been extended to include responsibilities to the environment. This has led to the development of the field of sustainability, which has also been referred to as sustainable business, sustainable development, and environmental sustainability. While business scholars and practitioners have studied and implemented sustainability topics and practices, a significant amount of sustainability research and practices operates under the same framework that places the ultimate attention on profitability at the micro level and GDP growth or efficiency at the macro level (Wolff, 2012), and thus simply cannot achieve a true measure of sustainability. At their worst, these research methods and practices simply become additional tools to reap ever greater profits and to place focus on social and environmental aspects of sustainability only where they might benefit profitability. At their best, these theories and practices are incomplete because they include the need to first serve the needs of the economy, businesses, and commerce, rather than seeing commerce as a tool that serves society.

The UN's Brundtland Commission in 1987 explored sustainable practices for development. This commission developed what is still today the most widely adopted definition of sustainability (Brundtland Commission, 1987): "development that meets the needs of the present without compromising the ability of future generations to meet their needs." While this commission and the corresponding definition presented hope that business interests would put more focus on environmental and social outcomes in both the long and short term, the definition was also clearly quite vague. This led to the concept of the triple bottom line (three Ps) of sustainability—People, Planet, and Profit—and the suggestion that businesses now would give all three goals equal footing (see Figure 3.1).

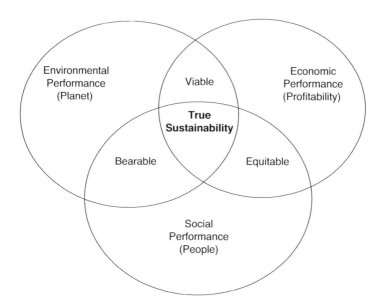

FIGURE 3.1 The Triple Bottom Line of Sustainability

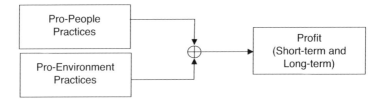

FIGURE 3.2 Sustainability in the Literature and Practice

Many business researchers filled the gaps in this vague definition by focusing on sustainability as a way to create firm value or profit. Even where business researchers suggest that businesses must take a triple bottom line approach, they often end up focusing on customer preference (i.e., sustainable operations will let you sell more stuff) (Elkington, 1994); justify sustainability by reference to the business case (i.e., potential to increase profit) (Aguilera, Rupp, Williams, & Ganapathi, 2007); create a competitive advantage (Hart & Millstein, 2003; Porter & Kramer, 2006); attract new customers (Bansal & Clelland, 2004); or cut costs (Christmann, 2000; Hart & Ahuja, 1996). In some cases, the focus has shifted from the short term to the long term—focusing on long-term profitability and how social and environmental goals may help organizations achieve long-term financial success (e.g., see Hart & Millstein, 2003). Through different media (e.g., articles, teaching materials, etc.), many research ideas from business schools have an impact on current as well as future business leaders. Therefore, it is apparent that the idea of sustainability being important if it achieves competitive advantage, profit, or shareholder wealth and to be ignored if it does not is a part of current business practices (Figure 3.2).

As a result, while a few organizations such as Interface Carpet, the SAS Institute, and others have practiced true sustainability, the global economy as a whole is still mired in the same (if not greater) destructive practices.

In some cases, the Planet aspect has become a new form of environmentalism. It is fairly easy to understand that without a planet there can be no profit, and protecting the planet may indeed be about protecting the source of this profit (Carter & Rogers, 2008). However, we can no longer afford to allow sustainability to be co-opted into supporting the destructive business practices that are harming the people and the planet. Instead, we must take back sustainability in terminology, research, and practice in such a way as to achieve the true goals as set out by the Brundtland Commission.

Critiques of These Theories of the Social Role of Business

While these theories of the purpose of the firm all recognize a role for business beyond the mere profit motive or the production of wealth for shareholders, it is also clear that these theories have not prevented the current destruction we see under the global economy. Perhaps some of the critiques of these systems will help to explain why we continue to see this destructive system, despite the long history of theories about the social responsibilities of business.

Voluntarism Does Not Work

Lieberwitz (2005), Marens (2008), and Compa (2008) all make the argument that business leaders will not undertake meaningful social responsibility on a voluntary basis. Marens (2008) informs us that from the earliest point of the development of the scholarship around the social role of the business, scholars were at best skeptical of whether businesses would ever voluntarily adopt any social responsibility. Lieberwitz (2005) echoes this argument for the modern era by presenting evidence that corporations have failed to meet any level of social responsibility despite the decades of social responsibility literature and research. Jenkins, Pearson, and Seyfang (2002) also have found that voluntary codes of conduct have not changed the destructive practices of the corporations developing these codes. Lance Compa (2008) presents a slightly different approach to voluntary CSR, suggesting it is important, but it is not enough. Compa suggests that voluntary CSR should be part of a three legged stool that also includes "strong laws strongly enforced . . . and strong, democratic trade unions."

INFORMATION BOX 3.3   VOLUNTARISM VS. MANDATORY CSR

The debate over whether corporations will ever engage as a whole in socially responsible business practices or whether the only path to social responsibility is through mandated actions is a long-standing debate. It is discussed here in this chapter, and it should be considered in light of the evidence from Chapters 1 and 2 as well as by students as they move forward through this text. CSR researchers vary in their positions on this debate—from the voluntary proposals by Carroll and Matten and Crane to the call for mandates from Lieberwitz and Marens to the balancing act by Compa, we see the viewpoints run across an entire spectrum.

Corporate Hijacking of Theories as Strategic Tools

Because these theories are voluntary, it is easy to have a fox guarding the hen house type of problem. Business leaders have oftentimes been quick to adopt these broad concepts and adapt them to meet and even further the Chicago School type of goals of businesses. Many of the theories discussed earlier in this text are also critiques as having been hijacked for business purposes. Corporate codes are oftentimes viewed as a way to attract new customers—they are more of a marketing tool than a meaningful step towards meeting social responsibility. Business ethics, as Marens argues, is perhaps the epitome of hijacking the field of the social responsibility of businesses. By defining the parameters of ethical behaviors, business leaders are able to establish their own rules of the game and to deflect the attention from others who might question their practices. Banerjee (Banerjee, 2008) points out that this has also occurred in the fields of corporate citizenship and CSR.

Business leaders often seem to conflate sustainability with viability (Springett, 2003). Indeed, an early business case on sustainability at Hewlett-Packard (admittedly recognized as a leader in the field) contains a motivation section entirely preoccupied with economic aspects (Preston, 2001). The alignment is still to a single, solitary goal of profit maximization; the only issue is whether sound environmental practices and people-friendly practices help organizations to achieve these goals. Sustainability researchers from Elkington to Hart and Milstein all point to sustainability as a business tool to attract more customers, cut costs, or increase profits. If the goals of the system have not changed, these social responsibilities will continue to be ignored as long as there are more effective, cheaper, or easier ways to make a profit or increase shareholder wealth as we see is so often the case. Jenkins, Pearson, and Seyfang (2002) critique the corporate code movement as being ineffective because too often the presence of codes becomes a marketing tool that really has little impact on business practices. Banerjee (2008) goes a step further and suggests that CSR, CC, and sustainability have all been misappropriated to serve corporate interests and to "curtail the interests of external stakeholders."

Thus, sustainability becomes focused on "sustaining" corporate profits and simply becomes another business tool to achieve financial outcomes. Corporations meet social responsibility as long as it produces more benefit for the company than refraining from such activities; i.e., corporations will be good citizens to the extent it serves their internal interests. In theory, this direction could be fine, as long as the sustainable or responsible operations always lead to the best profit margin—i.e., the interests of corporations and the rest of society are completely aligned. However, as we have seen in Chapter 2, this either is not the case or many business leaders do not believe this to be the case, as we continue to see destructive rather than sustainable business practices.

The Problems Are Systemic, and the Theories Do Not Question the System

Another critique of CSR is that it simply accepts the current economic system and fails to question whether the lack of focus on social outcomes is a result of systemic issues rather than individual decisions (Banerjee, 2008; Lieberwitz, 2005; Freeman & Liedtka, 1991). Perhaps part of the reason we see that social responsibility, corporate citizenship, and even sustainability are all eventually twisted towards the goals of profit and shareholder wealth is because these concepts have been placed within a system that sets out these financial interests as the primary or only goal. Researchers such as Lieberwitz (2005); Banerjee (2008); Freeman and Liedtka (1991); and Carbo, Langella, Dao, and Haase (2014) have all critiqued these theories as failing to question the very system that creates the destruction not when it is broken, but when it is operating as intended. Burawoy (1979) explored how employers convince workers to accept a very narrow set of parameters within this system of advanced capitalism and then convince them to compete for the few rewards available within this system. Marx and Engels argued that the system of capitalism itself would always lead to exploitation of workers, the environment, and any other resource that could produce a profit. Freeman and Liedtka (1991) suggested that a shortcoming of CSR is that it accepts the system within the terms established by Friedman and the idea of the corporation as a profit maximizer. For these critics, a meaningful exploration of the reasons for the destruction we see in the current systems of commerce around the globe and a path to a socially sustainable global economy must entail at the least an openness to a critique of the system.

The critique of these concepts is not to suggest that they do not have value. Each of the concepts calling for reform of the capitalistic system does indeed provide some important guidance. Many of the concepts help us to focus on specific social goals. They also present us with processes that may play a part or even processes that we know are unlikely to succeed and perhaps should be avoided. If nothing else, these past concepts give us a history of the types of measures that have or have not led to the furthering of social goals. The views of the firm discussed in this chapter and in Chapter 1 and the definitions and critiques of these views are summarized in Table 3.3.

TABLE 3.3 Summary of Critiques of Views of the Firms

View of the Firm	Definition	Critiques
Chicago School—Friedman	The unfettered free market system will regulate itself.	Does not work—leads to inequality, poverty, exploitation, and alienation. Corporate leaders will not pay attention to social outcomes.
Marxist critique	The division of labor from the ownership of the means of production leads to the negative outcomes we see under capitalism. A worker revolt is needed to overthrow the system.	There has been no worker overthrow of the system. When there has been an overthrow of the system, this has led to state despotism and tyranny.
Strategic stakeholder—Freeman	Firms create value for all stakeholders. All those affected by firm activities have a legitimate stake in corporate actions.	Language hijacked as management tool. Relies on corporate voluntarism. Exceedingly difficulty to meet all stakeholder needs without trade-offs.

(Continued)

TABLE 3.3 (Continued)

View of the Firm	Definition	Critiques
Social responsibility— early scholars	Voluntarism will never work. We must have tighter control of corporations. Scholars need to focus on issues of inequality, the role for a strong labor movement, and the role of an independent political process to rein in excesses of corporate power.	Critique from business leaders and the need for funding from businesses led to these ideas being cast aside first by academia then by the public and businesses.
Social responsibility— Carroll	Socially responsible employers must meet four responsibilities— economic, legal, ethical, and philanthropic—for a number of stakeholders.	Still places focus on economic outcomes. Relies on voluntary CSR. Does not question the system.
Corporate citizenship— Carroll	Good corporate citizens meet four responsibilities—economic, legal, ethical, and philanthropic.	No real advance from CSR. Still relies on voluntarism, even more focus on economics.
Corporate citizenship— Matten & Crane	Corporations should use their power in the citizenship structure to assure citizen rights where nation states either cannot or do not.	Once again, voluntarism does not work. State actors are duly elected and selected by citizens; corporations are not. Corporations exploit their power rather than use it to protect citizens.
Catholic Social Tradition	The focus is on the inherent value of the human being. All humans should be treated with dignity both inside and outside the workplace.	Voluntarism does not work. Corporations look at the workers as part of the means of production.
Corporate codes of conduct	Internal and external codes that corporations promise to follow.	Hijacked as a marketing tool. Too easy not to follow. Relies on voluntarism.
Sustainability	Development that meets the needs of the present without compromising the ability of future generations to meet their needs.	Hijacked by corporate power. Has become a marketing and/or strategic tool. Too often focused only on environmental issues.

Conclusion

Despite the plethora of past ideas, concepts, and even policies, we continue to see destructive results, and in many cases, the destruction is expanding and even accelerating. We continue to see businesses and the economic systems both nationally and globally run under the assumptions of the Chicago School view of the role of the firm. While Stakeholder Theory, CSR, CC, and other conceptions of the role of the firm are given some consideration internally by organizational leaders and occasionally in the public eye (especially after crises such as the Enron bankruptcy or the 2008 financial crisis), business continues to operate with a focus on economic measures. Profit, shareholder wealth, GDP, and the Dow Jones index all continue to be the markers of a "successful" business or economy. Measures of human well-being and planetary sustainability, much less human and ecological flourishing, are not discussed in the business section of newspapers or news channels, and too often they are discussed if at all as side concerns in business schools. As a result, we continue to see massive growth in shareholder wealth, executive pay, profits, and GDP, while we see continued destruction of the environment; the extinction of species of plants and animals; the destruction of natural resources; and harm to workers, consumers, communities, and the vast majority of society. If these concepts of the social role of the firm were not effective to put an end to the destructive system of commerce, then what is the solution?

Discussion Questions

1. Despite the various theories and concepts of how to assure that corporations operate in a socially responsible manner, the practices and outcomes shared in Chapters 1 and 2 continue to pervade our system of commerce. What have been the reasons for the failures of these concepts?
2. Compare and contrast the various theories and concepts of business and society. What are the similarities and differences? Are there common themes across these theories?
3. Marx and Engels suggest that there can never be a focus on social goals under a system of capitalism. Do you agree or disagree? Why? What is the evidence to support your argument? What is the counter evidence?
4. Many of the critics of the voluntary forms of CSR suggest that corporations and business leaders will simply never place social outcomes above the maximization of profit or wealth. Do you agree or disagree with these critics? What is your reasoning?
5. Should social goals be part of businesses' responsibility? Why or why not? If so, how will we assure such goals are met?

References

Adler, P. S. (2002). Critical in the name of whom and what. *Organization, 9*(3), 387–395.

Aguilera, R. V., Rupp, D. E., Williams, C. A., & Ganapathi, J. (2007). Putting the S back in corporate social responsibility: A multilevel theory of social change in organizations. *Academy of Management Review, 32*(3), 836–863.

Alvesson, M., & Deetz, S. (2000). *Doing Critical Management Research*. London: Sage Publications.

Baker, M. B. (2007). Promises and platitudes: Toward a new 21st century paradigm for corporate codes of conduct? *Connecticut Journal of International Law, 23*, 123–163.

Banerjee, S. B. (2008). Corporate social responsibility: The good, the bad and the ugly. *Critical Sociology, 34*(1), 51–79.

Bansal, P., & Clelland, I. (2004). Talking trash: Legitimacy, impression management, and unsystemic risk in the context of the natural environment. *Academy of Management Journal, 47*(1), 93–103.

Brundtland Commission. (1987). *Our Common Future: Report of the World Commission on Environment and Development.* UN Documents Gathering Body of Global Agreements.

Burawoy, M. (1979). *Manufacturing Consent: Changes in the Labor Process under Monopoly Capitalism.* Chicago: University of Chicago Press.

Carbo, J. A., Langella, I. M., Dao, V. T., & Haase, S. J. (2014). Breaking the ties that bind: from corporate sustainability to socially sustainable systems. *Business and Society Review, 119*(2), 175–206.

Carroll, A. B. (1991). The pyramid of corporate social responsibility: Toward the moral management of organizaitonal stakeholders. *Business Horizons, 34*(4), 39–49.

Carroll, A. B. (1998). The four faces of corporate citizenship. *Business and Society Review, 100*(1), 1–7.

Carter, C. R., & Rogers, D. S. (2008). A framework of sustainable supply chain management: Moving toward new theory. *International Journal of Physical Distribution & Logistics Management, 38*(5), 360–387.

Christmann, P. (2000). Effects of "best practices" of environmental management on cost advantage: The role of complimentary assets. *Academy of Management Journal, 43*(4), 663–680.

Compa, L. (2008). Corporate social responsibily and workers rights. *Comparative Labor Law and Policy Journal, 30*, 1–10.

Elkington, J. (Winter 1994). Towards the sustainable corporation. *California Management Review, 36*(2), 90–100.

Ferrell, O. C., Thorne, D., & Ferrell, L. (2016). *Business and Society: A Strategic Approach to Social Responsibility and Ethics.* Chicago: Chicago Business Press.

Francis, P. (2015, July 9). *Apostolic Journey of His Holiness Pope Francis.* Retrieved March 15, 2017, from The Vatican: http://w2.vatican.va/content/francesco/en/speeches/2015/july/documents/papa-francesco_20150709_bolivia-movimenti-popolari.html

Freeman, R. E., & Liedtka, J. (1991, July–August). Corporate social responsibility: A crtical approach. *Business Horizons, 34*(4), 92–98.

Friedman, M. (2017, March 16). *Milton Friedman.* Retrieved from Wikiquote: https://en.wikiquote.org/wiki/Milton_Friedman

Greenspan, A. (1963, August). The assault on integrity. *The Objectivist Newsletter, 2*(8), 118–121.

Hart, S. L., & Ahuja, G. (1996). Does it pay to be green? An emperical examination of the relationship between emission reduction and firm performance. *Business Strategy and the Environment, 5*, 30–37.

Hart, S. L., & Millstein, M. B. (2003). Creating sustainable value. *Academy of Management Executive, 17*, 56–67.

Jenkins, R., Pearson, R., & Seyfang, G. (2002). *Corporate Responsibility and Labor Rights: Codes of Conduct in the Global Economy.* London: Earthcan Publications.

Kennedy, R. G. (2006). Corporations, common goods, and human persons. *Ave Maria Law Review, 4*, 1–32.

Lieberwitz, R. L. (2005). What social responsibilty for the corporation? A report on the United States. *Managerial Law, 47*(5), 4–19.

Marens, R. (2008). Recovering the past: Reviving the legacy of the early scholars of corporate social responsibility. *Journal of Management History, 14*(1), 55–72.

Marx, K., & Engels, F. (1996). Manifesto of the Communist Party. In M. L. Writings, & T. Carver (Eds.), *Marx: Later Political Writings*, Cambridge, UK: University Press.

Matten, D., & Crane, A. (2005). Corporate citizenship: Toward an extended theoretical conceptualization. *Academy of Management Review, 30*(1), 166–179.

Mintzberg, H., Simons, R., & Basu, K. (Fall 2002). Beyond selfishness. *MIT Sloan Management Review, 44*(1), 67–74.

Moody, K. (2014). *In Solidarity: Essays on Working Class Organization in the United States.* Chicago, IL: Haymarket Books.

Naughton, M. (2006). The corporation as a community of work: Understanding the firm within the catholic social tradition. *Ave Maria Law Review, 4*, 33–75.

Porter, M., & Kramer, M. P. (2006). Strategy and society: The link between competitive advantage and corporate social responsibility. *Harvard Business Review, 84*(12), 78–92.

Preston, L. (2001). Sustainability at Hewlett-Packard: From theory to practice. *California Management Review, 43*(3), 26–37.

Shaw, W. H., & Barry, V. (2007). *Moral Issues in Business* (10th ed.). Belmont, CA: Thomson Wadsworth.

Springett, D. (2003). Business conceptions of sustainable development: A perspective from critical theory. *Business Strategy and the Environment, 12*, 71–86.

Trumka, R. (2010, April 7). *Remarks by AFL-CIO President Richard L. Trumka at the Institute of Politics, Harvard Kennedy School, "Why Working People Are Angry and Why Politicians Should Listen".* Retrieved March 16, 2017, from www.aflcio.org

Wolff, R. (2012). *Democracy at Work: A Cure for Capitalism.* Chicago: Haymarket Books.

CASE 3   CHILD LABOR ACROSS THE GLOBE

The use of child labor is a clear violation of human rights and thus clearly not a part of socially sustainable business systems. However, child labor has had a long history as part of destructive advanced capitalism. Throughout the American industrialization, child labor played a critical role. It is estimated that in 1900 one in five US children between the ages of 10 and 14 were employed in the mines and mills of the United States. Many of these children worked long hours in dangerous jobs (Budd, 2013, pp. 75–76). While the Fair Labor Standards Act passed in 1938 banned the worst forms of child labor in the United States, child labor has continued to be a part of both the global and American system of commerce.

According to the ILO, 168 million children worldwide are engaged as child laborers and more than half of these are engaged in hazardous work. While child labor is often equated with developing countries, child labor is still an issue today even in the United States. According to a Human Rights Watch (HRW) report, children aged 16–17 years old regularly work on the tobacco farms in North Carolina. These children work 11–12 hour days, six days a week, in extreme heat without consistent access to water. While the law allows for children as young as 12 to work the fields, the farmers have entered a voluntary agreement to hire workers only 16 years of age or older. One of the child laborers interviewed reported working in the tobacco fields since she was 13. Another explained that the employer confirmed her age simply by asking her if she was over 16, never asking for any further verification. However, according to the HRW report, whether or not employers actually abide by this agreement is questionable. The HRW report concluded that the majority of children they interviewed suffered from nicotine poisoning, exposure to pesticides, and heat exposure. Further, the report concluded that these children should not be treated as adults, as they are still in critical developmental stages that are put at risk by this work (Human Rights Watch, 2015b).

Child labor across the globe is a tremendous problem. According to the Department of Labor, there are nearly 140 products from seventy-five countries listed as products produced by child labor (Perez, 2016). These products are used throughout the globe including in developed countries in North America and Europe, and many of the goods, such as cotton and produce, are hidden within the supply chains of American, European, and Asian MNCs. Toys and Christmas decorations made in China are often made by child laborers before they are enjoyed or opened by children in the United States and other developed countries. Many of the workers killed in the Rana Plaza disaster were child laborers making clothes for consumers in the developed world. At least one in four Afghani children between the ages of 5 and 14 works to help their families to survive. Afghani children often work alongside their debt-ridden parents in the brick kiln industry to pay off their debt, receiving no pay, and suffering long and terrible working conditions. These children also work in the metal works industry, the carpet industry, and the informal employment sector (Human Rights Watch, 2016b). In Ghana, children as young as 8 work in the gold mines, often exposed to high levels of mercury, mining and processing gold for export (Human Rights Watch, 2015a). Children in the Philippines also work in the same types of conditions in the gold industry in their country (Human Rights Watch, 2015c). In Indonesia, children are exposed to hazardous working conditions in the tobacco fields much like the American children working the fields of North Carolina (Human Rights Watch, 2016a).

While much of the worst forms of child labor take place in the developing countries of the world, many US and European MNCs benefit from this child labor in their supply chains or through the direct production of their goods. In 2010, Apple admitted that child labor had been used in the production of its computers and devices in its Shenzhen facility (Moore, 2010), and Nestlé has been found to have been benefitting from child labor picking its cacao beans in West Africa (Haglage, 2015). Child labor is so common in the cotton fields that other textile and clothing industries almost assuredly benefit from the child labor, but due to the complexity of the supply chain are not held accountable (Moulds). According to an Amnesty International report, children as young as 7 work and die in the mines of the Congo for the cobalt that is used in batteries for Apple, Dell, HP, Samsung, Sony, Volkswagen, and other MNCs (Muhawesh, 2016).

From the bricks, carpets, and coal of Afghanistan to the rice, furniture, coffee, and cashews of Vietnam, child labor is part of the current system of global commerce. The vast majority of these goods are produced for export, and they are sold across the globe. Many of the goods end up buried deep within the supply chains of products. Even in the industrialized countries, child labor continues to be a reality. US, European, and Asian MNCs benefit from the child labor of suppliers and even direct producers of their goods.

Discussion Questions

1. Is the use of child labor ever ethical? Why or why not?
2. Can child labor be a part of socially sustainable business systems?
3. Is child labor indicative of the DAC system?
4. What are the solutions to the global child labor problem?

References

Budd, J. W. (2013). *Labor Relations: Striking a Balance* (4th ed.). New York: McGraw Hill Irwin.

Haglage, A. (2015, September 30). *Lawsuit: Your Candy Bar Was Made by Child Slaves.* Retrieved from The Daily Beast: www.thedailybeast.com/articles/2015/09/30/lawsuit-your-candy-bar-was-made-by-child-slaves.html

Human Rights Watch. (2015a). *Precious Metal, Cheap Labor: Child Labor and Corporate Responsibility in Ghana's Artisanal Gold Mines.* New York: Human Rights Watch.

Human Rights Watch. (2015b). *Teens of the Tobacco Fields: Child Labor in the United States Tobacco Farming.* New York: Human Rights Watch.

Human Rights Watch. (2015c). *"What . . . If Something Went Wrong?" Hazardous Child Labor in Small-Scale Gold Mining in the Philippines.* New York: Human Rights Watch.

Human Rights Watch. (2016a). *"The Harvest Is in My Blood": Hazardous Child Labor in Tobacco Farming in Indonesia.* New York: Human Rights Watch.

Human Rights Watch. (2016b). *"They Bear All the Pain": Hazardous Child Labor in Afghanistan.* New York: Human Rights Watch.

Moore, M. (2010, February 27). *Apple Admits Child Labour Used at Its Assembly Plants.* Retrieved from The Telegraph: www.telegraph.co.uk/finance/newsbysector/mediatechnologyandtelecoms/7332405/Apple-admits-child-labour-used-at-its-assembly-plants.html

Moulds, J. (n.d.). *Child Labour in the Fashion Supply Chain: Where, Why and What Can Be Done?* Retrieved January 18, 2017, from Unicef: https://labs.theguardian.com/unicef-child-labour/

Muhawesh, M. (2016, April 6). *From Apple to Volkswagon, Tech Boom Fueled by 40,0000 Congolese Child Miners.* Retrieved December 8, 2016, from Mintpressnews: www.mintpressnews.com/from-apple-to-volkswagen-tech-boom-fueld-by-40000-congolese-child-miners/215364

Perez, T. (2016, September 30). *List of Goods Produced by Child Labor or Forced Labor.* Retrieved January 18, 2017, from US Department of Labor: www.dol.gov/ilab/reports/child-labor/list-of-goods/

4

SOCIALLY SUSTAINABLE BUSINESS SYSTEMS

Social Justice is about the treatment of inequalities of all kinds.

Brian Barry (Barry, 2008, p. 10)

All human beings are born free and equal in dignity and rights. They are endowed with reason and conscience and should act towards one another in a spirit of brotherhood.

Article I of the Universal Declaration of Human Rights

We have come to a clear realization of the fact that true individual freedom cannot exist without economic security and independence. "Necessitous men are not free men." People who are hungry and out of a job are the stuff of which dictatorships are made.

FDR State of the Union Address, January 11, 1944 (Roosevelt, 1944)

Introduction

Socially sustainable business systems entail a new way of looking at business practices, business policies, and business regulation in such a way as to assure the sustainability of the planet and all of its inhabitants. From the people side of the equation, this means more than mere survival. As McGhee and Grant (2016) suggest, it is about flourishing, or thriving. It means ensuring all human rights for all humans at all levels and assuring socially just procedures and outcomes. From a planetary standpoint, it no longer merely means not destroying the planet, but it also today means healing much of the damage that has been done to the planet. SSBS is not just about meeting these goals; SSBS is also about establishing the system and the path to the system that will assure we work towards these goals.

SSBS has a content component (substantive outcomes and goals) and procedural component (systems and processes). The idea of SSBS also takes a systemic approach. Perhaps for business students, the best analogy would be to the content and process theories of motivation. The content theories explain the *what*, and the process theories explain the *how*. SSBS is a combination of both content and process—the *what* we are looking to achieve as well as the *how* to achieve it.

When we reviewed the various concepts and theories around social responsibility of businesses in Chapter 3, one of the strongest critiques of these concepts is that they have failed to work because they have *failed to question the system*. "Critiques" are often attempts to make minor changes within the current system or to change some of the inputs or influences from the outside to the current system of business practices. SSBS is predicated on the idea that the current system itself is flawed and that to overcome and to halt the destruction we see within the current system, we must fundamentally change the system itself. The system itself drives the behaviors and the destructive practices and is too strong to be overcome by minor internal changes or external influences. As Meadows (2008, p. 2) explained, "The system, to a large extent causes its own behavior! An outside event may unleash that behavior, but the same outside event applied to a different behavior is likely to produce a different result." We are currently stuck producing the same destructive results because we have not fundamentally changed the system. The application of different events or influences to such a strong system such as DAC is not likely to change behaviors or outcomes. SSBS is a fundamental change to the current system. It is not a modification of capitalism; it is a replacement for the current system of commerce that we define as DAC.

The largely voluntarist concepts of CSR, CC, and business ethics discussed in Chapter 3 are not going to be enough to change the behaviors within the system of DAC. These voluntarist ideas have not been enough to change the system over the past several decades. As we saw in Chapter 1, the destructive behaviors if anything are accelerating. Voluntarism has not worked. The system is too strong to be influenced. SSBS is about changing from within that very system that leads to the destructive behaviors and outcomes discussed in Chapters 1 and 2. SSBS is a broad-based system that includes the systems of commerce, politics, and ecology around the globe. SSBS includes establishing new parameters, new rules, new institutional structures, and new goals to meet the goals of the system.

The key to any systemic change is to begin with the end goal of our system in mind. We must have a marker that tells us whether the fundamental changes to the system are indeed working to drive us to the desired outcomes. If we are to accept the goals of the system as being profit generation or the creation of shareholder wealth, or perhaps even increases in GDP, then we might adopt the current system; but, even if we adopt a different system, it would still likely lead to the same destruction. However, as Adler has suggested, we must look towards broader and different goals. Socially sustainable systems require a focus on the goals of sustainability and "flourishing" of the people, the planet, and all of its inhabitants, today, tomorrow, and well into the future, meeting the needs and rights of the people, the needs of the planet today, and assuring those needs will be met tomorrow. Socially sustainable systems are also about more; they are about creating a system where not only are needs met, but all can thrive—all of the people and all parts of the ecological systems of the planet.

This is a much different system than the current system of destructive capitalism. However, if we step back and consider the stated goals of nearly every concept of business, commerce, markets, and economic systems, we see that SSBS is really a return to these goals. Adam Smith's free market system was supposed to create the greatest benefit for all. If it has not (or perhaps did not, as DAC is markedly different from Smith's concept), then of course we should try to figure out why it is not achieving its stated goal. Likewise, the goal of Marx was also to create the greatest good for the people within the system. These goals are consistent; unfortunately, under the current system of DAC, these goals are now ignored. The system is no longer assessed based on the meeting of these goals, but instead is assessed based on economic measures, perhaps as a result of the erroneous belief that a rising tide of prosperity will lift all boats (Mintzberg, Simons, & Basu, Fall 2002).

Establishing the Mission/Vision: The Content or Goals of SBSS

A New Model for a New Era: Socially Sustainable Business Systems or Socially Sustainable Systems

All of the different concepts regarding the role of business as being more than just profit outlined in Chapter 3 still have some level of relevance today. As both the early scholars of business and society and the Critical Management Studies group have pointed out, it is important to consider where we devote our attention and what goals we focus on within our system. If we continue to engage in a system that is focused only on profits, then the outcomes will not change. To truly achieve socially sustainable business practices, we can no longer afford to focus on profit at the expense of all else. We cannot merely focus only on profit or even only on profit and the planet. Any truly socially sustainable business system must indeed focus on goals of sustaining our society. This means that the ultimate dependent variable or the overarching mission of any organization or structure within this system must be to meet societal needs both today and into the future.

CMS teaches us that we need to be aware of for whom and what we are being critical. Sustainability helps us to begin to answer these concerns. The work in sustainability also helps us to understand the general directions in which our attention should be pointed—people and the planet. The field of sustainability adds a planetary concern that cannot be ignored if there is to be a future for anyone or anything, yet this concern is often lacking in the earlier concepts. We can take this to argue that we are critical in the name of human and planetary thriving.

The Catholic Social Tradition, business and society, social contract theory, and corporate citizenship all begin to help us answer these questions in more detail, especially about the people side. For the early scholars of corporate social responsibility, the focus was on three broad areas—inequality, employee representation, and the independent regulation of business. CST points us to focus on what it means to be a complete human being, the human need for growth and social development, and the human right of dignity and self-worth. These concepts provide guidance to the goals of social sustainability.

The People Component of SSBS Goals

The people side of the goals of SSBS is based on the rights and needs of human beings. A socially sustainable system must at a minimum meet the human needs and rights of all individuals in that society. Duncan Green (2008, p. 104) defines development as "transforming the lives and expectations of a nation's inhabitants . . . [t]he starting point for this effort must be guaranteeing that all people enjoy their basic rights and the ability to exercise them." Green (2008, p. 25) defines these rights expansively, to include "demands on those in power," "rights and the ability to exercise them," and civil and political rights—negative rights to be free from actions and "economic, social and cultural or 'positive rights', such as the right to education," and finally collective rights. As can be seen by the destruction to people discussed in Chapter 1, many of these rights are simply unmet or trampled upon under our current system.

As human beings, all of us have certain rights, and these rights are thus recognized as human rights. In discussing human rights, there is a general consensus that human rights are rights one has by virtue of the simple fact of being a human. Further, most would agree as the result of this that these rights apply to all humans regardless of race, color, gender, national origin, immigration status, etc. Taking this a step further, the key to human rights is that the enforcement and enjoyment of these rights are what make us human in the first place. These rights apply to all. This is readily recognized in the UN's Universal Declaration of Human Rights (UDHR):

> Article 1: All human beings are born free and equal in dignity and rights.
> Article 2: Everyone is entitled to all the rights and freedoms set forth in this declaration, without distinction of any kind.

Human rights exist not only as the requisites for health but to fulfill those needs for a life worthy of a human being (Donnelly, 2003). Human rights include not only those things that are needed to live, but those that are needed to live as humans. Spitz (2005, p. 318) takes this further and suggests that we should implement a system that ensures the rights and freedoms that are integral to "human flourishing." Most business students will be familiar with Maslow's Hierarchy of Needs and other needs-based theories of motivations (such as Herzberg's two factor theory, Aldefer's ERG theory, and McClellands's Learned Needs theory). However, what is often lost is that these researchers themselves defined their theories around human "needs." These were not defined as wants, or even as motivators, terms that could have been used, but were not chosen. Though the practical applicability of Maslow's hierarchy has received little empirical support, his description of the many and varied needs of humans is elucidating. These needs include not only the basic needs, such as the need for food and water (physiological needs), but also include higher level needs such as esteem, acceptance, and, ideally, self-actualization. Maslow himself recognized these needs as a legitimate basis for human rights. Other human rights scholars have also agreed that Maslow's work at least sets out a number of those things that should be included in human rights (Donnelly, 2003, p. 13). For other needs theories, factors such as rewarding work, recognition, growth, achievement, affiliation, and even power have been recognized as needs. These theories all give us at the least a starting point to understanding human needs and thus the types of goals towards which our systems should be working.

In addition to the needs defined by Maslow, we can also turn to well-established, internationally accepted documents to help us to define human rights. For instance, under the Universal Declaration of Human Rights, rights include life, liberty, and security (Article 3); freedom from slavery (Article 4); and freedom from cruel and inhumane punishment (Article 5). In addition to these, the UDHR also recognizes human rights that are clearly violated under the current unsustainable social economy. These include the right to peaceful assembly and association (Article 20); the right to social security (Article 22); the right to work, free choice of employment, and remuneration for such employment that ensures "for himself and his family an existence worthy of human dignity" (Article 23); and a right to a standard of living adequate for the health and well-being of oneself and one's family including food, clothing, housing, medical care, and necessary social services; and the right to security in the event of unemployment, sickness, disability, widowhood, old age, or lack of livelihood in circumstances beyond one's control (Article 25). In today's unsustainable social economy, due to the vast inequality of wealth and income, these rights are violated for billions of citizens throughout the world. Even in the United States, one in four workers does not earn enough to support themselves and their family (Quigley, 2003).

INFORMATION BOX 4.1   FDR'S SECOND BILL OF RIGHTS

By 1944, US President Franklin Delano Roosevelt believed the American people were prepared to accept and recognize a new bill of rights that protected every American's economic rights. In his 1944 State of the Union Address, FDR called for a Second Bill of Rights guaranteeing the right to a useful and remunerative job; the right to earn enough to provide adequate food, clothing, and recreation; the right to a decent home; the right to adequate medical care; the right to a decent retirement; and the right to education. More than seventy years later, the United States has failed to guarantee these rights for its citizens, and as inequality continues to grow, for more and more Americans, these rights seem like an impossible goal.

Starting with those whose fundamental rights are currently unmet is a critical component of SSBS. We cannot only look forward, but we must assess where we are now and correct any gaps where human rights are not being met. Green suggests that looking at those in poverty is an appropriate starting point. Those in poverty in the United States and around the globe struggle to meet their most basic needs. Many lack access to food, water, and shelter. Green (2008) explains that poverty around the developing world often entails a lack of control over one's home or shelter. Even in the United States, hunger and food insecurity are very real problems. The first goal of SSBS is to meet the basic needs of all human beings, to assure that every person has access to adequate food, water, shelter, health care, and security. SSBS means assuring that water supplies are safe, consumer products are safe, and medicines are safe and accessible.

Once the basic needs are met, the higher level needs must also be met. SSBS is not only about survival but also about flourishing. The higher level rights under the UDHR must be assured—the rights to just employment, fair wages, social security, paid time off, and health care, as well as the right to assembly. The upper level needs as described by Maslow, Herzberg, Aldefer, and others must be met. The opportunity for growth, development, social belongingness, and even self-actualization should be likewise goals of SSBS.

Even once human needs are met, a socially sustainable system will also require a just distribution of the surplus assets in a society. Human rights include the rights to a just system. In terms of economic justice, at a minimum, such a sustainable system must adopt what Peters (1997) defines as non-egalitarian justice. Peters suggests that distribution of income or assets must be made on only relevant factors and not irrelevant factors. Similarly, Dworkin (1981) suggests that disparities in resources should not be the result of brute bad luck or good luck, but instead should only be justified by earlier decisions made by individuals (i.e., the decision to trade off resources for leisure, or to forego leisure to accumulate resources). Miller suggests that equality is the "primary principle of justice" (1999, p. 31), while needs and deserts may also be just claims from citizens. Barry (2008, p. 10) explains that social justice is about addressing any inequalities that exist. The concepts of Dworkin, Peters, Miller, and Barry all suggest that, to have a just system, there must be a certain level of equality and that inequalities must have some legitimate basis (choice, relevant factors, needs, deserts). As discussed in Chapter 1, in the United States inequality is at an all-time high. Inequality has also increased recently in many other countries around the world. We see that poverty clearly exists in every industrialized country, while there are also those with tremendous, exorbitant levels of wealth.

A socially sustainable economy must be one that has the goal of assuring these rights as enumerated under the UDHR. Further, this goal must be to assure that these rights are met for all citizens of the global society. A socially sustainable system will be one in which the goals are to assure that all citizens have access to dignified jobs that will pay a living wage for all citizens that are able and willing to work. The living wage (a wage that permits the worker to raise a family adequately), as has been called for by many renowned economists, is where this standardization should start. One should note that the wage level itself should depend on the costs prevailing in the location of the worker. In this manner, a worker in the United States would not receive the same as a worker in India, but both would be compensated to have roughly the same (sufficient) standard of living. Also, working conditions, such as overtime, paid vacation, health (including insurance for the worker and their family), and safety measures, and the right to collectively bargain should be universal. For those who are unable to work, a socially sustainable system must assure some form of income security fitting to the dignity of a human being. All members of sustainable society must have access to the education that will qualify them for gainful employment as well as allow them to actively participate in their national and global citizenship as a full member of society and perhaps most importantly allow them to reach their own human fulfillment and potential. From a human rights perspective, education should be about self-fulfillment and at least the possibility of reaching Maslow's self-actualization. A socially sustainable system should be one that strives to provide adequate health care for all members of society, not merely to assure profits for insurance companies and health care providers. A socially sustainable system is one that ensures that all members of society will have a natural environment where they will be able to live safely, securely, and in good health. This environment would not be one where members of society must worry about the safety of their groundwater, the diseases in their food system, or the level of toxins in the air. A socially sustainable system must be one that ensures equality through a fair and sensible distribution of the surplus of that society. A socially sustainable system is not necessarily one of entirely equal outcomes, but it is one where the differences and disparities between members of that society make sense and one where one member's greed would never be allowed to violate another's rights or needs. First and foremost, this will mean that all human rights are met. Second, the distribution of any surplus should be based upon reasonably agreed upon relevant criteria and not any irrelevant criteria (Peters, 1997).

INFORMATION BOX 4.2   UNION REPRESENTATION AND RIGHTS: FRANCE AND THE UNITED STATES

In France, 93% of workers are covered by a collective bargaining agreement. French workers are also guaranteed protections from any form of moral harassment in the workplace. Mothers are provided with sixteen weeks of paid maternity leave, and employees can be fired only for just cause and such termination must be put in writing. Employees are also entitled to five weeks of paid vacation. In comparison, in the United States around 10% of workers are covered by a collective bargaining agreement, harassment is unlawful only if it is based on a protected status, and workers can be fired for any reason with or without notice and there are no guarantees to any paid time off.

These human-based goals can indeed be achieved. Even in terms of meeting the positive rights as defined earlier in this chapter, the impediment to meeting these rights is not an issue of feasibility, but instead one of political will (Donnelly, 2003, p. 29). It is hard to imagine the acceptance of an argument that individuals should live as less than human. However, when we step back and assess what this means, to truly define the rights and needs of human beings, what it means to not only survive but to thrive, we see that the current system of DAC indeed denies both the negative and positive rights and many of the needs of human well-being.

The Planetary Component of SSBS Goals

We cannot forget the other Ps in the triple bottom line of sustainability. People are not the sole inhabitants of the planet and do not have exclusive rights to the planet. There are planetary goals that exist even in the absence of these goals serving some human need or desire. First, the outcomes of the planet are of course critical to meeting human needs both today and into the future. If our air is poisoned and our water polluted, simply meeting our most basic physiological needs will become impossible. Further, as the planet warms, it becomes less and less habitable, farmland needed to supply food needs is destroyed, land needed for housing is swallowed up by rising sea levels, and water supplies are poisoned by the rising seas invading the water supplies. However, the planet also has its own merits without even the concern of human outcomes. We are far from the only species on this planet. Instead, we share the Earth with nearly ten million other species of plants and animals (How Many Species on Earth? About 8.7 Million, New Estimate Says, 2011). As one of millions of inhabitants of the Earth, we do not have the right to engage in practices that destroy the Earth for these other inhabitants. One needs only to look at the evidence for the rapid increase in the extinction rate in recent years to have great cause for concern (The Extinction Crisis, 2017).

A socially sustainable system assures that we preserve the planet not only today but into the future for the welfare of humankind as well as the millions of other species of plant life and animal life that call the Earth home. A socially sustainable system is also one that ensures that all members of society will have a natural environment where they will be able to live safely, securely, and in good health. This system must also assure that not only will today's planet be a safe, livable planet, but this will also be assured for future generations.

This means that we must put a halt to the practices that pollute the planet, our water system, and our air. We must put a halt to the burning of greenhouse gases that lead to the climate change impacting both developing and developed countries. We will need to put an end to the production and sales practices that have led to the massive swells of garbage in our oceans and the filling of landfills across the globe. We will need to begin to engage in practices that will help us to heal the damage that has been done to the planet: to drive innovations that will clean the oceans and scrub the air, and to drive practices that will allow the Earth the time to also heal itself of the toxic destruction it has suffered in the pursuit of profit. Just like the goals for the people of the planet, these environmental goals are also well within reach. Again, meeting these goals is not an issue of feasibility; it is an issue of political will. The reality is that we already have the technology needed to switch to renewable energy sources.

The Role of Profit in SSBS

The third P (profit) is no longer an end goal as indeed it never should have been. Profit also allows a business to continue to run. Adam Smith recognized this role as the sole role of profits—to be reinvested into the productive capital of the business. However, even this does not give us any real answer as to the purpose of profit. For the first (people), the purpose is clear—so that people can live their lives with the inherent dignity of being a human. The second P, planet, likewise has a clear purpose—it is critical for meeting the needs of people, but also there is an inherent value to the planet and the planet is clearly valuable to the non-people inhabitants of the planet. However, the final P, profit, is not a naturally occurring construct; it is a man-made construct and one that lacks any inherent value. We need to answer the question, Why is profit valuable? In fact, when reviewing the purpose of sustainability as presented by the Brundtland Commission, the inclusion of profit as one of the three equal end goals becomes questionable. We need to step back and take the time to ask why the pursuit of profit is a goal. Of course, high profit margins might indeed draw additional investors, create additional money for innovation, and provide opportunities to expand businesses and thus employment and wage levels of workers. However, these outcomes are not a natural outcome of profits. Profits could just as easily lead to repurchasing of stock shares, further increases in executive salaries and bonuses, hoarding of retained earnings, or large dividend distributions to wealthy stockholders. In the former use of profits, they are indeed valuable to society. In the latter, they benefit only a select few members of society. The question for profits will be whether they are truly helping to meet the needs of current and future generations. In other words, profit will be only an intermediary goal of this system and will exist only at this level if indeed it is used to drive other factors that lead to socially sustainable practices.

The idea of profit has always been that it serves an interest—the interest generally of people (and perhaps conceivably of the planet). The people could be any of the stakeholders we see in Freeman and Carroll's models. For the owners of a business, there is a legitimate expectation of some return for their risk—a *fair* return. It should be noted that fair returns are a very different animal from maximum returns. Fair profits serve the legitimate interest of one stakeholder, the owner. Profits also serve the interest of the communities, employees, suppliers, and even consumers who depend on the organization or business as a going concern. Profit also plays the role of establishing a level that a business must contribute back to society as a whole—as a percentage of tax on these profits. So, SSBS does not reject the notion of profit. Rather, SSBS demands that profit's importance should be re-understood. First, profit must always be subordinate to the interests of the people and the planet. Second, profit should be viewed as a predictor of outcomes rather than an outcome unto itself. In theoretical terms, profit should not be a dependent variable; it should be an independent variable that predicts the accomplishment of all legitimate stakeholder goals. This view of the third P is critical to creating a truly sustainable rather than destructive economic system and business practices. The goals of SSBS are set out in Table 4.1.

TABLE 4.1 Goals of SSBS

Group	Goal	Path
People	Meet all human rights and needs first	Human rights standards in all trade agreements and as part of WTO sanctions; strengthen the ILO and use enforcement powers that exist
	Sustainable level of equality that still supports motivation to achieve, but prevents negative outcomes; differences based on justifiable, relevant criteria	Labor unions, living wage ordinances, steeply graduated tax system
	Pursuit of happiness for all, improved health, quality lifespans, improved families and communities	Laws that provide mandatory leave and time off from work—vacation, family leave, and sick leave Universal health care
People: consumers	Safe products that meet needs first, wants second, and do not harm consumers or destroy environment	Consumer protection laws that place the burden on the corporation to prove safety
People: workers	Full employment with a right to a job at a living wage, positive right to dignity in the workplace, and positive right to be free from dangerous working conditions	A worker's bill of rights, a just cause standard of work instead of the at will employment, a full employment act, government subsidizing work when not filled by the private sector
People: students	Education accessible to all who are qualified and desire it at every level	Publicly funded education at all levels Free college education
People: citizens	Representative government that looks out for the interests of all of the people of the globe	Public campaign financing Strong laws against any form of voter suppression
	Empathy, responsibility, and hope (protection and empowerment)	Truth in campaigning laws
	Protection of rights from anybody who would infringe—including corporations	
Planet	Zero damage to the environment and steps to improve our ecological system	Environmental legislation Green jobs initiatives, backed by public funding if needed
	Not just maintaining the planet, but fixing current economic destruction	Public funding for sustainable energy sources, environmental repair
	Addressing climate change, safe drinking water, and air quality; ending the "death of birth"; protecting all species	End of public funding and tax rebates for climate damaging energy

Group	Goal	Path
Profit: macro level	Sustainable economy that assures all *needs* are met Creative destruction that involves all citizens, and has a broad goal of societal improvement	An inclusive economic system Right to a job to assure all are contributing members Living wage ordinances to assure that demand exists in the economy Redistribution of income through tax policy to assure economic demand, needed resources for public goods (infrastructure, schools, libraries, fire, police, courts, etc.), and to promote production of goods and services not yet economically viable on their own, but necessary for future development and well-being (i.e., public support of renewable energy sector)
Profit: micro level	Incentive to produce innovations to better society, fair returns to all stakeholders	A focus on business serving society and being a social institution with a great deal of power and thus responsibility to other components of society

Establishing the System—The Process Component

The goals of SSBS can indeed be met. As Klein (2014) has pointed out, the path to fully renewable energy sources exists. We can put an end to the harm that we are inflicting on the planet. There is nothing that ties us to the current system of factory farming; there is no reason that we must pollute our rivers, oceans, and air and water supplies. Likewise, we can indeed assure the human rights for all of the people of this planet. The failure to do so is more of a political choice about priorities than it is an issue of feasibility (Donnelly, 2003).

However, as we saw in Chapter 1, the current system of DAC is far from meeting the goals of SBSS. The goals of protecting human rights and protecting the planet cannot be achieved under the current system of DAC. Further, the band-aid of voluntary CSR or corporate citizenship does not present a path to achieving these goals. Voluntarism has not worked to prevent the destruction to the people and the planet in this system marked by relentless pursuit of profit and wealth. Achieving the social and environmental goals will require a fundamental change to the current economic system, the rules of that system, and the current business practices within that system. There is a great deal of evidence at this point to suggest that Marx's argument that a system that created such a division between the owners of capital and the workers (and we would add all other stakeholders—consumers, communities, the environment, and society at large) will always lead to this form of destruction. The owners will pursue their self-interest and are doing so indeed under such a system, convinced that their role is to pursue such self-interest (Mintzberg, Simons, & Basu, Fall 2002).

Any truly sustainable system must focus on all three pillars—the Earth, the people, and the macroeconomy. The narrow ownership interests under the current capitalistic system get in the way of such a broad view. The owners of capital hire the managers to represent their interests. These owners are often separated by time and space from the actual operations of the business. They look at the business as a financial investment. The managers or executives in turn rely upon the owners for their jobs and income. As a result, these owners, or the growth of shareholder wealth, become the primary focus of the business (Mintzberg, Simons, & Basu, Fall 2002). A new system will clearly need to have a new focus. Green (2008) suggests a very strong beginning to a new way of looking at sustainability. Green suggests that sustainability must start with a focus on the poor people in the world, a focus on those worst off and in the most immediate danger. He suggests that, first and foremost, government policies and business practices must be directed to address the issues with which those in poverty around the world are confronted. For Green, sustainability means a redistribution of the wealth around the world as well as a focus on growth. This is indeed just a starting point. The first step to redefining sustainability is indeed redefining the parameters. We must begin to think of sustainability not in corporate terms, but in societal terms, and then to ask what roles corporations play in assuring societal sustainability.

To address social sustainability, there must be a renewed focus on the fact that corporations are a part of a larger society, and this larger society has goals that must be met. Just as the strategic management literature suggests that there is a need for alignment to achieve organizational goals, the same is true of societal goals and corporations as well as all other parts of society that must be aligned to achieve these. The corporation would not allow a division or department to act outside of the corporation's interests in order to look out for the division's self-interest, nor should society accept a corporation acting outside of society's goals in order to pursue its own self-interest. A new system will need to view ownership in a different manner. All stakeholders must begin to be viewed as owners and must have the full rights of ownership. This broad group of stakeholders will be much more likely to take into account the broader interests of a business, will be more concerned about the potential impacts of a business, and will be more interested in a broader base of outcomes for the business.

Those in favor of the current system of DAC and those who benefit from this current system will not readily adopt a new system. The failures of voluntary social responsibility theories from CSR to corporate citizenship to sustainability all demonstrate the strong ties to the current system. Breaking out of this current destructive system will require a true social movement. These changed viewpoints will come only through increased discussion, participation, and discourse from societal members who have interests other than those of corporate power. These interests and this discourse must become a part of academia and in particular a part of the business school curriculum and research. Further, organizations, activists, and individual members of these other stakeholder groups must also play an active role in this discourse.

To create this social focus and to transform the focus of business, we must engage in discussions about the role of business and its responsibilities to the broader society. Courses such as the course you may be sitting in now will have to become a much more common part of the business school curriculum. As Marens (2008) has suggested, we will need to see a return to the ideas of the early scholars of business and society and a focus in terms of research and teaching on the societal impacts of business—as Wood (1991) points out, the field was referred to as "Business in Society" in the past, suggesting a much greater integration. We will need to see business students and academics discuss the subjects of these early scholars—inequality, the role of labor unions, and the need for an independent political process, as well as newer issues such as the destruction of the planet and the need for measures to protect our global ecosystem.

These discussions will have to go beyond the classroom and the walls of academia and involve all stakeholders—workers, managers, families, and communities. This will require a democratization of the corporation, a renewed democratization of business regulations (Marens, 2008), and a democratization of the workplace (Wolff, 2012). As all stakeholders become involved in the decisions around business and the decisions within businesses, this will spur the type of social movement that is needed to fundamentally change the current system (Bachmann, 2001). As these broad groups of stakeholders become involved, they are less likely to accept practices that lead to the loss of their jobs, destruction of their communities, and pollution of their air and water. They are more likely to push for the type of legislation that is needed to assure that businesses do not engage in the destructive business practices discussed in Chapter 1. This broad involvement will have the possibility of creating the virtuous cycle depicted in Figure 4.1.

The remainder of this book focuses on helping students to develop both their critical thinking as well as practical business practices, tactics, strategies, and ideas. It is meant to engage the reader to think about how and why we can make our systems truly socially sustainable as well as provide guidance concerning the business practices that can drive social sustainability. Students will be led through various business fields to consider tactics that will assure social sustainability in each field of business. Students will also be asked to engage in critical thinking to develop ideas beyond those presented here that will help to achieve social sustainability. Students will be engaged to consider the psychological barriers to social sustainability as well as the psychological processes that will open the door for a new socially sustainable economy. In the following chapters, students will explore socially sustainable supply chains and business operations, the role of strategic management in achieving social sustainability, the people practices that push us towards social sustainability, the role of leadership in achieving SSBS, the role of Information Systems in achieving SSBS, the psychology of sustainability, and

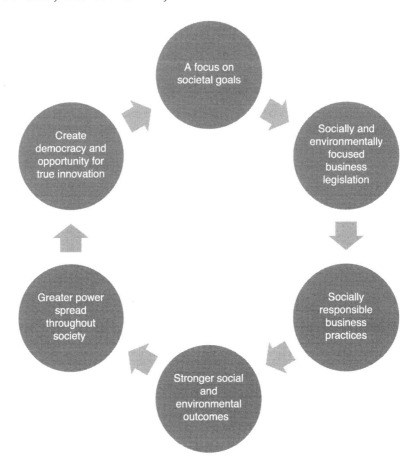

FIGURE 4.1 The Virtuous Cycle of SSBS

finally some thoughts about the paths forward that students can engage in both in the short term and in the long term to achieve SSBS.

As students engage in this exploration of potential paths towards social sustainability, Alvesson and Deetz offer some critical advice. First and foremost, we should be skeptical of any knowledge, idea, or solution that claims to be the exclusive solution. Second, the researcher's (and we would say the students') role today is more appropriately one of enabling more open discourse among the various members of organizations, and between them and external social groups and the larger societies in which they serve (Alvesson & Deetz, 2000, p. 17). This text is meant to drive students towards engaging in skepticism, in particular skepticism about the notion that the current economic system is the only viable solution. This text is also meant to drive students to engaging in the discourse as well as helping to create the paths for the much needed discourse among all stakeholders in the current global economic system.

Conclusion

SSBS is about assuring that the planet and its inhabitants are not harmed in the pursuit of profit or economic growth. SSBS is a system that focuses on human rights and the thriving of the ecosystems of our planet rather than the micro- and macro-economic systems that currently favor a few at the expense of the many. To achieve truly socially sustainable business systems, we must assure the human rights of all people across the globe. We also must assure that business practices do not harm our ecosystems, but instead are geared towards improving the many environmental challenges and problems we face today. SSBS is a marked change from our current system of destructive advanced capitalism. Such a change will require a radical reformation. This reformation will require a movement of people and the support of institutions. To achieve such a change, we must be willing to engage in meaningful discussion and analysis. We must be willing to focus our discussions and analyses on the outcomes to the people and the planet. We will need to break free from the ideology of our system of capitalism that focuses on monetary rather than meaningful outcomes. Such a transformation is possible, but only if we all collectively are willing to play a part in creating the virtuous cycle presented in Figure 4.1.

Discussion Questions

1. Compare and contrast the current system of DAC and SSBS.
2. What steps will be needed to achieve a system of socially sustainable business? What are the obstacles that will need to be overcome?
3. What are your thoughts about the goals of SSBS? Do they make sense? Are they being met under the current system of commerce? Why or why not?
4. What are the barriers to socially sustainable systems? Are these barriers created through ideology or empirical evidence?
5. How do current power structures within society promote or inhibit the path towards socially sustainable business systems?
6. What are your initial thoughts about the potential paths towards socially sustainable systems? What role can you play in driving the global economy towards social sustainability? What actors will need to be involved to create socially sustainable business systems?
7. We must think about pieces of the system that drive behavior, as well as influences from the outside that can change the system and change the behaviors. What leads to systemic change? What leads to cultural change? What pieces of the system continue to support destructive practices? How do we change or replace these pieces?

References

Alvesson, M., & Deetz, S. (2000). *Doing Critical Management Research*. London: Sage Publications.

Bachmann, S. (2001). *Lawyers, Law and Social Change.* Bloomington, IN: Unlimited Publishing.

Barry, B. (2008). *Why Social Justice Matters.* Cambridge, UK: Polity Press.

Donnelly, J. (2003). *Universal Human Rights in Theory and Practice* (2nd ed.). Ithaca and London: Cornell University Press.

Dworkin, R. (1981). What is equality? Part 2: Equality of resources. *Philosophy and Public Affairs, 10*(4), 283–345.

The Extinction Crisis. (2017, January 17). Retrieved from Center for Biological Diversity: www.biologicaldiversity.org/programs/biodiversity/elements_of_biodiversity/extinction_crisis/

Green, D. (2008). *From Poverty to Power: How Active Citizens and Effecitve States Can Change the World.* Oxford, UK: Oxfam International.

How Many Species on Earth? About 8.7 Million, New Estimate Says. (2011, August 24). Retrieved January 17, 2017, from Science Daily: www.sciencedaily.com/releases/2011/08/110823180459.htm

Klein, N. (2014). *This Changes Everything: Capitalism vs. the Climate.* New York: Simon & Schuster.

Marens, R. (2008). Recovering the past: Reviving the legacy of the early scholars of corporate social responsibility. *Journal of Management History, 14*(1), 55–72.

McGhee, P., & Grant, P. (2016). Teaching the virtues of sustainability as flourishing to undergraduate business students. *Global Virtue Ethics Review, 7*(2), 73–116.

Meadows, D. H. (2008). *Thinking in Systems: A Primer.* Junction, VT: Chelsea Green Publishing Company.

Miller, D. (1999). *Principles of Social Justice.* Cambridge, MA: Harvard University Press.

Mintzberg, H., Simons, R., & Basu, K. (Fall 2002). Beyond selfishness. *MIT Sloan Management Review, 44*(1), 67–74.

Peters, C. J. (1997). Equality revisited. *Harvard Law Review, 110*, 1210–1264.

Quigley, W. P. (2003). *Ending Poverty as We Know It: Guaranteeing a Right to a Job at a Living Wage.* Philadelphia, PA: Temple University Press.

Roosevelt, F. D. (1944, January 11). *FDR Library Marist.* Retrieved March 17, 2017, from 1944 State of the Union Address: www.fdrlibrary.marist.edu/archives/stateoftheunion.html

Spitz, L. (2005). The gift of Enron: An opportunity to talk about capitalism, equality, globalization and the promise of a North-American charter of fundamental rights. *Ohio State Law Journal, 66*, 315–396.

Wolff, R. (2012). *Democracy at Work: A Cure for Capitalism.* Chicago: Haymarket Books.

Wood, D. J. (1991, July–August). Toward improving corporate social performance. *Business Horizons, 34*(4), 66–75.

CASE 4 WORKER SELF-DIRECTED ENTERPRISES—A PATH TO SOCIALLY SUSTAINABLE BUSINESS SYSTEMS?

In *Democracy at Work*, economist, author, and professor Richard Wolff suggests that Worker Self-Directed Enterprises (WSDEs) might be a "cure for capitalism." Wolff's proposal might indeed be a cure for DAC and a path towards socially sustainable business systems. WSDEs under Wolff's proposal would be fully controlled by the workers engaged in the "productive" work of the organization. These workers would be the only individuals eligible to serve on the board of directors of the organization. The workers would be in charge of the broad strategy *and* the day to day operations of the enterprise. Most importantly, Wolff explains that in a WSDE, "the appropriation and distribution of the surplus are done cooperatively and . . . the workers who cooperatively produce the surplus and those who cooperatively appropriate and distribute it are identical" (Wolff, 2012, p. 122).

Wolff suggests that WSDEs would be more environmentally responsible, because the workers making the decisions "live, play and raise families" around the work-site and would experience the impacts of poor environmental practices. They would be less likely to make decisions that would harm their environments than the current system of detached and distant boards of directors. WSDEs are also more likely to have fairer compensation systems, for both the minimum and maximum levels of pay for the various jobs in the organization. Employees would be less likely to make the decision to chase low wage labor, to send work offshore, to violate labor laws, or to look for ways to avoid paying corporate taxes that benefit their neighborhoods. All of these possibilities suggest that WSDEs could indeed be a path towards socially sustainable business systems. Further, there are examples of organizations that are at least close to Wolff's description of WSDEs that support Wolff's claims.

The Mondragon Corporation in Spain is presented as an example of a corporation taking steps towards a WSDE by Wolff. The Mondragon is the largest worker co-operative in the world, with more than twelve billion euros in annual revenue, 261 companies, and more than 74,000 workers. Eighty-four percent of the workers in the Mondragon are also owners. The Mondragon is committed to the types of values that align with socially sustainable business systems. The Mondragon's value principles include open admission, democratic organization, sovereignty of labor, instrumental and subordinate nature of capital, participatory management, education, and social transformation (Mondragon, 2017). Its commitments are to its workers' safety, development and wage solidarity, sustainable development, protection of the environment, and a fair and equitable society (*Commitments*, 2017).

The Mondragon has demonstrated this commitment to the worker-members while also being financially successful. Even during the recent severe recession in Spain, the Mondragon was able to remain successful and committed to its people. Workers agreed to wage cuts during the recession, but the Mondragon was able to prevent the shedding of workers. Because of the co-operative organization of the Mondragon, it moves people and finances around to other co-ops when needed. If one company is overstaffed, rather than laying off workers, it will move workers to another company within the Mondragon. When one company is struggling, others within the huge co-op will contribute to keep it afloat. In fact, according to an HR director of the Mondragon, Mikel Zabala, many of the companies that have needed help at times are today the most successful companies within the Mondragon (Tremlett, 2013).

New Era Glass is also an example of an organization that is very similar to Wolff's WSDE. New Era is a worker-owned co-operative that took over the company from a corporate owner who decided to shut down the plant in pursuit of cheaper labor. New Era formed after the Republic Windows and Doors Company was nearly shut down during the economic downturn in the United States in 2008. The owners of Republic Windows and Doors announced that the company would shut down and all of its workers would be laid off immediately. The workers, members of the United Electrical Radio and Machine Workers of America (UE) led by Ricky Maclin, staged a sit-in demanding the wages they were owed and an opportunity to keep the plant open. The workers won their wages, and the facility was purchased by Serious Energy. However, Serious Energy also decided to shut down the plant, and again the UE workers stood their ground. This time they decided to come up with a plan to take ownership of the company. With the help of their union, the Working World, and the Center for Workplace Democracy, the workers made their plan a reality and formed the New Era Windows Cooperative (Our Story). In 2015, the Eastern Conference for Workplace Democracy renamed its biennial award in honor of the late Ricky Maclin (Ifateyo, 2015).

The United Steelworkers (USW) also teamed up with the Mondragon to form unionized, worker-owned co-operatives. USW defines union co-ops as "for-profit businesses that are owned and directed by workers, which utilize the collective bargaining process and are guided by the core principles of sustainability, solidarity, accountability, and community" (United Steelworkers). The position of the USW is that co-operatives will shift true control and ownership to the workers and as Wolff argues will provide them control over the surplus value the workers create. Rob Witherell (2013) explains that the unionized model of a co-op is necessary to maintain accountability and worker control as the co-op increases. The Mondragon has a similar model with social councils playing the role of the union. In addition to Wolff's argu-ments for WSDEs, Witherell argues that unionized co-ops are more likely to reinvest in production rather than the stock repurchases that we often see today in pursuit of increased stock prices. Witherell suggests that "together, union and cooperatives have the potential to create sustainable jobs that support sustainable communities" (Witherell, 2013, p. 252). Based on the success of many co-ops under the USW/Mondragon plan, the Mondragon itself, and New Era Windows, Witherell and Wolff may indeed be right.

Discussion Questions

1. How might WSDEs or unionized co-ops meet the goals of socially sus-tainable business systems?
2. Why might a large co-operative need to be unionized to meet the goals of socially sustainable business systems?
3. Look to find examples of worker co-operatives in the United States and abroad. Are these co-operatives successful? Why or why not? How did you define success, by DAC or SSBS standards? Why did you use the definition of success that you chose?

References

Commitments. (2017). Retrieved January 18, 2017, from Mondragon: www.mondragon-corporation.com/eng/corporate-responsibility/commitments/

Ifateyo, A. N. (2015). *New Era Windows Cooperative Recognized for Co-Op Innovation.* Retrieved January 18, 2017, from Grassroots Economic Organizing: www.geo.coop/story/new-era-windows-cooperative-recognized-co-op-innovation

Mondragon. (2017, January 18). Retrieved from Our Principles: www.mondragon-corporation.com/eng/co-operative-experience/our-principles/

Our Story. (n.d.). Retrieved Janaury 18, 2017, from New ERA Windows and Doors: www.newerawindows.com/about-us/our-story

Tremlett, G. (2013, March 7). *Mondragon: Spain's Giant Co-Operative Where Times Are Hard but Few Go Bust.* Retrieved January 18, 2017, from The Guardian: www.theguardian.com/world/2013/mar/07/mondragon-spains-giant-cooperative

United Steelworkers. (n.d.). *Union Co-Ops Overview.* Retrieved January 18, 2017, from USW: www.usw.org/union/featured-projects/union-co-op-overview

Witherell, R. (2013). An emerging solidarity: Worker cooperatives, unions and the new union cooperative model in the United States. *International Journal of Labor Research, 5*(2), 251–268.

Wolff, R. (2012). *Democracy at Work: A Cure for Capitalism.* Chicago: Haymarket Books.

5

SOCIALLY SUSTAINABLE BUSINESS SYSTEMS, EMPLOYEE RELATIONS, HR MANAGEMENT, AND EMPLOYMENT POLICY

A human being has a right to be free from domination regardless of the source. Wagner's Act (the National Labor Relations Act) was based on the understanding that servility is incompatible with human rights. . . . People can be rendered powerless not only by totalitarian states but also by those minimalist states that do not outlaw or take effective steps to prevent the violation of people's rights by private non-state actors.

James Gross—Workers' Rights as Human Rights (Gross, 2003, p. 4)

To be in the working class is to be in a place of relative vulnerability—on the job, in the market, in politics and culture.

Michael Zweig, The Working Class Majority (Zweig, 2000, p. 13)

The class war between employers and workers over the product of Labor goes on without letup. "Settlements" in wage movements, whether these are accompanied by strikes or not, are at best only truces in the ceaseless struggle, only turning points where the struggle takes on new forms. The employers will continue to try to destroy the workers' standard of living and break the unions; the workers will continue to build their unions and to advance their interests. Organization campaigns, strikes, settlements and their aftermath, are but various phases of the one great process of class struggle under capitalism.

William Z. Foster, Strike Strategy (Foster, 1926)

Introduction

The employment realm has a great impact on whether business practices are socially sustainable or whether they are destructive. In the current system of DAC, workers across the globe suffer a great deal of harm. For workers in the United States, many earn sub-poverty level wages. Even in the best of times, the presence of work is tenuous and the possibility of being unemployed is rather high. The United States working relationship has become one of fractured work, with many workers being employed through temp agencies, or engaged in contract work that could end the next day (Weil, 2014). In much of the developed world, the working environment is often even worse. Chinese workers in Apple's Shenzhen facility have jumped to their deaths reportedly to escape the sweat shop working conditions in the factory (Bilton, 2014). More than 1100 garment workers were crushed to death in an avoidable disaster in the Rana Plaza in Bangladesh (Bangladesh Factory Death Toll Soars Past 1,100, 2013), and millions of children across the globe toil in work and often the most dangerous forms of child labor (Hazardous Child Labour, 2017). To move from these destructive employment practices to a socially sustainable employment environment, we will need to follow Compa's (2008) three-legged stool as a solution. This three-legged stool suggests that we will need to adopt strong laws with strong enforcement, we will need a strong labor movement, and we will need to rely on progressive employers to adopt and follow SSBS practices.

The current system of DAC is wrought with the exploitation and alienation of workers. Employers squeeze or steal more and more of the surplus value of labor by forcing workers to produce more and more per hour while wages stagnate or even decline (Moody, 2014). Workers' lives seem to be viewed as a disposable part of the production process, as evidenced by the Shenzhen and Rana Plaza tragedies, as well as the Upper Big Branch, Sago Mine, and Deepwater Horizon tragedies discussed in earlier chapters. In the industrialized world, the stress levels of work have led to the United States being termed a Prozac nation, with anti-depressants and antacids becoming top selling pharmaceuticals, while the opiate and alcohol industries also boom as workers self-medicate to create their own escape. There is no need for employers to engage in this exploitation of their workers. In fact, a human rights approach demands that this exploitation end. Socially sustainable business systems require that employers meet and assure the rights and needs of all workers. The physiological, safety, esteem, and growth needs must be met to assure a socially sustainable business environment. SSBS employers must uphold the dignity of all workers and must assure all of the human rights of all workers. This standard applies to workers in the developed world as well as the developing world. Workers in Bangladesh have the same human rights as workers in Germany, the United Kingdom, and the United States. The standard applies to the workers employed directly, as well as those that employers now employ indirectly through the fissured workforce. When big box warehouses hire workers through temp agencies, they still owe these workers the same protections and assurances of their dignity and human rights. The employer must assure the rights of all the workers related to their supply chains—the workers in the home country and the host country, direct employees, and employees of suppliers. Apple cannot escape the responsibilities for Shenzhen simply because Foxconn is a mere supplier of its products.

Beyond assuring the human rights of workers, employment practices also impact other goals of socially sustainable business systems by impacting what is produced and how it is produced. Employment practices under the current DAC system support a relentless pursuit of profit and shareholder wealth. Jobs are set up to produce products as quickly as possible to get these products out to consumers to produce revenues. There is no concern for the environmental impacts of these practices, nor is there concern for the safety or rights of consumers and communities. As Leonard (2010) describes, jobs are structured to support a system that produces massive amounts of waste and pollution and destruction of natural resources. As discussed in Chapters 1 and 2, employers are focused on producing products that will need to be replaced by consumers due to the consumer preferences or the planned obsolescence of the product. Socially sustainable HR practices would change this. The emphasis would be to produce products in an environmentally sustainable way, to prevent the production of toxic pollution in the processes, to minimize the waste from production and disposal, and to look to protect and preserve the natural resources of the Earth. Employment practices and jobs would be set up to support and promote workers to innovate in socially and environmentally sustainable ways.

In addition to the changing employment practices of employers, labor unions also play an important role in socially sustainable systems. Labor must become a full member of the social sustainability community if we are to achieve the goals of SSBS. Labor must come on board to the commitment to transition away from destructive industries and practices. Labor can no longer defend the growth of environmentally destructive industries such as coal, natural gas fracking, and pipe-lining of greenhouse energy sources. This does not mean that labor should not continue to fight for the needs and rights of their members and all workers and especially the workers in these industries. In fact, the labor movement will need to be expanded to fight for worker rights on a global scale, and the leaders of labor will need to intensify their fight for workers in these destructive industries. Labor will need to take up the fight for the development of a Green Collar Economy (Jones, 2008). Labor will need to push for the guarantee of a job at a living wage and for a new full employment act on a global scale (Quigley, 2003). The labor movement should also focus on true employee ownership and control, such as Wolff's Worker Self-Directed Enterprises (2012) or the examples we see in the Mondragon and German works councils. Labor must expand the fight to truly address all of the needs of workers. The labor movement cannot ignore the life of workers outside the workplace. The labor movement cannot support employment practices that assure decent wages, while harming the health of workers and their families both inside and outside the workplace. The fight by the labor movement must expand to fight for all of the human rights of workers in all aspects of their life. It must fight for the bread and butter issue of decent pay, but it must also fight for a clean environment, to assure the air that workers breathe, the water that they drink and the food that they eat does not cause harm or even kill them or their families.

INFORMATION BOX 5.1   VOLUNTARISM VS. MANDATORY SSBS

One of the debates concerning corporate social responsibility in all of its forms (CSR, business and society, corporate citizenship, sustainability) has been whether socially responsible practices should be promoted and then engaged in voluntarily by corporations (voluntarism) or whether socially responsible practices should be mandated (mandatory). The idea of socially responsible business practices dates back as far as business. In that time, voluntarism has rarely worked on a micro scale (firm level) and has never been effective on a macro scale (social outcomes). While progressive organizations can help to push us towards SSBS by engaging in socially responsible practices, to achieve a truly socially sustainable system of commerce, we will need a mandatory system of socially sustainable practices. We will need to see strong laws with strong enforcement across the globe, applied in developed countries and developing countries to assure the rights of workers, citizens, and the Earth itself.

Voluntarism (see Information Box 5.1) has not worked as a whole in driving businesses to socially sustainable options and likewise will not be enough to drive socially sustainable employment decisions and practices. Further, while the labor movement and strong unions will also play an important role, unions currently are not strong enough to force the types of changes needed to the system. As Rosenfeld (2014) has pointed out, unions are no longer able to influence wages, benefits, social mobility, and equality the way they were able to just a few decades ago. To truly have socially sustainable business systems, we will also need to have strong labor and employment laws that are strongly enforced. These laws will need to focus on the human rights and needs of workers, shifting from a negative rights focus that we see in the United States to a positive rights focus that has been adopted at least in parts of the European Union, in Australia, and in parts of Asia.

Employee Relations and Human Resource Management

Noe, Hollenbeck, Gerhart, and Wright (2007) define human resource management (HRM) as the policies, practices, and systems that influence employees' behavior, attitudes, and performance. Employee relations (ER) is often defined in much the same way, but perhaps a bit broader as the interactions between employer and employee (Leat, 2001). The practices of human resource management and employee relations are often based on studies from the field of organizational behavior (OB)—or the "interdisciplinary field dedicated to better understanding and managing people at work" (Kinicki & Kreitner, 2003, p. 9). In fact, we could consider HRM and ER as putting OB theories into practice. When these HR practices are directed towards helping organizations to achieve their overall goals, this is often referred to as strategic HRM (SHRM). These HR practices will play a large role in determining whether business practices are socially sustainable.

HRM practices include determining wage levels, schedules, time off allowance, raises, and medical and retirement benefits, as well as making decisions about lay-offs, offshoring, the outsourcing of work, discipline, the structuring of jobs, and the assigning of job tasks. HR practices also include the recruitment of talent and the management and motivation of people in the organization. All of these will have a direct impact on the sustainability of the employees, the families, and the communities of an employer. These practices can also drive employees to behave in ways that can either increase or decrease the sustainability of those inside and outside the organization as well as the sustainability of the planet. Employee behaviors can either drive organizations towards innovations that will create sustainable organizations and development or drive organizations down the current destructive path.

Employee Relations/HRM and Worker Rights

Returning to Chapter 4, we can consider the goals needed for employees to live sustainable lives. Again, this focus will be on the rights and needs of employees, the rights not just to sustain life, but the rights to a life worthy of human dignity, as well as upholding the concept of social justice in the employment setting—the recognition of a fair distribution.

In terms of the rights and needs, the HR practice would be to shift away from using needs-based theories to drive behavior, to viewing these as a list of requirements that employers must meet. In looking at Maslow's Hierarchy of Needs, socially sustainable HRM will assure that employees are safe at work—physically and psychologically—and that their basic needs for food, shelter, medical care, and other necessities of life are met through their wages, as well as that they are able to meet their social needs, esteem needs, and the need to grow and develop through their work. The socially sustainable employer will also consider other needs of employees such as those described in McClelland's work on learned needs (affiliation, power, and achievement), Herzberg, and other needs-based theories. In addition, the socially sustainable employer will also consider the myriad of human rights that assure their workers the right to the dignity deserved by all humans. The socially sustainable employer will pay attention to internationally recognized documents of human rights such as the Universal Declaration of Human Rights and the International Covenant on Economic, Social and Cultural Rights (ICE-SCR); International Labor Organization conventions; rights recognized under the Catholic Social Tradition; corporate citizenship theories and social responsibility theories discussed in Chapter 3; and human rights theories from philosophers such as Kant and Rawls. In short, the socially sustainable employer will assure all of its employees' rights and needs that are listed as goals of socially sustainable business systems in Chapter 4.

INFORMATION BOX 5.2 SLAVE LABOR IN THE MODERN DAY UNITED STATES

There is perhaps no starker example of DAC HRM practices in the United States than the case of the John Pickle Company (JPC) and the Chellen workers. Chellen workers from India were recruited to come to the United States to work for JPC. All of these workers were skilled workers, left decent jobs to come to America, and were paid a large recruitment fee in return for a promise of work to match their skill, decent wages, and decent living conditions. However, when they reached the United States they instead were confronted with terrible working conditions, low pay, and unskilled work. Upon arrival at the JPC facility, the Chellen workers' passports, visas, and return flight tickets were all taken by Christina Pickle. The workers were forced to refurbish their own living quarters (a converted building with one door and one light switch), were not allowed to leave the premises, were threatened with arrest or deportation if they left the premises, were forced into unskilled labor, and were paid around $3 per hour (while also having to pay JPC for their living expenses). Only by escaping under a fence were the Chellen workers able to expose the practices of JPC.

For more details about the Chellen workers and JPC, see *Chellen v. John Pickle Co, Inc.* and *EEOC v. John Pickle Inc.* Case No. 02-CV-85-EA (M).

As we begin to think about the practices and functions of HRM, we can explore the specific HRM functions and tactics and consider what these will look like for the socially sustainable employer. We can explore the staffing, training, development, compensation, and organizational climate management practices that we should see in the socially sustainable employer. Much like the Universal Declaration of Human Rights, these practices are aspirational. There is no expectation that employers are engaged in all of these practices, much less that *all* employers are engaged in *all* of these practices. Nor is the expectation that these changes will occur overnight. However, as we have described in Chapters 1–4, if we are to escape from the current destructive business practices, we must be pursuing these ER/HRM goals.

Staffing

One of the key features of human rights is that people should be free from discrimination. Under the conception of rights in the United States, all should have equal opportunities. Discrimination interferes with that equality and interferes with a fundamental right. According to Article 7 of the Universal Declaration of Human Rights,

> All are equal before the law and are entitled without any discrimination to equal protection of the law. All are entitled to equal protection against any

discrimination in violation of this Declaration and against any incitement to such discrimination.

A socially sustainable employer must assure that its staffing practices—sourcing of candidates, recruitment of candidates, selection of candidates, and placement of new hires—are not discriminatory either covertly or overtly, intentionally or unintentionally. In the United States, federal equal employment opportunity (EEO) laws make it unlawful for an employer to discriminate based upon a candidate's race, color, national origin, gender, religion, disability, or age status over 40. The National Labor Relations Act (NLRA) also makes it unlawful to discriminate against candidates based on union status or activity. However, there are many gaps in the coverage of these EEO laws. The laws allow for a myriad of business exceptions to this discrimination—bona fide occupational qualifications (BFOQs), business necessity, legitimate business reason, and valid selection technique predicting job success. Further, the EEO laws leave many bases for discrimination open to employers—height, weight, gender identity, sexual orientation, political affiliation, tattoos, piercings, clothing choice, and conviction records are all examples of bases from which employers are allowed to discriminate (and really these are just the tip of the iceberg).

Even with these gaps in coverage, employers continue to discriminate based on these uncovered as well as covered areas. Further, there is often covert, perhaps even unintentional, discrimination that falls outside this scope—partnership tracks, working hours, the refusal to allow flexibility in work, etc. There are also inherent biases with interviewers that are ignored rather than addressed.

Job Structure/Development

The structuring of jobs and assigning of tasks are other typical HRM/ER functions that have a huge impact on the rights and needs of employees. Under Article 23 of the UDHR, it is recognized that "Everyone has the right to . . . just and favourable conditions of work and to protection against unemployment." These just and favorable conditions must mean that working conditions are fair and safe. Workers must be safe from physical and psychological injuries on the job. While injuries and even deaths are inevitable, socially sustainable employers will take every feasible step to minimize them. The current practices are far from achieving this sustainability. According to Spieler (2003), Occupational Safety and Health should be, but is not, treated as a core labor right or human right. According to Spieler (2003), in the United States approximately 65,000 workers die each year from work-related illnesses and injuries. Many if not most of these deaths are preventable, and the socially sustainable employer will take all steps necessary to prevent these deaths. Socially sustainable employers will also look to prevent workplace injuries—both physical and psychological injuries. The socially sustainable employer will implement ergonomic measures to eliminate the pain and strain of cumulative trauma injuries. Safety equipment will not be provided based on a cost-benefit analysis; instead, all feasible safety equipment and measures will be implemented. The socially sustainable employer would never engage in the types of practices seen at the Upper Big Branch Mine, where cutting corners on safety measures led to the death of twenty-nine miners. While not perfect, regulations over the past forty to fifty years have reduced the rates of workplace injuries and workplace deaths (Occupational Safety and Health Administration, n.d.). One must always be cautious, however, because these regulations are often ignored by employers in examples like those discussed earlier and there is always a push to roll back regulations, especially in the United States. Of course, many countries lack even these basic protections.

Compensation and Benefits

Determining the compensation and benefit plans of workers is another function of HRM/ER. Again, these determinations can have a tremendous impact on whether workers' needs and rights are being met. First, and perhaps most obvious, one cannot be a socially sustainable employer unless one assures employees are paid a living wage. Paying less than a living wage is a clear violation of the basic human rights of workers. The rights recognized at the first level of Maslow's Hierarchy of Needs and under Article 23 of the UDHR (3) state that everyone who works has the right to just and favorable remuneration ensuring for oneself and one's family an existence worthy of human dignity, and supplemented, if necessary, by other means of social protection.

Socially sustainable employers will also address the human rights and needs of employees with regard to both health care and retirement. Unlike the vast majority of other industrialized countries, the United States does not assure access to health care to all individuals. Health insurance still largely depends on employment relationships and is part of the compensation packages negotiated by employees— whether they are organized or not. Article 25 of the UDHR recognizes the access to medical care as a very clear fundamental human right:

(1) Everyone has the right to a standard of living adequate for the health and well-being of himself and of his family, including food, clothing, housing and medical care and necessary social services, and the right to security in the event of unemployment, sickness, disability, widowhood, old age or other lack of livelihood in circumstances beyond his control.

While access to health care is not an issue in many countries, it clearly is an issue in the United States. Therefore, to be a socially sustainable employer, an organization will have to assure employees have decent medical coverage, at a rate that will not impact their financial ability to meet their other needs. This access to health care is also an issue in many of the developing countries where American, European, and Asian multinational companies operate. These employers will need to take steps to assure access for their workers across the globe.

INFORMATION BOX 5.3 THE OVERWORKED AMERICAN

The Center for Economic and Policy Research found that in the absence of government standards almost one in four Americans has no paid vacation and no paid holidays. American workers who do have vacation average less than half of the paid time off of their European counterparts. Working a fifteen-hour day is not unheard of or uncommon in much of corporate America. The overwork and undervacation of the American workers are not only costly (costing businesses more than a trillion dollars per year) but deadly—shortening the lives of the typical American worker.

Vacations, holidays, and paid time off are also generally a part of the employment agreement in the United States. Employees in the United States are not guaranteed under the law any type of paid time off (again, unlike the majority of workers in the rest of the industrialized world). The first and foremost concern here should be a recognition that motherhood and childhood are entitled to special care and assistance. All children, whether born in or out of wedlock, shall enjoy the same social protection (Article 25 of the UDHR). The recognition of this should include providing access to paid maternity and paternity leave to assure the safest pregnancy possible and to assure a time for both parents to bond with their children. Time off is a necessity of life, and this necessity is recognized under the UDHR even if it is not recognized under US laws. Therefore, socially sustainable employers will recognize the right under Article 24 of the UDHR and provide employees with the "right to rest and leisure, including reasonable limitation of working hours and periodic holidays with pay."

Pensions are yet another part of employee compensation that must be considered from the realm of worker needs and rights. The same security, safety, and physiological needs apply to employees after they retire. Employers must take steps to assure that employees will be able to meet these needs upon retirement. In many cases, such as in the United States, the state retirement scheme is merely a supplement and not nearly enough to provide for these needs at retirement. Socially sustainable employers will provide workers with a secure retirement plan that will assure a dignified retirement. Such a plan should avoid the risks of the current 401(k) defined contribution plans we see in the United States. These plans, even in decent economic times, have created a multi-trillion dollar retirement gap (and approximately 40% of the retirement age population in the United States does not have a retirement account) (Morrisey, 2016). In the worst of times, during the economic crash of 2008 and during the Enron bankruptcy in 2000, millions of retirees were left with nothing in their retirement savings. Further, these plans allow for brokers to charge exorbitant fees, making millions of dollars off retiree savings for doing little or nothing in return. There can be no true social sustainability without a return to a secured and assured retirement—defined benefit plans.

The socially sustainable employer also must recognize the social justice issues in total compensation packages. Barry (2008) suggests that social justice entails addressing all unfair inequalities. Peters (1997) explains that non-egalitarian justice requires that any differences in outcomes must be based on relevant factors, while Dworkin (1981) argues that luck (good or bad) should not impact the distribution of material goods. In the current global economy, it is clear that these conceptions of social justice and just distribution are not followed. CEOs in the United States receive salaries that are hundreds of times what their average employees earn. The gap between the richest and the poorest is larger than it has ever been. Employers across the globe compete in a race to the bottom, chasing low wage labor to further build the already exorbitant shareholder wealth. While we have a long way to go to achieve meeting everyone's basic economic needs, even once we achieve this we will still be far from a just distribution.

Organization Climate

HRM and ER also entail managing the climate of organizations. Again, remember that workers have a right and a need for a psychologically safe working environment, an environment of just working conditions, and a right and need to share their voice—all to develop socially. A socially sustainable HR system will assure workers are safe from harassing and bullying behaviors. At the same time, these systems will also assure workers have a right to voice concerns in terms of the work they do and to have the opportunity to engage with their co-workers.

Workplace bullying and harassment are rampant across the globe. While many countries have taken steps to prevent and eliminate workplace bullying through the legal process, in the United States only harassment based on specific protected statuses is prohibited. Even with these laws in the United States, studies suggest that between 30% and 80% of employees face workplace bullying and harassment (Carbo, 2017). This harassment leads to drastic outcomes for targets—up to and including suicide or homicide. A socially sustainable employer will take steps to eliminate these harassing behaviors from their climate, not because they are required to by law or to avoid legal liability, but because they respect the rights and needs of their employees.

INFORMATION BOX 5.4   THIRTY YEARS OF WORKPLACE HARASSMENT IN THE UNITED STATES

In 2015, the United States Equal Employment Opportunity Commission (EEOC) put together a Select Task Force (STF) to study workplace harassment. EEOC Chair Jenny Yang and Commissioners Lipnic and Feldblum organized this task force due to the recognition that workplace harassment persisted as a major problem in the workplace nearly thirty years after the Supreme Court of the United States (SCOTUS) ruling in *Meritor Savings Bank* made such harassment unlawful. On June 30, 2016, the commissioners released a report based on information collected through the STF, other experts, and their internal studies and data. In addition to finding that harassment continued to be a persistent problem in the United States, the EEOC concluded that the business case for preventing harassment has not been enough to put an end to the problem; that too many times harassment goes unreported; and that retaliation for filing reports of harassment plays a large role in this underreporting. The EEOC recommended changes to organizational training, organizational policies, and organizational culture as part of the solution to these problems. Further, in January 2017, the EEOC put new enforcement guidance on workplace harassment forward for public comment.

Taking steps to prevent and eliminate workplace harassment and to assure civility is a good start, but that does not assure a socially sustainable workplace climate. As Kennedy (2006) and Naughton (2006) have both pointed out, workers also have social needs and work should provide an opportunity for workers to meet these needs. The need for belongingness was recognized by Maslow and the need for affiliation by McClelland. These needs must also be met for an employer to truly be a socially sustainable employer.

Labor Relations

A final area of HRM/ER practices is defined as labor relations. *Labor relations* is the interaction between management and workers, and assesses how workers do or do not engage in concerted activities, including forming or joining labor organizations (unions), and how employers react to these decisions. The process includes the organizing of concerted activity, the negotiations of collective bargaining agreements, and the day to day managing of these agreements. Just like all of the other HRM/ER functions, the labor relations function also directly impacts employee rights. Article 19 of the UDHR, Article 8 of the International Covenant on Economic, Social and Cultural Rights, as well as the core International Labor Organization conventions recognize the human right to form and to join labor organizations (unions) for mutual aid and protection. These conventions recognize the right to engage in concerted activity and to engage in collective bargaining as well as the right to refrain from such activities.

The European Union also recognizes this right in its social charter, and for the most part the companies within the European Union tend to follow suit in recognition of this right. In several European countries, the workers' right to engage in concerted activity and to have a voice in the company is also secured through works councils. In Japan, enterprise unionism is common, and unions are often seen as partners with management with employees following career paths that might take them from one side of the table to the other. However, in the United States, there clearly is a lack of recognition of labor rights as human rights. Employers engage ever harsher anti-union campaigns, push for legislation to limit labor rights, and threaten and fire workers who engage in these labor rights (Brofenbrenner, 2009). Companies that engage in these actions cannot be considered socially sustainable because they are violating the human rights of their workers. However, as will be discussed later in this chapter, this anti-union sentiment and these anti-union actions also have a broader negative impact on what is needed to be a socially sustainable society.

Maintaining Competitiveness

HRM and ER, of course, are expected also to allow companies to be competitive. As discussed in Chapter 4, organizations will need to be profitable to survive and to be able to meet the needs of their workers. Protecting and assuring workers' rights as discussed earlier in this chapter throughout the HRM process should not have a negative impact on the organization's ability to survive. While in some cases, meeting these needs might indeed mean redirecting revenue from within the organization, it does not mean that a company cannot be profitable. Perhaps the share of revenues going towards shareholder wealth and executive salaries and bonuses will need to decrease—in fact, social justice would require such a decrease. However, in all other ways, engaging in these practices will lead to better outcomes for organizations. In a service setting, Heskett and Schlesinger's (1994) service profit chain has long been confirmed. The better employees are treated, the better they will treat customers, and this leads to customers coming back. Catlette and Hadden (Catlette & Hadden, 2001) use the analogy of contented cows and present a compelling case that it is only when employees are treated well that they will provide discretionary effort—the very effort needed for any organization to be successful. While a business case can be made for SSBS practices in HRM, truly socially sustainable employee relations systems do not come from a focus on the potential for firm outcomes, but instead are focused on assuring the rights and needs of workers.

SHRM and Aligning to Sustainable Innovation

Organizational behavior is about predicting and understanding behavior in organizations, but also about changing these behaviors. HRM and ER are often about putting these OB theories into practice. So, beyond simply assuring internal worker rights and needs, HRM and ER can also play a role in directing the behaviors within their organization towards social sustainability. Perhaps most importantly, HRM and ER practices can drive organizations to engage in socially sustainable innovations both internally and externally.

Employees can be motivated and empowered to make their workplaces more socially sustainable. The training and development of employees can include training on environmental safety, waste reduction, process improvements, ergonomics, and workplace safety. Workers can be rewarded for coming up with ways to cut energy use, developing safer methods for work processes, and helping employers to meet socially sustainable goals. Workers will need to be empowered to make changes to their processes, to bring ideas forward, and to take risks that can lead to long-term improvements to social sustainability.

HRM and ER practices should also be used to drive external innovations that can lead to sustainable practices and products. The "creative" destruction of the current system of DAC has largely focused on innovation to increase revenues and profit. As a result, it has led to destruction. However, a different form of creative destruction can indeed spur innovation, creativity, and the improvement of the lives of the majority of members of society. Creative destruction can often be enabled by collaboration and the desire for purpose. The Federal Reserve study provides a direct look at how organizations can indeed drive creative innovations that can lead to socially sustainable practices. This study tells us that when people are driven by a higher purpose and given the autonomy to create, they will do amazing things and come up with amazing solutions. By refocusing on sustainable goals and providing the empowerment that workers need to be creative, organizations can drive the type of groundbreaking solutions Annie Leonard suggests are needed to save our planet, and we suggest are also needed to save the people of our planet. This socially focused creative destruction presents a path towards achieving what Jones refers to as the Green Collar Economy (2008). Only by breaking down the old systems of production and reliance on fossil fuels will we ever be able to achieve good paying, environmentally friendly jobs and to make the environmentally friendly and safe products that Jones envisions. Society should also ask the question, What kinds of skills do we want people to learn and develop further expertise with across time? What kinds of work do people find rewarding? Society then should take steps to make sure that jobs requiring those cherished skills are not eliminated by automation (simply for the sake of efficiency and profit motives). Automation should be reserved for improving human safety and perhaps also for those jobs that most people find boring or meaningless.

Strong Labor Unions

The second prong of our three legged stool is a strong labor movement. As discussed previously, the right to form and join unions is a human right, and for that reason it should be protected. However, a strong labor movement plays an even larger role in assuring socially sustainable systems. There is clear evidence that a strong labor movement, with strong unions, helps to assure many of the human rights of all workers. According to Jake Rosenfeld (Rosenfeld, 2014), "for generations now the labor movement has stood as the most prominent and effective voice for economic justice in the United States." Unfortunately, as labor has lost its power not just in the United States, but also across the globe, the ability to be this voice has also waned. A declining labor movement has led to or contributed to a number of the worst outcomes of the current system of destructive advanced capitalism. Rebuilding a strong labor movement is a necessary part of achieving a socially sustainable economy. The current political environment in the United States will require a change in tactics from labor, as more and more states enact "right to work" laws. There is good evidence that a strong labor movement comes from its members in a bottom-up fashion, rather than through top-down leadership, political dealing, or often seen "business unionism" processes (Carbo, Hargrove, & Haase, 2017).

One of the clear problems under the current system of DAC is that workers are not paid enough to survive. The presence of unions clearly raises the wages for both union workers—known as the union wage premium—and other workers due to the union threat effect or the union spillover effect. This wage premium has ranged from 14% to 30% (Yates, 2009; Rosenfeld, 2014). However, Rosenfeld points out that as the labor movement strength has declined in the United States, the ability of unions to influence the wages of people has dropped by 40% since 1973. In other words, as the labor movement as a whole has weakened, the wages for its members have begun to stagnate and decline. This has also led to the same declining influence over non-member wages—i.e., a weaker union threat effect or spillover effect. The decline in union strength and the decline in union density have been shown to lower the wages of union and non-union workers (Rosenfeld, Denice, & Laird, 2016).

Inequality is another one of the destructive outcomes of the current economic system, and again labor strength plays a clear role in inequality. Wage and wealth inequality is at an all-time high in the United States. As discussed in Chapter 1, inequality across the globe is at shockingly high levels. According to Western and Rosenfeld (2011), the declining union power in the United States has directly caused 20–33% of the increased inequality over the last several decades.

One of the promises of the current system is that the opportunities provided by capitalism will lead to social mobility (in particular upward social mobility). However, the reality is that as inequality has increased and wages stagnated, mobility has also decreased. This declining social mobility is seen in the United States and in much of Europe. Once again, a strong labor movement plays an important role in social mobility. Freeman, Han, Madland, and Duke (2015) found that there is a direct correlation between union density in a region or area and upward class mobility. First, they found that having a parent as a union member had a positive and significant upward effect on a person's wages as an adult. Second, and perhaps even more interestingly, they found that there is a profound spillover effect on mobility as not only was there stronger upward mobility for children of union members in areas of high union density, but also a strong upward mobility for children of non-union members.

Union presence or absence also has an impact on the safety and security of union workers. Lance Compa's Human Rights reports, Unfair Advantage (2000), and Blood, Sweat, and Fear (2004) demonstrate that in the absence of a union, employers will exploit even the safety and well-being of their workers. The Upper Big Branch mining disaster is a clear example of an employer exploiting worker safety in the name of profit. Unions have been found to increase enforcement of the Occupational Safety and Health Act in the United States (Mishel & Walters, 2003) and improve the safety performance in mines (Morantz, 2013). While union workers report more injuries (perhaps as a result of having the protection to feel confident to report injuries), overall their workplaces are safer.

Union workers also enjoy greater economic security. Nearly every collective bargaining agreement (CBA) contains a "just cause" clause. Union workers can be disciplined or terminated only if their employers can show just cause for the discipline. While this is also the standard in many other industrialized countries, where employment at will is the standard as in the United States, it is through organizing and collective bargaining that workers can win due process rights.

A strong labor movement is more likely to assure the human right to a decent retirement. More than 70% of union workers in the United States have pensions, while fewer than 44% of non-union workers do as of the early 2000s (Yates, 2009). Unions decrease the wage gap between white workers and Hispanic workers, white workers and black workers, and male and female workers. Union members are more likely to have all of the benefits discussed earlier as necessary to a dignified life—health care, paid time off, and maternity leave—than are non-union workers.

A strong labor movement also fights for social and economic justice on a large scale. Where we continue to see strong labor movements in the global economy, those countries have lower levels of inequality and lower poverty rates, and are more likely to have universal health care coverage, decent pensions systems, strong social safety nets, and paid time off.

There is no reason that we cannot see a more just economic distribution of the wealth and income in our society. As Yates writes, "Workers make low wages not because the market dictates that this is so but because they are not powerful enough to make their employers pay them more" (2009, p. 42). The same is the case for the upholding of all worker rights—the right to safety, health care, retirement, paid time off, and fairness—none of these are withheld out of some market necessity. They are withheld due to the power of employers to exploit their workforce. A strong labor movement helps to equalize that power differential between workers and management and is a key requirement to achieving socially sustainable employment practices.

Legislation and Strong Enforcement

As James Gross has recognized and made abundantly clear, the United States system of employment laws has simply never really had a human rights focus (2004). However, if we are to move towards socially sustainable business systems, the laws will have to change in the United States and in many other countries. While human rights and the right to dignity are more commonly addressed in employment laws in Europe, Australia, and parts of Asia and South America (and even in the South African Constitution), more must be done nationally and globally to assure the rights of employees under SSBS.

Much like the HRM/ER practices mentioned previously, the employment laws must focus on the human rights and needs of workers. In the United States, we have typically taken a negative rights approach—i.e., the things employees are free from. This includes freedom from discrimination, freedom from harassment based on a protected status, and freedom from unsafe working conditions. However, we have not ever taken a true positive rights approach—what employees should be entitled to. The European Union through its social charter takes such an approach. The very first article of the European Charter of Fundamental Rights states that human dignity is inviolable. It must be respected and protected. The charter goes on to explicitly protect the rights to engage in concerted activity, to form unions, to collectively bargain, to have just conditions of work, to be fairly remunerated, to receive paid time off, to receive maternity leave, to receive medical care, to have just cause in the workplace, to receive education, and many other positive rights that should be viewed as human rights.

The impact of this charter on fundamental freedoms can be seen in member state laws such as the focus on workers' right to dignity in the Moral Harassment Workplace bullying laws in France and Belgium. We also see this positive rights approach play out in the just cause standards applied to termination and discipline in the majority of developed countries. Workers have the right to just cause, to procedural and substantive due process in the workplace, in opposition to the United States model of employment at will, where workers can be fired for any reason with or without notice.

Spitz (2005) has suggested that the countries of North America should adopt the European Union model and develop a North American Charter of Human Rights. We adopt a similar model to Spitz as the route to assuring socially sustainable employment practices, but also expand the role of international agreements and the International Labor Organization.

First, the substance of employment laws must change. As stated earlier, the focus must be on the right to dignity, and there must be recognition that this dignity exists only when the rights enumerated under the UDHR and ICESCR and those described by Maslow, Herzberg, Alderfer, and McClelland are upheld. The laws must first and foremost guarantee the right to work and the right to work that pays a living wage—a wage that is enough to support not only oneself, but one's family in such a way that workers and their families live a dignified life. This right to work and the right to a living wage are recognized under the UDHR and the ICESCR, and have on many occasions been brought forth even in the United States via full employment acts proposed by FDR and Hubert Humphrey.

Workplace safety laws will need to be strengthened to assure that all feasible steps are taken to assure the physical and psychological safety of workers. If work cannot be done safely, perhaps that work should not be done. As Namie and Namie (2009) have stated, work should not hurt—that includes physical and psychological pain. When employers allow workers to be hurt in pursuit of profit, there must be stronger penalties. These penalties should not only include fines, but they should also include criminal charges. When a worker is hurt on the job, they have been assaulted and the employer should be held responsible. When workers are killed on the job, the employer has committed murder. At the very least, when employers allow for avoidable deaths such as those in the Upper Big Branch and Sago Mines, the Deepwater Horizon, or the BP Texas Oil refinery, the executives should receive an economic death penalty, preventing them from ever running a company again and preventing them from putting workers in harm's way. To protect workers' dignity, they must also be protected from psychological harm. Workers should be assured a right to a civil workplace, a workplace free from bullying and harassment of any type, not just the narrow protections from status-based harassment provided in the United States EEO laws.

Employees must also be provided with security. They must be provided assurance that employment decisions are made for good cause. They should be assured that all employment decisions are made in non-discriminatory ways and are made for legitimate business reasons. They should be afforded both substantive and procedural due process. Laws should directly address discrimination in all forms, including the structure of work and working conditions that may have an adverse impact. Further, non–job-related criteria should be banned from use by employers in making employment decisions.

There is also a need to have laws that will protect the economic rights of workers. Minimum wage laws will need to assure a living wage for the worker and their family. There must also be a recognition of the positive right to employment. As Quigley (2003) has argued, there should be a guarantee to a job that pays a living wage. Without this basic guarantee, the most fundamental of human rights of workers are violated. Such economic security also requires access to affordable medical care. Whether this comes through the employment relationship or through national legislation will need to be determined. The economic security of retirees should also be assured. This will require that employers provide access to stable, suitable pensions.

In addition to rights at work, workers also must have legal rights to be away from work. Employees should be assured the legal right to maternity and paternity leave, sick leave, and paid time off for rest and leisure.

The right to form unions, the freedom of association, and the right to engage in concerted activity and collective bargaining have long been recognized as human rights and core labor rights. The laws around the globe must catch up to this reality. In the United States, the laws around these rights must be modified. The current employer right to engage in captive audience speeches against this right should be prohibited. While employers should be free to say what they want, employees should not be required to attend these speeches. There must be a limit on use of strike breakers and permanent replacements that in essence nullify any rights to engage in concerted activity.

While it is clear there is a great need for substantive changes to the employment laws both in the United States and across the globe, there is also a need for changes to the procedures enforcing these laws. The enforcement must change in three ways: the strength of enforcement, the level of global consistency, and the access to a remedy. The penalties for violations of these employment laws must be stronger. Currently, in the United States the most common remedy for a violation of the NLRA is a cease and desist order. This does very little to convince an employer to follow a law they would rather ignore. The penalties must provide a meaningful incentive to assure that employers comply with the law. Employers also must be likely to be caught. Administrative agencies must be employed to do a better job of discovering and remedying violations. We can no longer simply rely upon the self-report or employee actions to address these violations. At the same time, we must take steps to protect these types of employee actions. Workers will need to be afforded better access to a remedial process, whether this is extending administrative remedies and expanding the power of these administrative agencies, or developing labor courts that are much more affordable and timely for aggrieved workers. Finally, there will need to be much more international cooperation and consistency. For instance, when workers are protected in Germany, German MNCs should not be able to race to China to take advantage of a lack of worker rights. This will require a stronger enforcement from the ILO as well as trade agreements. The World Trade Organization (WTO) can also play a role by changing the focus away from assuring and protecting corporate profits to punishing the violation of human rights as an unfair trade practice—this should also be extended to environmental issues and rights.

The Role of Labor in Sustainability

As Van Jones (2008) has pointed out, the labor movement and workers' rights activists have oftentimes been placed at odds with the environmental movement through the creation of a false dichotomy of good jobs or good environmental conditions. By framing the arguments around the current DAC and the jobs within this system, workers are told that if they support the elimination of polluting carbon fuels, this means that coal miners and others in these industries will be left unemployed and without any way to support their families. However, by first implementing methods to guarantee human rights, including the right to decent work, we can destroy this false dichotomy once and for all and turn our collective efforts towards saving and even improving the environment. Workers can be assured work and work at a decent wage, but workers and their representatives should also take steps to assure that the work they do is not harming the planet or the rights of other individuals. Work should not harm communities the way that we have seen work polluting the water and air supplies of communities with toxic chemicals. Work should not harm the environment the way we have seen logging lead to the destruction of forests and mountain top removal lead to the destruction of entire ranges of mountains and the surrounding communities. To truly achieve socially sustainable business systems, labor will need to join with the environmental movement to demand access to green jobs that are safer and cleaner for workers and that end this cycle of destruction under the current system of advanced destructive capitalism. As Van Jones puts it, it is time for a Green Collar Economy.

Achieving Socially Sustainable HRM—A Systems Approach

As we discussed in Chapter 4, the issues of social sustainability have existed for decades if not centuries. While the urgency of many issues, especially environmental issues, has increased over the past several decades, the social issues of worker safety, poverty, exploitation, and alienation from work have been a presence in the American workplace and much of the global workplace for as long as the employment relationship has existed. While Human Resources Management is often considered a newer discipline—replacing the role of the older function of personnel—the reality is that employers have engaged in HRM as a practice, tactic, or function also for as long as the employment relationship has existed. While the turn to strategic HRM led to some hope to address the issues of social sustainability, the outcomes described in Chapters 1 and 2 indicate that SHRM has failed to achieve any type of socially sustainable HRM systems.

So, the question becomes, If voluntary HRM, under our current system, will not achieve socially sustainable results, then how do we move forward? As discussed in Chapter 4, to achieve socially sustainable systems, including a socially sustainable employment relationship, we will need to change the current system. As Meadows (2008, p. 2) explains, "The system to a large extent, causes its own behavior! An outside event may unleash that behavior, but the same outside event applied to a different system is likely to produce a different result." Likewise, the same outside event (or perhaps a similar event) applied to the same system is likely to produce the same result. This is what we see under the current system. When we look at the history of the United States employment system, we see it is consistently far from a sustainable system. In the early industrialization period, we saw that workers toiled in dangerous working conditions, child labor was exploited, and many workers were paid less than a living wage. While there were some shifts under the New Deal era with wage levels increasing, the advent and growth of the middle class, and increasing levels of equality, we can easily see that this was a changed system. The New Deal era ushered in a system that was regulated externally by legislation and strong enforcement of the legislation—the Fair Labor Standards Act, the Wagner Act, the Social Security Act, and eventually the Civil Rights Act. This was a regulated system versus an unregulated system from the earlier era. At the very least, we had changes to the elements of the system.

Interconnections were changed, and various regulations were put in place in the system. For instance, in addition to the new legislation that required more of the "stock" of revenue or profit to be shared with workers (minimum wage and overtime rules under the Fair Labor Standards Act), new tax laws also required employers to pay more money into the federal income tax system, and those who had been receiving the majority of the flows of the stock of revenue had to pay a steep marginal tax rate. This fundamentally changed how the system worked. Further, the prior unmitigated relationship between the employer and employees now had external regulators and growing internal regulators (a growing labor movement as a result of the Wagner Act). At the very least, what we saw during the New Deal era was a number of balancing loops put in place to control the flow of the stock of revenues, but also to control the flow of power between employer and employee.

Unfortunately, during that New Deal era, the overarching goal of the system was still the same. The idea of capitalism continued to be for the owners of capital to make money off the capital they owned. The exploitation of the surplus value of the labor produced by the workers working the capital continued to be a viable way to earn more money. Rather than working within the new constraints built into the system, the owners of capital looked for ways to get rid of the inhibitors—to break down the balancing loops and re-establish an unfettered relationship between worker and employee. Very quickly, there were legislative reactions, such as the passage of the Taft-Hartley Act limiting the power of labor in 1947. There were also reactions directed towards researchers who had helped to usher in the New Deal era, such as Malott's veiled threats towards business schools that would dare teach the economic system as espoused by centrist economists such as Galbraith (Marens, 2008). There were attacks on the interconnections of revenue to taxes as lobbyists began to argue for cuts to taxes by the 1960s.

By the 1980s, Meadows was proven right and the power of the system had in essence led us back to the same types of conditions we had seen in the early period of industrialization in the United States. Regulations had been weakened, labor density had dropped and would continue to drop, the wage levels of workers began to stagnate and would decline for the next 30+ years, and inequality began to rise at times with rapid increases. These types of changes, even though they were considered rather extreme changes, were not enough to change the underlying system, and eventually the changing system prevailed. By 2003, Quigley (2003) reported that the percentage of American workers earning less than a living wage was not much different than the percentage toiling in the mines and mills before the New Deal era. Child labor was not only again alive and well in the United States, but US, Asian, and European MNCs were exploiting and continue to exploit child labor abroad. Hertz reported that worker safety had again taken a back seat, and this was again confirmed by Speiler in 2003 as well as by the tragic accidents at the Upper Big Branch Mine, the Sago Mine, Deepwater Horizon, and the Rana Plaza to name just a few.

If we are to achieve a socially sustainable employment relationship, we must have a fundamental change to the system. In Chapter 4, we suggested a large part of this fundamental change is changing the goals of the system. Harthill presents an example of how changing the goal (or at least focusing on the goal) of the system to one of assuring worker dignity led to the United Kingdom nearly passing a specific bill to protect against workplace bullying and later led to addressing bullying through already existing legislation (Harthill, 2008). This same fundamental change to the view of the goals of the employment relationship has been suggested as a step to eliminating workplace bullying in the United States (Carbo, 2017). In countries such as France, Sweden, and Belgium where dignity of the worker is an explicit goal of the system, anti-bullying laws exist and are strongly enforced (Carbo, 2017). However, this again would appear to be a modifier of the current system rather than a fundamental change. Perhaps as we have suggested in Chapter 4, we must move to an alternative to the current system of capitalism. In Chapter 4, we have called for a system that bestows upon all stakeholders a true ownership role. The German system with works councils presents at least a partially different system.

Wolff presents one model that comes very close to this system. Wolff (2012) argues for a system of Worker Self-Directed Enterprises, where the ownership of capital and the labor that works on the capital would no longer be separated. Unlike some current systems of employee stock ownership, in the case of WSDEs, the employees would have control over the organization. The employees—all employees—would be sole owners and would make decisions collectively. Wolff has argued that this system would be much more sustainable because workers would be less likely to make decisions to pollute their communities, to move jobs overseas, to exploit their co-workers, or to refuse to pay taxes into the systems upon which their families rely for schooling, roads, parks, libraries, and so on. Wolff's model is but one model for a way forward. However, any model must contain the two fundamental pieces of Wolff's WSDEs: no exploitation, and democratic control by all employees (Wolff, 2012, p. 166). The Mondragon in Spain also presents a form of WSDE. We would go a step further and suggest that we must also see some level of democratic control or involvement from all stakeholders—communities, society, and environmental protectors.

Conclusion

The treatment and outcomes of workers play an extremely important role in determining whether or not our system of commerce is socially sustainable or whether the system is destructive. Many of the human rights enumerated in the Universal Declaration of Human Rights relate to the workplace or depend upon the conditions of work. In the United States, many of these rights are not guaranteed through legislation and are not voluntarily provided by employers. American workers often do not earn enough to support themselves, much less their families; they lack even paid time off for maternity and paternity, much less paid time off for vacations; and they often work in unsafe conditions, in tenuous jobs. In the developing world, conditions are often even worse with workers engaged in sweat-shop labor or working under unsafe conditions, and employers exploiting child and slave labor. To move towards truly socially sustainable business systems, we must see a change to these employment practices. While progressive employers adopting and following codes of conduct can play a role, a voluntary path to SSBS has proven to be elusive at best. To achieve truly socially sustainable employment practices, we will need to see strong laws, with strong enforcement. These laws will need to be adopted by nation states, but also must be part of global agreements. A renewed labor movement not just nationally, but internationally, also must play a role in protecting worker rights and pushing for environmentally and socially sustainable jobs and industries.

Discussion Questions

1. Gross suggests that employment laws in the United States have never focused on human rights. Even if he is correct, should employment laws focus on human rights, or would this unnecessarily impede efficiency? How should we balance efficiency, profit, and employees' human rights?
2. As you look at the current business environment, are human rights of workers protected? If not, what specific rights are not protected?
3. Should everyone able and willing to work have a right to a job that pays a living wage? If not, what should the alternative be to such a guarantee? What should happen to those unable to secure employment or unable to meet their basic needs through their employment?
4. If you have taken a human resource management course, think back to the content of this course. How often were human rights discussed in the course? How often was profit or efficiency discussed? Did the course provide the right balance between these two concerns?
5. Consider the quote from Zweig at the beginning of the chapter. What are the specific vulnerabilities that he suggests exist for members of the working class? Do you agree or disagree? Why? What is the evidence to support your position? What is the evidence that is contrary to your position?
6. Consider the quote from Foster at the beginning of the chapter. He suggests that there is a sort of inherent conflict between employer and employee. Do you agree? How would Foster define the conflicting goals of employers and employees? Can these goals be aligned? If so, how?
7. Wolff has suggested that Worker Self-Directed Enterprises would be a path to achieving socially sustainable employment relationships. Can we achieve this level of social sustainability without fundamentally changing the system? Why or why not?

References

Bangladesh Factory Death Toll Soars Past 1,100. (2013, May 11). Retrieved from CBC News: www.cbc.ca/news/world/bangladesh-factory-death-toll-soars-past-1-100-1.1370852

Barry, B. (2008). *Why Social Justice Matters.* Cambridge, UK: Polity Press.

Bilton, R. (2014, December 18). *Apple 'Failing to Protect Chinese Factory Workers'.* Retrieved from BBC News: www.bbc.com/news/business-30532463

Bronfenbrenner, K. (2009). *No Holds Barred: The Intensification of Employer Oppostion to Organizing.* Washington, DC: Economic Policy Institute.

Carbo, J. A. (2017). *Understanding, Defining and Eliminating Workplace Bullying: Assuring Dignity at Work.* London: Routledge.

Carbo, J. A., Hargrove, M. B., & Haase, S. J. (2017, forthcoming). Democracy, militancy and union revitalization the DeMReV model of union renewal: A sustainable, strategic model expanding on Voss and Sherman. In David Lewin and Paul Gollan (Eds.), *Advances in Industrial and Labor Relations.* Bingley, UK: Emerald Books.

Catlette, B., & Hadden, R. (2001). *Contented Cows Give Better Milk: The Plain Truth about Employee Relations and Your Bottom Line.* Germantown, TN: Saltillo Press.

Compa, L. (2000). *Unfair Advantage: Workers' Freedom of Asssociation in the United States Under International Human Rights Standards.* New York: Human Rights Watch.

Compa, L. (2004). *Blood, Sweat, and Fear.* New York: Human Rights Watch.

Compa, L. (2008). Corporate social responsibily and workers rights. *Comparative Labor Law and Policy Journal, 30,* 1–10.

Dworkin, R. (1981). What is equality? Part 2: Equality of resources. *Philosophy and Public Affairs, 10*(4), 283–345.

Foster, W. Z. (1926). *Strike Strategy.* Trade Union Educational League.

Freeman, R., Han, E., Madland, D., & Duke, B. V. (2015). *Bargaining for the American Deam: What Unions Do for Mobility.* Washington, DC: Center for American Progress.

Gross, J. A. (2003). A long overdue beginning. In J. A. Gross (Ed.), *Workers' Rights as Human Rights* (pp. 1–22). Ithaca, NY: Cornell University Press.

Gross, J. A. (2004). Incorporating human rights principles into US Labor Arbitration: A proposal for fundamental change. *Employee Rights and Employment Policy Journal, 8,* 1.

Harthill, S. (2008). Bullying in the workplace: Lessons from the United Kingdom. *Minnesota Journal of International Law, 17,* 247.

Hazardous Child Labour. (2017, January 17). Retrieved from International Labour Organization: www.ilo.org/ipec/facts/WorstFormsofChildLabour/Hazardouschildlabour/lang—en/index.htm

Heskett, J. L., & Schlesinger, L. A. (1994). Putting the service-profit chain to work. *Harvard Business Review, 72*(2), 164–174.

Jones, V. (2008). *The Green Collar Economy: How One Solution Can Fix Our Two Biggest Problems.* New York: HarperOne.

Kennedy, R. G. (2006). Corporations, common goods, and human persons. *Ave Maria Law Review, 4,* 1–32.

Kinicki, A., & Kreitner, R. (2003). *Organizational Behavior: Key Concepts, Skills, & Best Practices.* New York: McGraw Hill Irwin.

Leat, M. (2001). *Exploring Employee Relations.* Oxford and Woburn, MA: Butterworth Heinemann.

Leonard, A. (2010). *The Story of Stuff: How Our Obsession with Stuff Is Trashing the Planet, Our Communities, and Our Health—and a Vision for Change.* New York: Free Press.

Marens, R. (2008). Recovering the past: Reviving the legacy of the early scholars of corporate social responsibility. *Journal of Management History, 14*(1), 55–72.

Meadows, D. H. (2008). *Thinking in Systems*. White River Junction, VT: Chelsea Green Publishing.

Mishel, L., & Walters, M. (2003). *How Unions Help All Workers*. Washington, DC: Economic Policy Institute.

Moody, K. (2014). *In Solidarity*. Chicago: Haymarket Books.

Morantz, A. D. (2013). Coal mine safety: Do unions make a difference. *ILR Review, 66*(1), 88–116.

Morrisey, M. (2016). *The State of American Retirement*. Washington, DC: Economic Policy Institute.

Namie, G., & Namie, R. (2009). *The Bully at Work: What You Can Do to Stop the Hurt and Reclaim Your Dignity on the Job*. Naperville, IL: Sourcebooks, Inc.

Naughton, M. (2006). The corporation as a community of work: Understanding the firm within the catholic social tradition. *Ave Maria Law Review, 4*, 33–75.

Noe, R. A., Hollenbeck, J. R., Gerhart, B., & Wright, P. M. (2007). *Fundamentals of Human Resource Management*. New York: McGraw Hill Higher Education.

Occupational Safety and Health Administration. (n.d.). Retrieved from Department of Labor: www.osha.gov/Publications/safety-health-addvalue.html

Peters, C. J. (1997). Equality revisited. *Harvard Law Review, 110*, 1210–1264.

Quigley, W. P. (2003). *Ending Poverty as We Know It: Guaranteeing a Right to a Job at a Living Wage*. Philadelphia, PA: Temple University Press.

Rosenfeld, J. (2014). *What Unions No Longer Do*. Cambridge, MA and London: Harvard University Press.

Rosenfeld, J., Denice, P., & Laird, J. (2016). *Union Decline Lowers Wages of Nonunion Workers*. Washington, DC: Economic Policy Institute.

Spieler, E. A. (2003). Risks and Rights: The Case for Occupational Safety and Health as a Core Worker Right. In J. A. Gross (Ed.), *Workers' Rights as Human Rights* (pp. 78–117). Ithaca, NY: Cornell University Press.

Spitz, L. (2005). The gift of Enron: An opportunity to talk about capitalism, equality, globalization and the promise of a North-American charter of fundamental rights. *Ohio State Law Journal, 66*, 315–396.

Weil, D. (2014). *The Fissured Workplace: Why Work Became So Bad for So Many and What Can Be Done to Improve It*. Cambridge, MA and London: Harvard University Press.

Western, B., & Rosenfeld, J. (2011). Unions, norms, and the rise in U.S. wage inequality. *American Sociological Review, 76*(4), 513–537.

Wolff, R. (2012). *Democracy at Work: A Cure for Capitalism*. Chicago: Haymarket Books.

Yates, M. D. (2009). *Why Unions Matter* (2nd ed.). New York: Monthly Review Press.

Zweig, M. (2000). *The Working Class Majority*. Ithaca, NY: Cornell University Press.

CASE 5 COSTCO—A SOCIALLY SUSTAINABLE EMPLOYER?

Costco was founded in 1983 by Jim Senegal and Jeffrey Brotman. Since that time, the company has grown to more than $118 billion in annual revenues, more than seven hundred warehouses, and more than 126,000 full-time employees (Yahoo Finance, 2017). Costco also has been extremely profitable with more than $15 billion in gross profit and more than $2 billion in net operating income in 2016 alone. While Costco has been a tremendous success from a financial standpoint, it is perhaps just as well known for its progressive employment practices. Costco is consistently ranked as one of the best employers to work for both within the retail industry and across all rankings.

According to a 2014 survey by Glassdoor, Costco ranks second in terms of employee satisfaction with compensation and benefits. Costco ranked behind only Google and only by fractions of a point, ranking ahead of companies such as Microsoft and Facebook (Cohn, 2014). Costco was also ranked second on Forbes's list of best employers in 2014 (Forbes, n.d.).

Costco takes care of its employees. The company pays a living wage, and the CEO, Craig Jelinek, believes in raising the minimum wage for all workers (Short, 2013). Costco pays its employees an average hourly wage of $11.50 to start. After five years, the average Costco employee earns $19.50 an hour and receives a bonus of more than $2000 every six months (Lutz, 2013). "Hourly workers make an average of more than $20 an hour—well above the national average of $11.39 for a retail sales worker—according to a 2013 Businessweek story" (Taube, 2014). Costco also has a history of taking care of its workers when tough times hit. After the recession of 2008, Costco approved wage increases for workers while their competitors were laying off workers (Short, 2013).

Both full-time and part-time employees are eligible for benefits and on average spend only 12% of their pay for benefits coverage (Lutz, 2013). As a result, 88% of Costco's 185,000 employees partake in company health and welfare benefits (Taube, 2014). Both full- and part-time employees receive health and dental insurance; can participate in a 401(k); and receive paid holidays, vacation, and sick time (Entis, 2014). Costco has also been committed to staying closed on Thanksgiving because it believes its workers deserve the time off to spend with their families (Short, 2013).

Costco is also committed to equity and equality. Costco's CEO, CFO, and even the founder all received base pay less than $1 million in 2016 (Yahoo Finance, 2017). Jelinek, the CEO, makes about 48 times the wage of the average Costco employee, in comparison to Walmart's CEO who earns as much as 796 times the average Walmart worker (Short, 2013). Costco is also committed to inclusion:

> It always has been and continues to be Costco's policy that employees should be able to enjoy a work environment free from all forms of unlawful employment discrimination. All decisions regarding recruiting, hiring, promotion, assignment, training, termination, and other terms and conditions of employment will be made without unlawful discrimination on the basis of race, color, national origin, ancestry, sex, sexual orientation, gender identity or expression, religion, age, pregnancy, disability, work-related injury, covered veteran status, political ideology, genetic information, marital status, or any other factor that the law protects from employment discrimination.
>
> *(Costco, n.d.)*

Costco embraces equality. Costco scored extremely well (90/100) on the Human Rights Campaign's Corporate Equality Index—an assessment of LGBT policies in the workplace (Short, 2013). Costco provides access to its diversity data directly on its website. According to its Type 2 Employer Information Report, 2800 of its 11,271 managers are female, and about 1600 are minorities.

As a result of these pro-employee practices in addition to the financial success, Costco's turnover rate for employees who have been there a year or more is only 5%, an extremely low rate for an industry that averages 66% (Peterson, 2015). Costco also averages $814 in sales per square foot, while Sam's Club makes just $586 per square foot (Lutz, 2013).

Discussion Questions

1. Is Costco a socially sustainable employer? Why or why not?
2. Which goals of the SSBS employment systems are met by Costco? Are there any that are not met? Are there any that are not covered in the case? If so, are you able to find out whether Costco also meets these goals?
3. There have been suggestions that Costco will be under financial pressure to open its doors on Thanksgiving and to be less generous with employees. If so, what does this suggest about the mechanisms for achieving socially sustainable employment systems?

References

Cohn, E. (2014, May 23). *Costco Employees Happier With Pay Than Many in Silicon Valley.* Retrieved January 18, 2017, from Huffington Post: www.huffingtonpost.com/2014/05/23/costco-pay-benefits-glassdoor_n_5375193.html

Costco. (n.d.). *Inclusion.* Retrieved from Costco: www.costco.com/inclusion.html

Entis, L. (2014, May 23). *The 25 Best Companies for Employee Compensation and Benefits.* Retrieved January 18, 2017, from Entrepreneur: www.entrepreneur.com/article/234183

Forbes (n.d.). www.forbes.com/pictures/mlf45ejldl/2-costco-wholesale/?utm_ source=finance.yahoo.com&utm_medium=partner&utm_campaign=full%20 text&partner=yahoo#64b80a912ccd

Lutz, A. (2013, March 6). *Costco Is the Perfect Example of Why the Minimum Wage Should Be Higher.* Retrieved January 8, 2017, from Business Insider: www. businessinsider.com/costco-ceo-supports-minimum-wage-hike-2013-3

Peterson, H. (2015, October 23). *Walmart, Target, and TJ Maxx Are Facing a Worker Crisis.* Retrieved January 18, 2017, from Business Insider: www.businessinsider. com/walmart-target-and-tj-maxx-are-facing-a-worker-crisis-2015-10

Short, K. (2013, November 19). *11 Reasons to Love Costco That Have Nothing to Do with Shopping.* Retrieved January 18, 2017, from Huffington Post—Business: www.huffingtonpost.com/2013/11/19/reasons-love-costco_n_4275774.html

Taube, A. (2014, October 23). *Why Costco Pays Its Retail Employees $20 an Hour.* Retrieved January 18, 2017, from Business Insider: www.businessinsider.com/ costco-pays-retail-employees-20-an-hour-2014-10

Yahoo Finance. (2017, Janaury 18). *Costco Wholesale Profile.* Retrieved from Yahoo Finance: http://finance.yahoo.com/quote/COST/profile?p=COST

6

SUSTAINABLE OPERATIONS MANAGEMENT

In the future, people like me will go to jail.

Ray Anderson, Interface (Kinkead & Gunn, 1999)

Introduction: What Is Operations Management?

There are functional and support areas of business, all of which contribute to the success of the firm. Functional areas include marketing, operations, and finance and accounting. Marketing deals with generating and manipulating demand through the classic four p's of marketing: product, placement, price, and promotion. Finance and accounting deal with cash flow, investment, and information for external and internal stakeholders. Operations management is concerned quite simply with the *fulfillment of demand*. Support areas include those disciplines that affect all of the functional areas, viz. human resources and Information Systems. Every functional area needs the right people and effective Information Technology, and support areas are as important as the functional areas. Everyone has a job to do, and only by people getting very good at their job and doing it their best can the firm be successful in its mission.

Every product that is demanded is either a good or a service, or a mix of the two. Goods and services have some distinguishing characteristics. Starting with goods, they are those products that are tangible, can be inventoried, have well-defined quality conformance standards, and require less interaction with the customer. On the other hand, a service is a product that is intangible, cannot be inventoried, has specific quality standards that are often difficult to measure, and requires a high degree of interaction with the customer. A frozen pizza or a textbook are good examples of goods, whereas an accounting tax return preparation or a haircut are some examples of services. That all said, most products are a mix of the two extremes of "pure good" and "pure service." When you buy a car, you are purchasing not only the physical automobile, but also a spare parts network, customer service, and a warranty. When you get your taxes done, your accountant likely provides some tangible copies, files, and other physical material to you. Generally, products are often thought of as on a continuum where pure good is on one side, pure service is on the other, and products occupy various positions between them. This easy to visualize line with two extremes and products as dots between them reminds us that we need to consider both the good as well as the service part of the product. Where goods are produced in factories and move though a distribution network, services are often provided close to the customer (the aforementioned examples of accounting and haircut coming to mind), since the product cannot be transported or inventoried. Sometimes, the customer is willing and must travel to where the service is provided, with Walt Disney World coming to mind. For us, it does not matter whether we discuss goods or services, and we must discuss both, for each of these can be produced and delivered in a more sustainable and socially responsible manner.

To fulfill the demand, we must as managers make many decisions regarding the question of how it is best to fulfill the demand. First, we can decide on the design of the product, where collaboration with marketing, as well as every functional and support area inside the firm if done best, is essential. Demand must also be forecasted, since most if not all of our decisions depend on the amount of demand we will have to fulfill, and this is another clear interface with the marketing discipline. Next, location decisions present themselves, and we must decide on where to locate factories and distribution centers. Closely linked to this is the decision on capacity for each facility and transportation system connecting the facilities. Quality control systems are designed through qualitative methods (voice of the customer from six sigma) as well as quantitative ones (statistical process control). The layouts and process technology inside the facilities are examined and decided upon, something changeable only in the long term, so these decisions have far-reaching impact on cost and our ability to fulfill demand. The design of jobs themselves, measuring performance, and attempting to align incentives are very important inside our setting, and interfacing with human resource professionals is advantageous and highly recommended if not utterly inevitable. Scheduling personnel is also an important decision, one that affects their quality of life, as does the design of their job. Lastly, the planning of how much to order, produce, store, and move are the classic decisions in this field. Just in Time and Toyota Production Systems, it must be noted, always emphasized treating workers as knowledge workers and providing good salaries, working conditions, and benefits. For each of these decisions, we can consider how not only cost is affected but also environmental impact and social responsibility.

And operations management is costly, as is easy to see on any financial statement. The cost of revenue includes the costs of goods sold as well as costs of marketing. In most firms dealing with goods, the cost of goods sold is the major component of the cost of revenue. In services, the costs of providing that service (mostly labor and benefits) is often called the cost of service, which in those organizations is mostly the majority of the cost of revenue. Cost of revenue itself often represents the majority of the total revenue the firm takes in, leaving the gross profit after being subtracted. Easy examples to find include Walmart, Apple, and Disney. That the cost of fulfilling demand represents a majority of the cost, a measurement of economic effort, alludes to the fact that it is of prime importance in building and running environmentally sustainable and socially responsible enterprises.

The Triple Bottom Line and Operations Management

Until recently, our field was predominately concerned with minimizing costs and thereby maximizing profits. Under a triple bottom line, we must consider people and planet alongside profit when making decisions (see e.g., Souza (2012)). This is made difficult because while in some cases we may be able to improve all three metrics, it is more often the case that a decision will improve some goals, but other goals will be adversely affected. It must also be said that aggregating the people and planet metrics is difficult, since each of them has various dimensions. In looking out for the planet, we would seek to, among other things, reduce water and energy uses and stack emissions. For people, we would need metrics for both the workers as well as the communities in which we operate. Though it will never be easy to arrive at a perfect solution balancing people, profit, and planet, we should always be thinking that we have an ethical responsibility and, even though we may never be able to say that we are perfect, that incremental improvements are fine in this journey. In those cases where there are improvements to all three metrics, these can be enjoyed as long as it does not preclude more effort to improve the system once these easy decisions are made. In the next sections, we will examine some ways that we can be more efficient, sustainable, and responsible in the fulfillment of demand.

Design of Goods and Services

It may not be immediately apparent how important the product design is to sustainability and responsibility, though it should be. In terms of costs that will be incurred in the production of a product, say a computer, when we design the product we are making decisions implicitly on materials, technology, and processes. One design might allow for different materials and steps in the manufacturing process. So, while early in the life cycle of a product, as the product is being designed, it is not as if we need to pay the majority of the costs to produce all of the product we will produce over the entire life cycle; however, we are making decisions that will inevitably lead to those costs and in this manner we must be very careful at this stage. Expanding this thought to the triple bottom line, it becomes apparent that as we are designing the product, we are making decisions that affect the people and the planet well into the future, so if we are to fulfill demand in a sustainable and responsible manner, we are to start here.

First, we must remember that we should be designing a product with its end of life in mind. Here, we may be able to recover the product (discussed in more detail later under "Product Recovery Management") and thereby decrease the environmental impact of the product. It is easier to recycle products when there are less types of material in the product, so this should be kept in mind, although it has the potential to trade-off with cost.

Next, the materials we use should generally be selected with environmental impact and social responsibility in mind. Materials that are often the result of slavery, child labor, and the like should be considered to be substituted by material that is more responsible. Less sustainable material is substituted by more environmentally sustainable material. Of course, material *known* to be the result of child labor, slave labor, and the like should never be touched under any condition. (See also the Chapter 11 Case for possible ways to make these kinds of information available (transparently) to consumers (e.g., the "Reveal" system).)

Another interesting point is the size of the box for the product, and its impact on environmental metrics, specifically greenhouse gas emissions. A consultant once asked his client about the size of the box for its product, a toy. The box was oversized, so much of it was empty, perhaps to give the appearance that the product was larger than it was. Some defended the box's size saying that the transportation cost (freight) of the boxes was affected only by weight, not volume, so it made no difference if the boxes had a larger volume. The consultant convincingly countered that freight rates were set based on a certain "profile" (typical mix of packages that they handle), and that in the end, the freight rates were set accounting for empty air that was being transported. Make the box more efficient, he suggested, and this will lead (albeit with some lag) to lower freight rates. In exactly the same manner, we can argue that environmental impact and even social responsibility can be affected even by something as seemingly trivial as a box.

Processes themselves vary greatly in cost, environmental impact, and social responsibility issues such as worker safety and community impact. So once again, rather than merely juxtaposing costs, we must consider people and planet alongside profit. Here it is worthwhile to mention that as we will see in more detail later, making your product *able* to be recycled is one good thing, but actually incorporating recycled material to substitute for virgin material, thereby "closing the loop," is much better. All of this must be carefully considered when designing the product.

For an interesting glimpse into metrics for environmentally sustainable manufacturing, see the OECD's green manufacturing indicators (www.oecd.org/innovation/green/toolkit/oecdsustainablemanufacturingindicators.htm).

Product Recovery Management

Product recovery management deals with products that are at the end of their *use* or the end of their *life*. A product that is at the end of its use, e.g., a leased photocopier, might be sold to another customer, whereas a product at the end of its life would be otherwise destined for the landfill. Product recovery management is concerned with the return, the *reverse logistics*, of the products back to a factory where some of the value might be retained and environmental impact might be mitigated (in terms of substituted virgin material as well as foregone landfill space) through one process or another.

There are several process options, called *disposition decisions*—the most commonly known and an easy place to start is (material) recycling. In recycling, we take material, such as a certain plastic, gained from many different products, and through a physical transformation via production processes make it into some other product having the same material. There are pros and cons to this. Where material recycling saves landfill space and reduces virgin material use, and is relatively commonplace today, recycling requires energy to transform aluminum cans into a bird bath, for example, so while it is a good option for a lot of things, it is by no means always preferable. The reality is that, among the options, it is usually fairly low in preference, with the only lower options including landfilling or "heat recycling" where the material is simply burned for heat and the heat is "recycled."

Other options include *repair* where products are simply fixed to correct what caused them to cease function and then sold to, e.g., a secondary market, or *refurbishing* where products are not just repaired, but critical elements examined, leading to a product that has a "specified" quality, though it is less than "good as new" and is also typically sold in a secondary market.

Remanufacturing is arguably the most interesting product recovery option for a couple of reasons. In remanufacturing, products are taken apart and the parts are inspected to "good as new" quality standards. The bad parts are recycled, while the good parts can be reassembled into a remanufactured product meeting the same quality standards as a new product at a fraction of the price and saving landfill space and substituting for virgin material. In remanufacturing, it can also be mentioned that not only material from the returned products is saved, but also some of the value added in manufacturing such as the energy used to manufacture the part. On the social side, there are also potential benefits. First, this typically occurs relatively decentrally due to the lack of economies of scale and substantial transportation costs, suggesting that many communities would benefit from jobs. Second, these jobs tend to be higher skilled because the remanufacturers must learn to deal with many (model years of) products and exhibit good judgment on whether a part can be saved or whether it should be recycled. This lends itself to good wages, hopefully living wages, and jobs with benefits in keeping with our responsibility towards human rights. Not all products can or should be remanufactured, but for those that can, it could represent a very advantageous option, allowing for good profit, low environmental impact, and very good social responsibility.

Another novel option is *repurposing* where materials used for one product (such as tires or storage containers) are put into service for some other product (e.g., home construction). Other examples of repurposing include materials for works of art (http://m.huffpost.com/us/entry/12990094). All of these ideas can be part of the theme "Reduce, Reuse, Recycle" in that order, to improve overall environmental sustainability.

Even if goods cannot serve any useful purpose, they should still be required to be taken back and disposed of in an appropriately environmentally friendly manner. Consider the end of life vehicle ordinance in the European Union that requires manufacturers to take back and dispose of in an appropriate manner any vehicle that they have manufactured at any point in time when the consumer returns it. Before this legislation, cars that had no useful life or value were left in wooded areas or simply on streets after having their license plates removed. After this ordinance was enacted, manufacturers put systems in place to recover and dispose of cars (using a mix of disposition options from this chapter) and a fixed charge was added to each new car sold to offset the costs of this. It must also be mentioned that a system like this will incentivize manufacturers to design the product in such a way that hazardous materials are truly avoided since in the end the manufacturer will have to deal with the waste. Naturally, this enhanced product responsibility must be as broadly applied as possible to prevent responsible firms from being made uncompetitive when compared with other firms that are not held responsible.

Location and Layout

Location decisions typically involve where to locate various production and logistics facilities. Capacity of facilities and the number of facilities are related decisions in that we may want one facility with enough capacity for all of the demand, or two facilities each capable of half of the demand. Given a certain configuration, costs (fixed and variable production costs as well as transportation costs) are usually computed to arrive at an optimal result, given all of the information was correct, in practice almost never the case, but still a good guide on the network configuration.

This cost orientation must be augmented by people and planet indicators and concerns. Once again, there may be cases where all three indicators of people, profit, and planet might be collectively advantageously affected, but in many others, trade-offs will exist. A few words on some specifics follow. Some authors would suggest you avoid areas that are "pro union" or employ measures called "union avoidance tactics." We eschew this entire branch. We believe that the right to unionize is a basic human right stemming from the right to associate, and this right cannot be taken away from anyone. In any case, unions typically provide quality work, done safely, and so decrease uncertainty that makes operations difficult. Unions also facilitate the human rights of workers, specifically living wages that also reduce problems of income inequality, vacation, health insurance, and retirement benefits, all of which are accepted human rights. The world will indeed be a better place when these rights are universally mandated, allowing us to compete based on productivity rather than who is willing to sacrifice their needs the most. Profit is important and necessary for business, but it may never be allowed to dominate environmental and social concerns. In the end, the profit is good only if it also brings about benefits for the environment and society.

Job Design and Performance Measurement

We are also responsible for our workers in that we design their jobs and we divide total tasks among jobs that get assigned to people. Giving some (or a lot of) thought to how the design will affect the happiness and productivity of the workers is essential. Here, the terms *job enrichment* and *employee empowerment* come into play.

Job enrichment deals generally with the idea that rather than assign a small task to a worker to do thousands of times each shift, broaden their responsibilities and allow them to do a larger portion of the surrounding tasks. The classic example compares two factories producing cars, the first in assembly line fashion with workers performing one monotonous task for hours on end (albeit efficiently due to learning curve effects on a small assignment) versus a factory where teams of individuals work on a single car from start to finish. Naturally, the workers in the second factory can be presumed to have a much higher job satisfaction and happiness and achievement. While such a factory may not be immediately as cost effective at producing cars, some might suggest that a learning curve for the team building approach, though steep at first, might prove optimal in the long term.

Job enrichment and job enlargement are not the same. Where the former gives employees higher levels of tasks, the latter would merely give the employee more tasks on the same level. Job enrichment seeks to remove typically dissatisfying mundane, repetitive tasks, leaving employees to turn their attention to higher order tasks that will allow them to better utilize their skills. Typically, people prefer to use more of their skills, and this has generally a positive effect on job satisfaction and job performance. Job enlargement merely, as Frederick Herzberg put it, "enlarges the meaninglessness of the job" by giving workers higher goals to increase the challenge of the job. We should be careful not to confuse the two, which might appear similar at first but have a profound difference. The work of Herzberg on how to motivate employees remains very relevant here and is a worthwhile, classic read.

Employee empowerment is when we push decision-making authority down, allowing our people (supervisors, workers, etc.) to make decisions traditionally reserved for higher personnel. Before employee empowerment, if a worker saw an unsafe condition, he or she might have been forced to seek a supervisor before taking any action. Empowering employees generally increases not only their job satisfaction but also their self-esteem. It would also otherwise, even not considering that, be an advisable practice in that it has been shown to be much more efficient than more "command and control" environments. To do this, you teach some of your tasks (admittedly not the most critical ones, but typically routine ones) to your direct reports, by taking time to describe the decision, the impact factors, the trade-offs, the objective, and generally how you make that decision. Once this is done, you simply allow them to decide these for themselves without your involvement, though you might look over their shoulder the first time. In time, they will learn and mimic your decisions more and more. They will doubtlessly make mistakes, when they decide other than you would have decided, but these instances are typically minimal and easily compensated for by the fact that you can look for more potent uses of your time and you should look for higher level issues that will impact operations.

Conclusion

As we have seen, operations management is concerned with fulfilling demand for goods and services. The operations management function is usually the most costly function in an organization, and so we are not surprised that it has a large impact on social responsibility and environmental sustainability. Social sustainability demands that all operations management decisions consider social and environmental metrics. This starts with the design of the product, and the selection of materials and processes to make and move the product. Location, capacity, and layout decisions that result in a manufacturing and distribution network must likewise consider all three p's of People, Planet, and Profit. Product recovery systems have done a great job at reducing environmental impact and have the potential to generate socially beneficial jobs that require skilled workers and more usually occur decentrally. Job design would have us consider employee empowerment, hopefully leading towards happier, more fulfilled workers.

Discussion Questions

1. Do you agree that operations management, since it is usually the most costly function of an enterprise, has a large potential to contribute to socially sustainable business systems?
2. Imagine measuring "environmental impact" as we might costs. What are different factors in being environmentally sustainable? How can we aggregate this into a single metric? Is it possible to combine into a single metric at all?
3. Imagine measuring "social responsibility" in a similar manner to costs. What are different factors under social responsibility? Can we aggregate this into a single metric? If so, how? If not, how can we measure and therefore manage our social responsibility?

References

Herzberg, F. (1987). One more time: How do you motivate employees? *Harvard Business Review, 65*(5), 46–57.

Kinkead, G., & Gunn, E. P. (1999, May 24). In the future, people like me will go to jail: Ray Anderson is on a mission to clean up American businesses—starting with his own. *Fortune.*

Souza, G. C. (2012). *Sustainable Operations and Closed-Loop Supply Chains.* Chicago: Business Expert Press.

CASE 6 INTERFACE

Interface, Inc. has manufactured carpeting since the 1970s. For the first two decades, it operated in a traditional manner, converting petroleum products into carpeting that was sold to customers. With the advent of servitization and the prevalence of leasing, Interface became involved with the removal and disposal of old carpeting. If one were to examine its business model from a bird's eye perspective, one would see oil being extracted from the Earth, it being refined and used in an industrial process to manufacture carpet, the carpet being installed and used by the customer, and after use the carpet being removed, sent to a landfill, then replaced by new carpeting. This process would repeat every time carpeting was replaced, taking oil from the ground and putting old carpet into the ground. Like a button that for every time it is pressed results in harm to the environment, this system remained unchecked until Ray Anderson, the CEO of Interface (and the case study also for the leadership chapter), courageously changed it (Mission Zero, 2017).

In 1994, Ray Anderson went through an epiphany when he famously exclaimed while looking at a truck returning with used carpeting that was about to be landfilled that someday the people responsible (those who profit) for this environmental damage will be "sent to jail." He then championed the idea that Interface should aim to change its business model from the traditional "take-make-waste" to a sustainable "take nothing—do no harm" model where the company takes from the environment only what can be naturally replenished and has zero landfill waste.

Championed by Anderson, this idea resulted in the entire reengineering of the value chain. The production and manufacturing processes were changed to use as much recovered carpeting as possible, decreasing virgin material use and needed landfill space, and providing a "sink" for recovered material. The leasing process was changed to capture more product from the sphere of the consumer, ensuring that valuable material was recovered for reuse. This is an example of *material mortgage* where the consumer is seen to mortgage material rather than own it, and the manufacturer expects to recover material and has in many cases designed the product using more durable, recoverable material that can decrease the environmental burden of manufacturing the product. The very design of the product itself was changed to allow for more environmentally benign manufacture, recovery, and reuse.

According to a report by the Natural Step (2013), a framework of methodologies to facilitate sustainability and one used by Interface, the changes have resulted in reducing:

- landfill use by approximately 85%;
- virgin material use by roughly 50%;

- energy use by factories by about 40%; and
- greenhouse gas emissions by approximately 40%.

Of course, these reductions also result in substantial cost reduction, saving the company $450 million since the start of initiatives. While these cost reductions are advantageous, we remind ourselves that the true benefit of this was the immense reduction in environmental burden that was achieved by redesigning the process with the goal of taking nothing and doing no harm.

Discussion Questions

1. Is Interface socially sustainable or merely environmentally sustainable? What are some indications to support your opinion?
2. Given that the changes resulted in cost savings, is this not merely maximizing profit and minimizing cost as done before any considerations of sustainability?
3. If the changes did not result in cost savings, should the changes have had to be made?

References

Mission Zero. (2017). Interface. Retrieved from www.interface.com/US/en-US/about/mission?_ga=1.177618278.297804319.1486064153 (accessed January 30, 2017).
The Natural Step. (2013). *Interface: The Journey of a Lifetime.* White paper.

7

SUSTAINABLE SUPPLY CHAINS

Creating a strong business and building a better world are not conflicting
goals—they are both essential ingredients for long-term success.

William Clay Ford Jr., Executive Chairman, Ford Motor Company
(Ford Company 2009/10 Blueprint for Sustainability: The Future at Work)

Introduction: What Is a Supply Chain?

Supply chain management extends operations management in the following manner. Most demand for goods and services is fulfilled by a chain of firms from a
manufacturer, to a distributor, to a retailer, ending up at the traditional last "partner" in the supply chain, the consumer. Examining a can of one's favorite beverage,
one can imagine the "trip" the can (and that which is inside of it) has been on.
Starting with raw material ingredients such as malt, yeast, hops, and water, not to
mention cans, a factory transforms these inputs into palletized cases of beer. These
pallets form full truckloads for the trip from the factory to the distributor. The
distributor in turn takes these pallets of beer and fulfills orders from retailers for
the beer, orders that are mixed from various pallets. The retailer receives a ship-
ment of several amounts of cases for each type of beer. Lastly, the customer selects
from the retailer the quantity and type of beer. In this manner, each partner in the
supply chain has their role to fulfill, and supply chain management merely seeks
to fulfill the demand along this chain in the most (cost) efficient manner possible.

Figure 7.1 provides an illustration of an actual supply chain where several
suppliers provide inputs to two factories, which in turn supply products to whole-
salers and distributors, finally arriving at retailers where it can be purchased by a
consumer. We use certain terminology, and it becomes advantageous to introduce
upstream and *downstream*. Upstream is away from the customer, while downstream

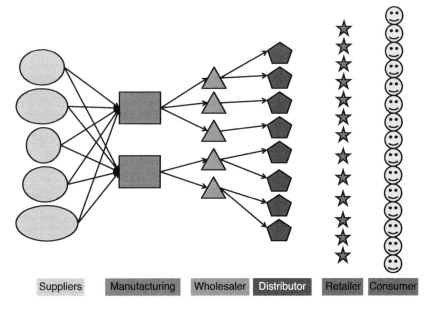

| Suppliers | Manufacturing | Wholesaler | Distributor | Retailer | Consumer |

FIGURE 7.1 An Actual Supply Chain With Names Deleted

is towards the customer. So, we say that the suppliers are upstream of the factory but the distributors are downstream of the factory. We also refer to the "levels" as *echelons*. So, the diagram would be said to have six echelons in the supply chain from the suppliers to the consumers.

Before the dawn of the field of supply chain management, it was being done, but being done in what we call an isolated fashion. Each partner decided on the amount to order from its upstream supply chain partners, and also on the price to sell to its next downstream supply chain partner. Each partner made a profit (typically invisible to other partners) depending on its costs and revenue—of course, revenue is influenced by the price. Each partner tried to maximize its profit, its individual profit. One can note that the sum of all of the revenue that the supply chain will see for the fulfillment of the demand is the price that the customer pays for it at the retailer. All other costs (the price of the product the retailer buys from the distributor, or the price the factory sells to the distributor for) merely carve up the revenue gained by the sale of the product to the customer. All other costs and prices simply allocate the revenue gained from the consumer.

Supply Chain Coordination

The true new contribution of the field of supply chain management comes from what we now do and what we now know better than how supply chains were run in the isolated fashion of the past. If one thinks of the isolated (or uncoordinated) supply

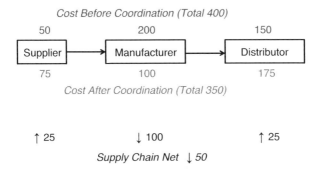

FIGURE 7.2 An Example of Supply Chain Coordination

chain, each partner had costs and revenues that led to profits. Each had information that it typically did not share with its partners, for one reason or another.

One can easily imagine that the true optimal solution, the best way to run the system, is to imagine if the entire supply chain was operated as one large profit-maximizing firm. These different divisions might share information more freely and make decisions that are optimal for the whole, rather than optimal for their single echelon. This is what is referred to as *supply chain coordination*, and it represents the novel, unique, and useful contribution of the field. Let's show an example to see if we can convince ourselves that it is useful.

Figure 7.2 contains a three-echelon supply chain of supplier, manufacturer, and distributor. At the top of the diagram, cost before coordination is given. As we can see, each echelon or partner has some costs. We ignore the revenue in this example under the assumption that the demand and the retail price are exogenous and outside our control, so we simply seek to minimize costs in this example, a very common (though by no means exclusive) assumption in the field.

As we can see, the supplier, manufacturer, and distributor incurred costs of 50, 200, and 150, respectively, for a total of 400. In coordinating the supply chain, the partners share information and make *globally* optimal decisions to maximize the *supply chain profit*, the revenue gained from the consumers minus the costs for all the echelons. Information sharing among the partners leads them to make better decisions. This is far from academic, and there are many examples of retailer point-of-sale data being immediately visible by the supply chain, leading to faster changes to unpredictable demand patterns. Making better decisions is the second effect of coordination, and this leads to decisions that will maximize the supply chain profit. Perhaps the retailer orders more product than it normally would because of holding costs, but this leads to higher product availability and better scale economies upstream in the supply chain. In the diagram, we can see the cost after coordination in the middle, and the net changes at the bottom. As we can see, although the supplier's and the distributor's costs have increased, the manufacturer's costs have decreased, and the sum of the costs has decreased.

This decrease in supply chain costs of 50 leads to a corresponding increase in the supply chain profit, but one can see that not all partners individually experience an increase in profit. Rather, some partners accept a disadvantageous increase in their isolated costs, and this potentiates the increase in other supply chain partner profits. There is a net positive effect, but for the individual firms, some experience positive effects while others make decisions that increase their isolated cost. Unless there is some method to compensate those who lose, there will be no sharing of information or mutual decision making that leads to optimal decisions for the supply chain as a whole. Supply chain *coordination mechanisms* are the ways that partners who gained from coordination compensate those whose costs had increased. This can take several forms, from periodic lump sum payments between partners to adjusting the prices that the partners sell and buy from each other. This coordinated supply chain does the best job at fulfilling the demand. In the next section, we will see what these basic lessons on supply chain management teach us about achieving sustainable and responsible supply chains.

Sustainable and Responsible Supply Chains

In the previous section, we learned the basics of supply chain management and the quintessential revelations of the field: that demand is satisfied by a chain of several firms, that the total costs of all of the members should be minimized, not only the individual echelons independently, and that this will bring about the most efficient solution. When we think about how to extend this idea that is focused exclusively on profit and cost to a socially sustainable business system where environmental sustainability and social responsibility are essential, we think about the triple bottom line of profit, planet, and people. In the previous section, we spoke only of costs and profit, a clear orientation on the first p. When considering all three, we would see an example where we are looking at not one number per supply chain echelon but three or more. Cost and profit are seen at each echelon, but also environmental impact and social responsibility (see e.g., Souza (2012)). Generally, we would seek to minimize cost or maximize profit, minimize environmental impact, and maximize social responsibility *along the entire chain*. Once again, we would argue that the latter two are essential, and profit should not be acceptable if the system is not environmentally sustainable or socially responsible.

When considering costs in a supply chain, it made no sense if one partner saved some money by ordering in a way that decreased its costs while increasing even more the upstream partner's cost. In the end, the sum of the costs along the supply chain were what counted. In an analogous manner here, we would orient our decision making not at individual firms but at the chain as a whole. It does us no good if some parts of the supply chain are "green" and "friendly" while other parts of the supply chain are "dirty" and irresponsible. In the end, the environmental and social performance of the supply chain should be optimized in the same manner in which we attempt to optimize costs and profits.

Of course, where theory seems straightforward, issues become complicated when applied in practice. This is because of several reasons. Real supply chains have many echelons, and multiple tiers of suppliers; first tier suppliers supply the manufacturer directly, where second tier suppliers supply first tier suppliers, and so on. This makes the supply chain look more like a "network" than a chain, while in this field we make no such distinction and refer to it as a supply chain, knowing that some are unwieldy and look like networks. Next, these supply chains are more and more geographically dispersed due to globalization. It is much more difficult to ascertain information and audit a supply chain partner through a physical visit when the partner is on the other side of the world. Lastly, Information Systems, absolutely crucial to global sustainable supply chains, must be able to capture accurately and transmit this information to all other parts of the supply chain. But the largest complicating factor is this: where the previous complications were present even just looking at one metric, e.g., cost or profit, we now must gather many more metrics (necessitating collaboration with MIS and HR professionals) to capture people and planet. And even worse, while sometimes we can make decisions where all three will be positively affected, in many cases there are trade-offs (where we better some objectives but adversely impact others) between the three metrics, exacerbated by the fact that these trade-offs exist throughout the complicated, geographically dispersed supply chain. We must keep in mind that although this is a daunting, seemingly impossible task to optimize the triple bottom line of a supply chain, we still have an ethical duty to do what we can, and incremental improvements are good steps in the right direction. Consumption of the low-hanging fruit, where all three are fortuitously affected, is fine as long as it never precludes making the more difficult decisions and seeking greater improvements that are more challenging.

As we have seen, sustainable and responsible supply chain management requires tracking environmental sustainability and social responsibility metrics alongside others up and down the supply chain. These metrics must be incorporated into decision making in a similar manner as cost and profit metrics assisted in supply chain decisions. This requires us to examine upstream and downstream partners, and this partner selection, evaluation, and relationship development provides arguably the best mechanism to bring about effective supply chain management. We will discuss this at length shortly; but first we will briefly spend some attention on other cases.

Taking the supply chain partners as given, or previously decided upon, the next step would involve supply chain coordination extended for the triple bottom line in an attempt to optimize (this term is used loosely here, as while a single mathematically optimal solution might exist in single goals, in multiple goals this is unlikely and the term is used more holistically) the supply chain. Here, the emphasis on the need for excellent management Information Systems cannot be understated. A good Information System would capture data along the supply chain comprehensively (from each partner, for each metric) and allow for what-if analysis that would help identify and exploit ways to make the supply chain more sustainable. The system would have to be scalable and able to be introduced in facilities spread over the globe.

Now, we return to situations where we do not take the partner selection as given, and can choose partners who are more sustainable and monitor their performance to motivate the partner to improve. Basically, this is an area known traditionally as *supplier selection* (a manufacturer's suppliers), but it takes on new complexity with sustainability as well as the knowledge that *downstream* partners (who would be a manufacturer's "customers") should also be evaluated in this manner.

It is helpful here to remind us of a few simple facts. First, a sustainable product will require a sustainable supply chain upstream and downstream. The manufacturer and suppliers can be very sustainable, but if downstream distribution and retailers exploit workers and disadvantageously affect the environment, obviously they are not. In the end, the entire chain must inarguably be considered. But, of course, traditionally we have not seen firms exercise control over downstream partners. This is likely due to the fact that the firm would not want to discriminate against "customers" by, e.g., selling to one retailer but not to another, in that it would not matter to do so because the revenue from the customer was what guided a decision to sell to them or not. That said, there have been cases where firms (e.g., the Snapper/Walmart case) have actually "fired a customer." In the Snapper case, its CEO famously traveled to Bentonville, Arkansas, headquarters of Walmart, to deliver the decision personally. With price concessions demanded by Walmart from its suppliers every year, Snapper foresaw a time when it would have to offshore production to manufacture to a target price. It also saw a better fit with smaller hardware stores that would be in a position to offer service to a premium brand of durable lawn mowers.

We now propose that all supply chain partners should be evaluated based on socially sustainable business system metrics and that these metrics should be used to select, terminate, evaluate, and develop partners. On a practical note, it must be seen that it would be virtually impossible in some cases to track the product along the entire supply chain, for the mere fact that the upstream supply side could be very lengthy, even containing circular influences (where a supplier of an input to our product also purchases our product for use in production somehow). In such cases, a standardized manner to limit the supply chain (e.g., only the first three tiers of suppliers must be included) complexity will enable data to be captured and metrics developed.

A good introduction to this topic and its practical ramifications can be found at the United Nations Global Compact website (http://supply-chain.unglobal compact.org/). The site includes resources and tools that can be used as well as case studies that illustrate application, impressively broken down by region and industry. One can see that it is interested in environmental impact as well as social responsibility.

The responsible sourcing tool (www.responsiblesourcingtool.org/) is exclusively concerned with human rights and worker protection. The tool is invaluable in several ways. First, it allows a company to understand and visualize its risk given the industry and country from which it sources inputs. This will enable analysts and executives alike to identify areas that should be adequately scrutinized, if not avoided entirely. Second, a key section on responsible recruiting, worker protection policies, and compliance monitoring provides a good glimpse into some of the shadier areas of global supply chains. Lastly, case studies are provided, broken down by country and industry, and a very detailed view into the supply chain for seafood is afforded.

Moving from the most general to the most specific, Ceres's supplier self-assessment questionnaire (www.ceres.org/resources/reports/supplier-self-assessment-questionnaire-saq-building-the-foundation-for-sustainable-supply-chains) provides a comprehensive list of questions and data that can adequately assess a supplier's environmental sustainability and social responsibility. The quality of this questionnaire is exceptional and comprehensive. In addition to environmental metrics that include air, water, waste, pollution, and transportation, social metrics include hours of work, compensation, health and safety, forced and underage workers, abuse and harassment, and workers' governance protections. While one can imagine other questionnaires being used, this is a perfect example of where we must be heading, towards a world where these questionnaires are used to ensure that entire supply chains, which fulfill consumer demand, act in an environmentally friendly and socially responsible manner.

Firms such as Ecovadis (www.ecovadis.com/) provide supplier assessments that take into account both people and processes (including environmental impact) and can be used by buyers to gather intelligence on potential supply chain partners or by suppliers to obtain a differentiating or qualifying criteria for future (continuing or not) business.

INFORMATION BOX 7.1   THE WAY FORWARD

The way forward must surely ensure that products are produced in an environmentally friendly, socially responsible manner from cradle (extraction of raw material) to grave (end of life disposition). The entire chain of the product must be sustainable and responsible. If we think of slave labor, would any of us argue that we should be able to buy a product made under such conditions? As supply chain professionals, we must behave in the same way for our employer as we exercise our duties. Better yet would be regulations that prohibited any firm from using inputs that are not sustainable and responsible. Of course, these regulations should be universally applied, and so a standardization of international environmental and social responsibility laws must happen. Legislation ensures that firms do not avoid participating voluntarily as a way to reap higher profits in the near term; standardization of laws prevents work from moving across borders to avoid environmental and social responsibility. In this manner, we can ensure that human rights are guaranteed, human beings derive benefit, and the environment is respected as we fulfill demand globally. We can leave the world a better place for future generations.

Also noteworthy is the NPO Global Reporting Initiative (www.globalreporting. org). Interested in both the environmental as well as the social, the website provides a comprehensive collection of metrics that enjoy some standardization worldwide as well as a consistent set of rules with which the metrics are calculated. This information would be provided to stakeholders generally but importantly also to potential supply chain partners up- and downstream.

Conclusion

As we have seen in this chapter, supply chain management entails fulfilling the demand considering that nowadays demand is fulfilled not by one firm but by cooperation between several firms. In traditional supply chain management, we seek to maximize profit along a supply chain by considering the entire chain in an integrated fashion. When we do this, we share information and decisions along the chain, resulting in a "global optimum." Socially sustainable business systems will require firms to consider not only costs but also environmental sustainability and social responsibility, along the entire supply chain. We should seek to operate in a manner that is socially responsible, environmentally sustainable, and profitable. We should seek to partner with suppliers, manufacturers, distributors, and retailers that also operate in sustainable and responsible ways. Just as it does no good for a supply chain to drive cost out of one part of the chain only to have it shift to another part of the chain, for a product to be sustainable and responsible, every step in the chain must be sustainable and responsible.

Discussion Questions

1. Imagine two supply chains, A and B, producing the same product, e.g., a computer. Supply chain A has very good environmental performance along the chain, and usually good social responsibility along the chain, but one link of the chain (company) uses slave labor. Supply chain B has mediocre (acceptable) environmental and social performance along the chain. Which chain should be preferred and why?

2. How can we quantify and trade-off metrics of cost, environmental sustainability, and social responsibility in supply chains? How should we incorporate these metrics when deciding on upstream and downstream supply chain partners?

References

Food Chain Workers Alliance. (2015). *Walmart at the Crossroads: The Environmental and Labor Impact of Its Food Supply Chain.* June 4, 2015. White paper.

Jobs with Justice. (2015). *New Findings on Conditions across Walmart's Garment Supplier Factories in Cambodia, India, and Indonesia.* May 2015. White paper.

Souza, G. C. (2012). *Sustainable Operations and Closed-Loop Supply Chains.* Chicago: Business Expert Press.

CASE 7   WALMART'S SUPPLY CHAIN

It would not be appropriate or fair to begin to scrutinize the nation's largest retailer without first mentioning that Walmart in many ways is an absolute pioneer in the field of supply chain management, and it is known to be very effective and efficient in its supply chain, if measured by the traditional profit and cost models. From "everyday low prices" to Hurricane Katrina, examples abound to illustrate its prowess in the field. It is also worthy to mention that it has started to pay attention to the environmental sustainability and in some cases the social responsibility of suppliers. The firm has a very large potential, in a way very few other firms do, to make business more sustainable and responsible. While it has made much progress, there are many examples of socially irresponsible practices. In the following paragraphs, we will provide some remarks on its food supply chain, followed by remarks on the supply chain for textiles and clothing. After this, we will discuss the Vlasic and Snapper cases, which provide some interesting insights into the sustainability of Walmart's supplier relationships.

In a report from the Food Chain Workers Alliance (2015), it was shown that while Walmart has a good supplier code of conduct and ethics, many violations were identified. These include failure to comply with local laws, and concerns over workers' age and status, working hours and rest periods, hiring decisions, compensation, worker housing, corruption, and health and safety, spanning much of the code of conduct and ethics. The report details the allegations, which, if true, would clearly indicate that there is a lack of social responsibility in the supply chain.

In another report, Jobs with Justice (2015) and the Asia Floor Wage Alliance detail findings of Walmart's textile and clothing supply chains in a similar manner. They find many instances that contradict the stated policy. Among these were suppression of the worker's right to associate and organize, the theft of wages, and a lack of protection against sexual harassment, physical violence, and unsafe, unhealthy working conditions.

Walmart is notorious for insisting on near perfect quality and delivery performance while demanding constant downward pressure on the cost and product prices. For both Vlasic, the pickle company, as well as Snapper, the manufacturer of lawn mowers, the relationship led them to uncharted territory: a situation where a firm "fires" its customers.

Vlasic, at the time the nation's top brand of pickles, had a profitable relationship with Walmart (Fishman, 2017). At some point, Walmart began to sell one-gallon glasses of whole pickles for less than $3. The effect was twofold for Vlasic. On the one hand, one-gallon glasses of whole pickle sales through the retailer Walmart spiked, providing revenue and market share. But on the other hand, Vlasic makes more margin on sliced pickles, and the $3 gallons at Walmart cannibalized sales from both other retail channels as well as other more profitable products. The case provides an interesting glimpse into Walmart's power in buyer-supplier relationships and its ability to make supply chain partners do things that are disadvantageous to the partner.

The Snapper case provides another example of buyer-supplier relationships with Walmart. Snapper is a manufacturer of durable lawn mowers that are made in America. They are sold through both big box retailers such as Walmart as well as smaller "mom and pop" businesses specializing in lawn mowers. At the small hometown businesses, employees are very knowledgeable on lawn mower selection and service, and spare parts are available to make investing in a durable lawn mower something that consumers would consider. At Walmart, on the other hand, while the customer does not receive expert advice or durable good service, the customer does receive a "good" price. And the price goes down every year as Walmart demands cost and price cuts for any standard product. The CEO of Snapper realized that Walmart was simply not a good fit for Snapper's strategy. In selling at Walmart, their product was side to side with very inexpensive, less durable products. Walmart lacked the personnel and ability to service the lawn mowers. Smaller stores were displeased that Snapper lawn mowers sold for less money at Walmarts. And lastly, and this is perhaps the most important message from the case, the CEO foresaw that because Walmart would demand cost reductions every year, Snapper would eventually be forced to move manufacturing offshore and to make its lawn mowers to much lower quality standards, resulting in products that are less durable and directly contradict Snapper's longtime differentiation strategy. The CEO, Jim Wier, who chose to no longer sell to Walmart (when most other companies would love to), has been dubbed "the man who said no to Walmart," and in comments betraying a humble nature exclaimed that on his tombstone will be written "the dumbest CEO ever to live."

Discussion Questions

1. Do you agree or disagree with Vlasic's decision? Develop arguments to support your opinion.
2. Do you agree or disagree with Snapper CEO Jim Wier's decision? Develop arguments to support your opinion.

References

Fishman, C. (2017). *The Wal-Mart You Don't Know*. Retrieved January 30, 2017, from Fast Company: https://www.fastcompany.com/47593/wal-mart-you-dont-know

Food Chain Workers Alliance. (2015). *Walmart at the Crossroads: The Environmental and Labor Impact of Its Food Supply Chain*. June 4, 2015. White paper.

Jobs with Justice. (2015). *New Findings on Conditions across Walmart's Garment Supplier Factories in Cambodia, India, and Indonesia*. May 2015. White paper.

8

INFORMATION TECHNOLOGY AND SUSTAINABILITY

Information Technology and business are becoming inextricably interwoven. I don't think anybody can talk meaningfully about one without talking about the other.

Bill Gates (Gates & Hemingway, 2000)

We have the technology to build a global paradise on earth, and at the same time, we have the power to end life as we know it. I am a futurist. I cannot predict the actual future—only what it can be if we manage the earth and its resources intelligently.

Jacque Fresco, American futurist (The Venus Project)

We do not inherit the earth from our ancestors; we borrow it from our children.

Native American proverb (Indigenouspeople.net)

Introduction

Rapid technological developments, particularly Information Technology (IT), over the last several decades have created radical changes within the global economy and business activities. IT and IT-enabled innovations have become key resources for companies to succeed. They not only provide the foundation for the production of goods and services but also define and shape the way firms operate. Additionally, the application of IT in business has also led to the advent of numerous new business models (e.g., online retailing) and fields (e.g., online travel booking, social media, etc.). Research has found that companies that have successfully developed appropriate IT strategy have been able to garner tremendous benefits from their investments and enjoyed significant business success. Therefore, modern companies spend up to 30% of all business investments on IT (Saunders & Brynjolfsson, 2016).

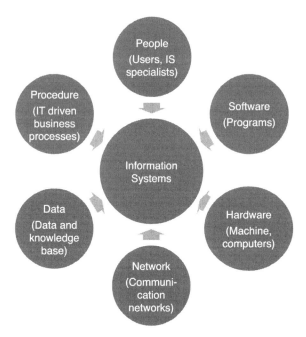

FIGURE 8.1 Information Systems Components

Research studying the business value of IT has found that it is not the purchase of technical systems that brings about benefits to companies. Rather, at the heart of application of IT to business activities are *Information Systems* (in this chapter, the terms Information Technology (IT) and Information Systems (IS) are used interchangeably) that help companies collect, process, organize, and distribute data. Information Systems thus comprise technological IT components (computers, databases, network equipment, etc.), business processes, and people who use and manage such systems (see Figure 8.1). Companies that have succeeded with their IT investments have been found to successfully combine (1) tangible technical components, (2) human technical and managerial IT skills, and (3) intangible IT-enabled resources such as knowledge and customer orientation to develop IT-enabled business initiatives to help them improve their business operations and competitiveness (Bharadwaj, 2000; Bharadwaj, Bharadwaj, & Bendoly, 2007). Similarly, such a combination of IT and business resources could enable companies to improve their sustainability performance. For example, by using IT to enable a new business model using an online movie catalog, rental DVDs shipping via USPS, and later online movie streaming, Netflix managed to successfully compete against rental industry giant Blockbuster. Netflix's business operation also contributes to sustainability by reducing environmental impacts of running brick-and-mortar stores.

Additionally, given IT's role in enabling collaboration, information exchange, business operations, and innovations within firms and across supply chain partners, it is arguable that IT resources should be critical in enabling firms to develop capabilities to address sustainability issues both within firms and across their supply chain through coordination with supply chain partners, including measuring sustainability performance and restructuring business processes for sustainability. In this chapter, we explore different aspects of IT's contribution to building more socially sustainable business systems.

IT Investments

Businesses and managers making decisions on IT investments usually have an operational and strategic focus in mind with regards to how/when/where such IT investments' benefit should be realized in terms of helping to improve their businesses' performance to justify such investments. Therefore, such IT investments are usually framed as IT-enabled business initiatives, which are a combination of IT and business assets and capabilities that are aimed at providing new capabilities targeted at enabling specific business operational activities.

Additionally, IT-enabled business initiatives are undertaken for a variety of purposes, and these different purposes have different effects on business performance. A popular framework that has been used to distinctly categorize IT-enabled business initiatives is the IT strategic role framework developed by Zuboff (1988) and Schein (1992). This framework categorizes IT investments in three categories:

- *Automate*—IT-enabled initiatives that help firms automate business processes, reducing or eliminating the hands-on role served by human assets to carry out work processes and work tasks faster, more efficiently, and/or more accurately. Examples of automate initiatives include a grocery store's self-checkout counters, or use of robots in retail companies' warehouses.
- *Informate*—IT-enabled initiatives that make available new, timely, more complete and relevant data to managers, employees, and external entities (e.g., customers and suppliers) such that these individuals better understand the work situations being faced to make better and faster decisions and carry out work processes and work tasks more effectively and/or more efficiently. An example of informate initiatives is a grocery retailer's initiatives to capture information about product purchases at its retail stores, then analyzing such data and combining the results with other data to determine the specific products and their quantities to be stocked at each retail outlet.
- *Transform*—IT-enabled initiatives that help firms restructure or reconstitute business assets, capabilities, practices, processes, and/or relationships that would fundamentally alter existing business processes, and/or models that enable an organization to create new products/services that position firms more favorably in the product-markets. Examples of transform initiatives include FedEx's overnight delivery model and Netflix's DVD rental and movie streaming model.

To support the development of such IT-enabled business initiatives, it is important that companies also make investments in their IT *infrastructure*, which comprises standardized IT services deployments (both technical and human, such as servers, networks, help desk, etc.) that provide platforms through which standardized technical services are provisioned and based on which automate, informate, and transform initiatives are developed and deployed to deliver their intended business objectives.

In the following sections, we will examine how investments in automate, informate, and transform IT-enabled initiatives and IT infrastructure will help firms improve their sustainability performance to become more sustainable businesses.

Sustainability Framework and IT Investments

In addressing sustainability issues, companies need to attend to all three aspects of the triple bottom line (People, Planet, Profits). In this section, we will examine the sustainability framework and how IT could help firms become more sustainable within this framework. The integrated sustainability framework was developed based on multiple frameworks. The framework stresses the importance of attending to People while balancing the Planet and Profit factors. Figure 8.2, which was introduced by Dao, Langella, and Carbo (2011), describes the four quadrants of the integrated sustainability value framework. By developing sustainability capabilities to pursue the sustainability objectives and practices within these four quadrants, firms may be able to achieve triple bottom line results and create sustainable value for both themselves and their stakeholders in economic, environmental, and social dimensions. In each quadrant of the framework, a sustainability strategy is listed, together with an IT strategy that helps firms to achieve the sustainability strategic goals of the quadrant.

Quadrant 1, Internal-Today

In this quadrant, the focus for companies to improve their sustainability performance is on their internal operation. Companies will look at current operations and determine how they will lead to improved People, Planet, and Profit outcomes. Activities helping companies to optimize their operations will lead to reduction in both waste and emissions and business operation costs. Additionally, firms focusing on this quadrant can also pay attention to social issues that are win–win conditions for them and their internal stakeholders (i.e., employees). Such sustainability targets are achieved by engaging in continuous process improvements of internal operations related to sustainability such as waste reduction, energy conservation, emission control, employee involvement, and employee safety and health. While increasing employee involvement and improving employee management practices that help increase employee morale could lead to improved internal operations that reduce environmental impacts, research has found that firms pursuing such strategies and practices end up reducing liabilities, cutting cost, and increasing profits, thus increasing sustainable shareholder value (Hart & Milstein, 2003).

	Internal	**External**
Today	*Sustainability Strategy:* o Prevent pollution via optimizing operation, to reduce cost and impacts on the environment. o Create organizational culture aimed towards sustainability; improve employee management practices within firms. *IT Strategy:* o Infrastructure's technical platform optimization. o Automate and informate initiatives. *Payoff:* Reduced costs, reduced environmental impacts, increased profitability, reduced risk, improved employee working conditions.	*Sustainability Strategy:* o Improve extended supply chain to reduce pollution through material and processes choices and closed-loop supply chain. o Extend organizational culture aimed towards addressing sustainability issues affecting both internal and external stakeholders. *IT Strategy:* o Infrastructure integration. o Informate initiatives. *Payoff:* Reputation and legitimacy, reduced environmental impacts, more socially and environmentally sustainable supply chain, increased competitive advantage.
Tomorrow	*Sustainability Strategy:* o Develop capabilities that enable radical clean technologies and processes that help solve social and environmental issues. *IT Strategy:* o Infrastructure flexibility. o Transform initiatives. *Payoff:* Innovation, strategic positioning, better and more sustainable products/services.	*Sustainability Strategy:* o Include core sustainability capabilities in all products, processes, and supply chains. o Sustainability vision: open new, previously ignored dialogues with stakeholders to solve social issues and locate growth opportunities. *IT Strategy:* o Informate initiatives. *Payoff:* Growth trajectory.

FIGURE 8.2 Integrated Sustainability Framework

In an operations context, internal-today would focus on cost minimization and risk management techniques. For example, firms would focus to decrease environmental burdens and associated costs of raw materials or disposal (e.g., product stewardship and product recovery management), and incorporate their internal stakeholders' (employees') concerns in decisions and ensure proper worker safety and health standards. Efficient utilization of land, water, energy, and other natural resources makes business more productive.

Through the product design decision, much of the product's environmental impact itself is determined through the sourcing of materials. Avoiding hazardous materials will result in decrease in both disposal costs of the product and risk of legislation and lawsuits. Additionally, improving business processes to reduce waste and energy consumption could also help firms reduce their environmental impacts. For example, when a distributor deliberates developing network alternatives (where to open distribution centers) to service, trade-offs must be considered between the two criteria of Profit and Planet.

IT could contribute to firms' internal-today sustainability strategy in several ways. First, on its own, IT could help firms reduce pollution by reducing the carbon footprint of their own IT technical infrastructure. This approach, commonly referred to as *Green IT*, has been approached as a win–win situation, reducing costs associated with IT infrastructure and at the same time reducing environmental impacts of IT infrastructure (Healey, 2009). Green IT is made up of two main venues: (1) IT infrastructure power consumption reduction and (2) sustainable IT assets management practices.

As companies increasingly rely on Information Systems for their operations, the scale of their IT technical infrastructure platform, which includes standardized technical IT services deployments through which standardized technical services are provisioned (e.g., hardware, software, networks, and data processing architecture) also increases. Together with such increase in IT infrastructure scale is the increase in the amount of energy consumed by such infrastructure. Companies thus could implement multiple approaches to optimize their IT technical infrastructure's power consumption, saving them money and reducing the carbon footprint of their IT usage. Such an optimization approach could be applied to personal computers used by individual employees and to data centers.

Energy Efficiency, Personal Computer Power Management

Many companies look to managing end-user device power consumption as an easy, effective way to reduce energy costs. For example, turning off PCs and monitors after work and utilizing the energy management features of operating systems can cut energy use per PC by as much as 40%, saving on average $150 per PC per year based on an average US utility rate of $.0855/kWh (Shehabi et al., 2016). Therefore, programs that promote use of both policies and best practices to reduce individual PCs' power consumption have increasingly become popular among businesses. These include, for example, using software that centrally manages energy settings of PCs and monitors, and enforcing standardized power settings on all PCs before distributing to end users, etc.

Energy Efficiency, Data Center Power Management

At the heart of Information Systems are data centers that include IT equipment that process (servers), store (storage equipment), and communicate (network equipment) digital data. Thus, data centers have become an essential part of the function of communication, business, academia, and governmental systems. These days, except for the smallest organizations, companies, universities, and governmental institutions all have some kind of data center needs, with large companies running tens or even hundreds of them. According to recent research by Ernest Orlando Lawrence Berkeley National Laboratory, data centers in the United States in 2014 consumed about 70 billion kWh of electricity, or about 1.8% of total US electricity consumption, costing around $4.8

billion, similar to the amount of electricity consumed by approximately 5.8 million average US households (Shehabi et al., 2016). At the global scale, Information and Communication Technology accounts for 2% of global carbon dioxide emission, roughly equivalent to what the airline industry produces. Therefore, Green IT practices aimed at improving energy efficiency of our computer systems' data centers will help us significantly reduce the environmental impacts of our IT infrastructure.

INFORMATION BOX 8.1   GREENING OF IT AT INTEL

Intel developed an IT Sustainability Framework that helps the company's IT department contribute towards Intel's emissions reduction goal by reducing Intel's consumption of IT-related and office energy and Intel's physical IT footprint while still allowing it to accommodate its growing computing needs. Initiatives driven by the framework include:

- Deployment of Intel Xeon® processor-based servers that help accelerate jobs by up to 17%, helping to avoid the addition of incremental server capacity and to decrease energy consumption, as well as helping Intel IT save nearly 120 million kWh in energy between 2010 and 2011.
- Implementation of cloud and virtualization strategies that increased Intel's virtualization percentage from 64% to 75%, helping Intel IT maintain flat energy and CO_2 footprints while significantly increasing Intel's compute, storage, and IT customer capabilities.

Intel's Green IT efforts led to Intel being recognized with awards by International Data Group (IDG) and Computerworld for efforts to use technology to conserve energy and lower CO_2 emissions in 2011 and 2012.

For example, companies have been able to use different technologies such as server virtualization and consolidation, blade servers, etc., to reduce the number of servers at data centers. The use of such technology has resulted in decreased energy required to run servers and storage, and a decrease in square footage needed to house the devices (which also need to be cooled and maintained). Additionally, by leveraging local climates and using free cooling strategies (e.g., Google and Facebook moving data centers to colder countries, or Microsoft placing data centers under the ocean), IT organizations can also decrease energy consumption of their data centers.

Besides Green IT practices aimed at optimizing power consumption, companies also adopt best IT asset management practices to reduce the carbon footprint of their IT infrastructure. Green IT asset management practices include initiatives that focus on purchasing computing equipment that is more energy efficient and environmentally friendly and programs to extend the equipment's useful life, and recycling them properly. By adopting practices such as extending the computer replacement cycle, companies could also reduce the environmental impacts of technology usage. By adopting responsible equipment recycling and discarding practices, companies would minimize IT waste sent to landfills. More than 80% of companies that adopt Green IT asset management practices are satisfied with their performance. Besides cost reduction, companies adopting Green IT asset management practices also get a big nod from their customers and employees.

INFORMATION BOX 8.2   AUTOMATE IT-ENABLED SUSTAINABILITY INITIATIVE AT JOHNSON & JOHNSON

At Johnson & Johnson, in 2013, a new data management system was developed to automate the process of collecting and managing workforce-related data such as retention rates, salary information, training and grievance data, etc. across the corporation. The data management system allowed Johnson & Johnson to track information more easily.

While Green IT practices have helped companies become more sustainable within quadrant 1, intelligent IT investment decisions would also help companies to develop IT-enabled initiatives that help them improve business operations' sustainability performance. For example, to achieve sustainable goals with employee management practices and operation management, companies must be able to measure their use of hazardous substances, emission of pollutants, and employee health and safety, and integrate such metrics within key business processes. Technologies, such as sensors, RFID, etc., that *automate* the collection and processing of such information and *inform* relevant employees about such information could help firms improve operational efficiency through increased organizational information processing efficiency and improved decision making with better availability of information. The availability of such information would also help HR managers regarding employee management practices (rewards, engagement, etc.) to improve firms' pollution prevention record.

Quadrant 2, External-Today

While many sustainability targets could be met by improving internal operations, being a sustainable business is not confined within internal business operation. As firms move into quadrant 2, it is important that they devise appropriate sustainability strategy and practices that take into account their interactions with external stakeholders (business partners, customers, shareholders, etc.) to be more sustainable.

As a company interacts with its supply chain partners, it is important that the supply chain partners also adopt sustainable practices. For example, a retailer such as Target could not be considered a sustainable business if its suppliers exploit laborers and/or cause environmental damage in the production of their products that are sold in Target's stores. Such practices would consequentially result in bad relationships with other stakeholders such as customers, regulators, etc., with regards to sustainability. As an example, according to the United Students Against Sweatshops, twenty-five campuses cut ties with Russell Athletic wear due to the sweat shop practices of its suppliers in Honduras.

Therefore, to become more sustainable, a company needs to actively engage in extensive interactions with its external stakeholders such as suppliers, customers, regulators, shareholders, NGOs, the media, etc. and integrate their sustainability view into the firm's business operation and strategy. Over time, a web of inter-action is formed, enabling a network of information and knowledge exchange between firms and their supply chain partners and stakeholders, helping compa-nies to steward the sustainability of their products and services.

Such product stewardship practices enable firms to deliver sustainability values to both their stakeholders and the organization. Such values can be gained from enhanced capabilities, lower environmental impacts, the addressing of social issues related to their internal and external stakeholders, reduced costs, increased profit-ability, and enhanced legitimacy and reputation.

To enable such a web of interaction, it is important that companies develop capabilities and organizational culture that support employees being open and receptive to exchange of sustainability information with outside stakeholders. Additionally, it is critical that sustainability metrics be used to measure business activities' sustainability and then communicate this information transparently across supply chain partners, upstream and downstream. This will enable com-panies to be able to select supply chain partners based not only on price but also on various triple bottom line metrics. On the other hand (with close information exchange), while a firm cannot control which retailers buy its products, it can limit its access to retailers failing to meet its sustainability performance criteria. This will not only ensure a good surplus for the members, but that the entire chain is working together towards a goal of becoming more sustainable.

INFORMATION BOX 8.3 INFORMATE IT-ENABLED SUSTAINABILITY INITIATIVE AT INTEL

Intel expects its employees and suppliers to comply with the Electronic Industry Citizenship Coalition (EICC) Code of Conduct. Intel also expects its suppliers to ensure that their suppliers abide by the EICC Code. The EICC Code sets forth standards and reporting guidelines for key areas of social responsibility and environmental stewardship, including human rights and labor standards (e.g., child/forced labor, freedom of association and collective bargaining, diversity and nondiscrimination, working hours and minimum wages, ethical practices, and worker health and safety).

Intel set up a Supplier Website that contains detailed information about the company's sustainability standards. The site provides numerous web-based tools designed to promote effective communication and help suppliers follow proper data collection procedures.

Intel's employee intranet portal, Circuit, is widely used and provides employees with information about workplace services and benefits. Employees are encouraged to utilize Intel's internal social media channels, such as blogs, wikis, and online forums, for both business and collaboration purposes. Intel believes that its employees are the best and most knowledgeable ambassadors of the company's sustainability efforts, and encourages its employees to participate in both internal and external social media channels to communicate with one another and the company's external stakeholders.

The web of interaction and information exchange among supply chain partners could be enabled by appropriate IT investments. First, companies could invest in informate IT-enabled initiatives to enable exchange of sustainability information with external stakeholders, helping them to gain more legitimacy with regards to sustainability. For example, a company would use web pages and/or web portals to provide external stakeholders with information regarding the social and environmental impacts of its products. Such web portals could also enable the company's employees to develop better collaborative relationships with external stakeholders, including potential employees, local communities, or various NGOs. Additionally, investments in appropriate informate IT-enabled initiatives could also enable a company to better exchange sustainability performance metrics with its supply chain partners to develop a sustainable supply chain. For example, companies could invest in inter-firm informate initiatives such as Electronic Data Interchange (EDI) or Enterprise Resource Planning (ERP) systems that could communicate their sustainability performance/requirements with their supply chain partners.

While informate IT-enabled initiatives could enable companies to communicate and exchange sustainability information with external stakeholders, such information exchange might be hampered by fragmented IT infrastructure between information exchange partners, constraining information flows and activity coordination. For example, if sustainability databases and computer systems across information exchange parties (i.e., supply chain partners) are not compatible, the information integration among the partners could not be conducted in real time and would require extra time and efforts for data conversion and systems connection.

Therefore, a well-integrated IT infrastructure among supply chain partners is critical to successful sustainability information exchange. This requires standards for data format, applications, and business processes to be negotiated and implemented among information exchange partners for seamless real-time connectivity. Therefore, besides appropriate investments in informate IT-enabled initiatives, it is critical that supply chain partners take appropriate steps to integrate their IT infrastructure, enabling informate IT-enabled applications to coordinate across inter-firm platforms. Such IT-enabled collaborations that deeply embed capabilities of IT platforms into organizational processes could facilitate firms in their coordination with suppliers and partners along the supply chain in the development and evaluation of sustainable technologies and processes.

Quadrant 3, Internal-Tomorrow

While it is critical for firms to examine current business operations and activities to make them more sustainable, it is also critical that companies look to the future and position themselves to be more sustainable and competitive by serving a particular set of customer needs better. These objectives could be achieved by the companies developing groundbreaking, radically innovative technologies, products, and/or processes that leapfrog and disrupt industry standard practices that not only improve social and environmental impacts but also help solve current and future social and environmental concerns. Success in doing so will also help companies to position themselves competitively for developing and exploiting future markets. An example is Toyota's success with the hybrid automotive technology integrated in its Prius cars, which emit as little as 10% of the harmful pollutants conventional vehicles produce while consuming only half as much gas. Success with hybrid automotive technology has placed Toyota in a competitive position that has enabled Toyota to establish its technology as a world standard.

INFORMATION BOX 8.4   TRANSFORM IT-ENABLED SUSTAINABILITY INITIATIVE AT COCA-COLA

Within its IT department, Coca-Cola has adopted the Lean Startup methodology to support its innovation process, enabling ideas to be generated and developed quickly and cost-effectively. Employees could access the Ideation Platform from their computers and smartphones to post ideas and rate other employees' ideas. Ideas that have received enough "likes" are developed into a proof of concept and presented to senior management for a decision on future investment.

Such practices have helped transform the innovation process at Coca-Cola's IT department, helping the company to learn and build its insights into its processes. The idea generation process has also started to expand to other areas of Coca-Cola's business.

Transform IT-enabled initiatives could have significant potential to enable companies to develop radical technologies, products, and/or processes for sustainability in this quadrant. For example, Netflix successfully developed transform IT-enabled initiatives to create a radically new business model, renting DVDs online and subsequently video streaming. Such innovations could not be acquired off the shelf but require deep understanding of current industry practices and IT's potential in enabling Netflix to structure its assets, capabilities, and processes to fundamentally challenge the dominant practices of the movie rental industry at the time. As a result, Netflix managed to position itself distinctly from other movie rental companies (e.g., Blockbuster), gaining new market share and competitive advantage, and at the same time reducing environmental impacts by not having to operate regular brick-and-mortar stores, and not having customers driving back and forth to rent and return DVDs.

While transform IT-enabled initiatives enable firms to develop radical product and process changes, such initiatives might not be feasible without appropriate IT infrastructure that is prepared for future anticipated needs. As IT infrastructure provides the foundation of computing, networks, shared data platforms, etc., on which specific IT-enabled initiatives are developed and deployed, it is critical that a company focusing on transform IT-enabled initiatives for sustainability develop appropriate IT infrastructure that is flexible enough to provide infrastructure support for its transform initiatives. Given the radically innovative nature of transform IT-enabled initiatives, it is difficult to predict future needs of different transform IT-enabled initiatives. Therefore, it is critical that the company's IT infrastructure is flexible in meeting such varied future requirements as they emerge.

A flexible IT infrastructure could be designed so that its hardware, operating systems, communication network, data, etc., could evolve and facilitate rapid deployments of IT initiatives as they emerge, supporting the continuous redesign of business- and IT-related processes and relationships. For example, United Parcel Service's flexible IT architectures enable data integrity and connectivity with customers' applications, providing real-time inventory information that can be leveraged by customers to improve inventory management, asset efficiencies, and market responsiveness.

Quadrant 4, External-Tomorrow

Within this quadrant, companies look to the future and beyond their boundaries to explore opportunities of unmet markets for sustainable new products/services that intersect with, and that could help address, the companies' business competency. By utilizing these opportunities successfully, companies could create value broadly for the society and at the same time create value and sustained competitive advantage for themselves.

INFORMATION BOX 8.5   INFORMATE IT-ENABLED SUSTAINABILITY INITIATIVE AT INTEL

As a technology company, Intel understands that its success rests on the availability of skilled workers, a healthy technology ecosystem, and knowledgeable customers. Meanwhile, the health of local economies where Intel operates depends on access to technology and quality education. Therefore, Intel has deployed multiple IT-enabled initiatives to provide technology education to local communities.

Intel designed and developed the Intel Learn Easy Steps digital literacy course to teach adults in developing countries computer skills that can be used in creating small businesses or micro-enterprises. The course was deployed through partnerships with NGOs and governments, and reached more than one million learners in twenty-two countries between 2011 and 2012.

To enable such a strategy, a company could include core sustainability capabilities in all products and processes, and, more importantly, develop a sustainability vision about the shared roadmap of growth between the company and its social context and communicate such a sustainability vision effectively to its internal and external stakeholders in addressing sustainability issues and seeking out the growth opportunities. For example, Johnson & Johnson, based on its sustainability vision, developed a sustainability goal for each of its business sectors and enabled the sharing of such sustainability goals with a growing number of customers who can choose to align their lives with their societal and environmental values to assist them in products choice and to help Johnson & Johnson explore unmet opportunities for sustainable products/services.

Supply chain partners are also critical to a company in exploring and addressing unmet sustainability market needs. Therefore, it is also critical that a company communicate its sustainability vision across its supply chain to enable it to select its supply chain partners based on their sustainability performance and to support these partners with sustainability activities. Doing so would help make the overall supply chain more sustainable over time. For example, a company could support its suppliers to improve performance over time through encouragement as well as training. The same company could also invest today in communities where the firm operates to have access to better employees tomorrow.

To enable open dialog, via sharing of the sustainability vision with external stakeholders to open up new pathways to sustainability growth in previously unserved/underserved markets, insightful leaders would recognize that informate IT initiatives play a significant role in enabling such communication. For example, appropriate websites and web portals enable Johnson & Johnson's employees to communicate effectively with its customers regarding sustainability. Informate initiatives would also better enable supply chain partners to exchange sustainability information and collaborate on future opportunities.

Conclusion

In this chapter, we have taken a deeper look at the role of IT in enabling companies to be more sustainable. More specifically, the chapter has provided insight on how investments in different aspects of IT infrastructure and different types of IT-enabled business initiatives (automate, informate, transform) would help firms develop sustainability capabilities for different sustainability objectives across the four quadrants of the integrated sustainability framework.

Discussion Questions

1. Define *automate IT-enabled initiative*. Give an example of an automate IT-enabled sustainability initiative.
2. Define *informate IT-enabled initiative*. Give an example of an informate IT-enabled sustainability initiative.
3. Define *transform IT-enabled initiative*. Give an example of a transform IT-enabled sustainability initiative.
4. As automate IT-enabled initiatives have increasingly replaced human labor with technology, how should businesses approach this in a more socially sustainable way? What roles do businesses and society have in helping workers whose jobs have been automated adapt to such consequences of technology evolution?

References

Bharadwaj, A. S. (2000). A resource-based perspective on information technology capability and firm performance: An empirical investigation. *MIS Quarterly*, 169–196.

Bharadwaj, S., Bharadwaj, A., & Bendoly, E. (2007). The performance effects of complementarities between information systems, marketing, manufacturing, and supply chain processes. *Information Systems Research*, *18*(4), 437–453.

Dao, V., Langella, I., & Carbo, J. (2011). From green to sustainability: Information Technology and an integrated sustainability framework. *The Journal of Strategic Information Systems*, *20*(1), 63–79.

Gates, B., & Hemingway, C. (2000). *Business at the Speed of Thought: Succeeding in the Digital Economy*. London: Penguin UK.

Hart, S. L., & Milstein, M. B. (2003). Creating sustainable value. *The Academy of Management Executive*, *17*(2), 56–67.

Healey, M. (2009, January). Analytics report: The eco-enterprise and the reality of green IT, *InformationWeek*.

Saunders, A., & Brynjolfsson, E. (2016). Valuing information technology related intangible assets. *MIS Quarterly*, *40*(1), 83–110.

Schein, E. H. (1992). *The Role of the CEO in the Management of Change: The Case of Information Technology*. Cambridge, MA: Sloan School of Management.

Shehabi, A., Smith, S. J., Horner, N., Azevedo, I., Brown, R., Koomey, J., & Lintner, W. (2016). *United States data center energy usage report*. Lawrence Berkeley National Laboratory, Berkeley, California. LBNL-1005775.

Zuboff, S. (1988). *In the Age of the Smart Machine: The Future of Work and Power*. New York: Basic Books.

CASE 8 SUSTAINABILITY AT INTEL

Intel's Background

Intel Corporation, which was founded in 1968, is currently the world's largest semiconductor chip maker, and is the inventor of the x86 series of microprocessors found in most PCs. Based in Santa Clara, California, Intel was among the earliest companies that helped establish the Silicon Valley area as the heart of the United States's IT industry.

Intel's Success Building Sustainability Into Bottom Line

Intel has had a track record of proactive engagement in sustainability efforts. Since the mid-1990s, Intel has taken voluntary steps and set aggressive goals to reduce the company's greenhouse gas emission. Since then, it has implemented a wide variety of sustainability initiatives and is currently the highest ranked technology company in the *Corporate Knights* (a magazine focused on Clean Capitalism) 2016 ranking of the world's most sustainable corporations.

To successfully embrace sustainability, Intel has tried to build sustainability into its bottom line through different strategies. For example, since 2008, Intel has linked a portion of every employee's variable compensation—from front-line-staff to CEO—to the achievement of sustainability goals, primarily related to environmental areas but also expanded to include social issues such as diversity.

Over the years, Intel has deployed its technological capability to improve its sustainability performance. We will examine several aspects next.

Intel and Green IT

Intel has engaged in multiple efforts to reduce the environmental footprint of its IT infrastructure. For example, Intel developed an IT Sustainability Framework that helps the company's IT department contribute towards Intel's emissions reduction goal by reducing Intel's consumption of IT-related and office energy and Intel's physical IT footprint while still allowing it to accommodate its growing computing needs.

In another example, Intel also serves on the board of the Green Grid, a global consortium of companies dedicated to resource efficiency in business computing systems, which has developed recommendations on best practices and technologies to improve data center resource efficiency.

Intel has pioneered a diverse set of hardware and software technologies that help measure and optimize energy use in computers and data centers.

Intel and IT-Enabled Sustainable Business Operation

Beyond the greening of its IT usage, Intel has also utilized its IT expertise to enable multiple initiatives aimed at improving sustainability performance of its business operation. For example, Intel has developed technology tools to use metrics and data within its decision making processes to help improve its business process management.

To better support its employees' professional performance and well-being and engage them in sustainability efforts, Intel uses a broad range of electronic and interpersonal channels such as an employee intranet portal, online community, etc., to provide employees with timely information and facilitate discussion between teams and individuals on sustainability topics. For example, Intel's intranet portal, Circuit, provides corporate and local Intel news, and information about workplace services and benefits. It is accessible through a web browser or mobile phone application. Intel's employees are encouraged to use its internal social media channels for business and collaboration purposes, and to build a sense of community across its global sites.

Intel and IT-Enabled Sustainable Supply Chain

Intel's focus on sustainability goes beyond its own internal operation. Intel is committed to developing a sustainable supply chain for its business. In 2014, Intel announced that the company was the first company to manufacture and ship only "conflict-free" microprocessors, which means that the computer chips do not include minerals that come from mines that pass their profits on to warlords in violence-ravaged parts of Africa.

Intel also uses its IT expertise to develop its sustainable supply chain. For example, Intel's Supplier Website contains detailed information about its supplier sustainability policies and metrics on human rights, ethics, the environment, health, and safety. The site also includes information on supplier diversity initiatives, supplier quality, and recognition programs. As such, the site helps Intel suppliers meet the companies' standards on sustainability.

Such initiatives help Intel's supply chain move from being opaque and turning a blind-eye on its sourcing to being more transparent for sustainability.

Intel Looking Beyond Its Supply Chain

Intel also utilizes its IT capabilities to help with sustainability efforts beyond its supply chain. For example, in addition to focusing on reducing its carbon "footprint," Intel also focuses on increasing its "handprint" by using its technology and expertise to help businesses in other non-IT sectors reduce their carbon footprint.

Intel also uses its technology to support multiple community development and education initiatives. For example, Intel developed the ICT training program called Intel Teach to support educators in multiple countries.

Discussion Questions

1. What different aspects of its sustainability has Intel been able to improve by utilizing its IT expertise?
2. How important is the role that IT plays in Intel's sustainability efforts?
3. What techniques should Intel utilize to advance SSBS at Intel as well as within the business community in general?

9

SOCIALLY SUSTAINABLE LEADERSHIP

In a truly great company profits and cash flow become like blood and water to a healthy body: They are absolutely essential for life but they are not the very point of life.

Jim Collins (Chapter 9, Good to Great, *2001)*

The frog does not drink up the pond in which he lives.

Sioux proverb[1]

Do your little bit of good where you are; it's those little bits of good put together that overwhelm the world.

Archbishop Desmond Tutu[2]

Introduction

Great organizations require great leadership; sustainable organizations require sustainable leadership. In this chapter, we will explore the role of leaders in creating socially sustainable businesses. This chapter will begin by introducing three categories of leadership taught across today's business schools. For each category, a path to Socially Sustainable Leadership will be suggested. In the final sections of this chapter, we will introduce two recent theories of leadership that have significant potential to promote Socially Sustainable Leadership: Level 5 Leadership and servant leadership.

Before we can describe different theories, we need to define the term *leadership*. Over the centuries, historians and philosophers have presented many different definitions of this term. During the last few decades, dozens of definitions have been posited by management professionals and scholars. Some focus on goal accomplishment, influence, and power. Warren Bennis, considered to be a pioneer and leader in the field of leadership studies, says, "Leadership is the capacity to translate vision into reality" (Kruse, 2013). Others focus on follow-ers. Bill Gates, founder of Microsoft, describes leaders as "those who empower others" (Ibid.). Peter Drucker, a management guru, offers perhaps the most parsimonious definition of all: "The only definition of a leader is someone who has followers." These definitions are just the beginning. One recent practitioner article on the Internet offers thirty-three current definitions (Helmrich, 2016)!

What is leadership in the business context? It is not simple; it combines many important factors. The very nature of business organizations is to do some-thing. Effective leadership involves *accomplishing objectives*. As Drucker points out, leadership requires *followers*. Leadership does not happen in a room with one person; that is self-management. So, leadership involves connecting people to objectives. For the purposes of this text, we define leadership as influencing followers to accomplish objectives. But, this book is not about leadership, but rather socially sustainable business systems. So, this book requires a definition for *Socially Sustainable Leadership*. Socially Sustainable Leadership is influencing fol-lowers to accomplish sustainable objectives while treating followers with dignity and respect.

Trait Leadership

Throughout much of history, leadership was considered a trait. Great leaders were able to command respect, accomplish large goals, and demand obedience from their followers. In psychology, traits can be defined as a set of stable characteristics that affect behavior. Many psychologists argue that traits stem from a combination of genetics and early childhood development. So, the trait theory of leadership holds that leadership is attributable to a range of characteristics that predict leader-ship effectiveness. In other words, leaders are born, not made.

This conceptualization of leadership dominated much of the discussion on the subject from ancient times through the first part of the 20th century. This conceptualization is consistent with the stratified, patriarchal societies that have prevailed throughout history and persist still today. What are these traits that make a good leader? The famous Chinese sage Sun Tzu (544–496 BCE) argued that these traits are wisdom, humanity, respect, integrity, courage, and dignity (Rarick, 1996). In his famous treatise on the acquisition and use of power *The Prince*, Machiavelli (CE 1469–1527) describes a darker set of traits: cunning, manipulation, and self-interest (Zaccaro, Kemp, & Bader, 2004). More recently, some authors continue to describe leadership in terms of traits. Phillips (2001) offers the founding fathers of the United States as exemplars of important lead-ership traits. Among the traits shared by these leaders are curiosity, intellectual capacity, self-confidence, integrity, courage, high moral values, and sense of des-tiny. Who has these traits that are so desirable for leaders? Of course, consistent with the prevalent patriarchal and stratified societies throughout history, they are predominately male, predominantly wealthy, and (in the case of the United States) predominately European.

In the management literature of the past fifty years, these notions of trait leadership have been largely, but not entirely, discounted. Modern scholars have investigated trait leadership in a more systematic fashion. Tim Judge, one of the foremost scholars in the field of organizational behavior, has led several of these investigations. A comprehensive 2002 meta-analysis of the relationship between personality and leadership found evidence of significant correlations among all five factors of personality studied (Judge, Bono, Ilies, & Gerhardt, 2002). Judge and associates also explored the relationship between intelligence and leadership and found a significant correlation (Judge, Colbert, & Ilies, 2004).

Notwithstanding these findings, modern management scholars have criticized trait theories of leadership from a variety of perspectives and looked for new explanations. Both feminist and Marxist critiques of trait leadership point to the many obvious problems associated with using historical models who are almost exclusively rich, powerful men to explain leadership effectiveness. Psychologists have argued that traits are far less powerful than situational context with regard to behavior. The stronger the situational context, researches argue, the weaker influence that traits have on behavior (Snyder & Ickes, 1985). Finally, and perhaps most importantly, is the futility criticism. If traits are acquired via genetics and early childhood, why bother concentrating on something that cannot be developed among adults? If leaders are born, then leadership is an accident of birth.

How does Socially Sustainable Leadership relate to trait theories? Socially Sustainable Leadership cannot be based on traits. Sustainable leadership is not inheritable, nor is it dependent upon neural pathways established during early childhood. The good news is that we do not need to have a time machine or genetic recoder. Every individual is capable of learning and developing durable psychosocial characteristics. Research provides evidence that people are able to intentionally develop characteristics such as resilience, optimism, and hope (Luthans, Luthans, & Luthans, 2004). We believe characteristics important for Socially Sustainable Leadership are similarly developable. So, every person is capable of learning to be a socially sustainable leader.

Sustainable leadership characteristics must be positive. They must be un-Machiavellian; trickery, deception, and self-interest are all antithetical to sustainable leadership. Characteristics must include love, respect, and care for followers. Sustainable leaders must be critical thinkers. They see the world for how it is and how it can be. Sustainable leaders must be committed to social and economic justice. So, what are some characteristics of socially sustainable leaders? Table 9.1 presents a set of five traits and their applicability to SSBS. We do not argue that leaders cannot possess or benefit from other characteristics than these five. We do argue that Socially Sustainable Leadership requires compassion, honesty, fairness, commitment, and prudence.

TABLE 9.1 Socially Sustainable Leadership Characteristics

Characteristic	Application to Socially Sustainable Leadership
Compassion	Compassion literally means having passion with another. It means having sympathy and concern for others. Compassionate leaders are not self-centered, controlling power-grabbers. Socially Sustainable Leadership demands the ability to recognize the needs of others and the ability to openly love and respect one's followers.
Honesty	Honest leaders tell the truth and do not deceive others. It is easy to tell the truth when the truth is pleasant. Socially Sustainable Leadership requires openness, frankness, and integrity even under difficult conditions in which the truth is painful. This is critical because many of the facts about the current destructive system, the plight of our planet, and current social conditions are extremely painful. Honest leaders do not steal. Socially sustainable leaders do not take from their followers. They do not take their wealth, their dignity, or their rights. Rather, they help their followers gain and maintain these possessions. Socially Sustainable Leadership requires real honesty, not technical honesty. Socially sustainable leaders do not hide behind technicalities that allow for miscommunication, misdirection, or misappropriation.
Fairness	Socially Sustainable Leadership demands a sense of fairness and a deep concern for justice. Fairness is interpreted in its broadest sense, not limited to instrumental mechanisms. Socially Sustainable Leadership requires the ability to recognize the way things are to strive to make them fairer. It includes the empathetic ability to place oneself in the shoes of another.
Commitment	The transition from DAC to SSBS will not be easy. It will not be without dislocation or disruption. Indeed, it is intended to disrupt and halt the existing destructive system. To accomplish this, socially sustainable leaders will have to be committed and maintain their commitment over time. Socially Sustainable Leadership requires commitment to followers and to the aims of making one's economic activities sustainable. Leaders must have fortitude, willpower, and hope to sustain their commitment.
Prudence	Prudent leaders think before they act. Socially Sustainable Leadership requires that leaders have the ability to gather, assess, and process information. They must have the wisdom to discriminate fact from falsehood, fact from argument, and fact from polemic. Prudent leaders do not act in an incautious or reckless manner. Socially Sustainable Leadership demands that leaders carefully act in accordance with a wise interpretation of the facts. Socially sustainable leaders do not imperil their followers, the people, or the planet by unreasoned or thoughtless action.

Contextual and Behavioral Leadership

As the problems with trait theories of leadership became apparent during the past fifty years, new theoretical explanations for leadership effectiveness were needed. Many of these theories have discounted the importance of traits and emphasized the importance of contextual clues, follower perceptions, and leader behaviors. These theories of leadership explore different sets of questions. Contextual and behavioral theories of leadership do not ask, Who is a leader? They ask, What does a leader do? and What should a leader do? In other words, these theories of leadership have moved beyond just describing leaders. Contextual and behavioral theories of leadership both describe effective leadership and prescribe effective leadership behavior.

During the late 1960s, several leadership theories focused on context and described leadership behavior. Blake and Mouton introduced a managerial grid (later renamed the leadership grid) in which they argued that leadership behavior is largely a function of leader attitudes about concern for people versus concern for results (Blake, Mouton, & Bidwell, 1962). In this model, situational cues drive behavior. For example, these authors would argue that leadership styles appropriate for a construction foreman working with a large number of temporary laborers for a short-term project would be completely inappropriate for a hospital manager supervising physicians. In the construction with temporary labor situation, Blake and Mouton would argue that a focus on results is appropriate and effective leaders exercise control and stress compliance with directions. In the hospital situation, effective leaders focus on concern for people rather than the task. In this context, the physicians are the experts, so control and compliance behavior is not effective leadership. Another descriptive theory of contextual leadership is Fiedler's Contingency Theory (1967). In Contingency Theory, leadership effectiveness is a function of the leader's style in relation to situational demands including stress and follower characteristics.

Other contextual leadership theories retain their focus on job and follower context but focus on prescribing rather than describing behavior. The Situational Leadership Model was offered a few years after Fiedler's theory by Hershey and Blanchard (1969). Like other contextual theories, Situation Leadership emphasizes that there is no one best leadership style. For Hershey and Blanchard, leadership behavior was a function of directive and supportive behavior. Depending on the follower and situation, leaders should engage in different leadership styles: delegating, participating, selling, or telling. Another prescriptive theory of contextual leadership is Path-Goal Theory (House, 1996). In this theory, goal accomplishment is predicted by follower path perceptions. Follower path perceptions are a function of the fit between leadership style, follower characteristics, and workplace characteristics. Effective leaders, then, ought to respond to follower characteristics such as ability and workplace characteristics such as task or organizational structure and respond with appropriate styles such as directive-, supportive-, participative-, or achievement-oriented behavior.

Other leadership theories stress the transactional nature of leadership. These theories view leader-follower relationships as a series of social and/or economic transactions. B. F. Skinner and other proponents of behavior modification argue that leaders can influence follower behavior by responding to interactions with appropriate rewards and punishments. Leadership as behavior modification is a prescriptive model in which leaders should first observe follower behavior and then respond to that behavior either positively or negatively.

Leader-Member Exchange Theory (LMX) recognizes that leaders form different relationships with different employees and that these relationships have consequences (Graen & Uhl-Bien, 1995). LMX focuses on the two-way relationships between employees (members) and their managers (leaders) and the impact of these relationships on the ability of leaders to influence behavior. Meta-analytic investigations into LMX provide evidence that follower characteristics, leader characteristics, interpersonal relationships, and contextual variables come together to predict a number of important attitudinal and behavioral outcomes such as job satisfaction, organizational commitment, turnover intention, and job performance (Dulebohn, Bommer, Liden, Brouer, & Ferris, 2012). To be effective within the LMX paradigm, leaders must have a great deal of situational awareness and pay constant attention to the quality of individual leader-follower relationships.

Contextual and behavioral theories offer many opportunities when viewed through the lens of social sustainability. The Leadership Grid, Contingency Model, and Situational Leadership Model describe and prescribe effective leadership in a variety of contexts. An application of Socially Sustainable Leadership would require leaders to maximize their concern for others. The contingencies suggested by these situational theories suggest that different levels of concern for tasks or for followers are more expedient or effective than others. Each of these theories suggests that there are situations in which it is appropriate and optimal to minimize concern for others. Minimizing concern for others is not socially sustainable. In other words, day-laborers performing temporary work should not be treated differently because they can be treated differently or because it is cheaper or more efficient to treat them differently. Day-laborers should be treated like the surgeon at the hospital to the degree that it is possible. Socially Sustainable Leadership allows leaders to adapt to situations but requires treating followers with the full caring and dignity to which each person is entitled.

Socially Sustainable Leadership can be directly applied within the Path-Goal model of leadership. In this model, leader behavior styles adapt to follower and workplace characteristics. The degree to which this is effective predicts follower path perceptions and, then, follower goals. Though adapting style to a situation is permitted and encouraged, Socially Sustainable Leadership requires more. These leaders are not passive observers of followers and workplace characteristics who then adapt their style accordingly. Socially sustainable leaders are not mere observers/adapters. Instead, socially sustainable leaders strive to develop followers and enable them to reach their full potential. They must strive to improve the conditions in which people spend their work lives. They have an obligation to change workplace conditions in such a way that employees can work in an environment that promotes health, thriving, and dignity. Socially Sustainable Leadership does not settle for a leader as observer/adapter; it demands leaders become developers/improvers.

Theories of transactional leadership are also not necessarily incompatible with Socially Sustainable Leadership. Behavior modification is permissible as long as followers are treated with a full schema of human dignity. This includes transparency of method. Behavior modification has the potential to be subtle and manipulative; this is not acceptable. The system rewards must be fully transparent and accessible to all. Punishment should be used sparingly or not at all; it is impermissible if it harms a follower. Similar to leaders in the contextual theories, socially sustainable LMX leaders must be developers/improvers. It is the socially sustainable leader's responsibility to care for every follower as they develop and maximize the quality of each leader-follower relationship. In addition, they must provide the resources that enable their followers to develop themselves. Finally, they must strive to improve working conditions, organizational culture, and other situational factors on which LMX depends.

Transformational Leadership

Transformational theories of leadership view leaders as visionaries who lead by transforming their followers. Professor Bernard Bass and his collaborators enumerated a number of techniques transformational leaders use to influence and change their followers. Transformative leadership behaviors include idealized influence, inspirational motivation, intellectual stimulation, and individualized consideration (Bass, & Steidlmeier, 1999, p. 185; Bass & Ronald, 2006). Idealized influence occurs when followers respect, admire, and trust a leader because the leader is a role model and acts consistently with integrity. This type of influence can change the values of individual followers and the norms of groups and teams. Inspirational motivation is a function of the transformative leader's ability to inspire and instill team spirit and enthusiasm. Transformational leaders often inspire their followers by challenging them with meaningful goals and setting high expectations.

Transformational leaders provide intellectual stimulation by encouraging followers to explore and question their assumptions, settled beliefs, and existing interpretations of facts. Transformational leaders stimulate their followers by helping them to reframe information and focusing on solution-finding. Transformative leaders allow mistakes and refrain from undue criticism. Followers may be changed by stimulation as they feel the freedom to innovate and are able to pursue new creative solutions. Finally, transformative leaders provide their followers with individualized consideration by acting as coach or mentor. By providing a supportive environment in which personal development is encouraged, followers are changed as they pursue their full human potential.

INFORMATION BOX 9.1 WANGARI MAATHAI (1940–2011)

In 1977, Kenyan environmental activist Wangari Maathai launched an NGO committed to environmental protection, environmental restoration, and women's rights. The NGO's mission is to "strive for better environmental management, community empowerment, and livelihood improvement using tree-planting as an entry point" (Green Belt Movement, n.d.). Since its founding, Maathai's Green Belt Movement has planted more than fifty-one million trees. As an internationally recognized leader in the ecofeminist movement, Maathai's contributions resulted in her being awarded the 2004 Nobel Peace Prize (Nobel Media AB, 2017). Maathai employed two key transformative leadership practices by inspiring her followers and showing every consideration for their well-being. Maathai challenged those around her with the visionary goal of improving the lives of women. She helped her followers to see how making women's lives better makes the world better. Additionally, Maathai consistently committed to the well-being of her followers. She showed consideration for her followers by providing opportunities that helped her followers achieve their full potential. Since its founding, Green Belt has trained more than thirty thousand women in forestry, food processing, bee-keeping, and other trades. Through her commitment to people and planet, Maathai exemplifies the transformative possibilities of Socially Sustainable Leadership (Green Belt Movement, n.d.).

FIGURE 9.1 Wangari Maathai

Transformative leadership need not be in conflict with Socially Sustainable Leadership. In fact, transformative leadership can be completely consistent with the goals of SSBS. The chief challenge for leaders who wish to be both transformative and socially sustainable is authenticity. To be sustainable, leadership behaviors must be real. With regard to idealized influence, there is nothing objectionable about leaders serving as role models to their followers, especially when they model positive behaviors and embody positive values. If followers respond with trust, respect, and admiration, that is positive. Similarly, leaders who transform their followers by inspiring them is positive in as much as the expectations set are achievable. Intellectual stimulation also does not present a sustainability problem. Socially sustainable leaders can and should encourage their employees to create and innovate. Like the other methods employed by transformative leaders, individual consideration is on its face desirable leadership behavior. Again, the key is that the support and development offered to followers must be authentic. To be transformative and sustainable, individual consideration behaviors must be free of subtext and guile. Socially Sustainable Leadership requires that people cannot be used as a means to an end.

Level 5 Leadership

" . . . almost everyone believed that CEOs should be charismatic, larger than life figures. Collins was the first to blow that idea out of the water."

(Collins, 2005, p. 136)

Another valuable lesson on Socially Sustainable Leadership arises from the work of Jim Collins. Since the 1980s, Collins had examined performance and attempted to derive the recipe for the proverbial secret sauce that distinguishes firms that exhibit outstanding performance from those that achieve only good performance. In the early 2000s, he began to focus on one of the seven key factors he identified, the role of leadership. He found that a key ingredient to move a company from "good" to "great" was the presence of an executive exhibiting an interesting mix of characteristics and behaviors. He termed this mix Level 5 Leadership. Table 9.2 is an adaptation of Collins's Level 5 Hierarchy.

In this section, we present the seemingly paradoxical facets of Level 5 Leadership, use anecdotal stories illustrating how it works, and provide empirical evidence to support its impact on business. It is our belief that Level 5 Leadership is an excellent model to which future socially sustainable leaders should aspire. By changing the way their firms view themselves, by enabling their businesses to consistently impact the world in a positive manner, and by selflessly valuing every human being within their organizations, Level 5 Leaders follow the path of Socially Sustainable Leadership.

Many business students will have never heard of Darwin Smith, and he would likely have secretly preferred this. He has been described as "shy, unpretentious, even awkward" and someone who "dressed unfashionably". This "mild mannered"

TABLE 9.2 Collins's Level 5 Hierarchy

Level 5	**LEVEL 5 EXECUTIVE**—Builds, develops, and achieves collective greatness. Possesses characteristics and employs behaviors that combine personal humility, selflessness, and indomitable will.
Level 4	**EFFECTIVE LEADER**—Capable of generating full commitment and enthusiastic pursuit of clear and compelling vision. She or he stimulates teams to achieve high levels of performance.
Level 3	**COMPETENT MANAGER**—Capably organizes people and resources to pursue and accomplish predetermined objectives.
Level 2	**CONTRUBUTING TEAM MEMBER**—A productive contributor in a group setting. She or he works effectively with others and collaborates to meet team objectives.
Level 1	**HIGHLY CAPABLE INDIVIDUAL**—A productive contributor who employs her or his abilities, knowledge, experience, and strong work habits.

Source: Adapted from Collins, J. C. (2001). *Good to Great: Why Some Companies Make the Leap . . . and Others Don't.* New York: Random House.

company lawyer starkly contrasted with the splashy personalities of most large company CEOs of the time, such as Jack Welch and Lee Iacocca. When he took over Kimberly Clark, which was underperforming in terms of stock relative to the market, he wondered if he were the right person for the job, and some even crassly reminded him that he lacked the qualifications for the job. As it turned out, he remained CEO for twenty years. During this time, Kimberly Clark consistently beat its competitors and enjoyed returns outperforming the market including blue chips such as GE, HP, 3M, and Coca-Cola. At his retirement, he admitted that he never stopped trying to be qualified for the job, betraying awesome humility. An interesting side note, he was once told by the Army's Officer Candidate School that he would never be a leader.

An even more appropriate example of Level 5 Leadership, one with a clear, courageous, and pioneering view of Socially Sustainable Leadership, comes from Hewlett-Packard CEO David Packard. When he was 39, he attended a meeting of business leaders concerned with increasing their companies' profits. After following the discussion and losing patience with the direction, he finally exclaimed that "a company has a greater responsibility than making money for its stockholders" and that "we have a responsibility to our employees to recognize their dignity as human beings" (Collins, 2003). This meeting took place in 1949 (and how far have we come?), and he found himself immediately isolated; not one person in the meeting agreed with ideas that were thought of as dangerous and socialist by his peers who believed him afterwards to be "not one of them" and "obviously not qualified" to run a large company. Unfazed, he continued to believe and put forth the idea that "those who help create wealth have a moral right to share in that wealth" (Collins, 2003). Always preferring to see himself and have himself seen as an HP man first and a CEO second, he preferred an open door workspace together with fellow engineers rather than a wood paneled CEO suite. He practiced management by walking around before that was even a term, and he shared equity and profit with all employees. He preferred to spend time with friends stringing barbed wire and, in spite of being a billionaire, continued to live in a small house he built with his wife. He donated with his partner Hewlett to Stanford University an amount of money equivalent to the initial endowment from the Stanfords, but refused to have his name appear anywhere until his death. A pamphlet for his eulogy identified the man who co-founded Hewlett-Packard as "Rancher, etc." Lastly and interestingly, he served for a couple of years as Under-secretary of Defense in the Nixon administration. There he did away with Robert McNamara's Total Package Procurement (TPP), a military procurement program that resulted in large cost overruns that were hidden from public view as they benefited shareholders of defense companies. The TPP was primarily credited to Robert H. Charles, an Assistant Secretary of Defense who started his career at McDonnell Aircraft, working his way up to Executive Vice President before turning to "public service." As Major General Smedley Butler USMC, who twice won the Congressional Medal of Honor, would say: war is a racket.

Level 5 Leadership, Collins explains, was an unexpected find. Looking for what distinguished good from great companies, Collins did not want to fall into the simplistic notion championed at the time (and perhaps even today) that success and failure are a result of the executive leadership. But again and again, the team kept encountering something unusual with the leadership characteristics discovered by looking at sustained, long-term performance of good versus great firms: the leaders at the great firms shared some common, paradoxical characteristics. The company size did not matter, and the industry the company was in did not matter; what mattered was the presence of a Level 5 Leader at a time of transition. As such, Level 5 Leadership is not some Pollyannaish, idealistic finding; it is an empirical, data-driven finding.

The common, paradoxical characteristics they shared were being modest and shy while being willful and fearless. Collins used Abraham Lincoln as a good example, someone who led our country through a civil war while being described as quiet, peaceful, and shy. Colman Mockler, the CEO of Gillette from 1975 to 1991, remained courteous, gracious, and reserved even as his company was attacked by corporate raiders. Like always, some conflated this niceness with weakness, something that more mature, intelligent, and humane people will quickly dismiss as hogwash.

Level 5 Leaders tend to downplay their role in any successes (crediting others or, when all else fails, "luck") while assuming full responsibility for failures. This selflessness is always something that touches our hearts, whether it is a soldier jumping on a grenade to save her or his comrades or a star sports team player who refuses to acknowledge an individual contribution and prefers to credit the team as a whole. On the other hand, selfishness and hubris do not inspire admiration, and they should not. Here, Collins points to Al Dunlap, the CEO of Scott Paper, who was paid around $100 million for 603 days (approximately

$160,000 a day) as he fired workers, halved the research budget, and put the company on "growth steroids in preparation for sale" (Collins, 2005, p. 142). Interestingly enough, years later, in 1996 this "Rambo in pinstripes" (as he described himself) took over Sunbeam Oster, where through accounting manipulations (Arthur Anderson was its accounting firm) the firm was forced into Chapter 11 bankruptcy in 2001. Today, the once great American manufacturer exists only as a brand. As an aside, the accounting manipulations were designed to make 1996 performance look worse than it was, to make 1997 performance look much better than it was. This West Point graduate provides a wonderful juxtaposition to Darwin Smith, who the Army said could not lead, and his view that the primary goal of any company is to make money for its shareholders nicely contrasts with David Packard, who claimed that workers had a "moral right" to share in the wealth they helped create. Dunlop is referred to nowadays as "the Boss from Hell," a "Corporate Psychopath," and a "Bum" (which is disparaging to bums), and ranks number 6 on CNBC's list of worst American CEOs ever.

So, the question becomes, Whom do we admire? Whom do we seek to emulate? What choice do we make? To believe that business is there to make shareholders money at the expense of employees, or to believe that workers have the moral right to share in the fruit of their work? As Camus might say, "These are games: one must first answer." Do human beings exist to serve corporations, or do corporations exist to serve human beings?

Having true leaders, leading with morals and convictions, with admirable humility and fierce professional will, will be essential to transforming business from destructive to sustainable. The humility of these managers meshes well with Mintzberg's criticism of "heroic leadership," although we would say that this humane, humble leadership where one truly cares about human beings (workers, communities, and future generations) is the true heroic leadership. We hope you join us in this belief.

According to Collins (2005, p. 145), "people who could never in a million years bring themselves to subjugate their needs . . . to something larger and more lasting than themselves" will never be able to be Level 5 Leaders. Some have the seed, and others do not. Those who have the seed can, under the right circumstances (among them, a great mentor, loving parents, a significant life experience, or strong religious faith), develop into Level 5 Leaders, capable of transforming companies in truly beautiful ways. One Level 5 CEO imagined retiring to a house and looking from the back porch on their blossoming former employer and saying, "I used to work there." To make the world a better place, we need more leaders like this, with perhaps a slight modification. The sustainable leader would retire and look from their back porch on a blossoming former employer, an Earth that was left in better shape than it was before, and remember many lives positively impacted through providing employees with meaningful work, living wage, health care, and retirement benefits that allowed families to thrive.

Servant Leadership

As is evident from the previous sections, some paradigms of leadership are more compatible with social sustainability than others. For example, Level 5 Leadership clearly aligns with Socially Sustainable Leadership, and traditional trait theory does not. In this final section, we will explore another leadership paradigm that we believe is fully congruent with Socially Sustainable Leadership. Servant leaders, like Level 5 Leaders, are prepared to subordinate their own interests to the interests of their followers. Servant leaders overturn the traditional power relationship between leaders and followers by giving away power rather than wielding it (Parris & Peachey, 2013).

Servant leadership is not a new idea. It has deep origins in both Asia and the West. Laozi (c. 500 BCE) was a Chinese contemporary of Confucius and is generally held to be the philosophical founder of Taoism. Taoist principles call on leaders to refrain from pushing, to serve, to be selfless, and to listen (Korac-Kakabadse, Kouzmin, & Kakabadse, 2002). A 4th century BCE figure from India, Chanakaya is credited with saying, "The king shall consider as good, not what pleases himself but what pleases his subjects" (Barrett, 2011, p. 276). Within the Christian tradition, one of the central themes of the gospel stories is the sacrifice that Jesus makes on behalf of His followers and of all humanity. Christians get direct guidance from Jesus on servant leadership. In the gospel of Mark (10:42–45), Jesus says,

> [42] So Jesus called them and said to them, "You know that among the Gentiles those whom they recognize as their rulers lord it over them, and their great ones are tyrants over them. [43] But it is not so among you; but whoever wishes to become great among you must be your servant, [44] and whoever wishes to be first among you must be slave of all. [45] For the Son of Man came not to be served but to serve, and to give his life a ransom for many."[3]

The medieval Christian friar Francis of Assisi (c. CE 1181–1226) is credited with saying, "Because I am the servant of all, (in Latin, '*servus omnium*') I am obliged to serve all" (Richey, 2016, para. 8). For more than two thousand years in both the East and West, spiritual thinkers have expounded the potential of leading by serving.

INFORMATION BOX 9.2   ANDREW CLANCY

Taking over his small family publishing business as a young man, Andrew Clancy has transformed his company, Publishing Concepts (PCI), into the nation's top company in alumni relations publishing and services. Clancy is committed to servant leadership and views his role as President and top leader to help his associates thrive in life (Clancy, n.d.). By building a culture based on values and committed to customer promises, Clancy typifies both the character and behaviors of a socially sustainable leader. PCI pays its call-center associates significantly more than market wages and treats them with respect and dignity. Associates are offered flexible work hours, learning opportunities, leadership programs, and an educational reimbursement program. As a result, PCI's turnover is well below the industry average. How have PCI associates responded? In 2015 and 2016, PCI was named Texas's #1 mid-sized company to work for (Best Companies Group, 2016).

FIGURE 9.2 Andrew Clancy

Robert Greenleaf (1904–1990) ushered servant leadership back into the modern management lexicon.[4] From 1926 until 1964, he worked at AT&T, then the nation's dominant provider of telephone service. During his career, he worked, traveled, and observed the operations of one of the United States's flagship corporations. Following his retirement, Greenleaf embarked on his career as a writer, speaker, guru, and "evangelist" for his leadership principles. Greenleaf embraced sustainable business concepts. He understood that profit could not be the justification for corporations: "The organization exists for the person as much as the person exists for the organization." Greenleaf's greatest passion was for servant leadership. For Greenleaf, leaders are servants first.[5] Servant leaders are not driven by the desire to acquire power or wealth. Instead, they seek to make a better world through serving others.

The Robert K. Greenleaf Center for Servant Leadership continues the work of its founder. This organization defines servant leadership as "a philosophy and set of practices that enriches the lives of individuals, builds better organizations and ultimately creates a more just and caring world."[6] These principles are fully in accord not only with Socially Sustainable Leadership but the entire premise of socially sustainable business systems. Fully consistent with the SSBS paradigm, practitioners of servant leadership should be committed to building a positive future. Similarly, servant leaders understand that businesses play a central role in making our world better for all people.

Larry Spears, one of Greenleaf's disciples and collaborators, offers a list of ten characteristics shared by servant leaders (Spears, 1998, 2010). Table 9.3 displays these characteristics and offers corresponding Socially Sustainable Leadership behaviors for each characteristic. Each of these behaviors has the potential to make the lives of people in organizations better. Each of these behaviors has the potential to help organizations better serve the societies in which they operate. Socially Sustainable Leadership requires not just characteristics—it requires action.

TABLE 9.3 Servant Leadership Characteristics and Socially Sustainable Leadership Behaviors

Servant Leadership Characteristics	Socially Sustainable Leadership Behavior
Listening	Leaders habitually listen more than they speak (two ears, one mouth). Leaders listen with a purpose. Leaders actively seek to identify the will of their followers and help their followers achieve that will.
Empathy	Leaders place themselves in the shoes of their followers. Leaders do not exclude followers or make them "other." Leaders seek to practice acceptance and understanding.
Healing	Leaders care for their followers in a holistic sense. They help their followers heal physically, mentally, and emotionally. They build workplaces where followers can flourish and achieve physical and psychological well-being.

(Continued)

TABLE 9.3 (Continued)

Servant Leadership Characteristics	Socially Sustainable Leadership Behavior
Awareness	Leaders are self-aware. Leaders acknowledge their own weaknesses and failings. Leaders are aware of their surroundings, the needs of their followers, and the challenges that their organizations face.
Persuasion	Leaders persuade their followers. Good leaders should not need to use force or coercion. Followers follow good leaders because they want to, not because they have to.
Conceptualization	Leaders dream and encourage their followers to dream. Leaders provide followers the freedom and resources requisite for innovation and creativity.
Foresight	Leaders respect and learn from history. Leaders learn from past positive and negative experiences. Leaders are aware of and grateful for the present. Leaders embrace the uncertainty of the future and move forward in hope of making it better.
Stewardship	Leaders subordinate themselves to followers. Leaders use their power to empower others. Leaders care for the resources under their care.
Commitment to the growth of people	Leaders nurture the whole growth of their followers. Leaders commit to providing the resources and opportunities to help every follower achieve their full human potential.
Building community	Leaders unite rather than divide. Leaders find win–win solutions to problems. Leaders help followers to promote harmony rather than generate counterproductive conflict. Leaders are inclined to build bridges to others rather than walls.

Conclusion

Leadership is important to business success. In this chapter, we have examined five theories of leadership and how they could be applied to SSBS to develop *Socially Sustainable Leadership*. We could also see that instead of relying on leaders to lead organizations towards SSBS, each individual could be capable of affecting change through individual leadership of personal change that could result in collective change.

Discussion Questions

1. The central goal of SSBS is to build a positive future for people and planet. Do you think that leadership is essential for a more environmentally sustainable and socially responsible world? Why or why not?
2. What styles of leadership are most compatible with Socially Sustainable Leadership? Which are least compatible? Explain your answer with examples.
3. What are some of the pitfalls that socially sustainable leaders should avoid? Draw on your personal experience to give an example of an unsustainable leadership practice.

4. Think about people who influenced or impacted your life. What character-istics did they possess that explain their impact? Were you left with a desire to emulate these role models and, if so, how? How do these characteristics connect or not connect to Socially Sustainable Leadership?

5. Use the Internet to identify a CEO of a Global Fortune 500 company. Read about this CEO's biography or management philosophy. Do you think he or she exemplifies Socially Sustainable Leadership? Why or why not?

Notes

1 http://izquotes.com/quote/336020 Retrieved March 16, 2017.
2 www.brainyquote.com/quotes/quotes/d/desmondtut387490.html Retrieved March 16, 2017.
3 New Revised Standard Version.
4 www.greenleaf.org/robert-k-greenleaf-biography/ Retrieved February 28, 2017.
5 www.greenleaf.org/ Retrieved February 28, 2017.
6 www.greenleaf.org/what-is-servant-leadership/ Retrieved February 28, 2017.

References

Barrett, R. (2011). *The New Leadership Paradigm*. Raleigh, NC: Lulu.com.

Bass, B. M., & Ronald, E. R. (2006). *Transformational Leadership*. London: Psychology Press.

Bass, B. M., & Steidlmeier, P. (1999). Ethics, character, and authentic transformational lead-ership behavior. *Leadership Quarterly*, *10*(2), 181–217.

Best Companies Group (2016). *Best Companies to Work for in Texas*. Retrieved March 27, 2017, from http://bestcompaniestx.com/index.php?option=com_content&task=view&id=53&Itemid=1

Blake, R. R., Mouton, J. S., & Bidwell, A. C. (1962). Managerial Grid. Advanced Manage-ment-Office Executive.

Chandler, A. (1962). *Strategy and Structure: Chapters in the History of Industrial Enterprise*. New York: Doubleday.

Clancy, D. (n.d.). *Servant Leadership*. Retrieved March 27, 2017, from PCI: www.publishingconcepts.com/default.aspx?page=ServantLeadership

Collins, J. (2001). *Good to Great: Why Some Companies Make the Leap . . . and Others Don't*. New York: Random House.

Collins, J. (2003, July 21). The greatest CEOs of all time. *Fortune*.

Collins, J. (2005, July–August). Level 5 leadership. *Harvard Business Review*.

Dulebohn, J. H., Bommer, W. H., Liden, R. C., Brouer, R. L., & Ferris, G. R. (2012). A meta-analysis of antecedents and consequences of leader-member exchange integrating the past with an eye toward the future. *Journal of Management*, *38*(6), 1715–1759.

Fiedler, F. E. (1967). *A Theory of Leadership Effectiveness*. New York: McGraw-Hill.

Freeman, R. E. (1984). *Strategic Management: A Stakeholder Approach*. Boston: Pitman.

Freeman, R. E. (May 18, 2012) *Edward Freeman: Businesses Should Be Driven by Purpose*. Retrieved February 27, 2017, from forbesindia.com: www.forbesindia.com/article/third-anniversary-special/edward-freeman-businesses-should-be-driven-by-purpose/32934/1

Graen, G. B., & Uhl-Bien, M. (1995). The relationship-based approach to leadership: Development of LMX theory of leadership over 25 years: Applying a multi-level, multi-domain perspective. *Leadership Quarterly*, *6*(2), 219–247.

Green Belt Movement (n.d.). *Who We Are: Our Mission.* Retrieved June 6, 2017, from www. greenbeltmovement.org/who-we-are.

Helmrich, B. (2016, April 5). *33 Ways to Define Leadership.* Retrieved June 6, 2017, from Business News Daily: http://reachingnewheightsfoundation.com/rnhf-wp/wp-content/ uploads/2016/12/33-Ways-to-define-Leadership.pdf

Hersey, P., & Blanchard, K. H. (1969). *Management of Organizational Behavior—Utilizing Human Resources.* Upper Saddle River, NJ: Prentice Hall.

House, R. J. (1996). Path-goal theory of leadership: Lessons, legacy, and a reformulated theory. *Leadership Quarterly, 7*(3), 323–352.

Johnson, C. Y. (2016, September 21) *EpiPen CEO to Defend Lifesaving Drug's Soaring Price in Front of Lawmakers.* Retrieved February 27, 2016, from Washington Post: www. washingtonpost.com/news/wonk/wp/2016/09/21/what-to-expect-when-congress-takes-on-epipen-maker-mylan/?utm_term=.44230827bd90

Judge, T. A., Bono, J. E., Ilies, R., & Gerhardt, M. W. (2002). Personality and leadership: A qualitative and quantitative review. *Journal of Applied Psychology, 87*(4), 765.

Judge, T. A., Colbert, A. E., & Ilies, R. (2004). Intelligence and leadership: A quantitative review and test of theoretical propositions. *Journal of Applied Psychology, 89*(3), 542.

Kaplan, R. S., & Norton, D. P. (1996). *The Balanced Scorecard: Translating Strategy into Action.* Cambridge, MA: Harvard Business Press.

Korac-Kakabadse, N., Kouzmin, A., & Kakabadse, A. (2002). Spirituality and leadership praxis. *Journal of Managerial Psychology, 17*(3), 165–182.

Kruse, K. (2013, April 9). *What Is Leadership?* Retrieved March 2, 2017, from Forbes Magazine: www.forbes.com/sites/kevinkruse/2013/04/09/what-is-leadership/#20f89b115b90

Luthans, F., Luthans, K. W., & Luthans, B. C. (2004). Positive psychological capital: Beyond human and social capital. *Business Horizons, 47*(1), 45–50.

Mintzberg, H., Ahlstrand, B., & Lampel, J. (1998). *Strategy Safari: A Guided Tour through the Wilds of Strategic Management.* New York: The Free Press.

Mintzberg, H., & Quinn, J. B. (1988). *The Strategy Process.* Harlow: Prentice-Hall.

Nobel Media AB (2017). *Wangari Maathai Facts.* Retrieved March 27, 2017, from Nobel-prize.org: www.nobelprize.org/nobel_prizes/peace/laureates/2004/maathai-facts.html

Parris, D. L., & Peachey, J. W. (2013). A systematic literature review of servant leadership theory in organizational contexts. *Journal of Business Ethics, 113*(3), 377–393.

Phillips, D. T. (2001). *The Founding Fathers on Leadership: Classic Teamwork in Changing Times.* New York: Grand Central Publishing.

Porter, M. E. (1979, March-April). How competitive forces shape strategy. *Harvard Business Review, 57*(2), 137–145.

Porter, M. E. (1980). *Competitive Strategy.* New York: Free Press.

Porter, M. E. (1985). *Competitive Advantage: Creating and Sustaining Superior Performance.* New York: Free Press.

Rarick, C. A. (1996). Ancient Chinese advice for modern business strategists. *SAM Advanced Management Journal (07497075), 61*(1), 38.

Richey, M. (2016). *Servus Ominium: The Importance of Servant Leadership Discussed at USF's Annual Breakfast.* Retrieved February 28, 2017, from Today's Catholic News: www. todayscatholicnews.org/2016/02/servus-omnium-the-importance-of-servant-leadership-discussed-as-usfs-annual-breakfast/

Snyder, M., & Ickes, W. (1985). Personality and social behavior. In G. Lindzey, & E. Aron-son (Eds.), *Handbook of Social Psychology* (3rd ed., pp. 883–948). New York: Random House.

Society for Human Resource Management. (2012, November 27). *Strategic Planning: What Are the Basics of Environmental Scanning?* Retrieved February 27, 2017, from www.shrm. org: www.shrm.org/resourcesandtools/tools-and-samples/hr-qa/pages/cms_021670. aspx

Spears, L. C. (1998). *Insights on Leadership: Service, Stewardship, Spirit, and Servant-Leadership.* Hoboken, NJ: John Wiley & Sons.

Spears, L. C. (2010). Character and servant leadership: Ten characteristics of effective, caring leaders. *The Journal of Virtues & Leadership, 1*(1), 25–30.

Stout, L. A. (2012). The problem of corporate purpose. *Issues in Governance Studies, 48,* 1–14.

Zaccaro, S. J., Kemp, C., & Bader, P. (2004). Leader traits and attributes. *The Nature of Leadership, 101,* 124.

CASE 9   RAY ANDERSON (ANDERSON, 2009; HAWKEN, 2011; MAKOWER, 2012)

Ray Anderson, as we have already spoken about, was CEO of Interface and is a fine example of leadership that led to a transformation to make the world a better place. Interface had for years sold and leased carpeting to firms; the latter is a good example of servitization, where rather than purchasing the product, we purchase the service. When carpeting is leased, it is replaced every several years with new carpet. This results in a lot of carpet coming back to Interface that has to be disposed of in some fashion. Ray Anderson famously exclaimed, when looking at a truck returning full of carpet that was to be disposed of in a landfill, that "someday they will put people like me in jail." This led to an epiphany of sorts, where Anderson challenged his company to become environmentally neutral by 2020. Transformation ensued. Interface reorganized its product recovery processes to gain as much material from the old carpet as was possible and its production processes to use the recycled material. He unabashedly exclaimed that the globe has been harmed by the major culprit, business and commerce. But he also believed that business has the ability, opportunity, and responsibility to reverse the current trend. He has been often described as "humble," which fits very well with our glimpse into Level 5 Leadership, as well as the fact that his religious faith (one of several possible triggers for Level 5 Leadership) had a role in the way that he saw the world and his responsibilities in it. He believed until the end that business could be better, that it could be a solution to the problem of sustainability that it almost certainly had caused. Believing that we cannot change the system leads often to the conclusion of helplessness, makes excuses for the bad behavior of others and ourselves, and makes it far less likely that we will transform businesses and society to ensure that future generations enjoy what we have been given to protect: life itself. Ray Anderson passed away in 2011, and in his eulogy, a mentor called his passing "startling, a summons, maybe even a provocation" (P. Hawken as quoted in Walsh 2011). To make the world a better place, we need leaders who like him are motivated by responsibility more than self-interest, who have the intelligence to look at the truck of used carpet and to recognize the problems it presents to the world, and then have the courage and honesty to communicate this concern to others. We are all challenged by his vision.

Discussion Questions

1. Discuss how Ray Anderson's leadership is relevant to Level 5 Leadership.
2. Could Ray Anderson be viewed as a servant leader? Explain.

3. Do you see any characteristics of transformative leadership applicable to Ray Anderson's leadership in the case? If so, what are they?

References

Anderson, R. (2009). *The Business Logic of Sustainability*. Retrieved from Ted Talks: www.ted.com/talks/ray_anderson_on_the_business_logic_of_sustainability

Hawken, P. (2011, August 11). *Reimagining the World Was a Responsibility*. Retrieved from Green Biz: https://www.greenbiz.com/blog/2011/08/11/reimagining-world-was-responsibility

Makower, J. (2012, August 6). Why Aren't There More Ray Andersons? Retrieved from Green Biz: www.greenbiz.com/blog/2012/08/06/why-aren%E2%80%99t-there-more-ray-andersons

Walsh, B. (2011, August 19) *Ray Anderson: A Summons, Maybe Even a Provocation*. Retrieved June 6, 2017, from Healthy Building News: https://healthybuilding.net/news/2011/08/19/ray-anderson-a-summons-maybe-even-a-provocation

10
SOCIALLY SUSTAINABLE STRATEGY

The underlying principles of strategy are enduring, regardless of technology or the pace of change.

Michael Porter,[1] *professor, Harvard University*

Strategy without tactics is the slowest route to victory. Tactics without strategy is the noise before defeat.

Sun Tzu,[2] *author of* The Art of War

We know that the profitable growth of our company depends on the economic, environmental, and social sustainability of our communities across the world. And we know it is in our best interests to contribute to the sustainability of those communities.

Travis Engen, CEO, Alcan[3]

Introduction

In the current economic system of DAC, business strategy largely comes down to one question: How does this firm maximize value for the owners? As was discussed in previous chapters, this question results from the premise that the purpose of business organizations is to generate value for their shareholders. Therefore, strategic outcomes are always ultimately evaluated in terms of dollars and cents for the owners. In some of the literature on sustainability and in much of the practice of sustainability, sustainable practices are often looked at as a strategy to achieve the traditional firm goals of profit and shareholder wealth. However, this view of sustainability is no real advance from DAC. Instead, it is a hijacking of sustainability to meet profitability goals. This is oftentimes referred to as greenwashing from an environmental viewpoint.

In this chapter, we look to flip the equation. Sustainability will not be a means to achieve the business's overall strategy. Instead, we will look at how strategic management theories and tools can be utilized to help us to achieve socially sustainable business practices. As discussed in Chapters 2 and 3, sustainability requires the achievement of a triple bottom line—People, Planet, and Profit. Strategic management is used to align organizations towards their goals to keep them on the path to achieving these goals. Under SSBS, the goals have changed. The people and the planet have become primary, but at the same time, the organization must remain at the least viable and ideally profitable. The profitable company will be better able to provide for employees, reinvest in renewable, sustainable, innovative technologies, and engage in risks to create products and processes that can help to create a sustainable future. Strategic management tools should be utilized to help the SSBS organization to achieve these three goals.

First, we define strategic management and review the important theories of strategic management. We then discuss the strategic management process. Afterwards, we will flip the equation and examine how strategic management tools and concepts could be used to enable companies to evolve towards SSBS goals.

Definition of Strategy

Strategy is not a new field of study. Since the inception of agriculture and human civilization, leaders have engaged in strategic activities. In the earliest Mesopotamian city-states, princes and priests set long-term objectives for their people whether it be the storage of grain or the completion of large-scale construction projects. In ancient times, military strategy was an important subject for philosophers and generals alike. Many concepts found in business texts today trace their origins to the classic military and political principles from such ancient strategists as Sun Tzu, Thucydides, and Marcus Aurelius. Like their ancient counterparts, later thinkers from Machiavelli to Clausewitz have impacted modern strategic theories and practices.

Business strategy became a serious matter of scholarship during the 1960s. Definitions of strategy continued to be developed over the next fifty years. In 1962, Harvard Business School professor Alfred Chandler defined strategy as "the determination of the basic long-term goals of an enterprise, and the adoption of courses of action and the allocation of resources necessary for carrying out these goals" (Chandler, 1962). Another Harvard professor, Michael E. Porter, defined strategy as "broad formula for how a business is going to compete, what its goals should be, and what policies will be needed to carry out those goals" (Porter, 1980). Porter continued describing strategy as the "combination of the ends (goals) for which the firm is striving and the means (policies) by which it is seeking to get there" (Ibid.). In 1998, McGill University professor Henry Mintzberg and his colleagues performed a comprehensive review of the many definitions of management strategy (Mintzberg, Ahlstrand, & Lampel, 1998; Mintzberg & Quinn, 1988). Mintzberg held that strategy is a complex and fluid set of activities that include planning intended outcomes, recognizing patterns of intended and emerging activities, positioning an organization within an environment, making specific maneuvers to outperform competitors, and executing a "theory of the business." For the purposes of this book, we define strategic management as the process of developing and implementing long-term, top-level organizational objectives.

Seminal Theories of Strategic Management

In Table 10.1, four seminal theories of strategic management are presented. These are not only the important theoretical frameworks developed over the past half-century of scholarship, but they are theories that have played and continue to play a significant role in strategic thinking within the current economic system. The first three theories, as originally conceptualized, support the profit-driven motives typical of DAC. In each of these theories, good strategy is assessed as maximizing value for owners. However, each of these theories has the potential to be modified and utilized within a new SSBS framework. The final theory, Stakeholder Theory, is a foundation upon which to build socially sustainable business strategy.

Transaction Costs Economics

Transaction Costs Economics (TCE), as its name implies, has its roots in classic economics. Within TCE, firms are loci of transactions, internal and external. Internal transactions vary from the significant to the banal. For example, an automobile manufacturer might have significant internal transaction costs with regard to the logistics of moving parts within a manufacturing facility and the much less significant costs of maintaining onsite human resource records. External costs might include the price of purchasing raw materials or the amounts paid to government in the form of fees and taxes. In either case, TCE argues that good strategy seeks to minimize these costs to produce more profits for the owners. TCE has the potential to be utilized within SSBS by expanding the notion of costs to include *all* the costs of organizational activities. For example, internal costs such as wages could not simply be sought to be minimized. Wages would have to be socially sustainable. Similarly, external costs such as emissions and wastes would have to be accurately measured to reflect the costs to the commons rather than just the cost to the organization.

Agency Theory

Agency theory is closely associated with the Chicago School and, therefore, often used to explicitly justify strategic processes within the current destructive system. Agency theory holds that officers and directors have a duty as agents of the owners; all interests must be subordinated to ownership interests. Any strategic activity that does not serve shareholders is a violation of this duty. In other words, good strategy means good for the owners. Any other strategy is an impermissible infringement

TABLE 10.1 Four Seminal Theories of Strategic Management

Strategic Theory	*DAC Approach*	*SSBS Potential*
Transaction Costs Economics (TCE)	Firms reduce internal and external transaction costs by creating economic efficiencies. Good strategy enables some firms to reduce transaction costs more than others. Reduction in transaction costs creates value for stockholders.	Definition of *costs* can be expanded to include costs to the commons and human costs. Good strategy would decrease economic, environmental, and social costs of business transactions. Firms differentiate themselves by reducing the economic, social, and environmental costs creating value for stakeholders.
Agency	Officers and directors are agents of owners and have fiduciary duty to act in the best interest of stockholders. Focus on stockholder "value" maximization is the only legitimate strategic goal.	Definition of the duties of officers and directors can return to historical and legal norms. Officers and directors are fiduciaries of the corporation rather than stockholders. Good strategy maximizes the value of the corporation rather than the value for stockholders. Corporate value is not measured only by maximizing profits but by generating profits while acting in the interests of all stakeholders.
Ecology	Organizations function in an economic and social environment. Some organizations have better ecological fitness than others. Good strategy exploits internal resources and external resources in an ecological niche. Strategic success is evaluated by continuous environmental adaptation, continued survival, and growth.	Notions of economic and social environment can be expanded to include the legitimate interests of the planet and people. Good strategy would entail using organizational resources in such a way that matches the capabilities of an organization with the needs of the social and economic environment. Strategic success is evaluated by continuous adaptation to evolving internal and environmental demands. Survival and growth are desirable only in as much as the organization serves the legitimate interests of stakeholders, the planet, and society.
Stakeholder	Firms seek to maximize value to stakeholders by providing needed goods and services more effectively than competitors. Value is maximized without a system of trade-offs in which one stakeholder wins at the expense of another.	The interests of stakeholders are maximized. Stakeholders would not be limited to those narrowly impacted directly by the activities of an organization. Rather, stakeholders would be conceptualized in a broader or even global sense. Stakeholders would include all those significantly affected by the direct or indirect activities of an organization.

of the owners' "rights." This view has come to the current economic system, particularly within the United States. This view has dominated despite its incompatibility with the historic purpose of corporations and the legal requirements of corporate governance (Stout, 2012). Directors and officers who set corporate strategy often act as if they are fiduciaries of the shareholders alone. To modify traditional agency theory into a socially sustainable framework, the duty of officers and directors must return to the historic purpose of corporations—to generate wealth for the common good—and the actual legal requirements of corporate governance—to act in the best interests of the corporation. In addition, the best interests of the corporation must include the legitimate interests of people inside and outside the organization and of the planet on which the corporation depends.

Ecological Theories

Ecological theories of strategic management are exactly what they sound like. Just as biologists view organisms living and evolving within an ecosystem, organizational ecologists view firms operating and adapting within an economic ecosystem. Strategy, then, is the process of adapting organizational resources to best fit within an economic environment. This theory is incompatible with SSBS only because of the way that outcomes are measured. As in most other cases with DAC institutions and conceptualizations, the evaluation outcomes must be modified to be sustainable. Organizational ecology has the potential to be useful as a sustainable strategic framework if two modifications are made. First, organizational success must be redefined from *mere survival to survival while providing a social good without damaging the planet*. Second, the *economic environment* in which a firm operates must be modified to reflect the *actual environment*. All organizations depend upon the planet for their survival and people to produce and consume their goods and services. Therefore, sustainable ecological strategies must reflect that dependence by protecting the legitimate interests of planet and people.

Stakeholder Theory

Stakeholder Theory, first explicitly elucidated by Professor Edward Freeman in 1984, offers a radically different perspective on the purpose of a corporation compared to the previous theories. For Freeman, the purpose of a corporation was not to maximize value for shareholders but to maximize the value for stakeholders. Stakeholders were defined as "any group or individual who can affect or is affected by the achievement of the organization's objectives"(Freeman, 1984, p. 46). In Stakeholder Theory, the purpose of corporations is not to produce profit for the owners. Profit is the outcome of activities that create value for the stakeholders. Freeman makes a famous analogy explaining that the purpose of the human body is not to produce blood, but human bodies depend upon the production of blood to survive; similarly, the purpose of corporations is not to produce profit (Freeman, 2012). Critically, good strategy within

Stakeholder Theory does not mean pitting one group of stakeholders against others. Rather, the strategic process is to find value maximization without trading off legitimate interests of stakeholders. To be fully compatible with SSBS, Stakeholder Theory must simply expand Freeman's original definition of stakeholders. Social stakeholders of organizations must be viewed in the broadest possible sense: all people affected directly or indirectly by the activities of an organization. Additionally, the local and planetary environment must be viewed as a legitimate stakeholder.

Strategic Management Process

Besides the seminal theoretical frameworks discussed earlier, other strategic management tools and concepts could be utilized to help the SSBS organization to achieve the three goals of the triple bottom line. Figure 10.1 illustrates the strategic management process. This section will examine how strategic tools and frameworks within the strategic management process could be used to help business practitioners and students develop better strategy for businesses to become more sustainable and achieve their goals of SSBS.

Crafting the Vision and Mission Statements

An organization mission statement is the statement of the organization's purpose, its reason for existence (Hunger & Wheelen, 2014, p. 6). The mission statement allows the organization's members to stay focused. A strong mission statement can help employees to understand each and every day what they are trying to accomplish. Organizations also often go beyond the common mission statement

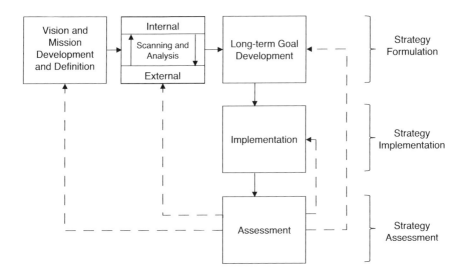

FIGURE 10.1 Strategic Management Process

and provide what is often a deeper, more meaningful and inspiring message. Some companies such as Medtronic include this as part of the entirety of their mission statement. For others, it might come through a vision statement (a statement of where an organization wants to be in the future). Other organizations might have a values statement or a credo.

INFORMATION BOX 10.1   JOHNSON & JOHNSON (N.D.) CREDO EXCERPTS

"We believe our first responsibility is to the doctors, nurses and patients, to mothers and fathers and all others who use our products and services . . . "

"We are responsible to our employees. . . . We must respect their dignity and recognize their merit. . . . Compensation must be fair and adequate, and working conditions clean, orderly and safe."

"We are responsible to the communities in which we live and work and to the world community as well. We must be good citizens . . . "

"Our final responsibility is to our stockholders. Business must make a sound profit . . . "

For instance, Johnson & Johnson has a well-known credo that focuses on its customers, employees, communities, and their responsibility to stockholders. Southwest Airlines credits a great deal of its success to the methods of communicating its mission statement. When the mission statement was first crafted, it was delivered to employees as a giant prize in a box of Cracker Jacks (Frieberg & Frieberg, 1996, p. 118). The company also posts its mission statement everywhere it can and then relies on employees to work towards achieving this mission each and every day. Interestingly, the Southwest Airlines mission statement does not mention profit. Instead, it focuses briefly on customer care, and then the focus turns to employees—stable work environment, opportunity for growth, creativity, and innovation. In essence, the mission statement reads like it was taken straight out of the goals of SSBS.

Internal and External Scanning/Analysis

The next step within the strategic management process involves companies scanning and analyzing their internal business and the external environment within which they operate. Based on their understanding of their internal and external situations, companies could develop their own long-term goals. In Table 10.2, four paradigms within strategic management are presented. Each of these paradigms provides a perspective to view the internal and external scanning/analysis process. Each provides insight into what organizational strategists ought to do. None of

TABLE 10.2 Four Strategic Management Paradigms

Paradigm	DAC Approach	SSBS Potential
Competitive advantage	Firms seek to develop competitive advantage by producing more profit and generating more stockholder value than competing firms. Firms develop and employ assets and practices that enable them to produce more profit than competitors.	The goal of competitive advantage is not to generate profits and maximize stockholder value better than competitors. The goal is to provide goods and services better than competitors while fulfilling the legitimate interests of stakeholders, the planet, and society.
Scanning (SWOT)	Organizations scan internally and externally to identify internal strengths and weaknesses and external opportunities and threats. The function of strategy is to use strengths to exploit opportunities and avoid threats and minimize challenges presented by internal weaknesses. SWOT analyses within the shareholder value paradigm often underestimate the weaknesses and threats connected with environmental and social damage. Similarly, profit-focus causes firms to ignore the external opportunities organizations have to improve conditions for the people of the planet.	Assessment and definition of SWOT need to be expanded to include social and environmental impact. Internal scanning must include an expanded view of the legitimate interests of workers. Threats must include the possibility of causing environmental and social damage. Opportunities must be limited to those that protect the legitimate interests of the people and planet. Opportunities must be expanded to include those that may not maximize shareholder value but do maximize stakeholder, social, and environmental value.
Five Forces	Strategic desirability is determined by assessment of buyer power, supplier power, threat of potential entrants, threat of substitutes, and industrial rivalry. The function of strategy is to exploit opportunities that minimize the negative potential and maximize the positive potential of controlling one of these forces. Firms avoid situations in which they are powerless and seize on situations in which they are powerful. Firms avoid entering markets in which the threat of potential entrants, the threat of substitutes, or intense competitive rivalry make the market unattractive.	Accumulation of organizational power is permissible only in as much as it serves the legitimate interests of stakeholders, the planet, and society. Firms are free to seek to provide goods and services that are unsubstitutable. Firms are free to avoid markets that are easily accessible by new entrants. Firms are free to avoid intense competitive rivalry.
Resource-based view	Firms seek to develop, maximize, and care for tangible and intangible internal resources that are valuable, rare, inimitable, and non-substitutable. Possession of these resources leads to competitive advantage as measured by the maximization of shareholder value.	Development, maximization, and care for resources that do not harm the legitimate interests of stakeholders, society, or the planet are fully permissible. Resources that lead to providing needed and acceptable goods and services more effectively than competitors lead to competitive advantage.

these paradigms as originally formulated explicitly addressed the legitimate interests of people and planet foundational to SSBS. All of these paradigms have been utilized to focus on shareholder value maximization and have, therefore, been servants of the current destructive system. However, all have the potential to be useful within an SSBS framework. Each can be modified in such a way as to support the outcomes of SSBS. This requires the focus of each strategic paradigm to move beyond the profit motive.

Competitive Advantage

The concept of competitive advantage underpins many notions of strategic management. The idea of competitive advantage concerns the ability of organizations to perform at a higher level than others within the same industries or markets; Porter emphasized that competitive advantage was an outcome of "many discrete activities" rather than a firm level attribute (Porter, 1985, p. 36). He argued that firm activities contribute to relative cost position, create a basis for differentiation, and determine strategic relevant activities. In other words, some firms do activities better than others. Critically, *performing* and *doing better* are almost exclusively measured in terms of financial performance. In DAC, profit is synonymous with performance; creating shareholder value is the measure of doing better.

Voluntary regimes such as CSR have not altered the view of competitive advantage as a means to achieve financial success. It is, however, possible to reformulate the concept of competitive advantage to fit within the SSBS framework. Socially Sustainable Competitive Advantage (SSCA) could be viewed as the ability of some organizations to provide stakeholders with value better than others while not damaging people and the planet. Within SSBS, the purpose of good strategy would be to generate an organization's SSCA rather than outperform other companies financially. To achieve SSCA, organizations would need to seek those strategic resources and implement strategic objectives that served the social good rather than the narrow interest of shareholders. Shareholder value could be a legitimate outcome of Socially Sustainable Strategy, but not its purpose. Strategies that achieved SSCA would attend to the legitimate interests of shareholders, but not seek to maximize them.

Strengths-Weaknesses-Opportunities-Threats (SWOT)

Closely related to ecological theories of strategic management is the strategic management paradigm of environmental scanning. The Society of Human Resource Management describes environmental scanning as "a process that systematically surveys and interprets relevant data to identify external opportunities and threats. An organization gathers information about the external world, its competitors and itself. The company should then respond to the information gathered by changing its strategies and plans when the need arises" (Society for Human Resource Management, 2012). Just as organisms evolutionarily develop the traits adapted to their ecosystems to thrive and reproduce, strategic managers seek to adapt to their competitive environments to thrive and survive. Perhaps the most commonly utilized form of environmental scanning is the SWOT analysis. The process of assessing an organization's internal strengths and weaknesses and assessing external strengths and opportunities has been a common feature of strategic management for the past fifty years. Within the current destructive economic system, SWOT analyses are designed to produce adaptive strategies that maximize competitive advantage.

SWOT analyses have the potential to fit within the SSBS framework if the purpose of the analysis is modified and the scanning of internal and external factors is expanded. Sustainable SWOT analyses must be aimed at developing SSCA. In other words, SWOT analyses must move way beyond assessment of factors that might maximize profits and shareholder value. With regard to internal scanning, sustainable SWOT analyses must greatly expand the view of legitimate interests of internal stakeholders, especially employees. For example, low labor costs could no longer be a strength if wages did not provide all employees with the ability to thrive and have their human rights and dignity preserved. Any internal activities that compromised the legitimate interests of the planet and its people would have to be carefully and frankly assessed. With regards to external opportunities and threats, expanded analyses would also be required. Strategic opportunities would include only those possibilities that promoted the social good without compromising people or the planet. Activities with the potential to do environmental or societal damage would have to be assessed as unacceptable strategic threats. For example, a sustainable SWOT analysis would carefully assess the threat of carbon emissions or other waste associated with organizational activities.

Porter's Five Forces

In 1979, Porter introduced what he called the "Five Forces analysis," which can be used to determine the attractiveness of an industry (Porter, 1979). Though the Five Forces model, strictly speaking, analyzes industries, it is often used as an analysis tool for an organization considering entering into a market. The Five Forces are (1) the threat of new entrants, (2) threat of substitutes, (3) bargaining power of buyers, (4) bargaining power of suppliers, and (5) competitive rivalry. Threat of new entrants describes the ease with which a firm can enter into a market. For example, the threat of new entry into the bauxite mining industry is low because entering this market is extremely expensive. Mineral rights must be obtained, expensive machinery must be purchased, and complex technical expertise must be developed. Similarly, the threat of substitutes in this industry is relatively low. Bauxite is required for the production of aluminum goods. No other mineral substitutes for bauxite. Other products might substitute for aluminum (plastic, glass, steel, or other metal alloys), but, assuming a demand for aluminum, bauxite is non-substitutable. Bargaining power of buyers and suppliers describes the relative power of those parties in the value chain. High bargaining power of suppliers indicates that an industry is highly dependent on materials and services that may be relatively hard to acquire. For example, there are only two large aircraft manufacturing companies; each has a limited manufacturing capability and faces limited price competition. This makes the airline industry relatively unattractive because there is high supplier power. The airline industry is attractive, however, from the perspective of the bargaining power of customers. There are many customers in this market and no powerful "super customers" that can determine market prices or make service demands on individual airlines. The final force, competitive rivalry, takes into consideration the interactions among competitors within an industry. For example, in the beer industry, there are many competitors, high advertising costs, and continuous product innovation. This makes the beer industry relatively undesirable because of this force.

Porter's Five Forces have the potential to contribute to socially sustainable business strategies. The Five Forces are consistent with SSBS as long as social and environmental factors are given full weight. However, these Five Forces are not sufficient to assess strategic decisions. Two new forces must be introduced: The threat to the planetary environment and the threat to human dignity and flourishing. In other words, Porter's Five Forces model must become a Socially Sustainable Seven Forces model. Importantly, the two new forces must take priority over the existing five. If a business activity includes a substantial threat to the planet or its people, then there would be no legitimate business strategy to pursue and the other five factors would be moot. In other words, if either the environment or humanity was threatened, the threat of new entrance and new substitutes would not matter, nor would the bargaining power of buyers and suppliers be relevant. Similarly, competitive rivalry within an industry would be unimportant if an activity threatened either the planet or its people. The Socially Sustainable Seven Forces model, therefore, has two necessary forces (threat to planet and threat to people) and five sufficient forces (threat of new entrants, threat of substitutes, buyer power, supplier power, and competitive rivalry).

Resource-Based View

The resource-based view (RBV) helps firms analyze their internal environment for strategy formulation. With its original focus on companies gaining and sustaining competitive advantage, RBV states that a firm develops competitive advantage by not only acquiring but also developing, combining, and effectively deploying its physical, human, and organizational resources in ways that add unique value and are difficult for competitors to imitate (Barney, 1991). The RBV differentiates resources and capabilities. Resources are inputs of the production process and include physical and financial assets, employees' skills, organizational (social) processes, and so on (Hart, 1995). Capabilities are defined as the capacities of a bundle of resources being brought together to perform particular value-added tasks or activities (Ibid.). RBV posits that firms' capabilities to create sustained competitive advantage are supported by resources that are immobile, unique, and not easily duplicated by competitors (Barney, 1991). Figure 10.2 illustrates the basic tenets of RBV over time (Wade & Hulland, 2004).

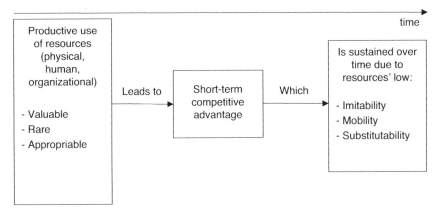

FIGURE 10.2 Resource-Based View Tenets

The RBV framework could be used to support firms in developing socially sustainable business strategies. Research has shown that environmental, social, and economic performance are positively linked, and a focus on sustainability could help firms improve operation, innovation, and strategic growth, while gaining a sustained competitive advantage and delivering sustainable values to the broader society (Colbert & Kurucz, 2007; Hart & Milstein, 2003; Porter & Kramer, 2006).

To develop capabilities to address social and environmental issues, a company needs to engage in wide-ranging activities within itself, such as changing business culture and redesigning business processes. Additionally, the company also needs to actively engage in extensive interaction with its external stakeholders such as suppliers, customers, regulators, shareholders, NGOs, the media, etc., and integrate their sustainability view into the firm's business operation and strategy. To successfully engage in such activities, the company needs to effectively coordinate bundles of complex human and non-human resources to develop capabilities for action. Such capabilities deliver sustainable values to the firm's stakeholders and help the firm gain sustained competitive advantage.

INFORMATION BOX 10.2   COSTCO'S SUSTAINABILITY-ENABLED COMPETITIVE ADVANTAGE

Multiple aspects of Costco's sustainability-oriented resources/capabilities are difficult to imitate, helping the company deliver sustainability while maintaining its competitive advantage. Such resources/capabilities include:

- a well-developed supply chain of sustainable products;
- an environmentally friendly operation; and
- well-treated employees who are loyal.

For example, for a company to enable its sustainable internal operation, it needs to train and develop employees to build the level of intellectual capital geared towards sustainability. Such employee development and employee safety and health would increase employee involvement in continuous process improvements for sustainability. Empirical studies found that firms pursuing such strategies and practices end up developing capabilities that enable them to improve performance in all three aspects of the triple bottom line and could be considered rent-earning capabilities that confer competitive advantage (Bansal & Roth, 2000; Vachon & Klassen, 2007).

Over time, as companies develop a web of interaction with external stakeholders for sustainability, a network of information and knowledge exchange between the firms and their external stakeholders helps them steward the sustainability of their products and services. Such product stewardship practices enable firms to deliver sustainability values to both their stakeholders and themselves. Studies have suggested that supply chain partners engaging in sustainability stewardship bundle their resources into capabilities that have the potential result of SSCA for the supply chain as a whole.

Long-Term Goal Development/Strategy Formulation

Once companies have finished their internal and external scanning and analysis, insights from such processes help them formulate long-term goals/strategy for their business. In this section, four generic business strategies will be discussed within the context of SSBS. Just as the previously discussed theories and perspectives with strategic management were not developed with the explicit goals of achieving social and environmental sustainability, these generic strategies were principally envisioned to help firms achieve financial goals to maximize profit and create shareholder value. Just as with the theories and perspectives, the generic strategies are generally not inherently opposed to social sustainability. Each, with modification, has potential to impact strategic formulation and implementation within a new SSBS paradigm. Table 10.3 presents four generic business strategies. For each strategy, both the DAC and SSBS interpretation are presented. Each of the four generic strategies will be briefly discussed. Next, three SSBS strategic necessities will be offered.

Cost Leadership

Cost leadership is the most basic generic strategy. In this strategy, firms seek to sell products or services more cheaply than their competitors. The ultimate goal of this strategy is to grow market share and produce profits based on high volume rather than high margin. Though low prices are not in and of themselves undesirable in SSBS, many of the predictors of low prices in the current destructive economic system are anathema to social sustainability efforts. As Marx and Engels pointed out in *The Communist Manifesto*, low prices are often tied to low wages.

TABLE 10.3 Generic Business Strategies

Generic Strategy	DAC Interpretation	SSBS Interpretation
Cost leadership	Firms seek to attract and retain customers principally by offering goods and services at a lower price. Growing market share is critical in this strategy. Firms pursuing this strategy must minimize costs to produce profits.	Often problematic in terms of SSBS. Minimizing labor costs is generally not consistent with aims of SSBS. Minimizing costs of raw materials and production is similarly problematic. Firms with too much market share may not be responsive to the legitimate interests of all stakeholders. Cost leadership strategies may be pursued under SSBS only if not based upon exploitation of employees, customers, or natural resources.
Differentiation	Firms provide goods and services that are distinct from those of other firms. Customers are attracted because the firm is the only provider of a more desirable product or service. Firms pursuing this strategy must develop human capital and the resulting intellectual property that sets them apart from their competitors.	Firms may pursue socially sustainable differentiation strategies by offering superior goods or services compared to competitors. Differentiation is in no way incompatible with SSBS provided that the good or service is produced in a sustainable manner and that the good or service is, in itself, sustainable.
Focus	Firms pursuing this strategy concentrate on a specific market niche whether it is a customer segment, a product segment, or a geographic market. This strategy requires companies to specialize and adapt to specific market requirements to outperform competitors.	Firms may pursue socially sustainable focus strategies by concentrating on a specific market niche. Focus is in no way incompatible with SSBS provided that the good or service is produced in a sustainable manner and that the good or service is, in itself, sustainable. Additionally, firms may not use their focus to exploit a particular market, especially labor or consumer markets. For example, the exploitation of a monopoly is not socially sustainable.
Diversification	Firms seek to minimize risk and maximize returns by expanding into a wide range of economic activities. In vertical diversification, firms seek to compete up and down the supply chain of a specific product or service. In horizontal diversification, firms seek to enter multiple customer or product segments.	Firms may pursue socially sustainable diversification strategies. Vertical diversification has the potential to reduce environmental impact and reduce costs without the exploitation of labor, natural resources, and the environment. Both forms are permissible if goods and services are produced in a sustainable manner and are, in themselves, sustainable.

The push for efficient production most often centers on wage earner exploitation. When apple growers or other agricultural producers seek to sell their goods at lower prices, they drive the wages for picking down to maintain profits. Similarly, lowering production costs in the current economic system often relies on unacceptable exploitation of natural resources or unacceptable production of waste products. For example, chicken farmers, beef producers, and other factory farm operations often keep prices low by compromising air and water quality. A more subtle problem with this strategy was mentioned in Chapters 1 and 2. Cost leadership often leads to the production of low-quality, "disposable" goods. For example, household consumer goods such as toasters have had their economic lives reduced to enable them to be sold at a "lower" price.

Differentiation

The differentiation strategy is pursued by firms that wish to offer a good or service that is perceived as superior to that of its competitors. These products are often more expensive than those offered by other firms. For example, Apple iPads are often significantly more expensive for the same amount of memory compared to tablets from other manufacturers. Apple offers a wide variety of electronic devices, and, as a rule, these products are more expensive than those offered by competitors. Presumably, Apple continues to acquire customers because consumers view the Apple product to be superior and, therefore, worth the price difference. In and of itself, Apple's or any other company's differentiation strategy is not inconsistent with SSBS.

Companies could pursue socially sustainable differentiation strategy by truly embracing sustainability values in their strategy and action. For example, as companies pay and treat employees well, the engaged employees could in turn provide superior goods and services to customers, an approach that many companies have embraced successfully, including SAS, Chobani, and Ben & Jerry's.

INFORMATION BOX 10.3   BEN & JERRY'S DIFFERENTIATION BY EMBRACING SUSTAINABILITY

Ben & Jerry's, the producer of ice cream, frozen yogurt, and sorbet, differentiates itself from other competitors as a company that places social and environmental sustainability at the heart of its business model while flourishing as a business. The company's mission is made up of three parts:

- product: offers high quality and environmentally friendly products;
- economic: provides sustainable financial growth that benefits its stakeholders, including employees; and
- social: uses the company's business in innovative ways to make the world a better place.

The company pays its entry-level employees a starting salary twice the minimum wage. Its workers get paid leave and health club memberships. The employees, in turn, deliver exceptional products and services.

Focus

Companies pursuing a focus strategy seek to outperform their competitors in a particular market niche. Some seek to dominate a particular product line. For example, Rolex focuses exclusively on luxury watches. Other companies focus on particular geographic markets or regional demands. For example, Vegemite (a food spread) is a household staple in Australia but almost unheard of in North America. Other companies pursue a focus strategy by providing goods or services to a particular consumer group. For example, Black Entertainment Television (BET) is programmed specifically for an African American audience, and this focus has led to its broad adoption as a basic cable and satellite channel. Rather than competing in the broader entertainment market, BET focuses on African American viewers and attracts advertisers specifically seeking this audience. Focus strategies, whether with regard to product, geography, or consumer niches, do not in and of themselves conflict with socially sustainable business practices as long as the consumers within these niches are not exploited. Intentional monopolistic strategies sometimes pursued under the guise of the focus strategy are not permissible. For example, the pharmaceutical company Mylan recently has raised the price of an EpiPen (an emergency injection device to halt allergic reactions) from $100 in 2007 to $600 in 2016 (Johnson, 2016). In most US markets, no substitute product was available for this generic medication.

Diversification

The final generic strategy discussed in this section is diversification. Firms employing this strategy do so in an effort to reduce risks or create efficiencies. There are two basic forms of diversification:

vertical: diversifying up or down a supply chain to create efficiencies and/or reduce risks. For example, a restaurant chain might vertically diversify up the supply chain into meat packing, beef production, and feed production to reduce final consumer product costs and avoid market risks concerning the price of a commodity.

horizontal: diversifying across markets can also be employed to create efficiencies and/or reduce risks. For example, an operator of ski resorts might diversify into golf resorts to reduce seasonality and might diversify into a consumer staple product such as dairy to limit economic risks associated with recessions.

Both forms of diversification are potentially socially sustainable. Socially sustainable systems are certainly permitted to reduce economic risks. Finding efficiencies that do not come from reducing wages or exploiting the environment are similarly desirable within the SSBS framework.

All of the generic strategies have the potential to be employed in a socially sustainable manner. It should be noted that most large corporations pursue more than one generic strategy. Oftentimes, this involves integrating two of the generic strategies. For example, cost leadership is often paired with focus. Discount Tires pursues a focus strategy (only tires and tire-related maintenance) and cost leadership (offering a low price guarantee). For firms that pursue integrative strategies, the SSBS opportunities are the same as for those of the other generic strategies.

Strategy Implementation and Assessment

Once companies have successfully formulated their long-term goals and strategy, they will engage in specific business actions to carry out such strategy. To implement these actions, companies will need to engage multiple business functions. The involvement of such business functions for sustainable business strategy and actions has been discussed in earlier chapters, including human resource management, operation management, supply chain management, and IT management. It is important that business resources and governance structures also be managed properly for sustainability. A majority of large US companies have also embraced the balanced scorecard approach in measuring their business performance (Kaplan & Norton, 1996; see Figure 10.3). While the balanced scorecard approach takes multiple perspectives towards measuring business performance, it was developed with the goal of profit maximization. We propose that besides the current perspectives, the balanced scorecard approach could be enhanced to include environmental and social perspectives to enable companies to measure their business performance in line with SSBS.

For example, in measuring the outcomes of companies' business actions, SSBS calls for a change in outcome measurement. The utility of business strategy and actions cannot be assessed merely in terms of profits. A broader view of outcomes that takes into account the legitimate interests of the people and planet must be adopted. To do so, we offer three Socially Sustainable Strategic Necessities:

1. Production of goods and services must not harm employees, vendors, or other persons in the supply chain. Instead, strategies are permissible only when they provide for a full scheme of human rights and dignity for the people involved in production.
2. Production of goods and services must not harm the environment in terms of either natural resources used or waste created. Instead, strategies are permissible only when they protect the environment up and down the supply chain, and all waste products must be environmentally sustainable.

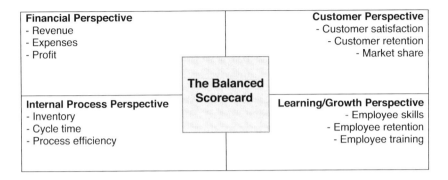

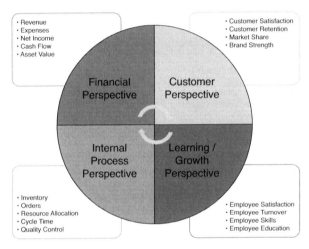

FIGURE 10.3 The Balanced Scorecard

Source: http://bi-insider.com/business-intelligence/balanced-scorecard-defined/

3. Products and service must be, in of themselves, sustainable and provide for a public good. It is not permissible to produce products that cannot continue to be produced over time or that harm the people or the planet (e.g., chemical weapons).

The three necessities then predicate companies' business strategy and actions. In other words, any business strategy and action may be pursued if it meets the requirements set forth in the Socially Sustainable Strategic Necessities.

Conclusion

In this chapter, we have examined in more detail the role of business strategic management in enabling companies to become more sustainable. More specifically, the chapter has examined different strategic management theories, perspectives, and tools, and proposed ways that they could be adapted to help companies in developing SSBS business strategy.

Discussion Questions

1. Develop a socially sustainable mission or vision statement for an organization of your choosing.
2. Develop a list of objectives to help you to achieve the mission/vision statement in Question 1.
3. Conduct a SWOT analysis or Porter's Five Forces analysis of a business of your choice; make sure to incorporate social and environmental values into your analysis.
4. What are some measures of social and environmental performance that you would recommend to be incorporated into an expansion of the balanced scorecard for SSBS?

Notes

1 www.brainyquote.com/quotes/quotes/m/michaelpor381636.html Retrieved March 16, 2017.
2 https://en.wikiquote.org/wiki/Sun_Tzu Retrieved March, 16, 2017.
3 www.interpraxis.com/quotes.htm Retrieved March, 16, 2017.

References

Bansal, P., & Roth, K. (2000). Why companies go green: A model of ecological responsiveness. *Academy of Management Journal, 43*(4), 717–736.
Barney, J. B. (1991). Firm resources and sustained competitive advantage. *Journal of Management, 17,* 99–120.
Chandler, A. (1962). *Strategy and Structure: Chapters in the History of Industrial Enterprise.* New York: Doubleday.
Colbert, B. A., & Kurucz, E. C. (2007). Three conceptions of triple bottom line business sustainability and the role for HRM. *People and Strategy, 30*(1), 21.
Freeman, R. E. (1984). *Strategic Management: A Stakeholder Approach.* Boston: Pitman.
Freeman, R. E. (2012, May 18) *Edward Freeman: Businesses Should Be Driven by Purpose.* Retrieved February 27, 2017, from forbesindia.com: www.forbesindia.com/article/third-anniversary-special/edward-freeman-businesses-should-be-driven-by-purpose/32934/1
Frieberg, K., & Frieberg, J. (1996). *Nuts!: Southwest Airlines' Crazy Recipe for Business and Personal Success.* New York: Broadway.
Hart, S. L. (1995). A natural-resource-based view of the firm. *Academy of Management Review, 20*(4): 986–1014.
Hart, S. L., & Milstein, M. B. (2003). Creating sustainable value. *The Academy of Management Executive, 17*(2), 56–67.
Hunger, J. D., & Wheelen, T. L. (2014). *Essentials of Strategic Management.* New York: Pearson.

Johnson & Johnson. (n.d.). *Our Credo.* Retrieved June 6, 2017 from www.jnj.com/about-jnj/jnj-credo

Johnson, C. Y. (2016, September 21) *EpiPen CEO to Defend Lifesaving Drug's Soaring Price in Front of Lawmakers.* Retrieved February 27, 2016, from Washington Post: www.washingtonpost.com/news/wonk/wp/2016/09/21/what-to-expect-when-congress-takes-on-epipen-maker-mylan/?utm_term=.44230827bd90

Kaplan, R. S., & Norton, D. P. (1996). *The Balanced Scorecard: Translating Strategy into Action.* Cambridge, MA: Harvard Business Press.

Mintzberg, H., Ahlstrand, B., & Lampel, J. (1998). *Strategy Safari: A Guided Tour through the Wilds of Strategic Management.* New York: The Free Press.

Mintzberg, H., & Quinn, J. B. (1988). *The Strategy Process.* Harlow, UK: Prentice-Hall.

Porter, M. E. (1979, March-April). How competitive forces shape strategy. *Harvard Business Review, 57*(2), 137–145.

Porter, M. E. (1980). *Competitive Strategy.* New York: Free Press.

Porter, M. E. (1985). *Competitive Advantage: Creating and Sustaining Superior Performance.* New York: Free Press.

Porter, M., & Kramer, M. (2006). Strategy & society: The link between competitive advantage and corporate social responsibility. *Harvard Business Review, 84*(12),78–92.

Society for Human Resource Management. (2012, November 27). *Strategic Planning: What Are the Basics of Environmental Scanning?* Retrieved February 27, 2017, from www.shrm.org: www.shrm.org/resourcesandtools/tools-and-samples/hr-qa/pages/cms_021670.aspx

Stout, L. A. (2012). The problem of corporate purpose. *Issues in Governance Studies, 48,* 1–14.

Wade, M., & Hulland, J. (2004). The resource-based view and information systems research: Review, extension, and suggestions for future research. *MIS Quarterly, 28*(1), 107–142.

Vachon, S., & Klassen R. D. (2007). Supply chain management and environmental technologies: The role of integration. *International Journal of Production Research, 45*(2), 401–423.

CASE 10   COSTCO'S STRATEGY FOR SSBS

Costco was founded in 1983 by Jim Senegal and Jeffrey Brotman. Since that time, the company has grown to more than $118 billion in annual revenues, more than seven hundred warehouses, and more than 126,000 full-time employees (Yahoo Finance, 2017). Costco also has been extremely profitable with more than $15 billion in gross profit and more than $2 billion in net operating income in 2016 alone. While Costco has been a tremendous success from a financial standpoint, it is perhaps just as well known for its progressive employment practices. Costco is consistently ranked as one of the best employers to work for both within the retail industry and across all rankings.

According to a 2014 survey by Glassdoor, Costco ranks second in terms of employee satisfaction with their compensation and benefits. Costco ranked behind only Google and only by fractions of a point, ranking ahead of companies such as Microsoft and Facebook (Cohn, 2014). Costco also ranked second on Forbes's list of best employers in 2014 (Forbes, n.d.).

Costco takes care of its employees. The company pays a living wage, and the CEO, Craig Jelinek, believes in raising the minimum wage for all workers (Short, 2013). Costco pays its employees an average hourly wage of $11.50 to start. After five years, the average Costco employee earns $19.50 an hour and receives a bonus of more than $2,000 every six months (Lutz, 2013). "Hourly workers make an average of more than $20 an hour—well above the national average of $11.39 for a retail sales worker—according to a 2013 Businessweek story" (Taube, 2014). Costco also has a history of taking care of its workers when tough times hit. After the recession of 2008, Costco approved wage increases for workers while its competitors were laying off workers (Short, 2013).

Both full-time and part-time employees are eligible for benefits and on average spend only 12% of their pay for benefits coverage (Lutz, 2013). As a result, 88% of Costco's 185,000 employees partake in company health and welfare benefits. Both full- and part-time employees receive health and dental insurance; can participate in a 401(k); and receive paid holidays, vacation, and sick time (Entis, 2014). Costco has also been committed to staying closed on Thanksgiving because it believes its workers deserve the time off to spend with their families (Short, 2013).

Costco is also committed to equity and equality. Costco's CEO, CFO, and even the founder all received base pay less than $1 million in 2016 (Yahoo Finance, 2017). Jelinek, the CEO, makes about 48 times the wage of the average Costco employee, in comparison to Walmart's CEO, who earns as much as 796 times the average Walmart worker (Short, 2013). Costco is also committed to inclusion:

It always has been and continues to be Costco's policy that employees should be able to enjoy a work environment free from all forms of unlawful employment discrimination. All decisions regarding recruiting, hiring, promotion, assignment, training, termination, and other terms and conditions of employment will be made without unlawful discrimination on the basis of race, color, national origin, ancestry, sex, sexual orientation, gender identity or expression, religion, age, pregnancy, disability, work-related injury, covered veteran status, political ideology, genetic information, marital status, or any other factor that the law protects from employment discrimination.

(Costco, n.d.)

Costco embraces equality. Costco scored extremely well (90/100) on the Human Rights Campaign's Corporate Equality Index—an assessment of LGBT policies in the workplace (Short, 2013). Costco provides access to its diversity data directly on its website. According to its Type 2 Employer Information Report, 2800 of its 11,271 managers are female, and about 1600 are minorities.

As a result of these pro-employee practices in addition to the financial success, Costco's turnover rate for employees who have been there a year or more is only 5%, an extremely low rate for an industry that averages 66% (Peterson, 2015). Costco also averages $814 in sales per square foot, while Sam's Club makes just $586 per square foot (Lutz, 2013).

Discussion Questions

1. Examine Costco's mission statement and its commitment to sustainability. Discuss how Costco's actions described in the case are tied to Costco's mission and commitment to sustainability.
2. Pick one of the seminal theories discussed in the chapter and apply that to analyze Costco's business in terms of sustainability commitment and actions.
3. Conduct an internal and external scanning/analysis for Costco.
4. What do you think are some social and environmental performance measures that could be used to evaluate Costco's performance in an expanded balanced scorecard approach?

References

Cohn, E. (2014, May 23). *Costco Employees Happier With Pay Than Many in Silicon Valley*. Retrieved January 18, 2017, from Huffington Post: www.huffingtonpost. com/2014/05/23/costco-pay-benefits-glassdoor_n_5375193.html

Costco. (n.d.). *Inclusion.* Retrieved from Costco: www.costco.com/inclusion.html

Entis, L. (2014, May 23). *The 25 Best Companies for Employee Compensation and Benefits.* Retrieved January 18, 2017, from Entrepreneur: www.entrepreneur.com/article/234183

Forbes. (n.d.). Retrieved from Forbes: www.forbes.com/pictures/mlf45ejldl/2-costco-wholesale/?utm_source=finance.yahoo.com&utm_medium=partner&utm_campaign=full%20text&partner=yahoo#64b80a912ccd

Lutz, A. (2013, March 6). *Costco Is the Perfect Example of Why the Minimum Wage Should Be Higher.* Retrieved January 8, 2017, from Business Insider: www.businessinsider.com/costco-ceo-supports-minimum-wage-hike-2013-3

Peterson, H. (2015, October 23). *Walmart, Target, and TJ Maxx Are Facing a Worker Crisis.* Retrieved January 18, 2017, from Business Insider: www.businessinsider.com/walmart-target-and-tj-maxx-are-facing-a-worker-crisis-2015-10

Short, K. (2013, November 19). *11 Reasons to Love Costco That Have Nothing to Do with Shopping.* Retrieved January 18, 2017, from Huffington Post—Business: www.huffingtonpost.com/2013/11/19/reasons-love-costco_n_4275774.html

Taube, A. (2014, October 23). *Why Costco Pays Its Retail Employees $20 an Hour.* Retrieved January 18, 2017, from Business Insider: www.businessinsider.com/costco-pays-retail-employees-20-an-hour-2014-10

Yahoo Finance. (2017, Janaury 18). *Costco Wholesale Profile.* Retrieved from Yahoo Finance: http://finance.yahoo.com/quote/COST/profile?p=COST

11

PSYCHOLOGY AND SOCIALLY SUSTAINABLE BUSINESS SYSTEMS

Indeed, environmentalists need all the help that they can get from psychology. Psychology has the keys we need. Most environmental social science literature assumes that rational economic self-interest (i.e., the cool-minded pursuit of the dollar or of material utilities) is the only human factor worthy of consideration. Psychologists are aware that humans are moved by emotion and mood, as well as by reason, and are also aware that humans distort information in predictable ways.

(Anderson, 2001, p. 457)

A squirrel dying in front of your house may be more relevant to your interests right now than people dying in Africa.

Mark Zuckerberg,[1] Facebook founder

Introduction

Psychology is defined as the science of behavior and mental processes (APA, 2016). Behavior consists of observable responses and is often thought to be shaped by experience and the environment, though many of our behaviors have a genetic predisposition. Mental processes include our thoughts, perceptions, and other activity that we consider to be part of the mind. Thus, psychological influences can arise from many factors, and it is often helpful, broadly speaking, to consider a number of perspectives when attempting to explain psychological phenomena, some of which are alluded to in Figure 11.1. Table 11.1 lists psychology's major perspectives and gives an example of how these perspectives can inform our understanding of sustainability issues. Similarly, we can understand psychological influences from various levels of analysis from the micro (small-scale) to macro (large-scale) and the interactions (mutual cause and effect influences) between various levels. In addition, when explaining psychological as well as physical conditions (such as heart disease

FIGURE 11.1 The Machinations of the Mind

Source: https://pixabay.com/en/thoughts-think-psyche-psychology-551263/ (retrieved July 2, 2016)

TABLE 11.1 Major Perspectives in Psychology

Perspective	Description	Sustainability Example
Behavioral	Looks at how rewards and punishments and learning through experience shape future behavior; how people adapt to their circumstances (adaptation is also biologically predisposed)	Increasing pro-social behaviors through incentives; realizing the positive feelings via interacting with nature and showing pro-social behaviors; coping with climate change
Biological	Looks at how brain structures, hormones, neurotransmitters, and our shared characteristics with other species and inherited traits shape behavior	Short-term needs are emphasized over possible long-term needs (consequences of current actions may not consider effects years down the road), drive for power and conquest but also a drive for altruism
Clinical	Looks at how people develop psychological problems and how to treat them	Rates of psychological disorders are higher in areas of poverty and poor environmental quality; helping people cope with the social and environmental consequences of climate change

TABLE 11.1 (Continued)

Perspective	Description	Sustainability Example
Cognitive	Looks at how we process information, think, remember, perceive, and make decisions	Difficulties (biases) people have in making logical decisions, difficulties in perceiving slow changes, what is perceived in the here and now is more pressing than that which is occurring elsewhere or more distant in the future (possibly also a biological predisposition)
Humanistic	Looks at our potential for good and self-understanding	When we have a high level of self-respect and awareness, we can more easily treat others with dignity
Psychoanalytic/ psychodynamic	Looks at unconscious influences on human behavior	Some people deny that there are sustainability problems or rationalize their current levels of unsustainability
Social-cultural	Looks at how groups and society influence behavior	Behaving in sustainable ways because others around us do so and/or because the community structure supports sustainable choices

or responses to stressors), a bio–psycho–social model is often used to explain the outcome. For example, one's outlook on life and social environment (culture) can moderate a genetic predisposition towards heart disease.

Recent Attention on Psychology's Contribution to Sustainability

Numerous publications beginning in the 1980s have recognized the relevance of psychology to solving problems of sustainability, not only academic (McKenzie-Mohr, 2000; Myers & Twenge, 2016; Swim, Clayton, & Howard, 2011) but also the community perspective (Manning, 2009). Though not new to the issue, in its earlier period, psychology tended to focus more on environmental issues (e.g., the eco-psychology movement beginning in the 1970s) while not striving to solve the broader issues and complexities of sustainability problems (Pelletier, Lavergne, & Sharp, 2008). Clearly, climate change related impacts on people and the environment are human-caused events, thus an understanding of human behavior is crucial if we are to solve the myriad sustainability problems we face today. Psychology informs us as to how behavior patterns are established, maintained, and changed. Furthermore, psychology helps us understand peoples' cognitive processing, which includes how they form and maintain attitudes, evaluate risks, perceive changes in their environments, and make decisions and attempt to solve problems. Primarily, the focus from psychology has been on addressing behavioral impacts on the environment and then impacts on people (Pelletier, Lavergne, & Sharp, 2008). We extend this work in this chapter by illustrating psychology's contribution to social sustainability, as well as addressing gaps in the psychology of sustainability. Thinking within the psychological domain and its relevance to sustainability has also provided new insights, among which is that the social and environmental are inextricably intertwined (e.g., Adams, 2014; Hiedanpää, Jokinen, & Jokinen, 2012), indicating that perhaps these two "pillars" of sustainability are not as separate as is often thought. However, given that the environmental aspects of sustainability tend to be emphasized to a greater extent (e.g., using more green sources of energy, recycling, etc.), we feel that the social impacts are especially relevant as we aim for the "true" sustainability we highlight in this book if we are to truly solve sustainability problems. We also acknowledge that there is no simple or universally agreed upon definition of sustainability and the emphasis that should be placed on its various dimensions, which is something you should consider as you develop your viewpoints on sustainability issues. It may also be necessary to consider that sustainability is a problem that is "beyond super wicked" (Revkin, 2011), in that the solution will not be solved by any one discipline, nor through interdisciplinary collaboration, but perhaps only via "transdisciplinary" research (Ernst, & Wenzel, 2014)—specific knowledge gaining methods that solve current problems, argued to avoid some of the pitfalls such as the time-lag involved in traditional academic/scientific approaches.

One issue we feel is important to consider in trying to solve all of the myriad sustainability problems is Urzell & Räthzell's (2009) distinction between *weak and strong sustainability*. "Weak" sustainability is basically the status quo: individuals continue to consume but do so using more environmentally sound ways. It focuses on the individual changing their behavior rather than the corporation per se (which will still produce as much if not more than before). It could also include minimal efforts towards sustainability, including "greenwashing," that are meant to enhance a corporation's view by the public, and even our own sustainability efforts that fall short (e.g., engaging in recycling, but doing little to reduce our overall carbon footprint). "Strong" sustainability questions the economic status quo such as the size of existing markets, and demands more active citizens' participation in the design and operation of our social institutions. Some investigators are aware of the distinction. For example, Corral-Verdugo, Mireles-Acosta, Tapia-Fonllem, and Fraijo-Sing (2011) argue that sustainability is defined as the simultaneous engagement of pro-environmental and pro-social behaviors.

As mentioned in Chapter 3, more attention is being placed on social sustainability than in the past (e.g., UN declaration 2015). Psychology is well-positioned, at least in some respects, to address not only environmental consequences but also social consequences of our behavior.

Mutually Interacting Causal Spheres of Social and Psychological Influences

To provide a framework for thinking about the various spheres of influence on people, it will be useful to consider *Bronfenbrenner's ecological framework* that has had

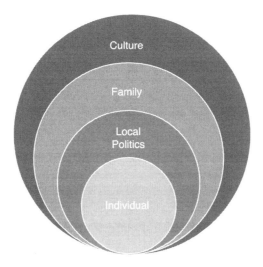

FIGURE 11.2 Bronfenbrenner's Ecological Theory of Development

Source: https://en.wikipedia.org/wiki/File:Bronfenbrenner%27s_Ecological_Theory_of_
Development.jpg

success in understanding influences on how we develop from infancy to adulthood (see Figure 11.2).

This model acknowledges that understanding human behavior and thinking is complex, and involves multidimensional levels that all interact (Bronfenbrenner, 1979). For example, this model can help explain how our behavior is influenced by our immediate surroundings such as family and peers, as well as macro-influences such as mass media and politics. It should be fairly obvious that changing behavior so that it is more socially sustainable will require interventions at multiple levels of scale, a point made in terms of implementing effective community interventions (Schensul, 2009). This is important because even if we decide on our own to change our behavior through self-regulation (e.g., Bandura, 1991), the influence of that change would be small unless adopted by a large fraction of the population (and as mentioned previously, the larger economic system might go unchanged). For example, one person, one group of people, or even one large city that embarks on a comprehensive recycling program just cannot stem the tide of waste. Changes such as "reduce, reuse, and recycle" cannot succeed in turning the tide of DAC if accomplished only at the individual or local level. At more macro levels of analysis, psychology has recently been applied to government policy using behavioral economics, for example, by showing how default settings can increase retirement savings (Sunstein, 2013; also some governments have established behavioral science offices to solve social problems, both in the United States (https://sbst.gov/) and in the United Kingdom (www.behaviouralinsights.co.uk/). More detail on these areas of influence will follow.

Micro-Influences

There are many examples of successful interventions for increasing sustainable behavior. As mentioned previously, people can take this up on their own, to change behavior in ways that not only benefit the environment but people as well (e.g., purchasing only eco-certified, fair trade products). Sometimes, behavior is easy to change. Other times, it might be problematic due to cost issues, etc. In other cases, such as energy consumption, outside influences might be needed. The micro-influences here are treated as such because they are targeted at the individual level. The most basic micro-level influence would be an individual behavior change program, as is often implemented in health management strategies such as weight loss and smoking cessation, but can also be applied in other settings such as marketing (Nord & Peter, 1980). The basic ideas here are to first track the problem behavior to establish a baseline. Next, a plan is implemented for increasing or decreasing the target behavior. The actual behavior is carefully monitored and recorded and compared to the goals that are set individually or in consultation with someone else (such as a physician or other expert). Typically, the person also decides on some reward as a motivator to be attained when the target behavior is achieved in a stable way. There has been application of behavior modification to work settings, though these methods are generally critiqued here (Schneier, 1974). While it remains to be seen, *behavior modification* could be applied to improve social sustainability if managers, executives, and other key decision makers were operating in an environment that incorporated behavior modification into their work (i.e., if these key decision makers were rewarded for good social sustainability practices). More recently, *Self-Determination Theory* has been applied to sustainability by incorporating cognitive/motivational factors into behavior (Kasser, 2009), such as interest and challenge, along with other outside, social factors such as shame. Kasser refers to the perceptual effects that can impair sustainability via the concept of "distancing." A problem that is close by has more impact on us compared to one that is more distant. Kasser discusses this in the context of, among other things, the weak labor standards and working conditions of products made far away—if the product is produced in that same harmful way locally, it may create more of an uproar from the consumer.

Other sustainability initiatives incorporate aspects similar to behavior modification programs. For example, *incentives* are commonly implemented to get people to switch to solar power, use less energy (e.g., by having the person's power bill reflect the energy usage of their neighbors), or purchase an electric/hybrid vehicle. Some of these are discussed in the context of *social influence tactics*, such as the comparison of energy use to that of one's neighbors (Cialdini, 2003), and *social proof* (people looking to others in their surroundings for cues for how to behave, which could be also considered a macro-influence as in Bronfenbrenner's model as well as an extension of conformity). Specific influence tactics such as the *foot-in-the-door phenomenon* (Swim, Clayton, & Howard, 2011) can also be useful for getting people to commit to bigger sustainability changes (after agreeing to a small change such as conserving electricity).

INFORMATION BOX 11.1   A RAY OF HOPE

Positive psychology (Seligman & Csikszentmihalyi (2000)) is an emerging field within the broader discipline that calls for a renewed focus on the psychological flourishing of healthy people. One stream of research within this movement concerns hope. Hope is defined as seeing the way to achieving a goal and having the will to stay on the path—*waypower and willpower* (Snyder, Rand, & Sigmon, 2002). Hope has been tied to many important positive individual outcomes such as psychological well-being and physical health. With regard to sustainability, we can remain hopeful if we recognize a path towards a more positive economic and societal future and have the will to stay on this path. SSBS offers one way. Are you willing to stay on this path?

Other theories that may provide explanation of sustainable and unsustainable behavior include social influences on individual behavior. *Social Learning Theory* (Bandura, 1991) and the vast body of empirical evidence supporting this theory explain why some actors might be willing to adopt sustainable behaviors in response to positive behavior modeled by others. Unfortunately, Social Learning Theory also explains the wasteful, unsustainable behavior practiced by so many of us as we respond to the negative societal norms promoted by DAC. Theories of *organizational justice* (Greenberg, 1987; Colquitt, 2001) suggest that individual behavior is frequently a function of a comparison between how an actor is treated vs. an actor's expectation of treatment. For example, an actor who feels that they are being treated unequally (distributively), without adequate processes (procedurally), or without dignity (interactively) are likely to commit antisocial and counterproductive behaviors, while those who are treated fairly are likely to engage in pro-social behaviors. If citizens are treated with disrespect at either the macro or micro level, they are much less likely to engage in sustainable behaviors.

There are additional barriers besides the fact that behavior can be difficult to change such as quitting smoking, losing weight, and exercising more, to name a few (see Table 11.2). Often, if behavior has been successfully changed based on an incentive, once the incentive is removed, behavior tends to *drift* back to its baseline levels (Breland & Breland, 1961), a process also known as behavioral extinction. Of course, some people maintain the positive behavior, perhaps after realizing indirect benefits (e.g., they feel better about contributing to the welfare of people and the planet, or realize the health benefits of walking or biking to work). Identifying barriers to change is an important step in the path towards sustainability, and one that is often not recognized (McKenzie-Mohr, 2000). As a result, specific sustainability programs have been implemented accounting for these barriers and have been shown to be more effective than information-only campaigns (McKenzie-Mohr, 2000). Another barrier to change is that some people *deny* that there is

TABLE 11.2 Psychological Barriers to Sustainable Behavior

Barrier	Description	Example
Availability heuristic	We often rely on memory retrieval to estimate the chances of something occurring.	People may overestimate the risk of air travel, based on remembering media stories of plane crashes.
Behavioral drift	After a behavior has been modified, there can be a tendency to return to the previous pattern, unless steps are taken to continually monitor for changes.	A person loses weight after following a program, but once they stop the program, they begin to gain weight.
Denial	Refusing to acknowledge a problem.	A sustainability intervention is undertaken, without realizing the importance of local leaders in preventing positive change.
Distancing	Difficulty in noticing a problem unless it is close to us in space/time.	Environmental changes at the polar ice caps are not thought to be serious, since for most people, these locations are very far away.
Adaptive self-deception	Intentional or unintentional self-deception regarding one's own relative strengths, weaknesses, and overall condition to maintain sense of self-worth and improve overall psychological functioning.	A person self-identifying as a "committed environmentalist" living a "green" lifestyle while simultaneously engaging in overt unsustainable activities. Or, a person may deny the existence of environmental problems to continue their current standard of living.

a problem with the environment or general social/working/living conditions of significant numbers of people (Cairns, 1998). Also, cognitive factors (belief systems/justification) can help us understand these challenges. For example, if a problem is not visible to a person directly, they might have difficulty believing there is a problem. Another example of *distancing* (Princen as cited in Kasser 2009; Spence, Poortinga, & Pidgeon, 2012) is that people have difficulty perceiving slow changes (e.g., year-to-year temperature increases might not be noticed unless graphed on a chart). Our perceptual systems evolved to register abrupt changes to our environment so that we could respond accordingly, e.g., to threats from predators. Thus, people may not notice that the planet is getting hotter and wetter, or that scores of people are now experiencing the impacts of climate change such as floods and droughts. (But note that here, the media can provide examples such as more intense storms or floods, sometimes creating controversy as well—are these driven by climate change or just infrequent catastrophic events?) Yet another possible explanation for unsustainable behaviors is *adaptive self-deception* (Baumeister, Campbell, Krueger, & Vohs, 2003), which suggests that an actor is likely to deceive herself or himself in light of uncertain information and self-interest. Because the forces of DAC have largely succeeded at disguising the crises facing our planet (e.g., climate change denial), many people may not modify behavior in a positive, sustainable direction. Alternatively, people may view themselves as environmentally responsible while acting in unsustainable ways. Distressingly, evidence indicates that those with a modest level of self-deception are often "happier" than those who have a more realistic self-understanding.

One must be cautious in a full explanation because of another psychological influence called the *availability heuristic.* People rely on memory for estimating events, and this estimation often is influenced by media stories involving accident risk. An example is that peoples' perceptions of the likelihood of dying from fire exceed that of drowning, whereas the opposite is true (Foulks, 1988). Distancing not only includes time and space, but also social distance, e.g., it is harder for people of a higher class to notice the impacts on a lower class (Liberman & Trope, 2008; Spence, Poortinga, & Pidgeon, 2012). Evidence suggests that asking people to focus on more distant events in time can reduce the effects of the normal distancing bias (Rabinovich, Morton, & Postmes, 2010).

Given these numerous barriers to sustainability, what can be done? One solution is that each person or group of people with similar interests such as farmers may have an environmental or social issue of relevance to them. Identifying that issue and pointing out the importance of addressing it can be key (Cairns, 1998). For example, many people who are not particularly progressive or pro-environmental might nonetheless support a sustainability issue if the issue is access to clean drinking water—an issue becoming more of a challenge in the United States due to loss of fresh groundwater resources and due to industrial pollution. Table 11.2 provides an overview of some of the psychological barriers to sustainable behavior.

Macro-Influences

Cialdini (2003), as mentioned previously, describes social influence processes that are very applicable to how people treat their surroundings. An important distinction he makes is between descriptive and injunctive norms and how these norms can sometimes work in opposition in social influence tactics such as public service announcements. *Descriptive norms* refer to what most people actually do in situations. *Injunctive norms* refer to what people ought to do from moral/ethical perspectives. To encourage situations that are desirable such as maintaining a clean environment, it is important to show the environment from the ideal, clean perspective that will activate the descriptive norm (i.e., that the environment *is* clean). Combined with this, the injunctive norm can illustrate, for example, that littering is discouraged by focusing on one person (a model) who litters and is called out for doing so by indicating to the viewer that this behavior is not acceptable. Cialdini empirically demonstrated how littering decreases when the environment is already clean compared to sullied (descriptive norm) and when a model is criticized for then littering. Counterintuitively, the message is less effective if the environment is shown to be already heavily littered and a model is criticized for littering. Cialdini describes previous public service announcements that did not present the message in an optimal way and show how aligning the descriptive with the injunctive provides the best outcome. Another important observation Cialdini makes is that it requires much less effort for people to follow descriptive norms (e.g., "following the herd"), compared to following injunctive norms, which requires greater cognitive effort. This observation has clear implications for educational interventions towards sustainable systems as well.

In addition, macro-influences include media stories on the need to become more sustainable. These then can establish social norms that are either helping or hindering sustainability efforts. Similarly, based on the slow impacts of climate change, new norms can be established that might prevent pro-sustainability behaviors (i.e., adapting to the change makes the new situation seem normal, rather than something that people would want to try to remedy/prevent).

Another important macro-influence is how economic factors and policies impact people. Dimaggio and Powell (1983) describe the "iron cage" of bureaucracy as one example. Also discussed are concepts such as reverse-legitimacy in that institutions are perceived to be legitimate when they are homogenized (e.g., the similarity of financial institutions in terms of how they operate and portray themselves). Though a financial paper, Riaz (2009) incorporates many psychological concepts such as the "cultural-cognitive" and normative institutions that maintain the status quo, as well as the relationship between descriptive social influence and how norms can change to delegitimize organizations via a "house of cards" awareness (i.e., the realization that the system is fatally flawed and about to collapse). One can also consider prior practices of organizations as a behavioral history of sorts that, like individual behavior, predicts future behavior. Riaz also discusses *New Institutional Theory*—the two-way influences between institutions and organizations, which is a more complex view of influence compared to the traditional sociological theory of the influence of institutions. Examples would include how think tanks (organizations) can influence institutions (e.g., Wall Street).

Moghaddam (2008) also illustrates macro-influences on individual psychology. He discusses the social contract and ethics and provides an alternative framework to Hobbes, Locke, and Rawls. Similar to Bronfenbrenner's approach, his approach is developmental in the Vygotskian sense that cognition occurs first in society and then in the individual (which Moghaddam refers to as the *dual nature of cognition*). This also dovetails with Jost's theory (e.g., Jost & Hunyady, 2005) about how cultural values become part of an individual's beliefs about how society should benefit/operate. His critique of social philosophers such as Hobbes, Locke, and Rousseau is in reference to their ideas about the social contract, which is that people rationally came to the conclusion that society has benefits for the individual (e.g., self-preservation). Also part of his argument against traditional approaches is that people logically decided to be subject to rulers and their laws. Moghaddam claims that these earlier social philosophers provided no empirical evidence to support their arguments. He also argues that more recently Rawls's (1999) *Theory of Justice* incorporates similar ideas (i.e., rationality) regarding the formation of social contracts. The key contributions from psychology regarding these issues are numerous research findings that humans are frequently irrational in their decision making (see Table 11.3). These ideas were first suggested by Herbert Simon in the 1950s with such concepts as *bounded rationality* in economic decision making (Camerer, 1999). In more recent years, Kahneman and Tversky added additional

TABLE 11.3 Examples of Human Irrationality

Human Cognitive Processes and Biases	Definition	Example
Bounded rationality	Limitations on human information processing in terms of space and time.	People cannot consider all of the relevant information when making decisions, but rather rely on shortcuts, such as using heuristics in making decisions and estimating probabilities.
Availability heuristic	Estimating the likelihood of an event, based on the ease with which a similar instance can be recalled from memory.	Thinking that it is more dangerous to fly on a commercial airliner than drive in a car, based on the ease of recalling media reports of plane crashes (the vividness and tragedy also increase the ability to recall an event).
Overconfidence and optimism bias—"positive illusions" (Anderson, 2001)	Believing one's own capabilities are better than in reality; believing that the future will be better than the present.	Believing that technology will solve our sustainability problems.
Hyperbolic discounting	The value of a present reward is greater than the value of a larger, future reward.	People will often choose to take a smaller reward now instead of waiting for a larger reward in the near future; examples could include cashing out retirement savings when leaving a job, instead of rolling them over into a 401(k). Other examples include the general difficulty in showing self-control and delaying gratification (impulsive behavior).
Confirmation bias	Searching for evidence that is consistent with one's beliefs, while ignoring evidence that would disconfirm the validity of the belief.	Believing that poor people are lazy because a few poor people were seen as behaving that way, when in reality most poor people work forty hours a week or more, some have two or more jobs paying minimum wage, etc.

(Continued)

TABLE 11.3 (Continued)

Human Cognitive Processes and Biases	Definition	Example
Cognitive dissonance	An emotional state that arises when one's attitudes and behaviors do not align. Motivational factors and rationalization can work to re-align attitudes with behavior (www.psychologytoday.com/blog/presence-mind/201305/are-you-sustainability-hypocrite). Self-Perception Theory (https://en.wikipedia.org/wiki/Self-perception_theory) is similar, but does not require the mental evaluation component—rather, one determines attitudes by current behavioral patterns.	Many people believe that action needs to be taken to create a sustainable future. However, for many of those same people, their behaviors do not change as the beliefs would imply (e.g., they still drive gasoline-powered vehicles too much, support policies that maintain harmful status quos for others, etc.). One example of what can happen as a result is that the individual will rationalize current behavior ("I will get an electric vehicle when the price is a bit lower and there are more charging stations around").
Learned helplessness	A behavioral pattern that emerges when an actor is repeatedly exposed to unavoidable and undesirable situations. Actors learn to behave helplessly even when the actor may have the power to change the circumstance (Seligman & Maier, 1967).	Many people today believe that the planet is on an irreversible negative trajectory and nothing can be done to alter this path. Others believe that poverty is an inevitable state of human suffering and that there is no way forward that will allow all people on this planet to share in the prosperity achieved by some. In either case, actors may be unwilling to engage in positive, sustainable behaviors because they feel helpless to change the situation or because they feel the situation itself is hopeless.

aspects of human decision making that deviated from rationality, such as their numerous examples of heuristics (e.g., that people use memory to estimate the likelihood of events, rather than considering actual probabilities—the *availability heuristic*). Other heuristics that are relevant to sustainability problems are *overconfidence* and *optimism, confirmation bias, cognitive dissonance,* and *hyperbolic discounting.*

Another famous example of human decision making that is relevant for resource use is *the tragedy of the commons* (Hardin, 2009). This relates to the ideas of selfishness and emphasizing short- over long-term goals. Specifically, this issue refers to the fact that, often, individuals (and corporations) will act selfishly with regard to common resources (such as land, fresh air, and water), by taking more than is sustainable or by polluting a common resource. It is assumed that everyone involved knows that the resources are limited or can tolerate only a certain amount of pollution from everyone. Yet, actors believe it is in their best interest (for maximizing profit) to utilize more of the resource than others. With a specific example such as pollution, there is another relevant concept in terms of business operation—*negative externality*. For example, the costs associated with pollution in generating electricity with coal are often not taken into account. Such costs include negative health impacts for workers, the community, and the natural environment (loss of land, water pollution, etc.).

Moghaddam's alternative social contract is that political socialization influences our beliefs. While this may seem obvious to some, many people believe their ideas are their own, especially in Western, *individualist cultures*, where one's own goals are seen as more important than group goals (*collectivist cultures*) (Myers & Twenge, 2016). Socialization also occurs via the family, and taken together with society at large, these influences fit in nicely with Bronfenbrenner's ecological framework and Vygotsky's sociocultural model of development. The interesting psychology here is that in many cases people are not aware of where their attitudes and behaviors actually come from. In psychology, this has been recognized for some time in both classical (Freudian) and modern (Lacanian) psychoanalysis (Newirth, 2006), and also behavioral theories of classical and operant conditioning (e.g., many of our habits were established based on environmental/cultural factors that we are no longer aware of). Mass media, according to Moghaddam, also provide a powerful force that shapes cultural attitudes. Examples include movies with hero plots, fairy tales, the representation of evil, and repetition of stories that become memes.

Psychological Well-Being

Psychological well-being (Ryff & Keyes, 1995) includes an array of psychological constructs that are very relevant to social sustainability. For a society to have social sustainability, peoples' needs must be met, and as Maslow (Donnelly, 2003) has argued, many of these needs are psychological (e.g., security, belongingness, etc.). Psychological well-being is thought to incorporate at least the following six dimensions: self-acceptance, positive relations with others, autonomy, environmental mastery (e.g., manages external activities such as work well), purpose in life, and personal growth (see Table 11.4).

Psychological well-being may also be important for how people are encouraged to change their own behavior. Kasser (2009) reviewed a number of studies showing that initiatives were more successful when people believed they were acting based on their own choice, rather than being forced to. This relates to the autonomy dimension of Self-Determination Theory as well. In addition, similar

TABLE 11.4 Components of Psychological Well-Being

Component	Definition	Example
Autonomy	Setting one's own course in life, rather than doing what others want us to do	Choosing a career based on what one has really determined for themselves is best, rather than on someone else's or society's wishes
Growth	Constant striving for improvement	Not being satisfied with the status quo or being satisfied that one is doing enough to solve current problems
Mastery	Becoming highly skilled at an activity	Extensive experience in one's profession. Over time, once the basics of the job are mastered, the individual can take on additional tasks and responsibilities and attain a more general mastery of their job (e.g., a so-called expert)
Positive relations with others	Expressing empathy, listening to others, treating others as equal	A manager who can take the perspective of an employee when making a decision, rather than just considering the decision from an economic point of view
Purpose	The idea that there is something more to life and finding out for one's self what that is	A person who experiences great setback and adversity, but realizes that these experiences are meaningful and can make one realize what needs to be done
Self-acceptance	Liking one's self rather than being too self-critical	Focusing more on other people rather than trying to be perfect

to autonomy, when peoples' goals are internally (intrinsically) set rather than based on external, materialistic rewards, they tend to have higher psychological well-being, show more sustainable interactions with the environment, and display more empathy when others are harmed. Similarly, Corral-Verdugo, Mireles-Acosta, Tapia-Fonllem, and Faijo-Sing (2011) discuss the importance of intrinsic over extrinsic goals in maintaining high levels of sustainable behaviors.

Another important consideration Kasser brings up is that the influences are bi-directional. Not only does psychological well-being make sustainable behavior more likely, but also sustainable social and physical environments enhance psychological well-being. There is in fact evidence that even brief interactions with nature have immediate psychological benefits (Berman, Jonides, & Kaplan, 2008).

Kahneman and Deaton (2010) provided empirical evidence on relationships between psychological well-being and income. Their research suggests (in the United States) that psychological well-being increases up to $75,000 household annual income, based on data from 2008–2009, and then tapers off as income further increases. This finding is important for showing how, at least at some point, money does not buy happiness. Note for that time period, the mean US income was about $71,500, but the median income was considerably lower, at $52,000, as reported in Kahneman and

Deaton (2010), based on the Census Bureau's American Community Survey statistics. Granted, they were able to disentangle psychological well-being (emotional components) from life evaluation (social status components, which do show further improved ratings as annual income increases to more than $75,000).

There are many negative outcomes related to low levels of psychological well-being. A good starting point is discussing the relationship of social circumstances such as one's living and working environments and stress responses. The psychological understanding of stress involves cognitive factors such as perceived threat and the coping responses at one's disposal. There are also biological factors and individual differences that relate to stress responses (one's learning history and predispositions to stressors). For example, if one is giving a speech, is that situation exhilarating or terrifying? The interpretation can then affect the physiological response such as increased heart rate, cortisol (a stress hormone) release, and other reactions that are triggered via sympathetic nervous system activation (the "fight or flight" response). Excessive stress reactions over time can lead to health problems such as cardiovascular disease and other illnesses that may be partly influenced via a suppressed immune system (thought to result from excessive cortisol release over time) (Tsigos & Chrousos, 2002). While these negative physiological responses can be moderated by exercise, meditation, etc., many people every day suffer the consequences of stress. There are situations where stressors can have positive results (referred to as eustress), and an untapped potential is for managers/supervisors to promote this in others (Hargrove, Becker, & Hargrove, 2015). In relation to sustainability, Reser and Swim (2011) discuss both the negative (vulnerability—for example, people living in poverty) and positive (resilience—high levels of community support and resources) aspects of how humans will respond to climate change. As in the beginning of this chapter, there is a complex interplay between the organism, the environment, and society (see their Figure 1, p. 279).

As mentioned previously, certain work conditions would tend to increase the chances for eustress (e.g., self-actualization, autonomy, attaining peak experiences or "flow" (Csikszentmihalyi, 1997). Specific to work environments, excessive stress often leads to burnout (Khamisa, Oldenburg, Peltzer, & Ilic, 2015). Because the factors related to burnout are often social (e.g., poor treatment of employees by managers, unpredictable work schedules, excessive workload, etc.), this area of present-day employment deserves great attention as a sustainability problem. In addition to the physical effects of stress and burnout, there are also negative social effects such as increased anger and social withdrawal.

Finally, one of the more interesting results of research on psychological well-being is that these research results have contributed to public policy changes. For example, many nations have set goals and recommendations to increase the happiness or psychological well-being of their citizens, and one nation (Bhutan) coined the term "Gross National Happiness" as an alternative to GNP as an index of a nation's health (Corral-Verdugo, Mireles-Acosta, Tapia-Fonllem, & Faijo-Sing, 2011; see also Chapter 13).

INFORMATION BOX 11.2 SOCIAL-CULTURAL PSYCHOLOGY

Social-cultural psychology has relevance to social sustainability in investigating and mitigating incidence of cultural bias. A classic example is the role of IQ tests (and similarly structured SAT tests) in academic and job placement. These tests historically (and perhaps still today) may be biased towards individuals who are not part of the dominant culture (e.g., in the wording of questions that often assumes tacit cultural knowledge). The tests may also measure skills that are learned in the dominant ("white") culture (www.huffingtonpost.com/ronnie-reese/test-bias-minorities_b_2734149.html). It was only more recently that psychology considered multiple frameworks of intelligence that researchers such as Sternberg and Gardner brought up (e.g., "practical intelligence," emotional intelligence, bodily-kinesthetic intelligence), compared to the more traditionally/culturally valued mathematical and verbal intelligence. Another current topic of discussion in sustainability relevant for the social-cultural approach is *environmental racism* (e.g., see www.ejnet.org/ej/).

Social Factors and Movements

Larger-scale social factors and social movements are also crucial for establishing socially sustainable business systems. One can look across history for examples such as workers' rights with the labor movement, women's suffrage, and civil rights. It is also the counterpoint that current social systems can maintain a status quo away from the goal of social sustainability. Psychology here has relevant points to make regarding the status quo and how to change it.

Jost (summarized in Jost & Hunyady, 2005) outlined a theory for why certain groups of people often argue against policies that would ultimately favor them. His *Systems Justification Theory* (SJT) encompasses a wide range of psychological beliefs and attitudes that people have towards policies, etc. These beliefs often reinforce a status quo that can, for example, maintain policies that perpetuate poverty. The basic idea is that many people rationalize the current system, perhaps out of fear for what an alternative might be. Jost and Hunyady also summarize interesting relationships between SJT and other psychological characteristics. For example, people high on the Big 5 personality trait dimension Openness to Experience are less likely to endorse SJT beliefs (high openness includes characteristics such as being willing to consider new viewpoints). Interestingly, Moghaddam (2008) argues that the roots of SJT were discussed by Marxist philosophers (see p. 891).

Contributions From I/O and Human Factors Psychology

Dilchert and Ones (2012) discuss the role that Industrial-Organizational (I/O) psychology can have for improving sustainability. They illustrate how organizational/

leadership beliefs influence an organization's sustainability efforts both positively and negatively. Examples include transformation— a moral belief that the company has regarding pro-social behaviors—and integration—the company emphasizes profit over people and the planet.

In terms of human factors, Metcalf and Benn (2012) apply psychological principles to understanding social and environmental sustainability (or lack thereof) of corporations. Human factors psychology generally applies principles of cognitive, behavioral, and social psychology to improve human interactions with technological systems. Basic examples include the design of computer and other display systems so that people can easily and intuitively interact with them (e.g., touch screens, graphical user interfaces, etc.). In terms of social sustainability, the application of human factors is more broad, such as looking at the corporation as a piece of technology and how that technology has failed in terms of how people interact with and are influenced by it. Their framework is one of several that argue against the idea that corporations' only function is to serve shareholder interests (e.g., Milton Friedman's shareholder perspective). Their alternative is to redesign the corporation (as one would redesign other failed technologies) to provide a better person-technology fit.

Metcalf and Benn provide a useful set of ideas to consider in moving towards more sustainable systems. For example, redesign to incorporate social and ecological values, which is not a new idea considering CSR initiatives, but recent history such as the 2008 global financial crisis illustrates continued shortcomings. Thus, in most cases, corporations continue to function primarily based on self-interest. They also mention that Management Science has recommended changes in the last fifty years such as increased conscientiousness that have yet to take hold as corporations continue to wreak social and environmental havoc in many instances. As in Jost's work, one barrier to change is that many people cannot see an alternative to the current system (cf. Carbo, Langella, Dao, & Haase, 2014; see also Chapter 13). Not that other alternatives haven't been proposed (see their review on p. 198), such as Eastern and Western religious-ethical approaches—Metcalf and Benn call for *systems thinking* that includes macro-influences such as regulatory structures and their influence on CSR, as well as broad perspectives such as life cycle analysis (p. 199). They refer to their approach using the acronym CIDEESS for "complex interconnected and dynamic environmental, economic and social systems" (p. 199). As a specific example, they discuss how the lack of transparency (e.g., withholding information to consumers) was partly responsible for the 2008 global financial crisis. Similarly, other design issues could improve transparency. One example, the Reveal™ rating system, is a symbolic indicator that incorporates *life cycle analysis* of a product on environmental and social dimensions. A life cycle analysis looks at all of the factors that go into producing a product from its beginnings in terms of physical labor and resources, to its disposal (or reuse, recycling). Such a system might move people to purchase more sustainable products if they had better access to information regarding how the product was made, under what conditions, etc. These ideas are further discussed in the Case at the end of this chapter.

Similar to our earlier work (Carbo, Langella, Dao, & Haase, 2014), Sovacool (2010) criticizes the corporation for failing to meet society's needs, based mostly on its design (e.g., "personhood" and its associated rights, maximizing shareholder return, etc.). In addition, similar to Metcalf and Benn (2012), Sovacool suggests we can gain a better understanding of corporations' shortcomings by analyzing them as a technological system and one that functions poorly:

> The corporation, distinct in its purpose, function, structure and personhood, is a type of technology. Moreover, reinforced by social structure and even the law, the corporation fails society by exacerbating financial inequality, socializing risk, commodifying human relationships and destroying the natural environment.
>
> *(p. 2)*

Other broad approaches towards sustainability encourage us to think about definitions. As mentioned previously, economic aspects are often emphasized over other components, with social aspects usually considered last and with less emphasis. Lamberton (2005) challenges the status quo with his definition of *sustainable sufficiency*. "Sustainable sufficiency is defined as achieving economic objectives consistent with the principle of *right livelihood*, ensuring the preservation of the natural environment and the welfare of each individual and society-at-large" (p. 61). "Right livelihood" is derived from Buddhist ethical principles applied to economics (Schumacher, 1973, as cited in Lamberton, 2005). There are also connections between this view and Maslow's Hierarchy of Needs. For example, in the Buddhist economic perspective, work is defined as something that gives people the opportunity to develop their skills, achieve dignity, and do so in a non-self-centered way—very similar to Maslow's concept of self-actualization. One of the differences between the status quo and the system Lamberton describes is that consumption is carried out in the most minimal way possible—still providing people with what they need, but not in the way that the current system promotes and markets excessive consumption. In contemporary psychology, there is an interesting connection between Buddhist philosophy and recent thinking on cognitive/perceptual processes—*embodied cognition* (Varela, Thompson, & Rosch, 1991). Embodied cognition also has relevance for the psychology of sustainability. At the theoretical level, embodied cognition describes how our cognitive and perceptual systems are linked to environmental constraints. This builds on ideas developed previously by Gibson in his discussion of affordances (i.e., what we perceive is at some level linked to what an object can be used for—a ladder affords climbing) and also bears some resemblance to Bronfenbrenner's model. At a more practical level of sustainability, we can see how the person-environmental link could affect a whole host of cognitive and other psychological processes. For example, what kinds of thoughts and feelings are evoked when people find themselves in clean, natural environments, compared to when they find themselves in dilapidated, polluted environments?

Challenges for Contemporary Psychology

Changing individual behavior may not be enough when the main problems are over-consumption, larger negative impacts from organizations (Stern, 2000), and industrial practices that largely maintain the status quo (Urzell & Räthzell, 2009). For many years, ecologists have discussed "carrying capacity" or ecological footprint and how sustainability relates to this—if everyone lived like the average American, we would need perhaps as many as four planets (Global Footprint Network, 2016). Similarly, the assumption that changing individual behavior will solve the sustainability problems may be a flawed one (Shove, 2010). Shove argues that this individual model (ABC—attitude, behavior, choice), while popularly adopted within the field of environmental psychology, ignores the important large-scale influences based on social change theory. Similarly, Anderson (2001) believed that the biggest barrier to change was a lack of solidarity (e.g., divisiveness and animosity among constituent groups) in real-world (e.g., community) settings where interventions are attempted. On more positive notes (while acknowledging the limitations of individual change and also the limitations of psychology), Swim, Clayton, and Howard (2011) eloquently discuss the "human element" in climate change, and also ways that psychology (via interdisciplinary work) can mitigate its effects and also help people to cope. Importantly, they recognize the importance of situational context in terms of whether an intervention will succeed or not. For example, programs targeted at individual change may be ineffective where there is not a supporting social network or values system. In fact, Swim, Clayton, and Howard (2011) is an excellent paper in regard to how we see the problems of social sustainability—as being ones that cut across many interacting levels, as Bronfenbrenner illustrated in his model (Figure 11.2).

Critical psychology is a sub-discipline of psychology that in general can suggest solutions where contemporary approaches have not succeeded. Public interest science can be a part of this, as Kimmel (1995, p. 103) states: "I believe it is the obligation of today's peace psychologists, researchers, and teachers to examine current international development ideologies, institutions, programs and policies, and, if they are not facilitating a sustainable community of world citizens, to assist in the creation of new world views."

INFORMATION BOX 11.3   GROSS NATIONAL HAPPINESS (GNH)

The four pillars of GNH are:

- sustainable development;
- preservation and promotion of cultural values;
- conservation of the natural environment; and
- establishment of good governance.

(See also Chapter 13.)

Note that Kimmel credited Milbrath (1989) in developing his view. Kimmel's ideas have similarity with Buddhist ethics and Gandhi's concept of Sarvodaya ("progress for all"). The American Psychological Association Division 48 (Society for the Study of Peace, Conflict and Violence: Peace Psychology Division) incorporates many of these ideas into its mission (e.g., psychological applications to reduce conflict and prevent violence). Division 48 also incorporated a long list of goals (eighty-seven!) for sustainable societies, including socio-economic equity, as well as the environment and health. Kimmel's suggestions dovetail with general human factors principles. He argues that sustainability indicators should be user-friendly and accessible to everyone, and that collaboration is needed in goal-setting (and a general "bottom-up" organizational philosophy as in the Buddhist and Gandhian Sarvodaya movement in Sri Lanka; see also Phorst (2012) for a discussion of the relevance of Buddhist principles to issues of sustainability and ethics). Much of critical psychology argues that we as researchers have traditionally held biases that favor the status quo in Western societies and that these biases may reinforce the status quo in terms of research agenda, while not directing attention towards marginalized individuals and other cultures (Fox, Prilleltensky, & Austin, 2009). To the extent that this is true among contemporary psychologists, one wonders what biases exist in those unfamiliar with the field.

INFORMATION BOX 11.4   EXAMPLES OF VALUES AND ETHICS OF INDIGENOUS PEOPLES

From a 1977 Native American UN speech based on realizations of the Iroquois Confederacy, *hau de no sau nee* (see https://ratical.org/many_worlds/6Nations/):

> But our essential message to the world is a basic call to consciousness. The destruction of the Native cultures and people is the same process which has destroyed and is destroying life on this planet. The technologies and social systems which have destroyed the animal and plant life are also destroying the Native people. And that process is Western Civilization.
>
> *(Basic call to consciousness, 1977, p. 9)*

The Iroquois Confederacy was apparently established via a peace-making effort among warring tribes. Perhaps through a process of strife and competition, ideas for a broadly sustainable culture resulted and were successfully implemented until Europeans began to colonize the Americas. Interestingly, the key to solving the problem was social—"laws were originally made to prevent the abuse of humans by other humans" (Basic call to consciousness (1977), p. 3). Klein (2014) also realizes the potential of indigenous rights (coupled with aggressive activism) in solving sustainability problems. She also echoes the problems of capitalism standing in the way.

A recent example of sovereign rights and sustainability was the (so far) successful protest and resistance to Energy Transfer Partners' planned Dakota Access Pipeline. One of the motivating principles for the Native American protesters was their spiritual beliefs regarding the purity of the land and water that they view as a nurturing force (www.nytimes.com/2016/12/10/opinion/sunday/how-to-stop-a-black-snake.html?smid=fb-share&_r=0).

Discussion Questions

1. Identify one aspect of your behavior that you could change to improve social sustainability. For this activity, you will need to record your behavior across the semester. Start by measuring your current level of behavior on some issue. For example, it could be the number of hours that you volunteer for community organizations each week. Your goal could be to start volunteering if you don't already or to increase the amount of time you volunteer if you do.

2. Identify a sustainability problem on your campus or in your town. Develop a brief, one- to two-page proposal for how you would go about improving the social or environmental condition. Be specific in terms of what you will measure, manipulate, and do to determine the program's effectiveness. What barriers do you foresee in implementing such a proposal?

3. Along with several of your classmates, list several beliefs that you think people have that make it difficult to establish social and environmental sustainability. Hint: think of some of the basic concepts discussed in this chapter that relate to SJT. What might be some ways that peoples' beliefs could be changed so that more sustainable approaches could be implemented and maintained?

4. When is the best time to implement a psychological intervention to change peoples' behavior? Why?

5. Can you identify an example of a "failed corporation" from a human factors perspective? Suggest a way to redesign it so that it would be more sustainable.

6. Which of the various ethical systems outlined in this chapter do you agree with most and why? How do you think it is best-suited to solving sustainability problems? Lastly, pick a specific sustainability problem and discuss it using ethical perspectives.

7. Some evidence suggests that people are more apt to act in sustainable ways when they believe they are doing so based on their own choice rather than being forced to do so. Which areas of sustainability are best suited to this approach and which areas do you think require more of a forceful/external approach?

8. Describe the economic values that you think most people from the United States and Western Europe have historically taken. Contrast this with the economic values from indigenous cultures.

9. Describe and discuss a social sustainability concept that you initially just understood theoretically or intellectually, but now understand better because of direct action or experiential learning on the issue.

> *Group activity*: Your instructor will distribute a number of cards equal to the number of members in your group. Each card will identify a specific culture/nation. Your task is to play the role of a person from that culture. You should research basic traditions, ideologies, etc., from the specific culture. Your instructor will also provide you with a sustainability problem (poverty, water/food shortages, etc.). Assume that the area where the problem is occurring is multicultural, so your task is to articulate from your assigned perspective how to best solve the problem. Adapted from Kimmel (1995).
>
> *Group activity*: During class, find an example company that you think produces high levels of employee burnout. What factors relate to this? Similarly, find an example company that creates a more positive work environment and resulting high levels of psychological well-being for its employees. You will present and discuss your findings to the class.
>
> *Decision analysis paper*: Describe the job characteristics/responsibilities for a career that you would like to obtain when you graduate or complete graduate school. Discuss the costs and benefits of this career from a social sustainability perspective. Include at least one example of *opportunity cost* that is relevant in this decision. Opportunity cost (Henderson, 2008) is what you give up when you choose one thing over another. For example, if you chose to go to a large university because of the greater variety of majors, one opportunity cost may have been smaller class sizes at a liberal arts college. Do you think your overall analysis supports this career as something that is socially sustainable? If not, what could be changed about this position that would make it more sustainable?

Note

1 www.brainyquote.com/quotes/quotes/m/markzucker416520.html Retrieved March 16, 2017.

References

Adams, M. (2014). Approaching nature, 'sustainability', and ecological crises from a critical social psychological perspective. *Social and Personality Psychology Compass, 8*, 251–262. doi:10.1111/spc3.12104

Anderson, E. N. (2001). Psychology and a sustainable future. *American Psychologist, 56*, 457–458. doi:10.1037/0003-066X.56.5.457

APA (American Psychological Association). Definition of psychology. Retrieved July 5, 2016, from American Psychological Association: www.apa.org/support/about-apa.aspx?item=7

Bandura, A. (1977). *Social Learning Theory*. Englewood Cliffs, NJ: Prentice-Hall.

Bandura, A. (1991). Social cognitive theory of self-regulation. *Organizational Behavior and Human Decision Processes*, *50*, 448–287.

Basic call to consciousness—Native people's analysis of modern world. (1977). The Hau de no su nee Address to the Western World, Geneva, 1977. Retrieved from https://ratical.org/many_worlds/6Nations/6nations1.html#cosmogony (accessed June 30, 2016).

Baumeister, R. F., Campbell, J. D., Krueger, J. I., & Vohs, K. D. (2003). Does high self-esteem cause better performance, interpersonal success, happiness, or healthier lifestyles? *Psychological Science in the Public Interest, 4*(1-44). doi: 10.1111/1529-1006.01431

Berman, M. G., Jonides, J., & Kaplan, S. (2008). The cognitive benefits of interacting with nature. *Psychological Science*, *19*, 1207–1212.

Breland, K., & Breland, M. (1961). The misbehavior of organisms. *American Psychologist*, *16*, 681–684. doi:10.1037/h0040090

Bronfenbrenner, U. (1979). Contexts of child rearing: Problems and prospects. *American Psychologist*, *34*, 844–850. doi:10.1037/0003-066X.34.10.844

Cairns, J. Jr. (1998). The Zen of sustainable use of the planet: Steps on the path to enlightenment. *Population and Environment: A Journal of Interdisciplinary Studies*, *20*, 109–123.

Camerer, C. (1999). Behavioral economics: Reunifying psychology and economics. *Proceedings of National Academy of Sciences*, *86*, 10575–10577.

Carbo, J., Langella, I. M., Dao, V. T, & Haase, S. J. (2014). Breaking the ties that bind: From corporate sustainability to socially sustainable systems. *Business and Society Review*, *119*, 175–206.

Cialdini, R. B. (2003). Crafting normative messages to protect the environment. *Current Direction in Psychological Science*, *12*, 105–109.

Colquitt, J. A. (2001). On the dimensionality of organizational justice: A construct validation of a measure. *Journal of Applied Psychology, 86*, 386–400.

Corral-Verdugo, V., Mireles-Acosta, J., Tapia-Fonllem, C., & Fraijo-Sing, B. (2011). Happiness as correlate of sustainable behavior: A study of pro-ecological, frugal, equitable, and altruistic actions that promote subjective wellbeing. *Human Ecology Review*, *18*, 95–104.

Csikszentmihalyi, M. (1997). *Finding Flow: The Psychology of Engagement with Everyday Life*. New York: Basic Books.

Dilchert, S., & Ones, D. S. (2012). Environmental sustainability in and of organizations. *Industrial and Organizational Psychology*, *5*, 503–511.

DiMaggio, P. J., & Powell, W. W. (1983). The iron cage revisited: Institutional isomorphism and collective rationality in organizational fields. *American Sociological Review*, *48*, 147–160.

Donnelly, J. (2003). *Universal Human Rights: In Theory and Practice*. Ithaca, NY: Cornell University Press.

Ecological systems theory. Retrieved from https://en.wikipedia.org/wiki/File:Bronfenbrenner%27s_Ecological_Theory_of_Development.jpg (open source image).

Ernst, A., & Wenzel, U. (2014). Bringing environmental psychology into action. *European Psychologist*, *19*, 118–126. doi:10.1027/1016-9040/a000174

Foulks, V. (1988). The availability heuristic and perceived risk. *Journal of Consumer Research*, *15*, 13–23.

Fox, D., Prilleltensky, I., & Austin, S. (2009). Critical psychology for social justice: Concerns and dilemmas. In D. Fox, I. Prilleltensky, & S. Austin (Eds.), *Critical Psychology: An Introduction* (pp. 3–19). Thousand Oaks, CA: Sage.

Global Footprint Network. (2016). Retrieved from www.footprintnetwork.org/en/index.php/GFN/

Greenberg, J. (1987). A taxonomy of organizational justice theories. *Academy of Management Review, 12*(1), 9–22.

Hardin, G. (2009). The tragedy of the commons. *Journal of Natural Resources Policy Research, 1*(3), 243–253.

Hargrove, M. B., Becker, W. S., & Hargrove, D. F. (2015). The HRD eustress model: Generating positive stress with challenging work. *Human Resource Development Review, 14,* 279–298. doi:10.1177/1534484315598086

Henderson, D. R. (2008). Opportunity cost. *The Concise Encyclopedia of Economics.* Retrieved from www.econlib.org/library/Enc/OpportunityCost.html

Hiedanpää, J., Jokinen, A., & Jokinen, P. (2012). Making sense of the social: Human-non-human constellations and the wicked road to sustainability. *Sustainability: Science, Practice, & Policy, 8,* 40–49.

Jost, J. T., & Hunyady, O. (2005). Antecedents and consequences of system-justifying ideologies. *Current Directions in Psychological Science, 14,* 260–265.

Kahneman, D., & Deaton, A. (2010). High income improves evaluation of life but not emotional well-being. *Proceedings of the National Academy of Sciences, 107,* 16489–16493. doi:10.1073/pnas.1011492107

Kasser, T. (2009). Psychological need satisfaction, personal, well-being, and ecological sustainability. *Ecopsychology, 1,* 175–180. doi:10.1089/eco.2009.0025

Khamisa, N., Oldenburg, B., Peltzer, K., & Ilic, D. (2015). Work related stress, burnout, job satisfaction and general health of nurses. *International Journal of Environmental Research and Public Health, 12,* 652–666. doi:10.3390/ijerph120100652

Kimmel, P. R. (1995). Sustainability and cultural understanding: Peace psychology as public interest science. *Peace and Conflict: Journal of Peace Psychology, 1,* 101–116.

Klein, N. (2014). *This Changes Everything.* New York: Simon & Shuster.

Lamberton, G. (2005). Sustainable sufficiency—an internally consistent version of sustainability. *Sustainable Development, 13,* 53–68.

Liberman, N., & Trope, Y. (2008). The psychology of transcending the here and now. *Science, 322,* 1201–1205. doi:10.1126/science.1161958

Manning, C. (2009). The psychology of sustainable behavior. *Minnesota Pollution Control Agency.* Retrieved from www.pca.state.mn.us/sites/default/files/p-ee1-01.pdf

McKenzie-Mohr, D. (2000). Fostering sustainable behavior through community-based social marketing. *American Psychologist, 55,* 531–537.

Metcalf, L., & Benn, S. (2012). The corporation is ailing social technology: Creating a 'fit for purpose' design for sustainability. *Journal of Business Ethics, 111,* 195–210. doi:10.1007/s10551-012-1201-1

Milbrath, L. W. (1989). *Envisioning a sustainable society: Learning our way out.* Albany, NY: State University of New York Press.

Moghaddam, F. M. (2008). The psychological citizen and the two concepts of social contract: A preliminary analysis. *Political Psychology, 29,* 881–901.

Myers, D. G., & Twenge, J. (2016). Social psychology and a sustainable environment. In *Social Psychology* (12th ed., in modules, pp. C1–C15). New York: McGraw-Hill.

Newirth, J. (2006). Jokes and their relation to the unconscious: Humor as a fundamental emotional experience. *Psychoanalytic Dialogues, 16,* 557–571.

Nord, W. R., & Peter, J. P. (1980). A behavior modification perspective on marketing. *Journal of Marketing, 44,* 36–47.

Pelletier, L. G., Lavergne, K. J. & Sharp, E. C. (2008). Environmental psychology and sustainability: Comments on topics important for our future. *Canadian Psychology, 49,* 304–308. doi:10.1037/a0013658

Phorst, C. (2012). An implementation of Buddhist environmental ethics for sustainable development in Cambodia. *Prajna Vihara, 13,* 137–144.

Rabinovich, A., Morton, T., & Postmes, T. (2010). Time perspective and attitude-behaviour consistency in future-oriented behaviours. *British Journal of Social Psychology, 49,* 69–89. doi:10.1348/014466608X401875

Rawls, J. (1999). *A theory of justice* (revised edition). Cambridge, MA: Harvard University Press.

Reser, J. P. & Swim, J. K. (2011). Adapting to and coping with the threat and impacts of climate change. *American Psychologist, 66,* 277–289. doi:10.1037/a0023412

Revkin, A. (2011). *"Conveying the Climate Story": Google Science Communication Fellows Workshop.* Retrieved from www.youtube.com/watch?v=lU_4OR3hOyo (accessed June 30, 2016).

Riaz, S. (2009). The global financial crisis: An institutional theory analysis. *Critical Perspectives on International Business, 5,* 26–35. doi:10.1108/17422040910938668

Ryff, C. D., & Keyes, C. M. (1995). The structure of psychological well-being revisited. *Journal of Personality and Social Psychology, 69*(4), 719–727.

Schensul, J. J. (2009). Community, culture and sustainability in multilevel dynamic systems intervention science. *American Journal of Community Psychology, 43,* 241–256. doi:10.1007/s10464-009-9228-x

Schneier, C. E. (1974). Behavior modification in management: A review and critique. *Academy of Management Journal, 17,* 528–548.

Seligman, M. E., & Csikszentmihalyi, M. (2000). Positive psychology: An introduction. *American Psychologist, 55*(5-14). doi: 10.1037/0003-066X.55.1.5

Seligman, M. E., & Maier, S. F. (1967). Failure to escape traumatic shock. *Journal of Experimental Psychology, 74*(1-9). doi: 10.1037/h0024514

Shove, E. (2010). Beyond the ABC: Climate change policy and theories of social change. *Environment and Planning A, 42,* 1273–1285.

Snyder, C. R., Rand, K. L., & Sigmon, D. R. (2002). Hope theory: A member of the positive psychology family. In C. R. Snyder & S. Lopez (Eds.), *Handbook of Positive Psychology* (pp. 257–276). New York: Oxford University Press.

Sovacool, B. K. (2010). Broken by design: The corporation as a failed technology. *Science, Technology, & Society, 15*(1), 1–25. doi:10.1177/097172180901500101

Spence, A., Poortinga, W., & Pidgeon, N. (2012). The psychological distance of climate change. *Risk Analysis, 32,* 957–972. doi:10.1111/j.1539-6924.2011.01695.x

Stern, P. C. (2000). Psychology and the science of human-environment interactions. *American Psychologist, 55,* 523–530. doi:10.1037/0003-066X.55.5.523

Sunstein, C. R. (2013). *Simpler: The Future of Government.* New York: Simon & Schuster.

Swim, J. K., Clayton, S., & Howard, G. S. (2011). Human behavioral contributions to climate change. *American Psychologist, 66,* 251–164. doi:10.1037/a0023472

Tsigos, C., & Chrousos, G. P. (2002). Hypothalamic-pituitary-adrenal axis, neuroendocrine factors and stress. *Journal of Psychosomatic Research, 53,* 865–871.

Tversky, A., & Kahneman, D. (1974). Judgment under uncertainty: Heuristics and biases. *Sciences, 185(4157),* 1124–1131. doi:10.1126/science.185.4157.1124

Urzell, D. & Räthzell, N. (2009). Transforming environmental psychology. *Journal of Environmental Psychology, 29,* 340–350.

Varela, F. J., Thompson, E., & Rosch, E. (1991). *The Embodied Mind: Cognitive Science and Human Experience.* Cambridge, MA: The MIT Press.

CASE 11 APPLICATION OF HUMAN FACTORS TO INCORPORATE PRINCIPLES OF TRANSPARENCY IN SUSTAINABLE PRODUCTS AND LABOR

The Reveal labeling system provides an interesting example of how to provide consumers with more direct information about how their products were produced, who produced them (e.g., corporate responsibility), and how they can be recycled (Shedroff, 2009). The basic idea is a "dashboard" that provides a 0–100 rating on a number of dimensions such as environmental impacts and labor standards. All the relevant dimensions can be summed to create an overall score for a product. Similarly, there are other examples of labeling systems used throughout the globe. Some products (e.g., snack foods) have multiple labels to inform the consumer (e.g., gluten-free, vegan, non-GMO, etc.). The Reveal system or some variant could simplify these multiple components and also provide information on social sustainability (typically, that is provided by either "union made" labels or concepts such as Fair Trade Certified™).

Shedroff discusses various labeling types. For example, a Type 1 label is third-party verified, and a Type 2 label is meant to be informative such as "organic." Some of these relate to concepts such as Shedroff's dashboard idea or typical nutritional information labeling (Category III), and there could also be a category for product safety such as UL™ (Category IV). Shedroff points out, however, that some of these labels are still lacking in that consumers may not understand what the labels mean.

There is also controversy on the accuracy of information that the labels imply or convey, at least in some cases, and there is a great variety regarding product labeling when it comes to sustainability issues (www.specialtyfood. com/news/article/36-food-labels-you-should-know/). Some are third-party verified, whereas others might merely be informational and therefore can have the possibility of misleading the consumer.

To start, there are labeling systems that have independent verification by outside organizations. An example is the 100% Vegetarian Fed, which if USDA verified, indicates that the animals were not fed animal feed or animal byproducts in their feed. In addition, they would not have been given supplements to their feed, but rather would have been fed on grasses, hays, or other pasture-edible plants.

Another example is shade grown coffee, often sought by consumers interested in purchasing more sustainable products. Generally, shade grown coffee requires less water (https://nationalzoo.si.edu/scbi/migratorybirds/coffee/). In addition, some shade grown coffee provides other habitat benefit such as for birds. Bird Friendly™ is a certification from the Smithsonian Migratory Bird Center. In addition to indicating that crops are organic and shade grown, the labeling requires farmers to adopt bird-friendly practices such as biodiversity of habitats beneficial to birds.

There is also labeling that can improve social sustainability, and Fair Trade Certified™ is one such example (www.specialtyfood.com/news/article/36-food-labels-you-should-know/). Fair Trade USA (http://fairtradeusa.org/) maintains a database of standards for their policies. These policies include participation by farmers in co-operatives and worker associations. Policies that guarantee minimum prices for workers are in place, and there are highly ethical labor standards in place such as worker safety, access to health care, and prohibiting child labor.

Several examples of labeling that are potentially less informative or misleading include the Cage Free label (www.specialtyfood.com/news/article/36-food-labels-you-should-know/). This type of label may imply that the birds are roaming freely on the farm; however, there are no standards that limit how crowded the space is for the birds (they may be raised indoors and may have less living space than is implied by the "Cage Free" term www.sfchronicle.com/food/article/What-does-cage-free-really-mean-exactly-7249746.php). Another potentially misleading label is "grass fed." This label might also imply that the animals such as cattle graze in an open pasture. However, they could be fed grass in an indoor stable and also be given antibiotics (www.sustainabletable.org/944/these-labels-are-so-confusing).

Discussion Question

Can you identify a product that has what you think to be a verifiable sustainability label and also identify one that is probably more of the "informational" type? For each, identify something other than the examples given, and list the characteristics that make the label a good one in your view and also identify misleading characteristics for an "informational" label.

References

www.specialtyfood.com/news/article/36-food-labels-you-should-know/ (discusses some examples such as the American Humane Certified label, 100% Vegetarian Fed label, etc.)

http://animalwelfareapproved.org/wp-content/uploads/2014/09/AWA-Food-Labels-Exposed-v10-ONLINE.pdf (provides information on how various labels stack up against various evaluation criteria)

www.sustainabletable.org/944/these-labels-are-so-confusing

http://agr.wa.gov/marketing/smallfarm/greenbook/docs/17.pdf (tips for making a good label)

http://kardish.com/blogs/wellness-blog/certification-marks-explained (discusses USDA Organic, Fair Trade, etc.)

Shedroff, N. (2009). *Design Is the Problem: The Future of Design Must Be Sustainable.* Brooklyn, NY: Rosenfield Media.

12

WHY ARE WE TIED TO DESTRUCTIVE ADVANCED CAPITALISM?

> What I question is not consumption in the abstract but consumerism and over-consumption. While consumption means acquiring and using goods and services to meet one's needs, consumerism is the particular relationship to consumption in which we see to meet our emotional and social need through shopping.
>
> *Annie Leonard,* Story of Stuff *(Leonard, 2010, p. 145)*

> What do you think would happen in this country if, for one year, they experimented and gave everybody a twenty-four hour work week . . . That is, I think, one reason rich kids tend to be fanatic about politics: they have the time. Time, that's the important thing. It isn't that the average working guy is dumb. He's tired that's all.
>
> *Mike Lefevre, in Studs Terkel's* Working *(Terkel, 1972, p. xxxiv)*

> I think the answer is far more simple than many have led us to believe: we have not done the things that are necessary to lower emissions because those things fundamentally conflict with deregulated capitalism, the reigning ideology for the entire period we have been struggling to find a way out of this crisis.
>
> *Naomi Klein,* This Changes Everything *(Klein, 2014, p. 18)*

Introduction

Despite the current system being unsustainable, violating human rights, destroying the environment, and rapidly depleting the natural resources of the Earth, we see that we are chained to this system, and that these chains run to nearly every group in society. Governments, industries, consumers, academia, the media, and society at large remain in bondage to DAC. These chains are unbroken despite the opportunity for SSBS to improve most of our lives over the short term and all of our lives over. We see workers buy into a system that has led to thirty years of stagnating wages because they see it as presenting an opportunity to get ahead (Burawoy, 1979; Zweig, 2000). We see academics support the system and rarely engage in research that would bring the system into question (Lieberwitz, 2002; Marens, 2008), and we see members of society wear their hats as consumers and buy into the idea that this system supplies low price goods and services (Leonard, 2010). The reality is that for the vast majority of people, this system is destructive and should be changed. However, rather than questioning the system and demanding change, people become attached to the system, and these ties reinforce themselves from each aspect of society. There are a number of reasons for these very strong ties that bind us. The bases for these ties work together to create a vicious cycle that tightens these ties or strengthens the bonds to the current system.

A vicious cycle of power and influence provides one explanation for DAC's grip on global society. The great beneficiaries of DAC are the owners of capital and the executives who serve their interests. In Chapter 1, we presented evidence that these individuals and the organizations they control own a disproportionately large share of the global (and national) wealth and income. Such wealth provides this group with a great deal of political and social power. This power is further used to influence other individuals and institutions, which is then used to gain more economic and political power. This, in turn, is used to again strengthen the ties to DAC, creating a hegemony that ties us ever tighter to a system that is destructive for the majority of people on the planet and the planet itself. This vicious cycle is depicted in Figure 12.1.

Influence Tactics and Weapons

The presence of the vicious cycle of power and influence and the pervasive and persistent negative impact of our attachment to DAC leave us with many questions. Authors such as Mike LeFevre, Naomi Klein, and Annie Leonard have sought to ask many of these important questions: Do we derive our social and emotional needs through spending? What are the signs of consumerism and how do these differ from consumption? Are working people too tired to participate in the process of making and understanding political decisions? As we see Americans work longer and longer hours, do other activities take a back seat? Is it harder to stay truly informed about issues? Do the links we receive in social media provide an in-depth understanding of business practices and economic decisions? Has our current system of commerce become an ideology? Do we no longer make decisions about our commerce based on evidence, but rather on assuring we follow the ideology of the free market system no matter the consequences?

These questions are not new. Almost since the advent of this system, the causes of destructive capitalism's grip on our society have been explored. In fact, all of the ideas from the three quotes that open this chapter have been discussed by other philosophers, researchers, academics, and activists. Karl Marx and Friedrich Engels in 1848, in *The Communist Manifesto*, put forward the argument that the system

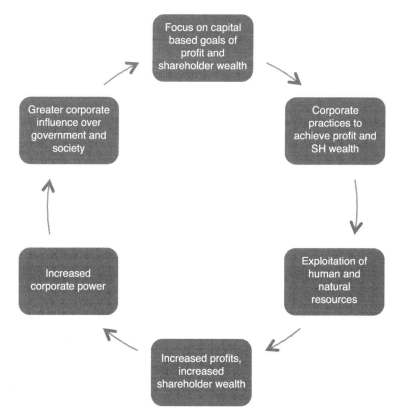

FIGURE 12.1 Current Destructive System of DAC

Source: Carbo, Langella, Dao, and Haase (2014)

exists as a result of political power and the control of institutions: "The power of the modern state is merely a device for administering the common affairs of the whole bourgeois class"; to continue to hold this power, the bourgeois would need to "continually revolutioniz[e] the instruments of production." The idea of revolutionizing these means of production is similar to Lenin's argument that capitalism continued to exist due to the commitment to reforming the system in minor ways to co-opt those or a subset of those who oppose the system or at least its current outcomes Moody K. (2014: p. 90). Gramsci, an Italian Marxist of the early 1900s, argued that those in power perpetuated the system by building an ideology around the system, or what he termed *hegemony*.

In more modern times, Burawoy, in his in-depth, participant observation study of "Allied Corporation," found that workers are sold on the current system through a sort of game playing, where workers are convinced that their best opportunities are to compete within the system, for a set of rewards that are of course bounded by those running the system. These rewards bind the workers to the system, much like the rewards from the reforms described by Lenin. Workers at Allied and the workers under the reforms are convinced that their opportunities will now rest in their own efforts and that the system provides them these opportunities. Those who do not succeed have only themselves to blame.

Zweig (2000) and O'Brien (2008), much like Leonard, focus on the push to convince all of us that we are consumers. Zweig (2000) suggests that working people are in essence convinced that their role as consumers is more important (to them and to society) than their role as workers. This has a negative impact on the solidarity they feel with other workers and thus decreases working class power. O'Brien (2008) suggests that we have been sold the idea of the "goods" life to take the place of a good life. She argues that we have been convinced that buying a bunch of stuff is the route to happiness and presents evidence that this simply is not the case.

Naomi Klein (2014, p. 149) argues that corporate lobbying plays a major role in perpetuating the system. In 2013, in the United States alone, the oil and gas industry spent just less than $400,000 a day lobbying Congress and government officials, and the industry doled out a record $783 million in federal campaign and political donations during the 2012 election cycle, an 87% jump from the 2008 elections. This lobbying gives corporations a great deal of control over the political processes, and these corporations, as Klein (2014, p. 100) explains, are not going to allow for legislation that is against their interests. Instead, they will make changes to their practices only if such changes are viewed as profitable. Much like Klein, Hertz (2003, pp. 120–124) has also focused on the political process as part of the reason for the ties to the system and suggests that corporate control over the political process has led to less commitment from citizens to the political process. She goes as far as to label political leaders as puppets on a string to corporate interests in her argument that corporations have engaged in a "Silent Takeover" of our systems of global commerce and politics (Hertz, 2003, p. 98).

Just one decade ago, a global financial crisis ensued, caused largely by corporate greed (e.g., the money corporations wanted could be made only by developing exotic financial instruments such as credit default swaps and collateralized debt obligations that even the leaders of financial institutions claimed not to understand). There was a lack of transparency in these "black box" instruments that were thought to adequately pool investor risk. The initial returns on such investments were too good to be true, but when mortgage borrowers could no longer make payments on the exuberant kinds of loans they were granted by institutions (e.g., "no doc." loans), the bonds began to fail, leading to freezing of credit markets, etc. Much of the history of this work is detailed in the Financial Crisis Inquiry Commission (FCIC) report and also in popular press books (and movies) such as Michael Lewis's *The Big Short*. Post-crisis, there is still great cause for concern as there are now fewer banks that hold even greater wealth than before the crisis, and the political climate will likely result in a repeal or partial repeal of legislation that was designed to prevent a similar crisis in the future (Dodd-Frank).

Cialdini's (2007) best-selling book *Influence* also presents us with an explanation for the powerful corporate influence over our institutions and members of society. When we step back and look at what Cialdini defines as six "weapons" of influence, we can see how these are each used by those who benefit from the current system of DAC. Within each of these weapons of influence, we can see the tactics discussed by Leonard and Lefevre as well as many others. Cialdini's weapons of influence include reciprocation, commitment and consistency, social proof, liking, authority, and scarcity. Each of these is utilized by corporations and those in power to maintain and to tighten their control and influence. We see many of

TABLE 12.1 Cialdini's Six Principles of Influence

Principle	Definition	Example of How the "Weapon" Is Used by Those in Power
Reciprocation	People feel obligated to return a favor or other received benefit.	1. The ownership society—we give you a stake in the company through stocks; now you should be devoted to assuring the company succeeds. 2. Consumerism—you get great prices and all kinds of stuff you can buy from these companies, now you must treat them well. 3. Pay off the privileged section of the working class: Burawoy's (1979) game playing—if you work hard within the system, you will be the most rewarded; Lenin's (Moody, 2014) explanation that you give part of the working class just enough for them to believe they are best served by the current system; Frank's Limousine Liberals (2016) who also benefit through a system they believe is a meritocracy where those on top get what they deserve because the system allows it.
Commitment and consistency	People increase their obligation over time; similar to the "foot-in-the-door" technique.	1. Convince people this is the way it has always been—the myth pointed out by Mintzberg, Simons, and Basu that the corporation has *always* existed to maximize shareholder wealth (Mintzberg, Simons, & Basu, Fall 2002). 2. Lenin's reformism takes hold; we must maintain the system, we simply need to tweak it—look at all of the great ideas for CSR and CC (of course, none of these has worked). 3. Commitment through the ownership society.
Social proof	People look to others for cues in terms of how they should act, especially when they are not sure of the best course of action.	1. Espouse that everyone agrees that this is the best system, the only viable system; ignore reporting on any other system and create doubts about any other system, creating a hegemony. 2. Examples of those who have done well, with statements that this proves the system works.

Principle	Definition	Example of How the "Weapon" Is Used by Those in Power
Liking	People respond positively to those whom they like and who are physically attractive. This can also include positive responses to similar attitudes and beliefs.	1. Make corporate leaders into heroes—a branding of the leaders themselves. 2. Turn the rich and powerful into celebrities. 3. Villainize those who think, for example, turning Marx into a villain, or trying to portray Bernie Sanders and Jeremy Corbyn as crazy (discussed later in this chapter). 4. Make those who do not thrive under this system appear to be at fault—the welfare queen myth, painting low wage workers as lazy or uneducated, or less worthy.
Authority	Most people in general respect authority and will often follow the orders of authority figures without questioning.	1. Convincing people of the importance and the expertise of those in power. Create "think tanks" to support the system; take over higher education and the research (Lieberwitz, 2002). 2. Get rid of academics and researchers who would argue against the system (Marens, 2008).
Scarcity	People tend to value things more when they are in short supply.	1. Game Playing described by Burawoy of convincing workers there is only so much in the system and they need to compete for it. 2. Horatio Alger stories—there is some out there, and if you work hard, you can be the one who gets it. 3. Austerity—there just is not enough to go around; we all must sacrifice. 4. You should be happy you have a job; they are scarce. 5. You should be happy you can get by; others cannot—especially when we refer to those in developing countries as a comparison to those in poverty and the working class in developed countries.

these weapons used in the previously described tactics. These weapons and the related tactics are further explained in Table 12.1.

Identifying the Influencers

If the ties to DAC are the result of influence, one of the first questions we should ask is, Who is doing the influencing? As is pointed out in Chapters 1 and 2, destructive advanced capitalism is not destructive for all; in fact, for some it has great value. In particular, those who benefit directly from corporate profits such as the owners of equity shares (who have no need to sell their labor to survive) and the corporate leaders such as CEOs and executives fare quite well under this system. In fact, the average CEO pay in 2011 was 231 times that of the average US worker (down from 351 times in 2007, but more than 10 times higher than the ratio of 20:1 in 1965 (Mishel, Bivens, Gould, & Shierholz, 2012, p. 289). CEOs are not alone in benefitting from this system. The top 1% and especially the top 0.1% in both the United States and around the globe have fared extremely well under DAC. In the United States, the incomes of the top 1% have grown from $428,000 in 1980 to more than $1.3 million as of 2014 (Levitz, 2016). Globally, the top 1% now holds nearly as much wealth as the rest of the world combined (Hardon, Ayele, Fuentes-Nieva, & Lawson, 2016). For these individuals at the top, the current system of destructive capitalism is working quite well. They are accumulating ever-greater shares of the national and global wealth and with this wealth a tremendous amount of power. It is this group that has a large incentive to see this system continue and this group that utilizes its wealth and influence to keep the rest of us tied to the system.

Corporate Influence Over Public Policy, the Political Systems, and Governments

The first linkage that starts this chain occurs between corporations and those with a self-interest in perpetuating the DAC system linking public policy to corporate interests. This initial link can be defined as the corporate influence or pressure on governments. This influence and pressure take three primary forms—campaign financing, lobbying, and threats. Researchers, including Hertz (2003), Klein (2007), Spitz (2005), and Yates (2003), have tracked this very progression of these business practices, the corporate influence and the governmental acquiescence, acceptance even further of the DAC practices described throughout this text. As a result of this governmental role, the corporations have become even more powerful and thus able to exert more and more pressure and influence on governmental actors. Hertz (2003, p. 13) suggests that, "Over the last two decades the balance of power between politics and commerce has shifted radically, leaving politicians increasingly subordinate to the colossal economic power of big business . . . whichever way we look at it, corporations are taking on the responsibilities of government." Matten and Crane (2005) propose that corporate power has overtaken much of the power of nation states and that, therefore, the corporation should take over many of the roles of the nation state, specifically in protecting and assuring rights. However, as we have discussed, corporations do not have the same goals as governments (at least not until and unless we see a shift towards socially sustainable business systems), and as a result nobody is left to defend or assure individual rights. The system in the United States presents a clear example of this corporate influence over government, but this example would also apply in most other governments across the globe.

Corporate Financing of Elections

At the national level, corporate financing of campaigns plays a critical role in the election of candidates. In fact, without the type of vast financing that can only come through corporations or those that have accumulated the wealth and income in our society, it might be impossible for a candidate to be elected today. According to Open Secrets, the average amount spent by a candidate running for the United States House of Representatives in 2016 was just less than $1 million, and for a candidate for Senate, the cost exceeded $4.8 million. The 2016 Presidential campaign is expected to cost more than $2.6 billion (Cost of Elections, 2016). Further, as a result of the recent *Citizens United* decision, we see that corporate interests can spend unlimited amounts on campaigns through a variety of alternative spending ads, movies, PACs, etc. The oil and gas industry doled out a record $73 million in federal campaign and political donations in the 2012 election cycle, an 87% jump from 2008 (Klein, 2014, p. 149).

Corporate Lobbying

In addition to campaign funding, lobbying is now a billion dollar industry (Klein, 2014, p. 149). In 2013, in the United States alone, the oil and gas industry spent just less than $400,000 a day lobbying Congress and government officials. As a result of these increased costs, politicians have become more and more dependent on the moneyed interests to fund their campaigns and careers. However, this funding does not come for free—there are clearly expectations that once in office these elected officials will execute, legislate, or make decisions in such a way that they benefit their benefactors.

Lobbyists even go as far as writing bills. Tom DeLay's bill entitled "Project Relief," which would have eliminated numerous workplace and environmental regulations, was written by lobbyists for more than 350 industries (Frank, 2008, p. 200). According to the website ALEC Exposed,

> Through the secretive meetings of the American Legislative Exchange Council, corporate lobbyists and state legislators vote as equals on "model bills" to change our rights that often benefit the corporations' bottom line at public expense. ALEC is a pay-to-play operation where corporations buy a seat and a vote on "task forces" to advance their legislative wish lists and can get a tax break for donations, effectively passing these lobbying costs on to taxpayers.
>
> *(Alec Exposed, n.d.)*

This lobbying by corporate interests can be extremely financially lucrative, leading to even more money to invest in influencing the government and other institutions. For instance, in 2004, a group of companies paid a lobbying firm $1.6 million to push for a small modification to the tax code—this small change led to these companies saving $100 billion in taxes (Frank, 2008, p. 200).

Corporate Threats

The influence does not just come about as a result of financing and lobbying. As Matten and Crane point out, businesses due to their large size and economic power can pose a very real threat to nation states—in essence, the threat that if the government does not work with them, then they will take their billions of dollars elsewhere. Consider the situation with Carrier Corporation in Indiana. This plant became a big campaigning point during the 2016 US Presidential election. Candidate Trump promised that he would keep the Carrier jobs in the United States by threatening to impose a 35% tariff on the company's products if they re-entered the United States. Shortly after winning the election, President Elect Trump claims to have negotiated a deal with Carrier to keep 40% of the jobs in the United States, while also giving Carrier a $7 million tax break from the state. Within days of the "agreement," Carrier CEO Greg Hayes explained that the company would begin to automate the plant, meaning the jobs that were saved would be eventually replaced by technology (Rupar, 2016). Carrier's threat to move a relatively small number of jobs was a big enough one to the largest national economy in the world that the possibility of a tariff was pulled off the table and the company was awarded a further tax break, while still allowing it to offshore 60% of the jobs, and further its goal of eventually eliminating the other 40% through technology. If these types of threats can so greatly influence what is perhaps the most powerful government in the world, consider the influence these threats would have over developing countries such as the economies in Bangladesh, India, and throughout Africa discussed earlier in this text and in several of the case studies. Could these threats lead to lax labor and environmental laws or lax enforcement of these laws? Might these countries give similar types of kickbacks as we saw the United States government provide to Carrier Corporation? The corporate threats are not only directed at nation states. In fact, they are often directed at specific politicians who stand up against the corporate influence or suggest an independent governmental regulation of business.

Corporate Insider Influence

Corporate influencers also exert their influence through a revolving door into government. Relying on both corporate confusion and Cialdini's weapons of influence, bankers from Wall Street are repeatedly appointed into positions within the United States government that are meant to regulate Wall Street and to drive the economy not for the benefit of banks, but for the benefit of the people. Consider the Presidential appointees to the Treasury over the past thirty-five years shown in Table 12.2.

Many appointees to governmental economic positions not only come from the financial industry and corporate America, but they also often return to jobs in these sectors to lobby on behalf of these sectors. The pay from the government appointed positions often pales in comparison to the pay from their prior

TABLE 12.2 Secretaries of the Treasury of the United States

Name	Appointed By	Year Appointed	Prior Career
Donald T. Regan	Ronald Reagan	1981	CEO, Merrill Lynch
James A. Baker	Ronald Reagan	1985	Attorney, Andrews and Kurth
Nicholas F. Brady	Ronald Reagan and George H. W. Bush	1988	Chairman, NY investment banking firm Dillon, Reed & Co.
Lloyd M. Bentsen	Bill Clinton	1993	Public service/elected politician
Robert Rubin	Bill Clinton	1995	Co-chair, Goldman Sachs
Lawrence Summers	Bill Clinton	1999	Chief economist, World Bank, and academic
Paul H. O'Neill	George W. Bush	2001	Chairman and CEO, Alcoa
John W. Snow	George W. Bush	2003	CEO, CSX Corporation
Henry M. Paulsen	George W. Bush	2006	Chairman and CEO, Goldman Sachs
Timothy Geithner	Barack Obama	2009	President and CEO, Federal Reserve Bank of New York
Jacob J. Lew	Barack Obama	2013	Managing director and COO, Citigroup
Steve Mnuchin	Donald Trump	2017	Partner, Goldman Sachs, and CEO, Dune Capital Management

jobs in finance and their succeeding jobs in finance and lobbying. The standard starting pay for a staffer moving from a job in government to a lobbying position is $300,000 per year (Frank, 2008, p. 180). This, of course, would not apply to a cabinet member or similar influencer who would move into lobbying.

Not only do the rich and powerful have influence on government, they directly wield power through governmental offices. This troubling trend of the direct influence of the wealthy is illustrated by the administration of President Donald Trump. Not only did an electoral college victory result in the election of a billionaire as President, his initial cabinet nominations contained at least four billionaires among his seventeen top appointees. News sources estimate the combined net worth of his cabinet members to be more than $13 billion. Inflation adjusted, this is five times greater than President Obama's and a whopping thirty-four times greater than President George W. Bush's (Rocheleau, 2016).

This idea of the expertise of these corporate insiders is not only used to obtain positions of power, it is also often used against those who question the system of DAC from gaining these same types of positions. For instance, we saw these types of implicit threats used against Bernie Sanders during the 2016 Democratic Presidential primaries by both Democrats and Republicans who believe in the corporate influence. Sanders's campaign positions for free higher education and health insurance for all Americans (a Medicare for all system) were labeled as naïve, socialist, and utopian despite the fact that these same policies exist in much of the rest of the industrialized world and in countries with far less economic power than the United States (Patterson, 2016). Third-party candidates are often dismissed as being fringe candidates, and despite the oftentimes high level of expertise and education among these candidates, they are considered fringe, while corporate-backed candidates and business people with much less education and even governmental experience are readily accepted as fit for office.

The Cumulative Effect of Corporate Influence on the Government

Because of this power shift away from governments and to corporate power, corporations are able to pursue a profit-maximizing agenda with nation state support. "Business is in the driver's seat, corporations determine the rule of the game, and governments have become referee, enforcing rules laid down by others" (Hertz, 2003, p. 8). The role of the nations has become one of assuring the best environments at the lowest costs for businesses. Both Klein (2007) and Spitz (2005) suggest that the globalization of this American form of free market advanced capitalism is a big part of the American government's agenda. As Spitz (2005, pp. 340–341) wrote about the George W. Bush administration, "it would appear that the necessity of developing nations accepting neo-American capitalism as the 'single sustainable [economic] model' is both a U.S. security interest and a military goal." Klein (2007) suggests this has been part of the agenda of the American government since at least the 1970s. Klein points to direct government intervention in the name of free markets such as Reagan's funding of attacks on Bolivia's coca farmers, followed by economic "shock therapy," as well as indirect government support for the unfettered role of corporations through "the Washington Consensus" takeover of World Bank and IMF policy in 1989 (Klein, 2007, p. 163). There has been little to change this corporate influence over the American political system as well as the political systems of the world. Thomas Frank points out in his book *Listen Liberals* that the Democratic Party is just as tied to and influenced by corporate actors (although perhaps a different group of corporate influence peddlers) as the Republican party. Frank (2016, pp. 143–144) writes, "the erudite Obama administration uses its mandate to continue the policies of the crude and tasteless Bush administration, essentially unchanged, at least for the first few years." Frank suggests that the Obama administration did not want to frighten Wall Street bankers, and as a result, there were no arrests, receiverships of banks, or even firings of Wall Street executives. Obama is also not the first Democratic President to have such influence; in fact, Bill Clinton played a large role in turning the Democratic Presidency to a party of Wall Street and tech corporations. Clinton had more millionaires in his administration than there were in the George W. Bush administration (Frank, 2016, p. 79). Like Obama, Clinton favored free trade agreements that were pushed by corporate lobbyists.

Corporate voluntarism has not protected the people and planet from the ravages of DAC. If we are ever to move away from this system that clearly serves those with wealth and power, governments around the world will need to restrict or overcome the disproportionate influence of corporations and the wealthy persons who control them. As Naomi Klein (2014) suggests, if practices are not seen as profitable, corporations will not pursue them voluntarily. Therefore, if we are to see changes to corporate practices that push us towards socially sustainable business systems, we will need to see businesses regulated by an independent government as the early scholars of corporate social responsibility suggested (Marens, 2008). For government to gain this independence, we will need to reform the campaign financing, end the billion dollar lobbying industry, prevent the threats from corporate America, and stop the revolving door between corporate influencers and government agents.

Corporate Influence Over Academia

This corporate influence also spills over into education at all levels and in particular higher education, which would normally be an area of discourse. Logically, business schools in particular might be most susceptible to this corporate influence. The critical view of the role of business may indeed have been part of the business school agenda in the past, but for all purposes, any questioning of the DAC has disappeared from the business school curriculum, research, and even service. Even the concept of corporate social responsibility has been hijacked by corporate interests. Marens (2008) points out that after World War II there was a collection of researchers interested in the field of business and society with a focus on the public good and the necessary restraints on businesses to assure the public good. In other words, these researchers and academics focused on a broader role for businesses as well as describing an alternative to DAC. It is no coincidence that during this time we saw a new model of the relationship between business and society, with greater regulations; increasing power, wages, and benefits for workers; and protections added for the environment and its resources. Marens suggests that in response to this new system of commerce, Robert H. Malott, a defense company CEO, published "Corporate Support of Education: Some Strings Attached" in 1978 in the *Harvard Business Review*. This article in essence stated that if business schools want corporate support, then they must turn their attention to Milton Friedman and away from Galbraith— clearly a push for an unfettered free market system with no constraints on business's pursuit of profit or, in other words, support for DAC. Marens suggests that after this point, academicians in the field of business ethics began tying their research to corporate interests, "abandoned any discussion" of constraining business practices through legislation, failed to measure the social and ethical outcomes of economic decisions, and even "faced potential career risks by advocating unionization, countervailing power" or any other form of potential discourse (Marens, 2008, p. 66). The new field of business ethics from that point forward focused on the idea of a voluntary call for businesses and business leaders to meet their ethical responsibilities. Unfortunately, there is little evidence to support that voluntarism has improved social justice or resolved the crises caused by DAC.

Much like Marens, Lieberwitz (2002) and Steck (2003) both suggest that academic research has been taken over by corporate interests. Lieberwitz (2002, pp. 761–762) points to the American Association of University Professors (AAUP) 1915 Declaration of Principles, and its emphasis on academic freedom that is "free from the influence of third parties," and shows how even in the life sciences, academic research today is greatly influenced by corporations. She suggests that corporate interests have had such a heavy influence on academic research that, "What had been 'third party' interests of individuals and groups outside the faculty now become the faculty's interests. Objective practices in academic research are altered to further these common financial interests of faculty, administrators, and corporate funders, such as restricting the public domain, increasing secrecy among faculty colleagues, and inviting greater intervention by industry." In defining the growing corporatization of academia, Steck (2003, p. 77) suggests that, "Perhaps most troubling for traditional academic culture is the host of commercial and corporate relations that breach the autonomy of research activity and crack, if not destroy, the wall between academics and commerce." This tying of corporate interests into academic research can indeed have direct and damaging effects on society. For instance, Klein (2007, p. 144) points out that the "Chicago School percepts about the supremacy of the free market" became the "unquestioned orthodoxy in Ivy League economics departments" during the 1980s. As a result of this, these free market policies became the policies of the United States economy as well as international and global policies, including international institutions such as the IMF and World Bank. Dissenters to these policies such as Joseph Stiglitz were simply pushed out of economic policy positions and even today still seem to be ignored or marginalized (Klein, 2007).

With the corporatization of the university and the tying of research interests to corporations (especially in business schools), it is not surprising that business school research even in the field of business ethics offers little discourse to the corporate agenda. Because of this growing ideology of the corporate mantra, the fact that so much of the sustainability literature reads like a strategy textbook is not particularly surprising. Not only does much of the literature fail to offer any countervailing arguments to corporate power and interest, but the research and the field have been taken over by corporate interests. By taking over the terminology and concepts of green business and CSR, corporatists are able to assure that these concepts do not interfere with their self-interest, and in fact may be used to further and justify their self-interest. In fact, taking over the language of these movements is "a powerful way of silencing the radical conceptions of sustainable development and the associated contestation of economic growth and the capitalist structures" (Springett, 2003, p. 73). Without this countervailing voice that might be offered by academicians, the corporate ideology goes unquestioned.

Corporate Influence Over the Media

The corporate influence is also seen in the media. Of course, sometimes it is hard to distinguish between the media and the corporate influencers. As Arudhati Roy (2016, p. 284) points out in *The End of Imagination*, six major corporations own nearly all of the primary media outlets in the United States, "six large cable companies have 80% of cable subscribers," and even social media and websites have become corporatized. She suggests that there is not just media support for DAC, but that the "media is the neoliberal project."

As Wolin (2008) points out in *Democracy, Inc.*, the media coverage of protests against the current system have been far from complimentary in recent history. Wolin (2008, pp. 215–216) points out that while coverage of the United States civil rights movement by the media was largely "benign," the opposition to the Iraq War received little coverage at all. During the 2004 election, the media either caricatured or ignored third-party candidates and even "pilloried as an extremist" the very "conventional" Democratic candidate Howard Dean. A Harvard study shows that Bernie Sanders's 2016 campaign, an anti-corporatist campaign, received much the same treatment as the third parties and labeled fringe candidates in 2004 (Patterson, 2016). Roy (2016, p. 284) suggests that "neoliberal corporatists" have learned how to infiltrate the components of a free democracy including the media. She suggests that in both the United States and India, the mass media have been a mouthpiece for governments (the Iraq War coverage) and corporations. The media in the United Kingdom appear to have similar problems. A report on the media coverage of left-leaning Jeremy Corbyn found the media had attempted to delegitimize Corbyn through lack of voice, scorn, ridicule, association, misrepresentation, and personal attacks (Cammaerts, Decillia, Magalhães, & Jimenez-Martinez, 2016).

In discussing the media coverage of labor, an institution one might expect to be anti-DAC, Dine explains that there is a great deal of research that shows labor receives either no coverage or negatively biased coverage. Media reports of labor use unappealing terms such as "labor bosses" to describe labor leaders. This lack of coverage and the tone of the coverage that does exist are often linked back to the corporate ownership of media and the dependence of media upon corporate advertisers (Dine, 2008, pp. 190–192). In a study of media coverage of social justice movements (the types of movements necessary to overcome DAC), Boykoff found that the media frame the global justice movement into five deprecatory frames—"the Violence Frame, the Disruption Frame, the Freak Frame, the Ignorance Frame, and the Amalgam of Grievances Frame" (Boykoff, 2006, p. 227). "Hostility to organized labor, permeates every part of the mass media: newspapers and magazines, film, television" (Zweig, 2000, p. 56). They have abandoned the working class in favor of the neoliberal business hegemony.

Corporate Influence Over Labor

Much like the media, labor is supposed to be another institution that provides a check on corporate power. In fact, the labor movement was founded directly as such a check on corporate power. Labor unions "are formed in response to the daily grind of working for others" (Yates, 2009, p. 35). Even Karl Marx and Friedrich Engels accepted that unions played an important role in fighting against the exploitation of workers (Moody, 2014, p. 15). However, over the centuries-long history of the labor movement, even this institution has been influenced in evermore powerful ways by corporations. While the labor movement is indeed the single remaining institution to fight for the rights of workers and to fight against the forms of exploitation of workers that we see under the current system of destructive advanced capitalism, it is clear that the labor movement (and in particular labor unions) has lost much of its power to protect workers in both industrialized and developing countries (Yates, 2009; Getman, 2010; Rosenfeld, 2014). At least in part, this loss of power can be traced to the movement's acceptance of the neoliberal system of capitalism that has created DAC.

Moody (2014, p. 45) suggests that post World War II, the true confrontation between labor and management ended, and "there were strikes to persuade a reluctant management and to demonstrate to the membership that union leaders still knew how to fight when circumstances demanded it. Genuine confrontation was viewed as archaic." The favorable economic conditions that emerged in the 1950s and the purge of labor activists as a result of McCarthyism both led to a more docile labor movement. Many labor intellectuals of this time period went into labor studies and universities where a business hegemony was emerging. A business unionism emerged from this time period, much in line with the early labor leadership of Samuel Gompers, a form of unionism that not only accepted the capitalistic system, but saw "capitalism, unionism and democracy [as] inextricably linked" (Moody, 1988, p. 56). It could be argued that labor as an institution has been co-opted by the capitalists through the type of reformism that Lenin had warned against. The blatant exploitation of workers had decreased, union workers were all doing well financially, and there was a growth of the middle class and opportunities for upward mobility. There was what became known as the labor accord, an accord where management accepted the role of unions, but unions also accepted that this role was limited to bargaining for wages and benefits and helping to maintain industrial peace. As a result, union leaders began to speak less about class consciousness and fundamental changes to the system and instead focused on providing services for their members. This played into an emerging "characterization of the working class" as a special interest (Zweig, 2000, pp. 52–53).

Even as it became clear during the 1970s and 1980s that management had broken and was no longer interested in this accord, labor as an institution clung to the ideology or perhaps hegemony of capitalism. Labor simply shifted from a broad labor accord towards the acceptance of the neoliberal, Democratic Party form of capitalism. This shift occurred at the very same time that the Democratic Party shifted away from viewing labor as its primary constituency. The Democratic Party moved into a belief in a meritocratic, capitalistic system that suggested that workers should be rewarded on their own individual efforts and that the system would assure that this would occur. Of course, since that time, inequality has skyrocketed in the United States, wages have stagnated, worker benefits have disappeared, work has become less safe, and union density has plummeted. Today, the labor movement is showing a willingness to break away from the ties of the DAC. The Fight for $15 movement, the broad social-based OurWalmart movement, and the emergence of workers' centers are examples of labor breaking away from acceptance of the system and its top-down, sclerotic bureaucracies. Unfortunately, with private sector union density at just more than 6% and overall labor density hovering around 10%, the strength of labor's influence is questionable.

Institutional Influence Over People

The corporate influence over these institutions leads to institutional influence over individuals. The influence is direct from corporations, but is also filtered through these influenced institutions. This influence impacts us as individuals in nearly every area of our lives—ourselves as workers, students, consumers, and citizens. In every avenue of life, members of society in the United States and increasingly around the globe are inundated with messages, propaganda that promotes the current system of destructive advanced capitalism. These messages are targeted to convince members of society that they should view themselves as consumers first. "Good" policies are those that lead to cheaper prices for lots of stuff. These messages drill into the notion that workers' problems are caused by their own poor choices. Headlines such as "Factory Closes Due to Union Demands" are not uncommon, while "Factory Closes to Maximize Stockholder Profit" is never the story in the mainstream media. In this mythology, workers who make good choices—i.e., support DAC—will benefit from the system. Workers who act in their own interest are viewed as disruptors, and their activities are often viewed as destructive. Fights to provide living wages in the fast-food industry and at Walmart are often presented as schemes that will increase consumer costs rather than acts of social justice. The messages sent by corporations and the media that too often supports their interests are consistent with Jost's Systems Justification Theory (why people often vote against their own interests, etc.—see Chapter 11).

Influence Over Our Role as Workers—The Chance to Get Ahead

One of the most important roles for nearly all of us nationally and globally is as an employee/worker. Each of us spends approximately one-third of our lives working. In many situations and as a whole, DAC is contrary to our interests as workers. However, despite this, even within this role, we see broad-based acceptance of this system. As Burawoy (1979) found in his study of Allied Corporation, not only do we see working class exploitation, but the working class does indeed participate in and accept the rules of this "game." While corporations and those who share in the corporate interests have pushed this agenda, the reality is that much of the rest of society has also bought into this agenda. Corporations and the agents of corporations have taken great strides to convince the members of society of the importance of the corporate interests. If they come to believe that capitalism is the best economic system or at least the only one that can be made to work in the modern world, they will be unlikely to spend time and energy seeking alternatives. So well has neoclassical economics spread the idea of economic man that "studies have shown that students who take a course in economics are more likely to behave selfishly than those who have not" (Yates, 2003, p. 161). The push of the ideals of the corporation has been so successful that Yates (2003, p. 160) suggests that neoclassical economics is no longer a "science but an ideology." Burawoy (1979) found that workers could become convinced to consent to the current system that leads to more surplus profit that is then simply expropriated by the owners of capital. Workers consent not to act in their own class interests, but instead to "play the game" as individuals often competing against each other to the benefit of their employers. Even when workers are organized, the labor union plays a role of assuring that workers play within the rules of the game as determined by the owners of capital.

While it makes sense for those who benefit from the current system to push these ideals, if the current system is so destructive to those whose interests lie outside the corporation, then this still leaves the question as to why so many have bought into this system. At the micro level, Burawoy found that workers would engage in a game of "making out." This game would be played in such a way that workers could better their positions within internal parameters set by the employer. Likewise, the workers' representatives, or labor union, also would have power, but only within the parameters of the game or current system. Through the benefits of the game, workers in the internal labor market would begin to see how their own interests were aligned with those of the company. Raises, bonuses, and promotions were all predicated on the employee performing well within the parameters of the game, and thus dependent on the well-being of the organization. According to Burawoy, it is the internal activities within a firm that drive this worker acceptance of the current system.

Influence Over Society Member as Citizen

While Burawoy makes it clear that the internal labor market of an employer can indeed lead to worker consent of the system, there are also external factors that drive this consent to their own demise. Mintzberg, Simons, and Basu (Fall 2002) offer at least a partial explanation that we as members of society have been convinced of a "series of half-truths." Through these half-truths, we have become convinced that the only role of the corporation is and always has been to pursue profit. However, we also have become convinced that this corporate pursuit of profit will benefit all and that growth in the economy will lift all of us. We have become convinced that to meet these corporate needs that will benefit all of us, corporations need heroic leaders that should be well compensated and must follow a "lean and mean" path to be successful. Finally, we have become convinced that we are all "economic man" (*homo economicus*) looking out for our own self-interest. As a result of buying into these myths, we accept corporate power, the pursuit of profit, the extreme compensation levels of CEOs and executives, and even the lay-offs and outsourcing of jobs to increase corporate profit. As Stiglitz (2012) has suggested, we share in a "national delusion" that the market will take care of all of us, and we simply need to allow it to run its course. We all become "capitalistic fools" serving the needs of the corporation even at our expense. We even lack any acknowledgement of these other issues of sustainability. According to an ILO report, the "challenge of creating productive jobs" for the growing global labor force is "barely recognized and its nature and magnitude are certainly well not understood." The employee concerns take a back seat to the corporate focus on economic growth (Ghose, Majid, & Ernst, 2008, p. 1).

As the owners of capital have indeed expanded this value to their own benefit, they have gained extraordinary levels of wealth and influence that allow them to set the rules of the game. These rules are set both internally, within firms, and externally, through laws and social conditions. We also see why working people and other members of society fall into the trap of buying into their own demise. From an internal perspective, employees and even labor unions buy into a game that allows them to gain or lose within a set of parameters set by the owners of capital. Employees become convinced that the well-being of their employers is directly tied to their own individual well-being. Further, from a societal level, we are convinced of a series of myths that as the capital owners do well, we will all do well, and that for these owners to do well, they must engage in practices such as the lean and mean production.

Influence Through Consumption—The Push to Consumerism

Zweig (2000, p. 46) suggests that consumerism became a reality after World War II, as more and more people identified themselves through their possessions rather than their work. The concept of "keeping up with the Joneses" emerged during this time frame and "seemed to become the very purpose of life." Through marketing and nearly every form of mass media, the consumption habits of the middle class are presented as a model to be followed by all, for the working class even if this means debt. This concept of consumption is a key to our economic system. Even in books pushing for changes to our system, there is often an acceptance of a "demand" driven economy, and there is often the argument that steps need to be taken to drive demand.

The push to consumerism starts early; as Yates points out, by the time children get to first grade in many of the wealthy capitalist countries, they will have seen tens of thousands of commercials and will continue to be "saturated: with commercialism" (Yates, 2003, p. 194). According to Yates, the message of marketing is always the same: "consuming things is what 'liberates' us." As O'Brien (2008, p. 291) explains, we have been sold on the idea of a "goods life" equating to a "good life." Leonard (2010, p. 145) describes the issue of consumption as not a problem with consumption but with "consumerism or overconsumption." She presents several numbers on spending to compare with social goals from 2004–05:

- spent on shoes, jewelry, and watches in the United States—$100 billion; spent on higher education—$99 billion;
- spent on cosmetics worldwide—$18 billion; reproductive health care for all women would have cost $12 billion; and
- spent on pet food in the United States and Europe—$17 billion; it would have cost $19 billion to eliminate hunger.

The DAC system and its influencers rope us into this consumerism. Leonard (2010, p. 147) points out that after 9/11, then President of the United States George W. Bush suggested that if we wanted to show that we were true Americans, we should go out and shop. Leonard (2010, p. 155) suggests this consumerism is driven by corporations' "incessant need for profit." Through planned and perceived obsolescence, astute marketers convince citizens to view themselves as consumers and their self-worth through the "stuff" they are able to purchase.

Conclusion

The influence to accept the current system of destructive advanced capitalism is overwhelming. As depicted in Table 12.3, the institutions that we all rely upon and participate in on a daily basis are following their roles in a system of DAC as opposed to the roles we suggest we would see from these institutions under socially sustainable business systems. Any one of these influences alone might not be enough to explain the rigid compliance to the current economic system despite the apparent harm to consumers, workers, communities, the environment, our water, land, and food. However, consider each of these influences as a wire or a pencil. Each wire makes the chain itself stronger, making an ever tighter and stronger bind. If we imagine these influences as pencils, we all realize how easy it is to break a single pencil. However, when we begin to place these pencils together in a stack of two, three, four, five, or more pencils, we see how difficult it is to break these pencils. The ties to DAC are numerous, and the number of these ties makes them extremely strong.

Any solution must change the influence structure to the people and assure that the influence stays there. In both failed Marxist economies and failed capitalistic economies, what we have seen is that the power becomes isolated in an institution that is controlled by a select few elite individuals. Perhaps the most well-known of the so-called Marxist experiments was the USSR. The Russian Revolution, of course, was hailed as a victory overthrowing a ruling class and providing true power to the proletariat or workers. Unfortunately, this power was not spread across the working class for long. Instead, a select few individuals took control of a

TABLE 12.3 Roles of Institutions

Institution	DAC	SSBS
Corporations	Dominant institution; all other institutions serve the desires and wants of the corporation.	The corporation is another institution within society that exists to serve the needs of the society—social justice, sustainability of the people and the planet, improvement of living conditions, and advancement of the human race.
Media	To distribute corporate messaging.	To inform the citizenry.
Government	Subservient to business interests—from the tax code to regulations (and lack thereof).	Of, by, and for the people. Interests of citizens are assured by policy empathy, responsibility, protection, and empowerment. Serving the people and assuring protection of the planet. Must assure human needs and rights are met and must protect against any violation of these needs and rights.
Academia	Job training and technical skills are emphasized.	Critical thinking, enlightenment, and betterment of society and the world are emphasized.
Labor	A cost to be minimized with an emphasis on efficiency of operations.	Creator of capital; emphasis on worker well-being, dignity, health, and safety.

government institution that was meant to represent the workers' interests. As is the case with any institution that becomes powerful and is controlled by a powerful few, what we saw was a self-interested select few using this institution to influence all other institutions for their own benefit and then using these other institutions to influence and control the members of society. In the United States today, just slightly more than 50% of individuals own any equity shares at all in a massive corporate marketplace (Gallup poll, 2016). What we see is that an elite few (the top 1% that own about 65% of the equity) control the most powerful institutions in our society. The solution lies not in any one specific system over another, but lies in the direction of influence and control—whether the influence and control flow from a narrowly controlled institution or whether the influence and control flow from the members of the society to these institutions.

Discussion Questions

1. Do we see broad-based support for a destructive system of commerce? If so, why?
2. Review Cialdini's tactics of influence. Have you ever been influenced by these tactics? If so, when and how? How can you overcome these influence tactics? Do we see these tactics used to support the current system of commerce? Provide an example.

3. Search through the popular press, academic works, and textbooks for examples of institutional support to the current system of commerce. Look for examples questioning the current system. Which are more common? What is the media source for these different pieces of information?
4. Review the proposed roles for the press, government, academy, labor, and corporations. How do these compare to how these institutions function today? Do we see the current functions as being closer to the system of DAC or SSBS? Explain.
5. What steps would you propose to begin to break the ties to DAC? What influence tactics could you use to help to spur changes?

References

Alec Exposed. (n.d.). Retrieved from ALEC Exposed: www.alecexposed.org/wiki/What_is_ALEC%3F

Boykoff, J. (2006). Framing dissent: Mass-media coverage of the global. *New Political Science, 28*(2), 201–228.

Burawoy, M. (1979). *Manufacturing Consent: Changes in the Labor Process under Monopoly Capitalism.* Chicago: University of Chicago Press.

Cammaerts, B., Decillia, B., Magalhaes, J., & Jimenez-Martinez, C. (2016). *Journalistic Representations of Jeremy Corbyn: From "Watchdog" to "Attackdog."* London: London School of Economics.

Carbo, J., Langella, I. M., Dao, V. T, & Haase, S. J. (2014). Breaking the ties that bind: From corporate sustainability to socially sustainable systems. *Business and Society Review, 119,* 175–206.

Cialdini, R. B. (2007). *Influence.* New York: Harper Collins.

Cost of Elections. (2016). Retrieved January 19, 2017, from Open Secrets: www.opensecrets.org/overview/cost.php

Cox, R. W. (1983). Gramsci, hegemony and international relations: an essay in method. *Millennium, 12*(2), 162–175.

Dine, P. M. (2008). *State of the Unions: How Labor Can Strengthen the Middle Class, Improve Our Economy, and Regain Political Influence.* New York: McGraw Hill.

Frank, T. (2008). *The Wrecking Crew: How Conservatives Rule.* New York: Metropolitan Books.

Frank, T. (2016). *Listen, Liberal: Or Whatever Happened to the Party of the People?* New York: Metropolitan Books.

Gallup poll (2016). Just Over Half of Americans Own Stocks, Matching Record Low. Retrieved from: http://www.gallup.com/poll/190883/half-americans-own-stocks-matching-record-low.aspx

Getman, J. G. (2010). *Restoring the Power of Unions: It Takes a Movement.* New Haven, CT and London: Yale University Press.

Ghose, A. K., Majid, N., & Ernst, C. (2008). *The Global Employment Challenge.* Geneva: International Labor Organization Publications.

Hardon, D., Ayele, S., Fuentes-Nieva, R., & Lawson, M. (2016). *An Economy for the 15.* Oxford, UK: Oxfam International.

Hertz, N. (2003). *The Silent Takeover.* New York: HarperBusiness.

Klein, N. (2007). *The Shock Doctrine: The Rise of Disaster Capitalism.* New York: Metropolitan Books.

Klein, N. (2014). *This Changes Everything: Capitalism vs. the Climate.* New York: Simon & Schuster.

Leonard, A. (2010). *The Story of Stuff: How Our Obsession with Stuff Is Trashing the Planet, Our Communities, and Our Health—and a Vision for Change.* New York: Free Press.

Levitz, E. (2016, December 8). *A New Study Shows How Severe U.S. Inequality Is—and How Little We're Doing about It.* Retrieved January 19, 2017, from The New Yorker: http://nymag.com/daily/intelligencer/2016/12/we-are-losing-the-battle-against-inequality-without-a-fight.html

Lieberwitz, R. (2002). The corporatization of the university: Distance learning at the cost of academic freedom? *The Boston University Public Interest Law Journal, 12*(1), 73–135.

Marens, R. (2008). Recovering the past: Reviving the legacy of the early scholars of corporate social responsibility. *Journal of Management History, 14*(1), 55–72.

Matten, D., & Crane, A. (2005). Corporate citizenship: Toward an extended theoretical conceptualization. *Academy of Management Review, 30*(1), 166–179.

Mintzberg, H., Simons, R., & Basu, K. (Fall 2002). Beyond selfishness. *MIT Sloan Management Review, 44*(1), 67–74.

Mishel, L., Bivens, J., Gould, E., & Shierholz, H. (2012). *The State of Working America* (12th ed.). Ithaca, NY: Cornell University Press.

Moody, K. (1988). An injury to all: The decline of American unionism. Verso.

Moody, K. (2014). *In Solidarity.* Chicago: Haymarket Books.

O'Brien, C. (2008). Sustainable happiness: How happiness studies can contribute to a more sustainable future. *Canadian Psychology, 49*(4), 289–295.

Patterson, T. E. (2016). *Pre-Primary News Coverage of the 2016 Presidential Race: Trump's Rise, Sanders' Emergence, Clinton's Struggle.* Cambridge, MA: Harvard Kennedy School Shorenstein Center on Media, Politics and Public Policy.

Rocheleau. (2016, December 20). *Trump's Cabinet Picks So Far Worth a Combined $13b.* Retrieved from Boston Globe: www.bostonglobe.com/metro/2016/12/20/trump-cabinet-picks-far-are-worth-combined/XvAJmHCgkHhO3lSxgIKvRM/story.html

Rosenfeld, J. (2014). *What Unions No Longer Do.* Cambridge, MA and London: Harvard University Press.

Roy, A. (2016). *The End of Imagination.* Chicago: Haymarket Books.

Rupar, A. (2016, Deccember 9). *Carrier Says It Will Spend Millions Automating Indiana Plant, Plans to Lay Off Workers Trump 'Saved'.* Retrieved January 19, 2017, from Think Progress: https://thinkprogress.org/carrier-automation-trump-deal-more-layoffs-db2554f46297#.gdmjniu8d

Spitz, L. (2005). The gift of Enron: An opportunity to talk about capitalism, equality, globalization and the promise of a North-American charter of fundamental rights. *Ohio State Law Journal, 66*, 315–396.

Springett, D. (2003). Business conceptions of sustainable development: A perspective from critical theory. *Business Strategy and the Environment, 12*, 71–86.

Steck, H. (2003). Higher education in the twenty-first century: Corporatization of the university: Seeking conceptual clarity. *Corporatization Annals of the American Academy of Political and Social Science, 585*, 66–96.

Stiglitz, J. E. (2012). *The Price of Inequality: How Today's Divided Society Endangers Our Future.* New York: W. W. Norton & Company, Inc.

Terkel, S. (1972). *Working.* New York: The New Press.

Wolin, S. S. (2008). *Democracy, Inc: Managed Democracy and the Specter of Inverted Totalitarianism.* Princeton, NJ: Princeton University Press.

Yates, M. D. (2003). *Naming the System: Inequality and Work in the Global Economy.* New York: Monthly Review Press.

Yates, M. D. (2009). *Why Unions Matter* (2nd ed.). New York: Monthly Review Press.

Zweig, M. (2000). *The Working Class Majority: America's Best Kept Secret.* Ithaca, NY and London: ILR Press.

CASE 12 FAST FASHION, EXPLOITATION, AND THE RANA PLAZA DISASTER

Many American and Western European consumers do not spend much time thinking about the impact of their purchasing decisions. However, the decision to engage in what has become known as the fast fashion industry has proven to have disastrous impacts for workers across the globe. The garment industry has always been a labor intensive industry. As a result, there has been a consistent push in the industry to lower labor costs. This push has led to technological advances in the industry, but most recently it has led to a push for cheap labor. The industry has seen a race to the bottom moving from decent paying union jobs in the industrialized centers of Western Europe and the United States, to sweat shops within the cities of these countries, to even cheaper sweat shops in China, and finally to the cheapest labor and perhaps least regulated source of labor in Bangladesh (Taplin, 2014). The $350 billion US fashion industry now produces less than 3% of its garments in the United States (Institute for Global Labour and Human Rights, 2014).

This race to the bottom occurred rapidly over a twenty-five year period (Institute for Global Labour and Human Rights, 2014). The race to the bottom was intensified as the fashion industry moved to the fast fashion or lean retailing model that exists today. This model moved from fashion seasons that lasted months to a system of clothes being on the shelves for four to six weeks or fewer, before they were shipped off for sale at discounters (Taplin, 2014). The push for quick turnover of the inventory and models leads to a push for faster and faster production at an ever lower cost. This push has led to the exploitation of workers across the global fashion supply chain.

There are five thousand garment factories in Bangladesh employing more than four million workers (Institute for Global Labour and Human Rights, 2014). These garment workers work twelve to fourteen hour days for a $40 monthly wage, and the majority of these workers are young women, as young as 16 years of age (Taplin, 2014). The child workers of Bangladesh are not the only workers being exploited in the garment industry. According to a US DOL report, 168 million children (10% of the global population of children) are engaged in child labor, many of them in the garment and textile industry. As just one example of child labor further down the garment industry supply chain, the cotton industry in Uzbekistan relies on child and forced labor. The majority of the cotton produced in Uzbekistan is shipped to China and Bangladesh to be used in the garment production mentioned previously (International Labor Rights Forum, n.d.). Classic Fashion, a supplier for Hanes, Kohl's, Target, and Walmart, has an expansive history of the worst forms of exploitation, according to a report from the Institute for Global and Human

Rights (2014). Classic Fashion workers in Sri Lanka, Bangladesh, India, Nepal, and Egypt work on average thirteen hours per day for 61 cents an hour (Kernaghan, 2011). The young women working at Classic Fashion have been the victims of sexual assault, rape, and even torture at the hands of Classic Fashion management (Kernaghan, 2011).

Corporate codes of conduct have failed to alleviate the disasters and exploitation in the garment industry. In fact, according to the Institute for Global Labour and Human Rights, "for the last 25 years, the garment industry has knowingly hidden behind their so-called 'Corporate Codes of Conduct' and voluntary monitoring schemes, which have had zero power to assure the rule of law" (Institute for Global Labour and Human Rights, 2014). In fact, despite these codes of conduct, the garment industry in Bangladesh experienced one of the worst industrial disasters on record.

> On Wednesday morning, April 24, 2013 at 8:00 a.m., **3,639 workers refused to enter the eight-story Rana Plaza factory building** [emphasis added] because there were large and dangerous cracks in the factory walls. The owner, Sohel Rana, brought paid gang members to beat the women and men workers, hitting them with sticks to force them to go into the factory. Managers of the five factories housed in Rana Plaza also told the frightened workers that if they did not return to work, there would be no money to pay them for the month of April, which meant that there would be no food for them and their children. They were forced to go in to work at 8:00 a.m.
>
> At 8:45 a.m. the electricity went out and the factories' five generators kicked on. Almost immediately the workers felt the eight-story building begin to move, and heard a loud explosion as the **building collapsed, pancaking downward, killing 1,137 workers** [emphasis added].
>
> Eighty percent of the workers were young women, 18, 19, 20 years of age. Their standard shift was 13 to 14 ½ hours, from 8:00 a.m. to 9:00 or 10:30 p.m., toiling 90 to 100 hours a week with just two days off a month.
>
> Young "helpers" earned **12 cents** [emphasis added] an hour, while "junior operators" took home **22 cents** [emphasis added] an hour, $10.56 a week, and senior sewers received **24 cents** [emphasis added] an hour and $12.48 a week.
>
> *(Institute for Global Labour and Human Rights, 2014)*

The workers in the Rana Plaza factory were producing garments for thirty-two European, Canadian, and American multinational companies, including the GAP, Walmart, Primark, and Benetton. Eighteen of these companies have pledged donations to the Rana Plaza Trust Fund, including a pledge of $9 million from Primark and $1 million from Walmart. Since the disaster of 2013, there have been some improvements in some of the Bangladeshi garment factories as a result of workers demanding changes and pushing for the right to form unions and engage in collective bargaining. However, to date, less than one-half of 1% of the garment manufacturers are unionized. Further, workers are still often threatened and even beaten for attempting to form unions. As a result, for the majority of workers in the garment industry, conditions remain much the same (Kernaghan, 2014).

Discussion Questions

1. Can fast fashion be a part of a sustainable economy?
2. What are the current problems that make the garment industry destructive? How can these be overcome?
3. How likely is it to see another disaster such as the one at Rana Plaza? How can such a disaster be avoided?

References

Institute for Global Labour and Human Rights. (2014, April 24). *Rana Plaza: A Look Back, and Forward.* Retrieved from Institute for Global Labour and Human Rights: www.globallabourrights.org/alerts/rana-plaza-bangladesh-anniversary-a-look-back-and-forward

International Labor Rights Forum. (n.d.). *Uzbekistan's Cotton Industry Relies on State-Orchestrated Forced Labor of Children and Adults.* Retrieved January 19, 2017, from International Labor Rights Forum: www.laborrights.org/industries/cotton

Kernaghan, C. (2011). *Sexual Predators and Serial Rapists Run Wild at Wal-Mart Suppliers in Jordan.* Pittsburgh, PA: Institute for Global Labour and Human Rights.

Kernaghan, C. (2014). *Unprecedented Changes: Garment Workers in Bangladesh Fight Back and Win: The Institute Initiates Turnaround in Major Apparel Producers.* Pittsburgh, PA: Institute for Global Labour and Human Rights.

Perez, T. (2016, September 30). *List of Goods Produced by Child Labor or Forced Labor.* Retrieved January 18, 2017, from US Department of Labor: https://www.dol.gov/ilab/reports/child-labor/list-of-goods

Taplin, I. M. (2014). Who is to blame?: A re-examination of fast fashion after the 2013 factory disaster in Bangladesh. *Critical Perspectives on International Business, 10*(1/2), 72–83.

13

HOW DO WE BREAK THE TIES AND MOVE FORWARD?

A journey of a thousand miles begins with a single step.

Laozi[1]

Each time a man stands up for an ideal, or acts to improve the lot of others, or strikes out against injustice, he sends forth a tiny ripple of hope, and crossing each other from a million different centers of energy and daring those ripples build a current which can sweep down the mightiest walls of oppression and resistance.

Robert F. Kennedy, "Day of Affirmation" speech, June 6, 1966
(RFK in the Land of Apartheid, 2017)

But I do not think that any of us Americans can be content with mere survival. Sacrifices that we and our allies are making impose upon us all a sacred obligation to see to it that out of this war we and our children will gain something better than mere survival.

FDR, State of the Union address, January 11, 1944
(Franklin D. Roosevelt Presidential Library and Museum, 1944)

Genius the world round stands hand in hand, and one shock of recognition unites them all.

Herman Melville (Melville, 2017)

Introduction

Now that we have come to our final chapter, what are your thoughts about the way forward? What do you see as solutions to the current destructive outcomes to the people and the planet? Can we make changes within the current system? What role, if any, can you play in creating socially sustainable business systems? What do the quotes at the start of this chapter say to you? What do these mean? How do we begin to break the strong ties to the current system of destructive advanced capitalism (DAC) discussed in Chapter 12?

In this chapter, we will present a number of options for what we see as paths forward. We will also discuss how we can create the inertia and a *virtuous cycle* that can propel us out of the ties to the broken system of destructive commerce and into socially sustainable business systems. In her video *The Story of Solutions* (Leonard, 2017), Annie Leonard suggests that solutions will have to be game changing. She suggests that the changes will have to focus on fundamental changes to the system or that solutions must break away from the assumptions and expectations of the current system. The system of DAC is the problem, and any solution to the problem must be big and must focus on changing the system itself. As Donella Meadows (2008) and other systems-thinking scholars have suggested, we must think critically about the system as a whole and how to change the entire system. To change from the current system of destructive capitalism to a socially sustainable system, we must finally break with DAC. We must turn to create a system focused on the well-being of the people and our planet. A new system will require new forms of ownership. This new system must be formalized by legislation and international agreements. To accomplish this transformation, it is critical that a healthy culture of critique and discourse be promoted to enable change. The following sections examine each of these components in more detail

A Change in Focus

Degrowth

The current system of DAC is focused on growth, and progress is measured in terms of money. The current system's relentless obsession with GDP or profit is at the heart of its destructive nature. A socially sustainable system must abandon monetary growth as the intended outcome of our economic activities. In fact, not only must the focus change away from growth, a socially sustainable system must, at least in part, focus on degrowth. The concept of degrowth can be defined as "a political, economic, and social movement based on ecological economics, anti-consumerist and anti-capitalist ideas" (https://en.wikipedia.org/wiki/Degrowth). It is also considered an essential economic strategy responding to the limits-to-growth dilemma (Assadourian, 2012).

INFORMATION BOX 13.1   GDP MEASUREMENT

GDP = C + I + G + (X – M), or GDP = private consumption + gross investment + (government investment + government spending) + (exports – imports)*

This sole focus on monetary value of GDP does not account for negative environmental and social impacts of economic activities. For example, while consuming and discarding goods are accounted for in GDP calculation, recycling is not.

* Source: "Calculating Real GDP." (August 8, 2016). *Boundless Economics.* Retrieved January 13, 2017, from www.boundless.com/economics/ textbooks/boundless-economics-textbook/measuring-output-and-income-19/ comparing-real-and-nominal-gdp-94/calculating-real-gdp-357–12454/.

"Degrowth thinkers and activists advocate for the downscaling of production and consumption—the contraction of economies—arguing that overconsumption lies at the root of long-term environmental issues and social inequalities" (Wikipedia, 2017). Naomi Klein in her book *This Changes Everything* has called for a degrowth movement. This would be a "game changing" event because it calls for the exact opposite of the goals of the current system. Klein specifically focuses on the need to reduce our consumption (especially in the developed economies), to "change how often we drive, how often we fly, whether our food has to be flown to get to us, whether the goods we buy are built to last or to be replaced in two years, how large our homes are" (Klein, 2014, p. 90). The focus on decreased consumption is a focus on reducing the energy usage across the consumption cycle. Klein suggests that those of us in the richest countries would need to return to a lifestyle closer to the one of the 1970s (Klein, 2014).

INFORMATION BOX 13.2   DEGROWTH MODEL

One example of a "degrowth model" comes from Svartedalens nursing home in Sweden (Euronews, 2017). There, the workers had six-hour days, five days a week, but earned the same amount of pay as they did prior to the reduction in hours. The results were impressive: not only did the managers of Svartedalens find an increase in worker morale (happiness) as one might expect, but they also found that productivity increased, and there were also improvements in worker health and "energy," and decreased sick days taken. Unfortunately, despite this success the program was abandoned by a newly elected right-wing majority at the City Council.

A socially sustainable system not only would break from the focus on GDP, but it would be fully supportive of decreases in GDP that produced positive outcomes for the people and the planet. A socially sustainable system must explore a broader perspective of measuring progress by examining other metrics such as GNH or the recently introduced Inclusive Development Index (IDI). Rather than consumers being "good Americans" by going to the mall and spending money as President

George W. Bush suggested in the days following the attacks of 9/11, we would be good global citizens by staying home, driving less, flying less, buying local, and buying goods that would last, even more/rather than buying goods engaging in the sharing economy (Leonard, 2010). Using these new metrics will require new accounting procedures that better represent the true costs of destructive activities and the true economic benefits of sustainable activities.

INFORMATION BOX 13.3   INCLUSIVE DEVELOPMENT INDEX

The World Economic Forum introduced IDI in 2017. The three key indexes of IDI are Economic Growth, Inclusion, and Intergenerational Equity, which are developed based on the following key pillars:

- education and skills development;
- basic services and digital infrastructure;
- sound institutions, business, and political ethics;
- productive allocation of financial resources;
- good jobs, wages, and livelihoods; and
- equitable taxation and social protection.

Among major advanced economies, while the United States is among the top countries in terms of GDP per capita, it ranks in the bottom 20% in terms of IDI.

Source: www.weforum.org/reports/the-inclusive-growth-and-development-report-2017

While this initially might seem like a great deal of sacrifice, the reality is that a key concept of degrowth is that reducing consumption does not require individual martyring or a decrease in well-being. Rather, "degrowthists" aim to maximize happiness and well-being through non-consumptive means such as sharing work and consuming less, while devoting more time to art, music, family, culture, and community. O'Brien (2008) makes the case that such degrowth is actually a path to sustainable happiness. In other words, the goal of degrowth is to increase human flourishing by changing the way we live and consume resources. These positive changes will predictably result in decreases to GDP as people make positive choices that increase well-being and decrease material consumption. Klein refers to this idea as selective degrowth and suggests we would refocus our consumption to the "caring economy" (2014, p. 93). Klein's "green transition" calls for a move away from maximizing profits to growing industries that are focused on improving human well-being and reducing human suffering. This idea is similar to Jones's

Green Collar Economy (2008), with a focus on solving poverty and joblessness while also addressing the environmental issues caused by the current system. The degrowth concept could also be related to the "Moderately Prosperous Society" vision studied and promoted among China scholars as well as Chinese leaders described in the following information box.

INFORMATION BOX 13.4   CHINA'S MODERATELY PROSPEROUS SOCIETY (MPS) VISION

This vision, which has been studied and promoted among China scholars as well as Chinese leaders, came from the realization that China in particular and the Earth in general could not have enough natural resources to support the huge population of China (currently around 1.4 billion) to live an American middle class life. The focus of MPS economy is to assure people comfortable economic means sufficient to escape the drudgery of life. However, the focus of MPS economy is not solely on economic advancement, but on the idea that growth needs to be balanced with social equality and environmental protection.

An important piece of degrowth under SSBS would be an understanding that not all societies would be affected in the same way. Much of the developed world needs to reduce specific expenditures and move away from consumption-focused lifestyles, while significant investments will be required in other parts of the word. Simply put, there simply are not enough resources for those in the developed world to consume a disproportionate amount of resources while much of the rest of the world lives in poverty. North Americans must abandon the quest for the 3000 square foot single-family exurban home, and economic activity and jobs must be refocused on providing sustainable housing with basic infrastructure to all the people on this planet. As part of the movement towards degrowth, SSBS must address the lack of access to clean water, healthy food, plumbing, decent homes, health care, and all other rights recognized under the Universal Declaration of Human Rights. A construction industry in the United States to build and install lawn sprinkler systems is hard to reconcile on a planet where one in ten people lack access to clean drinking water and one in three lack access to basic sanitation (http://water.org/water-crisis/water-sanitation-facts/). There are jobs building ranch houses in the Arizona suburbs; there are also jobs building clean water projects in Namibia. A socially sustainable economic system focuses on providing human rights and fulfilling the basic needs of all of the citizens across the globe. To assure these rights (especially in developing countries), we will need to address and eliminate destructive practices across the globe including addressing the wasteful planned and perceived obsolescence in industries ranging from technology to fast fashion. We must prevent consumers from following the path of the "goods life" while at the same time assuring the "good life" for all.

A Focus on the "Bottom of the Pyramid"

As Mintzberg, Simons, and Basu (Fall 2002) suggest, the primary focus of the current DAC system is on maximizing shareholder wealth. These shareholders largely come from the top 1–5% of socio-economic statuses. In fact, as of 2010, the top one-fifth of households in the United States held 90% of the stock wealth in the country (Mishel, Bivens, Gould, & Shierholz, 2012). So, this system that focuses on increasing shareholder wealth places a great deal of focus on a very small, already privileged group of individuals (often at the expense of workers, consumers, and communities). Green (2008) has suggested that any solution must focus on those in poverty. Similarly, Law Professor William P. Quigley (2003) has called for a Constitutional guarantee to a job at a living wage to put an end to poverty. This would clearly be a fundamental change to our current economic system.

Likewise, a call for a focus on the bottom of the pyramid from Banerjee (2008), among others, is a suggestion that we must first correct the problem for those living in poverty. Zweig's (2000) call for attention to be placed on the issues of the working class in the United States is another example of this bottom-up focus that is the complete opposite of the current concept of a trickle down economy. A system that is focused on making the rich ever richer is no longer sustainable in an era of record inequality. Rich getting richer has led to high levels of mental illness, stress, crime, incarceration, obesity, and imprisonment and lower levels of educational achievement, physical health, and social mobility. The only path to reverse these trends is to change the focus from those at the top to those at lower rungs of the pyramid, with particular focus on those at the bottom—away from the shareholders and towards the broader stakeholders.

As Donnelly (2003, p. 29) has stated, "the impediments to implementing most economic and social rights, however, are political. For example there is enough food in the world to feed everyone. Despite this, widespread hunger and malnutrition exist not because of a shortage of food but because of political decisions about distribution." Stiglitz (2012) provides evidence that raising the standards of those who are worst off would actually benefit the larger economy. Green (2008) also suggested that we begin by working on improving the lives of the most disadvantaged and then work our way outward.

A Focus on Human Rights

The UN's Universal Declaration of Human Rights provides a long-accepted model to follow for granting every person on the planet the dignity of basic human rights. Applied psychologists from Maslow to the present have recognized that the satisfaction of basic needs is a necessary but not sufficient condition for human thriving. Providing all citizens of the planet with basic needs and basic human rights must become the new focus of a sustainable economic system. A socially sustainable system would provide a healthy environment with healthy food, clean air, and clean water for every global citizen. Educational opportunities and equal access to the technological developments would no longer be the preserves of the rich in developed nations. In DAC, impoverished people have been victims of destructive practices such as industrial pollution, worker exploitation, and resource depletion. SSBS's refocus from profit to provision of rights and fulfillment of basic needs ends this unacceptable cycle.

Finally, to be truly sustainable, a new economic system must not only provide a better life for today's citizens, it must also protect and preserve the same high quality of life for future generations. Trade-offs that fulfill today's needs at the expense of future generations are equally unacceptable. Practices that privilege the present and exploit the future must be avoided in a new, socially sustainable system.

A Change in Ownership/Control Structure

The focus on growth and profit results from the current system of corporate ownership and the current schema of corporate law. In DAC, shareholders are paramount: shareholders choose corporate leadership, and corporate leadership acts in the interest of the shareholders. In DAC, corporate governance structures are beholden to shareholders and focus economic activity on maximizing shareholder interest most often at the expense of other stakeholders and the common good. This control and the resulting outcomes are demonstrated in the model of capitalism in Figure 1.2.

INFORMATION BOX 13.5   DAC AND THE CONCEPT OF PROPERTY

One of the contributors to DAC is the perverted aspects of property ownership—not so much the run of the mill property that most people own (basic houses, cars, etc.), but rather the larger scales of property owned by the rich and multinational corporations (e.g., think of a large corporate farm that owns thousands of acres in an area and contributes to unsustainable agricultural practices in the name of "property rights"). Similarly, think of the large mining company that extracts dirty resources from the ground to burn in order to generate electricity and pollutes the surrounding environment in the name of "property rights." Lastly, consider the wealthy, who rent out large swaths of land and living quarters, all the while enhancing their wealth through the rents that many can barely afford to pay—contributing to wealth inequality; Piketty has pointed out a "society of rentiers" (p. 264) in his book

> *Capital in the Twenty-First Century* (Piketty, 2014). In fact, ideas such as these are not new at all and were brought up by famous philosophers who had an influence on the formation of government outlined in the United States Constitution. Take Locke, for example, who argued that as free people, we have rights to personal property and resources, but only to an extent that these resources are available to other individuals as well. It really goes back to the old saying that each of us has the right to exercise our own freedoms, as long as those freedoms do not impair the rights of others to also be free. This is in line with the Brundtland Commission's statement on sustainable development mentioned in Chapter 3.

To change these outcomes, we must change the form of control of corporations. Economist Richard Wolff (2012) suggests that changing the ownership structure of corporations would help us to achieve socially sustainable goals. He proposes what he refers to as WSDEs. These entities were discussed in Chapter 4 and Case 4 earlier in the book. In a WSDE, there would be no division between the ownership of the productive capital of an organization and those who work that capital to produce the products or services. Instead, workers would have true ownership and true control over the organization. As Wolff explains, these workers would be less likely to engage in destructive practices that would harm their communities and their co-workers. They would also be more likely to have closer ties to the consumers of their products and services and thus less likely to harm them as well. The Mondragon, discussed in Case 4, and the various worker co-ops also present potential examples of this type of change in ownership and control.

The German model of codetermination also provides an example of a change in control without a change in ownership. Under German law, any employer with five or more employees must provide workers with representation on the board of directors of the organization. This representation must be through an independent works council that is run by the workers. The board representative(s) from this council will be chosen entirely by the workers and come from the workforce of the organization. The works council must be consulted on strategic business decisions and also has various rights to information, inspection, and supervision, and even the right to object and veto management decisions (Bamber, Lansbury, Wailes, & Wright, 2016, p. 189). These works councils exist in approximately 50% of German employers (Bamber, Lansbury, Wailes, & Wright, 2016), and studies have found that organizations with works councils are actually more efficient and productive (Hubler & Jirjahn, 2003).

The Need for Legislation

The current destructive system is supported by a framework of legislation and administrative law. For example, owners of corporations are protected by limited liability, and corporations are provided special access to sources of equity and debt. Achieving socially sustainable business systems will also require legislation. The simple reality is that social sustainability will not be achieved voluntarily. Without appropriate legislation and regulation, corporations will continue with destructive practices despite the fact that these practices are not in their long-term interests. Proponents of conscious capitalism and Stakeholder Theory are correct that long-term corporate interests require leaders to move away from the profit focus. However, voluntary-based systems have simply not been effective in achieving this transformation. As Klein (2014) has suggested, corporations will undertake socially responsible practices only if they are profitable, and the current system of accounting recognizes only past not future profits. Corporations are simply not likely to voluntarily abandon profitable activities whether or not those activities are socially responsible. As was discussed in Chapter 3, voluntarism has not resulted in a shift away from DAC except on the edges. The current crises facing the people and planet require transformative change now, not gradual adoption of sustainable practices. The difference between the impact of legislation on social outcomes and voluntary CSR is perhaps best explained by Marens (2008) in his article "Recovering the Past: Reviving the Legacy of the Early Scholars of Corporate Social Responsibility." While Marens's focus is on the scholars of business and society, he also explains that during the period of an independent regulation of businesses—the New Deal era of approximately 1940–1973—we experienced tremendous social and environmental outcomes. While the United States also experienced significant GDP growth during this time, the growth was shared across income groups. We also saw laws that led to greater equality across genders and races, cleaner air, and cleaner water. As these laws were slowly chipped away through repeal or lack of enforcement due to the backlash from corporate interests (see, e.g., Chapter 2), we have seen the stagnation and decrease of wages, increased inequality, increased poverty, and increased environmental destruction.

The lessons from the New Deal era give us an important starting point to consider the types of legislation that would be needed to create socially sustainable business systems. This has been recognized by a number of researchers and activists. For example, Van Jones, in *The Green Collar Economy* (2008), points to FDR's New Deal as an example of the type of government action we will need to solve the problems of inequality, poverty, and environmental degradation. Cass Sunstein (2004) also borrows from FDR's programs in calling for the adoption of what FDR termed the Second Bill of Rights during his 1944 State of the Union address. This Second Bill of Rights would guarantee work, decent pay, health care, housing, education, and retirement benefits for all of the peoples of the world. Sunstein points out how we have forgotten the historic impact of Roosevelt's State of the Union address that year, but that it laid the foundation for the Universal Declaration of Human Rights. Post 9/11, Sunstein argues that we need to reclaim Roosevelt's ideals, to combat the hyper-individualism that has taken hold over our more deeply human and cherished ideals as a nation. Much of this hyper-individualism is the basis for distrust of government and the kinds of programs that lead to the greatest levels of broadly shared prosperity that our nation has experienced, but no longer does. We need to reclaim the Second Bill of Rights. Quigley (2003) also builds from FDR's New Deal ideas in calling for a Constitutional amendment to assure a job at a living wage.

The Need for Global Agreements

DAC is supported internationally by both the existence of destructive international agreements and the absence of appropriate international agreements. Any path to create a socially sustainable economic system would require not only national legislation but broad international agreements. A schema of international agreements that contained enforceable rules ensuring sustainable practices would benefit all citizens of the globe. The lives of workers in the developed world who have been so harmed by the corporate race to the bottom would be improved along with the lives of the exploited workers in poorer nations who have been victimized to produce consumer goods for the developed world.

The UN project on sustainability calls for just such a global solution, but falls victim to the same form of voluntarism and emphasis on property ownership[2] discussed in the prior section of this chapter. Much like the need for national legislation, global solutions must have meaningful enforcement provisions. There are a number of current international examples with varying levels of strength and success. For example, the ILO, a branch of the United Nations, is tasked with developing conventions and directives that are then adopted (or not) by member states. The United States, the most critical player in the global marketplace over the last half of the century or longer, has consistently failed to ratify ILO conventions. While all member states are required to abide by the core conventions of the ILO, even these are not enforced in any meaningful manner. We also see some labor protections in some free trade agreements. For instance, the North American Free Trade Agreement (NAFTA) includes a side labor agreement. However, the language of the agreement and the enforcement of the agreement are far from assuring the human rights of the workers in the three countries involved in the agreement. The language and enforcement of worker rights in other trade agreements are similarly weak. On the other end of the spectrum, the European Union Charter of Fundamental Rights goes much further in protecting the rights of workers in all of the member states of the European Union. The protections under this Charter are much broader than those in these other trade agreements, and membership in the European Union requires nation states to assure these rights to workers. Spitz (2005) uses this EU Charter as her basis for a call for a similar North American Charter of fundamental human rights (Spitz, 2005). Spitz's recommendation and the European Union Charter are good starting points, but these protections must be truly global. These charters should be extended to all nation states as part of the global system of trade. Further, in addition to workers' rights, these charters should also address all forms of human rights as well as environmental protections. Only such a global charter will be able to prevent a race to the bottom by corporate interests to avoid labor and environmental regulations.

In addition to the need for national and global legislation to achieve socially sustainable business systems, there is also a need for progressive businesses and their leaders to take voluntary actions. As Compa (2008) has argued, legislation has been difficult to pass for the past twenty to thirty years, and even once passed the enforcement has often been weak. Further, enforcing legislation against every employer might indeed be an impossibility. There will be a need to have at the least a critical mass of organizations that voluntarily adopt socially sustainable practices. These organizations should be recognized. Consumers should be informed about the existence of these organizations, and hopefully consumers will in turn choose to buy products from these SSBS enterprises rather than from those engaging in the practices common in DAC. We see a number of steps being taken towards creating these socially sustainable corporations, such as the development of B-corporations, fair trade, and organic labeling, and even boycott lists. These voluntary actions play a role in SSBS, but as has been explained, they simply do not work as the sole solution to move from DAC to SSBS.

Creating Critique and Discourse to Fuel a Movement

Of course, we are not the first to suggest alternatives to improve our current economic system. Many of the alternatives suggested offer incremental changes to the broader system or focus on individual behavior at the micro level—for example, voluntary calls for a refocus on stakeholders or city recycling plans. These are laudable, but are unlikely to address the current crises in time. While not minimizing these efforts, it is important to recognize that while many viable paths towards a socially sustainable system of commerce have been suggested, none of these has been adopted in a wide enough fashion to combat the destruction of the current advanced capitalistic system. What is needed is not just an end solution, but a path to getting there. We must develop the path of how we can break the ties to the current system and create a new system that benefits all the people of this planet. This transformation threatens the power structures that dominate our society. One wonders if part of the problem is the fear of challenging corporate and government power and fear of changing the status quo.

To combat the inertia of the current system and create momentum for socially sustainable systems, we must use influence techniques and practices that will be strong enough to overcome the ties to DAC discussed in Chapter 12. We must create a *virtuous cycle* of influence between society, institutions, business practices, and government. As was alluded to in prior sections, a more substantive multi-level approach is needed. It remains to be seen whether these changes will be primarily bottom up (e.g., "Occupy" type influences) or top down (e.g., significant legal, governmental, or leadership approach changes). In this section, we highlight some areas of thinking in terms of potential large-scale progress in this area.

Many people simply assume that our current economic system is the only one that can possibly be successful. We must overcome that assumption. There are in fact many alternative systems that could be implemented and many that exist at more micro levels within the current system. WSDEs, as mentioned previously, and similar systems of worker control and ownership exist both at a micro level in small businesses and at a broader level in the Mondragon region of Spain. We also see significant worker control via the works council laws in Germany and other countries in the European Union. Many of the New Deal types of legislation proposed in the prior section are commonplace in the Scandinavian countries and other parts of the European Union. Even on DAC's US home turf, we can catch glimpses of worker control through such mechanisms as employee stock ownership plans and B-corporations that have changed the activities of a small number of US corporations for the better. Other corporations, such as Costco, have demonstrated their ability to be both sustainable and economically viable. Similarly, there are rays of hope within the realms of international agreements that address environmental issues and labor rights.

The current system of capitalism is the currently prevailing system, but its inevitability is no different from the inevitability of the pre-industrialization feudalism. The explorers of the "New World" must have been shocked to see indigenous peoples in the Americas thriving without European schemes of property ownership. But the fact is, societies and economies have always taken a variety of forms. DAC is not an inevitability; it is a choice. Importantly, social sustainability is also a choice.

To break the grip of destructive capitalism and make the sustainability choice, a vibrant social discourse is imperative. There must be a resurgence among the groups and people that should be leading such discourse. Academia, labor, and the press are three essential loci for social and economic critique and discussion. Unfortunately, each of these three centers of discourse has become intertwined and to some degree compromised by the current system of DAC. To achieve a socially sustainable system of commerce, we will need to see a resurgence of these traditional avenues of discourse. Academics, labor leaders, and journalists must reclaim their essential roles as societal critics.

Creating Academic Discourse

Society has invested and continues to invest billions of dollars in academia. This support comes through direct taxpayer support, state grants, federal grants, federal loan programs, and land grants. In exchange for this investment, society should have the expectation that these institutions are aligned to achieving social goals. As Marens (2008, pp. 68–69) has so aptly pointed out, academic researchers should return to the ideas of some of the "pioneers" of the field of business and society, to "remember that questioning the nature of the corporation and weighing the welfare of the entire society were legitimate topics of scholarship." To academics, especially those in business schools, it should be clear from a basic analysis of the current business systems and practices that the vast majority of people are not benefited by the current system. For example, in its most recent report, Oxfam reported that the eight richest people in the world own as much wealth as the bottom 3.5 billion people of the world (Oxfam International, 2017). The ecological and economic outcomes discussed throughout this text provide evidence that the current system does not benefit all. On the contrary, the current system to most people has compromised the health of the planetary ecosystem upon which we depend. Academics have a professional and social obligation to explore these outcomes. Academics must take steps to assure all voices are heard and to analyze the policies and practices of business with a view that is broader than the mere outcome of profits, shareholder wealth, or GDP. The dependent variables of academic research should be expanded to include environmental outcomes, poverty, inequality, happiness, well-being, and human rights. Models of business behavior that lead to social sustainability should be developed. Where business practices conflict with the goals of social sustainability, academics must point out where legislation and mandates will become necessary to assure better social outcomes. Academics must be willing to engage in meaningful critical analysis and critique of business systems, practices, and leaders.

As such, there must be a system in place that will support the academics willing to take on this mantle and undertake research and writing that addresses social sustainability. As Marens, Steck, and Lieberwitz have all pointed out, the majority of academic research in business schools has become corporate-centered. Noncorporatist academics have been systematically attacked by corporate leaders and undermined by institutional dependence on corporate funding. Intellectual independence has too often been sacrificed on the altar of private funding and institutional development. In short, academics must use their privileges and gifts to speak truth to power and protect the interests of the broader community. To do this, academics must not be beholden to corporate interests. Rather than funding institutions, research centers, journals, and programs through corporate financing, there will need to be an independent source of financing through the public so that academics can refocus on their duty to serve the public interest.

Reviving and Restoring the Role of the Labor Movement

Academia must not be the only dissenting voice. The other stakeholders in business practices (employees, consumers, the environment, etc.) must also be heard. Perhaps most importantly, employee voices must be heard through true employee advocates, organizations, and representatives.

Dean and Reynolds (2010) suggest that "the American labor movement remains the social force with the greatest capacity to foster a broad-based movement for social and economic change." Moody points out that unions are the most socially integrated of any form of organization—cutting across race, gender, national origin, and religion in ways no other social organization does (Moody, 2014, p. 81). The labor movement must indeed play a critical role in driving the discourse and critique of the current system and creating a social movement to break the ties to the current destructive system. However, the labor movement itself must first be revamped. The labor movement must become more democratic and militant (Carbo, Hargrove, & Haase, 2017) to create the excitement and inertia for a true movement of social justice. The labor movement will need to take advantage of the integration of diversity that exists in unions. The labor movement and labor leaders will need to work across broad swaths of activist organizations and interests to create the type of class consciousness that is needed to drive a social movement (Moody, 2014). To create a movement towards socially sustainable business systems, the activists in the movement must be convinced of a potential benefit and must be convinced of the potential success of such a movement (Chong, 1991).

INFORMATION BOX 13.6   A SOCIAL MOVEMENT

White (2016) suggests that successful social movements are never just scaled-up or rebranded versions of past social movements; rather, they may require novel tactics, as the opposing side will be prepared for the same-old, same-old. As one of the co-founders of the Occupy Movement and a former senior editor of the anti-consumerist website *Adbusters*, White also emphasizes personal epiphany and mental environmentalism (www.micahmwhite. com/social-change-theory/mental-environmentalism) as routes to success. Take the Occupy Movement, which had intense and massive support for a brief period of time. While the movement did raise the issue of income inequality to the national level, he feels the movement was a failure, given the negligible impact it had on our banking and financial system as a whole (e.g., the banks are even bigger today than they were before the 2008 financial crisis—thus a failure of protest). What do you think? How will social movements succeed in the future? Perhaps, there will be historical events spurring on the next broad-scale social action. For example, White notes the important influence of basic things such as increasing food prices that often mobilize the populace.

The labor movement must truly turn to a *social justice form of unionism*, with a focus on all of the broad issues that can create a socially sustainable system of business. The movement will need to focus on the rights of *all* workers, not just their members, thus bringing in a broad array of workers to the movement. The movement will need to focus on environmental issues, criminal justice issues, racial justice issues, and immigrant issues so that members of each of these groups will see the potential for benefit. While broadening the focus is one part of the requirement to bring together a broad-based social movement, the labor movement must also show that it can be successful. This is where unions must be willing to be more militant, to engage in direct actions, to engage in concerted activity during the day to day managing of a collective bargaining agreement, to engage in broader socially oriented direct actions, and to engage in meaningful contract and strike campaigns (Carbo, Hargrove, & Haase, 2017). Some of the actions taken by the Chicago Teachers Union, the Service Employees International Union (SEIU)-backed Fight for $15, and the occupation of the Chicago Glassworks by the UE all demonstrate the potential of such actions. To return to being the "natural anchor pull[ing] together the many currents of progressive activism" (Budd, 2013) (Dean and Reynolds, 2010), the labor movement will need to broaden its focus and fight to assure more and more examples of success.

A Need for Critical Media

In addition to the role for labor and academics, the media must play a role in driving critical discussion of the current business systems. We can no longer afford to have media that simply serve as cheerleaders of the current destructive practices. As discussed in Chapter 12, a major cause for the current state of the media in the United States is the corporate ownership of such media. It is unlikely that GE, Disney, and the other corporate owners of the media in the United States will give up their control of these media outlets any time soon. However, what can occur is a system that works around this corporate owned media. First, much like academia, we should see a renewed public funding of media. NPR, PBS, and newer web-based examples such as ProPublica are critical components of a free press, and they should be expanded and supported through tax dollars—again, the idea of media of the people and for the people. Further, alternative media sources can also play a role.

Independent news sources and muckraking journalists and novelists have played a critical role in driving social movements throughout history. Printers of pamphlets and newsletters were critical in driving support for the American Revolution. Likewise, labor presses played a role in the forming and advancement of the labor movement in the United States. Muckrakers such as Ida Tarbell and Upton Sinclair were critical in ushering in the progressive era and the regulation of business practices. Today, academics, labor activists, and others can help by becoming a part of new and independent media. A colleague of ours at Kutztown University began a small blog, *The Raging Chicken Press*, that has grown into a well-known regional media outlet with additional blogs and podcasts. This growing blog is an example of how an academic (and labor activists) can help to drive an open and independent press. *Labor Notes* is another example of an independent, labor-based press that engages in critical analysis of the current economic system. The proliferation of social media provides a path for a new form of independent press. This kind of press can play a critical role in informing people about the current destructive practices—informing them about the alternatives to the current system, informing them about socially sustainable business practices, and driving support for such practices.

To achieve a system of socially sustainable business practices, we will need not just a group of activists or networks, but a coalition to come together on economic, social justice, and environmental issues; to change the status quo, which never changes without a fight, large masses of people will have to pressure their governments to adopt sustainable practices. Similar successes have been seen in other past social movements such as during the Great Depression in the United States, where such movements forced FDR to create social safety nets and works programs. Roosevelt's initial political leanings would not have inclined him to adopt New Deal programs without pressure (Zinn, 1980). While he saw a deep need to reform the economy, he was very clear that he supported a free market system (for instance, see FDR's 1932 speech to the Commonwealth Club) and opposed welfare (Sunstein, 2004). There are numerous sources of information for groups undertaking these kinds of large-scale changes. White (2016) illustrates historically the successes of social movements while at the same time pointing out some of the shortcomings such as repeating the same tactics. The status quo learns from prior efforts to weaken their grip on control, and we see currently efforts to walk back decades of progress both in the United States and abroad. Chong (1991) pointed out important factors that get people involved in these causes including seeing the psychological and/or social benefit and that the movement will lead to the establishment of these benefits (Budd, 2013). The sources of energy for these movements should be broad and come simultaneously from the press, academics, activists, and everyday citizens. For sustainable change to come, a broad-based activists' movement must develop.

What Can You Do?

In this book, we have presented evidence of the crises resulting from DAC and the imperative need to create socially sustainable business. In this chapter, we have presented steps that can propel us towards a socially sustainable system. In Chapters 5 through 10, we presented you sustainable alternatives for business practices

As you move forward in your business career, ask yourself if you want your life to be about maximizing stockholder wealth. Is "Worked Hard to Make Owners Rich" what you want on your tombstone? We believe there is an alternative. We believe every businessperson has the real opportunity to help make the world better during their career.

Many of the actions you can take are small. Many may be difficult or even risky at the beginning of your career. But great things come from many people taking small actions just as terrible things come from many people going along to get along. Find ways that you can make your company's activities more sustainable. Choose to work for companies that make sustainable choices. Start new enterprises that serve the public good and provide meaningful work to your employees. Use your pocket book to support socially sustainable companies. Use your voice to promote social, economic, and political change. Use your time to volunteer and contribute to causes that improve your community and your planet.

In Chapters 11 through 13, we provided you with some of the psychological, social, and influence tools to help you to understand the destructive nature of the current system. Take these tools and messages to help others to understand the alternatives available. You can take steps as a worker, manager, community member, friend, or citizen to overcome the influences that create the ties to the current destructive system of commerce. You can take part in creating the type of movement that is necessary to achieve a truly socially sustainable global economy. Pay it forward!

Finally, we hope that this book has helped you to become a better critical thinker. No book, especially including this book, presents all the answers. However, as you have interacted with this text, we hope that you, your classmates, and your professor have wrestled with many questions. We hope that you and those around you hold the potential of finding new answers to the questions presented in this text and the new questions that will face you in your business career. We hope that you will move forward and use your critical thinking skills to develop your own answers and your own solutions, and to help to create a more socially sustainable future for all.

Discussion Questions

1. What are your reactions to the Information Boxes on degrowth? Do you think most people would find a suggestion for a shorter workweek to be preposterous and unreasonable? Why? Is a forty or fifty hour workweek just an idea or belief that we have that things must be this way?

2. It is expected that many people would be skeptical of the SSBS ideas we present in this book. It is possible that some of this skepticism is based on beliefs that free market capitalism is the only possible system. As an exercise, search for the assumptions required for efficient capital markets. Discuss as a class whether you think these assumptions are met in current capitalist frameworks.

3. What role do you play, if any, in perpetuating the current economic system? Do you currently take steps to drive our system to be a more socially sustainable system? What steps could you take to help to achieve SSBS?

4. Discuss the various potential solutions proposed in this chapter. Review the solutions posed by Naomi Klein, Van Jones, Cass Sunstein, Annie Leonard, the authors of this text, and others. Conduct a force field analysis of these solutions by identifying barriers or inhibitors and drivers (factors supporting these solutions). Can the barriers be overcome? Are there ways to produce additional drivers?

5. If there were more WSDEs, how do you think they would work through problems of competitiveness? For example, in the United States, many CEOs

argue that to be competitive, they must move their manufacturing facilities overseas, where labor costs are much lower. Such decisions have resulted in dramatic social and political consequences. If such a challenge occurred for a WSDE manufacturing a product, how might they continue to operate under competitive, international conditions? Or, do you think the only way they could succeed would be if all firms were WSDEs?

Notes

1 www.brainyquote.com/quotes/quotes/l/laotzu137141.html Retrieved March 16, 2017.
2 See http://americanpolicy.org/agenda21/.

References

Assadourian, E. (2012). The path to degrowth in overdeveloped countries. In *Moving Toward Sustainable Prosperity* (pp. 22–37). The WorldWatch Institute.

Bamber, G. J., Lansbury, R. D., Wailes, N., & Wright, C. F. (2016). *International and Comparative Employment Relations: National Regulation, Global Changes* (6th ed.). London: Sage.

Banerjee, S. B. (2008). Corporate Social Responsibility: The Good, the Bad and the Ugly. *Critical Sociology*, 34(1), 51–79

Budd, J. W. (2013). *Labor Relations: Striking a Balance.* New York: McGraw Hill.

Carbo, J. A., Hargrove, M. B., & Haase, S. J. (2017, forthcoming). Democracy, militancy and union revitalization the DeMReV model of union renewal: A sustainable, strategic model expanding on Voss and Sherman. In David Lewin and Paul Gollen (Eds.), *Advances in Industrial and Labor Relations.* Bingley, UK: Emerald Books.

Chong, D. (1991). *Collective Action and the Civil Rights Movement.* Chicago: University of Chicago Press.

Compa, L. (2008). Corporate social responsibily and workers rights. *Comparative Labor Law and Policy Journal, 30,* 1–10.

Dean, A. B., and Reynolds, D. B. (2010). *A New New Deal: How Regional Activism Will Reshape the American Labor Movement.* Ithaca, NY: Cornell University Press.

Donnelly, J. (2003). *Universal Human Rights in Theory and Practice* (2nd ed.). Ithaca, NY and London: Cornell University Press.

Euronews (2017). Retrieved June 6, 2017, from Euronews: http://www.euronews.com/2017/01/04/swedish-old-folks-home-abandons-six-hour-workday-experiment

Franklin D. Roosevelt Presidential Library and Museum (1944). Retrieved from http://www.fdrlibrary.marist.edu/archives/stateoftheunion.html

Green, D. (2008). *From Poverty to Power: How Active Citizens and Effecitve States Can Change the World.* Oxford, UK: Oxfam International.

Herman Melville. (2017, March 16). Retrieved from IZQuotes: http://izquotes.com/quote/252472

Hubler, O., & Jirjahn, U. (2003). Works councils and collective bargaining in Germany: The impact on productivity and wages. *Scottish Journal of Political Economy, 50*(4), 471–491.

Jones, V. (2008). *The Green Collar Economy: How One Solution Can Fix Our Two Biggest Problems.* New York: HarperOne.

Klein, N. (2014). *This Changes Everything: Capitalism vs. the Climate.* New York: Simon & Schuster.

Leonard, A. (2010). *The Story of Stuff: How Our Obsession with Stuff Is Trashing the Planet, Our Communities, and Our Health—and a Vision for Change*. New York: Free Press.

Marens, R. (2008). Recovering the past: Reviving the legacy of the early scholars of corporate social responsibility. *Journal of Management History, 14*(1), 55–72.

Meadows, D. H. (2008). *Thinking in Systems: A Primer*. Junction, VT: Chelsea Green Publishing Company.

Mintzberg, H., Simons, R., & Basu, K. (Fall 2002). Beyond selfishness. *MIT Sloan Management Review, 44*(1), 67–74.

Mishel, L., Bivens, J., Gould, E., & Shierholz, H. (2012). *The State of Working America* (12th ed.). Ithaca, NY: Cornell University Press.

Moody, K. (2014). *In Solidarity*. Chicago: Haymarket Books.

O'Brien, C. (2008). Sustainable happiness: How happiness studies can contribute to a more sustainable future. *Canadian Psychology, 49*(4), 289–295.

Oxfam International. (2017, January 16). *Just 8 Men Own Same Wealth as Half the World*. Retrieved January 18, 2017, from Oxfam International: www.oxfam.org/en/pressroom/pressreleases/2017-01-16/just-8-men-own-same-wealth-half-world

Piketty, T. (2014). *Capital in the Twenty-First Century*. London: Harvard University Press.

Quigley, W. P. (2003). *Ending Poverty as We Know It: Guaranteeing a Right to a Job at a Living Wage*. Philadelphia, PA: Temple University Press.

RFK in the Land of Apartheid. (2017, March 15). Retrieved from RFKS A Film: www.rfksafilm.org/html/speeches/unicape.php

Spitz, L. (2005). The gift of Enron: An opportunity to talk about capitalism, equality, globalization, and the promise of a North-American charter of fundamental rights. *Ohio State Law Journal, 66*, 315.

Stiglitz, J. E. (2012). *The Price of Inequality: How Today's Divided Society Endangers Our Future*. New York: W.W. Norton & Company, Inc.

Sunstein, C. R. (2004). *The Second Bill of Rights: FDR's Unfinished Revolution and Why We Need It More Than Ever*. New York: Basic Books.

Toolbox, N. H. (n.d.). *Becoming American: The British Atlantic Colonies, 1690–1763*. National Humanities Center.

White, M. (2016). *The End of Protest: A New Playbook for Revolution*. Knopf, Canada: Penguin RandomHouse.

Wikipedia (2017). Retrieved January 27, 2017, from Wikipedia: https://en.wikipedia.org/wiki/Degrowth

Wolff, R. (2012). *Democracy at Work: A Cure for Capitalism*. Chicago: Haymarket Books.

Zinn, H. (1980). *A People's History of the United States*. New York: Harper Collins.

CASE 13 THE FUTURE BELONGS TO YOU

Rather than providing a case study for this chapter, we suggest that students explore their own paths to creating socially sustainable business systems. They can engage in creating this path by creating their own case study if they so choose that looks at past movements as examples (for instance, the Civil Rights Movement, the Women's Suffrage Movement, the Labor Movement, or the Movement for LGBTQ equality might all provide examples of how a movement can be built to move from DAC to SSBS). Students might also choose to approach this task from a more micro level and discuss how they can engage in their jobs or even at the organizational level to create socially sustainable business practices. Students might want to explore organizations that are at least headed towards social sustainability such as Costco, Interface, or the Mondragon. Students might also explore social entrepreneurship and non-profit management or creation as options. Students could also explore how they might push for SSBS as community members, and they could find and study other successful community actions as guidance.

INDEX

Page numbers in italics indicate figures and tables.